"One of Lincoln's greatest speeches remains the least known. Carefully crafted to win the support of New York City Kingmakers, it lacked the charm of direct confrontations with Stephen A. Douglas and the poetry of Lincoln's presidential oratory. Without a Cooper Union Address, however, there would be no Gettysburg Address. Harold Holzer gives this great speech its due, with diligent rhetorical and historical analysis that brings today's reader back to Lincoln's transformation from prairie politician to potential president."

—John Y. Simon, Executive Director,
Ulysses S. Grant Association

"Elegant. . . . To sit with *Lincoln at Cooper Union* is almost to sit on the stage with Lincoln in the Great Hall. . . . Holzer lays out the rhetorical map of the Cooper Union speech in a dazzling analytical performance. . . . Wonderful narrative elegance of Holzer's writing."

—*Claremont Review of Books*

"Who better to write a book on Lincoln's Cooper Union Speech in Manhattan than the quintessential New Yorker himself, Harold Holzer. . . . In this superb book, Holzer sheds new light on the indispensable speech that made Lincoln president. . . . His engaging narrative furnishes the reader with a window into Lincoln the man and his times. Indeed, his well-crafted and accessible book will grip the scholar, general reader, and Lincoln aficionado alike. . . . Outstanding."   —*Lincoln Lore*

"Harold Holzer's latest gem of a book examines the circumstances, meaning, and consequences of one of Abraham Lincoln's most important speeches. . . . Holzer's analysis of the speech . . . is superb. . . . Outstanding. . . . Well researched, well written, and thought-provoking, it is a pleasure to read and stands out as one of the finest recent books on our sixteenth president."   —Townhall.com

"This is a delightful book to read and is fast-paced and breathtaking in its scope."   —Frank J. Williams, Chairman, The Lincoln Forum

"Nicely written and enlightening. . . . Holzer's analysis of the Cooper Union speech, how it was composed, how it was delivered, and the reaction it caused . . . is well worth any courtroom lawyer's careful study. For it is nothing less than a timely primer . . . on how to be a great communicator."

—*New York Law Journal*

"Through meticulous study of historical sources, Holzer portrays a vivid picture of Lincoln's triumph at Cooper Union. He conveys the enormity of what Lincoln had at stake, and how he prepared for the night that ultimately changed forever the course of his life and the nation. . . . Among the approximately 16,000 books and pamphlets written about Lincoln, *Lincoln at Cooper Union* is destined to rank among the top 100. . . . A delightful book to read." —*Civil War Book Review*

"The author does an impeccable job of re-creating the fascinating events of the time. . . . A surprisingly good book that should appeal to . . . all those who enjoy an authentic, vicarious window on the fascinating past." —*The Rail Splitter*

"Well told and well documented. . . . Holzer makes clear that if Lincoln had failed rather than triumphed at Cooper Union on that February evening, he might very well have failed to receive the Republican Party's nomination for president." —*The Washington Times*

"Few people know more about Abraham Lincoln than Holzer. This fine new work focuses on a widely known but little studied address that Lincoln delivered early in 1860 in New York City. . . . Surely no one will again overlook this masterful speech." —*Publishers Weekly*

"Holzer's research is prodigious. . . . Although Holzer is an unabashed (even effervescent) advocate for Lincoln—and for the significance of this speech—he also is careful to analyze the architecture and rhetoric of the remarks and to puncture some puffballs that have grown in the yard of Lincoln legends. . . . The enthusiasm is infectious." —*Kirkus Reviews*

"Holzer demolishes any lingering remnants of the myth that Abraham Lincoln stumbled accidentally into the presidency. . . . Engrossing . . . Pull this one out of the stream and savor it." —*Myron A. Marty, St Louis Post-Dispatch*

OTHER BOOKS BY HAROLD HOLZER

The Lincoln Forum: Rediscovering Abraham Lincoln
(coeditor with John Y. Simon)

State of the Union: New York and the Civil War (editor)

Prang's Civil War Pictures: The Complete Battle Chromos of Louis Prang

Abraham Lincoln The Writer: A Treasury of His Greatest
Speeches and Letters (editor)

Lincoln Seen and Heard

The Union Image: Popular Prints of the Civil War North
(with Mark E. Neely, Jr.)

Lincoln as I Knew Him: Gossip, Tributes, and Revelations from His
Best Friends and Worst Enemies (editor)

The Lincoln Forum: Abraham Lincoln, Gettysburg, & the Civil War
(coeditor with John Y. Simon)

The Union Preserved: A Guide to the Civil War Records in the
New York State Archives (editor)

The Lincoln Mailbag: America Writes to the President, 1860–1865 (editor)

Witness to War: The Civil War

The Civil War Era

Dear Mr. Lincoln: Letters to the President (editor)

Washington and Lincoln Portrayed: National Icons in Popular Prints

The Lincoln-Douglas Debates: The First Complete,
Unexpurgated Text (editor)

Mine Eyes Have Seen the Glory: The Civil War in Art
(with Mark E. Neely, Jr.)

Lincoln on Democracy (coeditor with Mario Cuomo)

The Lincoln Family Album (with Mark E. Neely, Jr.)

The Confederate Image: Prints of the Lost Cause
(with Gabor S. Boritt and Mark E. Neely, Jr.)

The Lincoln Image: Abraham Lincoln and the Popular Print
(with Gabor S. Boritt and Mark E. Neely, Jr.)

LINCOLN AT

⚓ *The Speech That Made*
Abraham Lincoln President

SIMON & SCHUSTER PAPERBACKS

COOPER UNION

HAROLD HOLZER

New York   London   Toronto   Sydney

SIMON & SCHUSTER PAPERBACKS
Rockefeller Center
1230 Avenue of the Americas
New York, NY 10020

First Simon & Schuster paperback edition 2005

SIMON & SCHUSTER PAPERBACKS and colophon are registered
trademarks of Simon & Schuster, Inc.

For information about special discounts for bulk purchases,
please contact Simon & Schuster Special Sales: 1-800-456-6798
or business@simonandschuster.com.

Designed by Paul Dippolito

Manufactured in the United States of America

1   3   5   7   9   10   8   6   4   2

The Library of Congress has cataloged the hardcover edition as follows:

Holzer, Harold.
Lincoln at Copper Union : the speech that made Abraham Lincoln
president / Harold Holzer.
p.   cm.
Includes bibliographical references and index.
1. Lincoln, Abraham, 1809–1865—Oratory.   2. Lincoln,
Abraham, 1809–1865—Views on slavery.   3. United States—
Politics and government—1857–1861.   4. Speeches, addresses, etc.,
American—New York (State)—New York.   5. Cooper Union for
the Advancement of Science and Art.   6. Lincoln, Abraham,
1809–1865—Political career before 1861.   I. Title.
E440.H65 2004
973.7'092—dc22   2003063344
ISBN 0-7432-2466-3
0-7432-2467-1 (Pbk)

For Edith

✣ CONTENTS ✣

*Let us have faith that right makes might, and in that faith,
let us, to the end, dare to do our duty as we understand it.*

—ABRAHAM LINCOLN AT COOPER UNION, FEBRUARY 27, 1860

*The speech at New-York, being within my calculation
before I started, went off passably well, and gave me no
trouble whatever.*

—ABRAHAM LINCOLN TO MARY LINCOLN, MARCH 4, 1860

MORE THAN NINE HUNDRED PEOPLE filled the Great Hall of Cooper Union in New York to hear Abraham Lincoln's great speech that night, many waiting hours on a long line that circled the building. The speaker—and the man assigned to introduce him—were called on stage by the school's African-American president. The orator made careful use of the microphone, aware that the event was being taped for television. Audience members could not help but notice how frequently he gulped Poland Spring water as he held the hot, floodlit stage for nearly an hour and a half. Only one cell phone rang during the entire evening.

None of the above happened on February 27, 1860, of course—the day Lincoln himself made history at Cooper Union in New York, albeit to a house only three-fourths filled. In Lincoln's time, electronic amplification, broadcasting, color-blind executive opportunities at major universities, and, for that matter, bottled water, were all unknown and unimaginable.

But it did happen just as described 140 years later, on May 5, 2000. That evening, to mark the publication of the clothbound edition of this book, actor Sam Waterston mesmerized a modern audience at Cooper Union in a re-creation of Lincoln's address.

I was privileged that night to sit on stage throughout the performance, having assumed the role of *New York Evening Post* editor William Cullen

Bryant, who had introduced Lincoln on February 27, 1860. I will not soon forget the thrill of listening to those seven thousand words up close, just as Bryant had. What a spellbinding oration it remains, in the hands of a speaker capable of squeezing nuance from Lincoln's canny repetition of phrases, and passion from his dazzlingly intricate peroration.

Aired repeatedly on C-SPAN, the re-creation—and the book—not unexpectedly rattled some archives, shaking hitherto unknown, but important information to the surface. The bad news is that the material came to light too late for inclusion in the original; the good news is that the paperback edition provides this opportunity to recognize and discuss new discoveries.

Chief among them is a long-lost letter that Lincoln wrote to Ohio Senator Thomas Corwin on October 9, 1859—just a week before receiving the momentous telegram inviting him to speak in the East. (Unbeknownst to Lincoln, Corwin would be asked to participate in the very same lecture series. The Senator went to Brooklyn as requested; Lincoln demurred, ending up, fortuitously, at Cooper Union). Their correspondence began when Corwin wrote Lincoln that he was worried that their party's incessant focus on slavery would doom its chances to elect a president in 1860. Lincoln believed otherwise—and in the newly unearthed, handwritten letter, emphatically so declared. Employing frank language to the man who came close to sharing the spotlight with him in New York, Lincoln insisted Republicans ought not to try attracting Democrats to their ranks by emphasizing irrelevancies like "tariff, extravagances, live oak contracts and the like—the very old issues upon which the Whig party was beat out of existence." The issue of slavery, Lincoln argued, not only offered moral, but political resonance:

> What brought these democrats with us? The Slavery issue. Drop that issue, and they have no motive to remain, and will not remain, with us. It is idiotic to think otherwise. Do you understand me as saying Illinois must have an extreme antislavery candidate? I do not so mean. We must have, though, a man who

recognizes that Slavery issue as being the living issue of the day; who does not hesitate to declare slavery a wrong, nor to deal with it as such; who believes in the power, and duty of Congress to prevent the spread of it.[1]

That we now have a letter in which Lincoln used the word "idiotic"— for the first and only time—to warn against abandoning antislavery ideals, sheds dramatic new light on his views on the eve of his New York trip. In a way, it is too bad that Lincoln did not speak so forthrightly there. His carefully modulated Cooper Union address instead encouraged generations of observers to conclude that it showed no real antislavery zeal, although this book contends otherwise. The newly discovered Corwin letter makes clearer what Lincoln had in mind when he wrote his first speech for the East: the twin goals of placing slavery "on the course of ultimate extinction," and of improving his party's— and his own—prospects in the 1860 presidential campaign.

Another issue, the controversy that erupted in 1860 over Lincoln's Cooper Union honorarium, continues to elicit interest—perhaps because modern politicians so often earn enormous fees for their speeches, a practice that arouses as much debate now as it did then. A number of readers wrote to inquire precisely what his $200 payment was really worth back in 1860. Actually, the precise value of Lincoln's honorarium remains open to interpretation. According to Inflation Watch, a much-consulted Internet website, the $200 New York fee would be equal to some $4,000 today—a sum far less than senators and governors earn nowadays for rotary club talks. But using other formulas that also take into account stock-market inflation, the $200 of 1860 might be

---

1. Abraham Lincoln to Thomas Corwin, October 9, 1859, original from the Corwin family archives, not in *The Collected Works of Lincoln*, courtesy of the Abraham Lincoln Book Shop, Chicago. The author held the original letter in his own hand, thanks to proprietor Daniel Weinberg. Corwin originally wrote to Lincoln on September 17, 1859, then replied to the newly found "explanation," as he called it, on October 17 ("Six months hence we shall see more clearly what at this time must remain only in conjecture.") Both of Corwin's letters are in the Abraham Lincoln Papers, Library of Congress.

worth tens, even hundreds of thousands of dollars in the 21st century.[2] That makes it easier to understand why the honorarium became a political issue. The last word on Lincoln's true value, however, properly belongs to one of those who paid for him to speak. And as co-host James A. Briggs wrote in the letter that accompanied his fee for lecturing at Cooper Union:

> Enclosed please find "check" for $200. I would that it were $200,000. for you are worthy of it. You "hit the nail on the head" here; & long, very long will your speech be remembered in this City. It did great good, it was so weaved & linked with truth, that it *convinced men*.[3]

Yet it apparently convinced more men in Manhattan than in Brooklyn—the place Lincoln expected to deliver it—reminding us how fortunate he was that his appearance was moved across the East River. On the day he was to appear at Cooper Union, in fact, the Brooklyn *Daily Eagle* lashed out with a querulous item, unknown and unpublished since, belittling the Republican party's recent, and popular, lecture series:

> Under the guise of literary entertainments, such men as G. W. Curtis, Wendell Phillips, and others, have in our lecture rooms preached the doctrines of [New York Senator William H.] Seward and [antislavery chronicler of the South Hinton] Helper. Many who habitually attend lectures are generally attracted more by the desire to see some celebrity than by the subject of his discourse; and many go to see Phillips, Harrison, and Cassius M. Clay out of mere curiosity to see the men, as they would as soon go to see

---

2. See http://westegg.com/inflation/. According to this website, which bases its calculations on the consumer price index, $200 in 1860 would be worth $3,910.57 in 2003, the last year for which data is available.

3. James A. Briggs to Abraham Lincoln, February 29, 1860, Abraham Lincoln Papers, Library of Congress. I am grateful to the Lincoln Studies Center at Knox College in Galesburg, Illinois, for providing the authoritative transcription, and Karen Needles of the Lincoln Group of the District of Columbia for reproducing it.

Barnum's mermaid. As a class, lecture-goers are a people who do not usually attend political meetings. Latterly the disguise of literary discourses has been thrown off, and the Republicans have openly announced their political lectures. But clinging to the claptrap of the lecture system, they have brought out only great guns from abroad, whose fame and notoriety had excited a curiosity to see them. A course of Republican lectures is now in progress at the Cooper Institute. Phillips, Giddings, and Clay have delivered themselves; to-night, Abraham Lincoln, Douglas's Republican competitor from Illinois, will hold forth.[4]

And so Lincoln did—unforgettably. In large part, he "held forth" by dramatically repeating the phrase "our fathers" no less than thirty times. Several readers wrote to point out that its use was not novel for "Barnum's mermaid" from Illinois. True enough. As Lincoln declared during the Lincoln-Douglas debates a year and a half earlier: "I say . . . there is no way of putting an end to the slavery agitation amongst us but to put it back upon the basis where our fathers placed it."[5] But not until New York did Lincoln make the notion the central theme of a major speech. At Cooper Union, the phrase "our fathers" echoed so often that one can imagine Lincoln basing the volley on a scene from one of his favorite author's best-known plays. After all, the constant reminder that *our fathers understood this [slavery] question just as well, and even better, than we do now* reverberates with the same kind of impactful frequency with which Marc Antony reminded friends, Romans, and countrymen that "Caesar was an honorable man," in the funeral oration from Shakespeare's *Julius Caesar*.[6]

---

4. *Daily Eagle* (Brooklyn), February 27, 1860, consulted on http://eagle.brooklynpubliclibrary.org/Archive.

5. Roy P. Basler, et al., eds., *The Collected Works of Abraham Lincoln*, 9 vols. (New Brunswick, N.J.: Rutgers University Press, 1953-55), 3:180–81.

6. Period testimony to Lincoln's love for Shakespeare is abundant, but one of the most interesting came from Lincoln himself, in a letter to actor James H. Hackett on August 17, 1863, in which the president came close to boasting that "Some of Shakespeare's plays . . . I have gone over perhaps as frequently as any unprofessional reader." See *Collected Works*, 6:392.

Finally, several readers wrote to ask if Lincoln invented the most famous line of his Cooper Union speech—his declaration that "right makes might." Truth to say, it is hard to know for sure. Lincoln once described himself as a "retailer," not an inventor, of his funniest stories,[7] and the same may be true about his serious writing. His "of the people, by the people, for the people" at Gettysburg, for example, owed much to a similar, earlier turn of phrase by Transcendentalist preacher Theodore Parker.[8] As for "right makes might," the expression was certainly percolating in the national vocabulary at the time, particularly within the roiling debate over slavery.

Writing in *Douglass' Monthly* three months before Lincoln rose to speak at Cooper Union, ex-slave and abolition advocate Frederick Douglass observed: "Slavery . . . shields itself behind *might*, rather than right." Did Lincoln read the newspaper and commit the sentiment to his extraordinarily elastic memory? We do not know for certain, but if he ever did consult the publication, November 1859 would have been the most likely month for him to do so. At precisely that time, fretting over his upcoming East Coast lecture, Lincoln was grappling with the political fallout from John Brown's recent, bloody abolitionist raid at Harpers Ferry. Douglass's interesting turn of phrase could be found in that month's editorial, "Capt. John Brown Not Insane." As usual, if Lincoln indeed "retailed" the phrase "might, rather than right," he also improved it—and made it immortal.[9]

HAROLD HOLZER
Rye, New York
February 12, 2005

---

7. Noah Brooks, "Personal Recollections of Abraham Lincoln," *Harper's New Monthly Magazine*, 31 (July 1865), quoted in Don E. Fehrenbacher and Virginia Fehrenbacher, *Recollected Words of Abraham Lincoln* (Stanford, Calif.: Stanford University Press, 1996), 49.

8. Garry Wills, *Lincoln at Gettysburg: The Words That Remade America* (New York: Simon & Schuster, 1992), 107.

9. Philip S. Foner and Yuval Taylor, eds., *Frederick Douglass: Selected Speeches and Writings* (Chicago: Lawrence Hill Books, 1999), 374–75.

﹣❧ INTRODUCTION ❧﹣

A MONG THE MANY tantalizing "what ifs" of the Civil War era—what if Stonewall Jackson had survived past 1863; what if George G. Meade had pursued the shattered Confederate army after Gettysburg; what if Abraham Lincoln had eluded assassination—is one question that must precede all the others. What if Lincoln the aspiring presidential candidate had failed his first, grueling, decisive test of political and oratorical skills in New York City?

In fact, it is entirely possible that had he not triumphed before the sophisticated and demanding audience he faced at New York's Cooper Union on February 27, 1860, Lincoln would never have been nominated, much less elected, to the presidency that November. And had Lincoln not won the White House in 1860, the United States—or the fractured country or countries it might otherwise have become without his determined leadership—might today be entirely different.

This is the story of that momentous speech: its impetus, preparation, delivery, reception, publication, calculated reiteration, and its enormous, perhaps decisive, impact on that year's presidential campaign. It seeks to ask and answer the question from which historians have long shied: Why did this voluminous, legalistic, tightly argued, fact-filled address prove so thrilling to its listeners, so irresistible to contemporary journalists, and such a boost to Lincoln's political career? How exactly did it transform its author from a relatively obscure Illinois favorite son into a viable national contender for his party's presidential nomination?

To find the answers required deep investigation into original reports and recollections and the shunning of the many, but fleeting, mentions of the speech in modern biographies, which have shed little light on the Cooper Union enigma.

For all of its universally acknowledged importance, Lincoln's Cooper Union address has for years enjoyed a peculiar reputation. It is widely understood to have somehow propelled Lincoln to the presidency. Yet it has been virtually ignored by generations of historians, most of whom have relegated it to the status of exalted footnote. Cooper Union remains, vexingly, the best known of Abraham Lincoln's speeches that no one seems to quote or cite; the most important of his addresses whose importance no one can quite explain beyond simply reiterating its importance; and the most famous of his speeches that almost no one today ever reads.

Myth and misunderstanding have conspired further to obscure Lincoln's accomplishment as thickly as the dense fog that enshrouded New York City only a few weeks before his arrival. Generally, when it has been mentioned at all, the Cooper Union speech has been celebrated for the wrong reasons, while its true virtues have oddly been ignored.

One thing may be said with certainty. Had Lincoln failed at his nerve-wracking, physically exhausting, do-or-die New York debut, history would long ago have relegated his name to the trash heap of obscurity. In the words of a twentieth-century song, had he not made it here, he might not have made it anywhere. He would never have won his party's presidential nomination three months later, or the bitter election that followed six months after the convention. He would never have confronted the agonizing choice between war and peace—to accept secession or fight to preserve the Union. And he would never have enjoyed the opportunity to strike a fatal blow against slavery, or to refashion American democracy into the global example he believed to be its rightful destiny. He would, to twist his own, later words, have "escaped history" altogether.

As far as his subsequently earned, exalted place in political literature—which Walt Whitman, Harriet Beecher Stowe, and Edmund Wilson, among others, have celebrated—it is probably fair to say that
without Cooper Union first, there would have been no Gettysburg
Address, no Second Inaugural, no further grand opportunities.

Then why is Cooper Union so little known today?

Perhaps its intimidating length—it is ten times longer than the Second Inaugural address, and some twenty-eight times the size of his masterpiece at Gettysburg—has discouraged recollection and analysis. So,
possibly, has the fact that, stylistically, it is so completely unlike anything
that Lincoln produced either before or after his New York appearance.
On the one hand, it is infinitely more restrained, intricate, and statesmanlike than the stem-winding oratory with which Lincoln earned his
reputation as a public speaker in the West. Yet it is also far less elegiac
than the monumental speeches that he delivered once he was elected to
the presidency and the Civil War began. In the Lincoln canon, it represents an altogether unique rhetorical watershed, the transforming
moment separating the prairie stump speaker and the presidential orator.

To further complicate matters, careful study reveals the complex
Cooper Union address itself to be, in a sense, three distinct speeches in
one, each ingeniously calculated to validate the antislavery platform of
Lincoln's Republican party through completely different approaches:
legal precedent, a hearty dose of ironic challenge, and a dazzling coda of
inspiring political faith. For this reason, too, Cooper Union has resisted
easy analysis. Remarkably, the speech has until now inspired only one
brief book, now forty years old.[1]

Modern readers consulting the few existing sources on the subject
might reasonably conclude that Lincoln was simply invited to New
York City, sat down and wrote out a fine speech, then went on to deliver
it successfully. They might think that he did so unaware of political
challenges confronting him at home and across the country from Democrats and fellow Republicans alike. They might suspect that Lincoln
was ambivalent or indifferent about the presidency, and unschooled in
the vast historical literature he was called upon to digest, explain, and

rebut in New York. They would likely fail to take into account the frenzied, partisan press that Lincoln knew would simultaneously praise and pillory his performance, and to which he tailored his address as surely as he crafted it for his "hearing" audience. The truth is, the full history of Lincoln's Cooper Union experience—its origins and its aftermath—is far richer, the context of Lincoln's New York debut more nuanced, and the challenge he faced far more daunting than earlier books have acknowledged.

Yes, the Gettysburg Address, Lincoln boasted, was "short, short, short," while the Cooper Union address is long, long, long. But Cooper Union has long cried out for study.

To properly appreciate its impact in its time and place, however, requires a significant leap of imagination. It may be hard for modern Americans accustomed to today's political sound bites and carefully timed question-and-answer-style presidential debates—which we view in the comfort of home on television—to appreciate the frenzied, all-consuming, society-defining political culture of the Lincoln era. But understanding that culture is crucial to understanding the Cooper Union address.

Lincoln's zealous contemporaries virtually lived and breathed politics—a passion manifested by the 80% voter turnout in the 1860 election. And they hungrily feasted on public oratory, flocking to hear candidates hold forth for hours at a time on the issues of the day.

In Lincoln's time, political speechmaking provoked the devotion of old-time religious revivalism and unleashed a level of community passion unequalled until the introduction of professional sports generations later. Citizens followed politics avidly, decorated their homes with pictures of their leaders, and took their families to political events as eagerly as they might visit church or the annual county fair.

Speeches and speakers might engulf entire towns, villages, and cities in waves of excitement. Crowds practically fought "a hand-to-hand conflict for even the meagerest . . . standing room" to hear politicians hold forth, as one journalist of the day observed with astonishment. Speeches and debates might inspire raucous parades, banner-waving, picnicking, drinking, brawling, and demonstrations bursting with fireworks, music, torchlights, and still more speeches. Hard as it is to conceive, during the Lincoln-Douglas debates of 1858, one audience, though exhausted after hearing three long hours of political argumentation under a scorching midsummer sun, happily headed off afterward to hear yet another speech, as if it could simply not get its fill of such oratory.[2]

Into this long-vanished political culture Lincoln emerged and thrived, developing into a shrewd crowd pleaser who even his lifelong political rival Stephen A. Douglas acknowledged to be "full of wit, facts, dates—the best stump speaker, with his droll ways and dry jokes, in the West."[3] Over time, Lincoln became wise not only in the ways of enthralling crowds, but in creating prose that could also be usefully reprinted in party-affiliated newspapers. For long before the introduction of newsreels, radio, and television, newspapers afforded information-hungry party loyalists scattered in rural isolation throughout the country their chief access to politicians and their unexpurgated ideas. Lincoln would want his Cooper Union speech to resound in print as effectively as it did in person, helping to magnify its impact and increase its influence.

The Cooper Union address tested whether Lincoln's appeal could extend from the podium to the page, and from the rollicking campaigns of the rural West to the urban East, where theaters, lecture halls, and museums vied with politics for public attention. Cooper Union held the promise of transforming Lincoln from a regional phenomenon to a national figure. Lincoln knew it, and rose to the occasion.

As if to illustrate his metamorphosis, the Cooper Union appearance also inspired the most important single visual record of Lincoln's, or perhaps any, American presidential campaign: an image-transfiguring Mathew Brady photograph. Its later proliferation and reproduction in prints, medallions, broadsides, and banners perhaps did as much to create a "new" Abraham Lincoln as did the Cooper Union address itself.

Supposedly, Lincoln volunteered when he encountered the famous photographer again a few months later: "Brady and the Cooper Institute made me President."[4] There is no corroborating contemporary evidence that Lincoln ever said anything of the kind. But he might as well have. Make him president, they undoubtedly did. This book attempts to explain how that happened.

A NOTE IS OFFERED to explain how Lincoln's speech is referred to in this book, and also how the text identifies Peter Cooper's academy, which still sits at Astor Place in Manhattan and continues to function as a free college for gifted students in the fields of engineering, architecture, and design.

Officially the school was—and remains—Cooper Union. But from the time its Great Hall began presenting speakers in 1859, a few months before the school even opened its doors to students, a so-called "People's Institute" established itself to organize public programs there for the further enlightenment of both its enrollees and the general public.

Thereafter, Lincoln and nearly all of his contemporaries, including journalists, began referring to the school itself as "Cooper Institute" or "Cooper's Institute." To most Americans of Lincoln's day, his 1860 speech thus became known as the "Cooper Institute" address. Readers will see on the pages that follow many references to the "Institute," not the "Union," from both Lincoln and his contemporaries.

Abraham Lincoln, however, lectured not for the "Institute" group, but for an independent political organization that rented the building's Great Hall for the evening. Therefore it is proper to say that he spoke at Cooper Union, not Cooper Institute. Besides, Cooper Union is the name by which the school ultimately came to be known, just as originally planned.

For the sake of accuracy and uniformity alike—with apologies for the resulting, unavoidable inconsistency—the narrative of this book employs "Cooper Union" throughout.

Chapter One

⊰ "Abe Lincoln Must Come" ⊱

T HE TRAIN BEARING a weary but exultant Abraham Lincoln
home from nearby De Witt County lumbered into Springfield,
Illinois, early on Saturday evening, October 15, 1859. No one was on
hand there to greet him. Lincoln disembarked, strode past the brick
depot, and commenced the brief, four-block walk along the gas-lit
streets that led to his house. The weather was "fine and bracing," with a
touch of frost biting the air.[1]

The practicing attorney had spent the last five days at Clinton, a village some forty miles to the northeast, busily "attending court," as he
innocuously put it. But ever the politician, he had kept one eye keenly
fixed on fast-approaching state election contests in Pennsylvania, Indiana, Iowa, Minnesota, and perhaps most crucial of all, Ohio. Just a few
weeks earlier, Lincoln had stumped tirelessly for Republican candidates
there, delivering rousing addresses at both Columbus and Cincinnati,
rebutting, one after another, earlier speeches by his perennial rival, the
"Little Giant" of the Democratic party, Illinois senator Stephen A.
Douglas. The night before Lincoln's return home, voters across the
country went to the polls, Republicans triumphed everywhere, and his
admirers in Clinton gathered to toast "Long Abraham" the "Giant

Killer." Convivial though it was, the party paled in comparison to the celebration awaiting him the next evening in Springfield.

Here, not long after he settled in at home, a surprised Lincoln was welcomed by a "vast multitude" of "several hundred" cheering Republicans. As a brass band serenaded Lincoln from the street, the crowd shouted for him to step outside and speak. Soon they would importune Lincoln to walk farther, and the procession would head boisterously over to the State House, for still more celebrations, speeches, and music.[2]

Before greeting his supporters, however, Lincoln surely glanced at the incoming mail that had accumulated in the house since his departure. Among the pile of letters was a telegram. It had arrived three days earlier at the town's Illinois & Mississippi Telegraph Company office on the north side of the Public Square. Ordinarily, operators would have promptly dispatched it to Lincoln's nearby law office. But most residents knew that Springfield's most famous citizen was out of town. So office superintendent J. J. S. Wilson probably sent a boy to run it over to his residence. There, Lincoln found it three days later.[3]

What Lincoln discovered when he tore open the envelope and read the telegram must have astonished and excited him. Here was another invitation to deliver yet another speech, but one that Lincoln, exhaustion notwithstanding, surely sensed immediately could advance his political ambitions on a grander stage than he had ever ascended. What the telegram brought was his first major invitation to speak in the East. And it marked the beginning of four months of negotiations, drama, and grueling work destined to lead him to the most pivotal public appearance of his career.

One can only imagine the satisfaction that Lincoln felt that night. A year earlier, through the summer and fall of 1858, he had debated Democratic incumbent Stephen A. Douglas face to face seven times in their bitter contest for the U.S. Senate. Lincoln had lost that race, sending him into a brief but profound depression. This autumn, at significant political risk, he had boldly followed the senator into Ohio to argue anew over the wrenching issue that divided not only them, but the rest of the country as well: the extension of slavery. As always, Douglas favored granting settlers the right to welcome or banish slaves from new territories. Just as vigorously, Lincoln opposed the spread of slavery anywhere, insisting that the institution be contained and allowed to die. Embracing Lincoln's arguments over Douglas's, Ohio, unlike Illinois the year before, had gone Republican by seventeen thousand votes. It was easy to believe that the tide was turning.[4]

An ambitious, ingenious politician who hungered for a return to elective office, Lincoln knew that the biggest prize of all, the presidency of the United States, would be decided only a year down the road. He sensed that Senator Douglas would likely become the Democratic candidate for the White House in 1860. Now, amidst the excitement of this night of triumph in Springfield, it suddenly seemed possible that the infant Republicans might actually hope to beat Douglas next fall—barely five years after organizing as a new national political party—that is, if they nominated an electable candidate. Improbable as it seemed just a few hours before the state election results had filtered in from across the country on October 14, Lincoln now had reason to imagine himself that man. And here was an invitation to introduce himself where he was least known: in the heart of the vote-rich East.

All this surely raced through Lincoln's mind as he heard the music begin to swell outside his windows on the evening of October 15. What did he say to his politically savvy, equally ambitious wife, Mary—herself once the object of an earlier Lincoln-Douglas rivalry, if local legends were to be believed? Did Lincoln share with her his mounting excitement over the party's triumphs and prospects? Did he dare speculate that while a major battle had been won, a larger one now loomed, with the presidency itself now in reach, and a major new forum to advance his ambitions suddenly, almost miraculously awaiting him in the East?

All we know for sure is that once inside his door—and sometime before the brass band persuaded him across town to further cheer the Democrats' recent election day "Waterloo"—Abraham Lincoln discovered the momentous telegram.

It had been sent on October 12 by a New York–based Republican activist named James A. Briggs, one of a growing number of easterners convinced that the only way the party could win the White House was by nominating a westerner who could attract votes from both sides of the country. The overwhelming favorite for the Republican presidential nomination was New York's own U. S. senator, William Henry Seward. But even as Seward's supporters worked with confident serenity to secure what seemed his destiny, a growing number of New Yorkers searched for alternatives. The anti-Seward forces remained fearfully certain that his nomination would ensure Douglas's election to the White House, and with it the unbridled spread of slavery nationwide.

Personally, Briggs, a onetime Cleveland attorney and businessman, now the head of the Ohio state agency in New York, counted himself a supporter of yet another rival aspirant for the 1860 Republican presidential nomination: Ohio governor Salmon P. Chase. But apparently he believed that to give Chase a chance at an 1860 convention victory Republicans must chip away at Seward's dominant strength by promoting a range of alternatives. The fall of 1859 found Briggs eagerly inviting several potential challengers from the West to declare their cases before eastern audiences—and, of course, before the influential eastern press. In other words, the original invitation to Lincoln was for the hosts, above all, part of an elaborate ploy to stop Seward and help Chase.

Into this complex political web came the terse invitation: twenty-five words that nonetheless held the prospect of changing Lincoln's life, and perhaps the nation's life. Lincoln must have understood so instantly.

Hon. A. Lincoln.
    will you speak in Mr Beechers church Broolyn [sic] on or about the twenty ninth (29) november on any subject you please pay two hundred (200) dollars.[5]

For all his peripatetic stump speaking, Lincoln had never spoken in the New York area in his life. Now, though not yet a presidential candidate, he was being handed the chance to appear in one of the nation's shrines to abolitionism—the so-called "Grand Central Station of the Underground Railroad," Reverend Henry Ward Beecher's Plymouth

Church in Brooklyn—and there to strike a blow against slavery, and for his own political future. The chance to lecture inside a house of worship surely seemed particularly appealing. Back in 1838, Lincoln had delivered his first great speech—to the Springfield Young Men's Lyceum—from the pulpit of the local Baptist church. For a man who had conceded more elections than he had won, but never lost his thirst for admiration and acclaim, here now was a chance at greater glory than even the most ardent hometown greeting could offer. The telegraph operator did not even know how to spell "Brooklyn"—he left out the "k"—but Lincoln certainly recognized the venue and the chance with no trouble at all. They represented, on the one hand, an extraordinary prospect for a national success, and on the other, a dangerous risk for failure.

As he prepared that night to head back outside his home to deliver an impromptu speech to his friends and then march with the local band over to the Capitol building, he likely sensed that his life had irreversibly changed. First, the clean Republican sweep on election day, in Ohio in particular. Now the invitation East: not just an invitation, but the opportunity of a lifetime.

In its next edition, Springfield's Republican paper would taunt the recently vanquished opposition with a tongue-in-cheek "apology" to local Democrats for keeping them awake on October 15 with the late-night hurrahs, music, speeches, and cannon fire. But the paper was dead serious when it added that the party's recent successes meant that Lincoln's "name was now inscribed high upon the roll of distinguished men spoken of in connection with the Presidency."[6]

A few days earlier, a Pennsylvania Republican journal had boldly proposed an 1860 national slate of Chase for president and Lincoln for vice president. "We think this ticket would suit the Republicans of Illinois better," came the quick and earnest reply from Springfield, "if the names were transposed."[7]

THE MAN WHO INVITED Lincoln East, James A. Briggs, had written him once before, in the heat of the 1858 Illinois Senate race, and it is possible that Lincoln—blessed with a politician's best weapon, a superb memory—recalled the name. Concerned at that earlier date that Senator Douglas was, in his "campaign tirades," unfairly labeling Chase an outright abolitionist (the political kiss of death for mainstream Republicans), Briggs sent along the text of a speech that his hero had delivered as a senator back in 1850, clarifying his position. Briggs hoped that the next time Douglas misrepresented the Ohio leader, Lincoln would "have the kindness to correct him from Gov. Chase's own speech." Added the New Yorker: "There is a deep interest felt here in the Illinois contest. I hope you will win a great and a glorious victory." Now, more than a year later, Lincoln's defeat in that contest still smarting, came Briggs's exhilarating telegram.[8]

Some Lincoln biographers have suggested that he was initially hesitant about the opportunity, but Lincoln was in fact elated about the invitation from the moment he received it, if for no other reason than that it offered the highest fee that he had ever earned as a public speaker. Two hundred dollars was a considerable amount of money in 1859. The potential political capital was of course even greater.[9]

Vexingly, Lincoln's path to what would become the Cooper Union address was paved with confusion. Postponements, conflicting invitations, changing venues, and a revolving roster of hosts all complicated matters, week after anxious week, before Lincoln finally boarded the train toward New York in late February 1860.

In a way, such difficulties were to be expected. Lincoln's America was still sixteen long years away from the invention of the great communications boon of the century, the telephone. Long-distance contact was still confined to handwritten correspondence sent through the U.S. mails or dispatched via private telegraph companies.

Nor was transportation to be taken for granted in the prewar era. To travel from Illinois to New York, half the breadth of the continental United States, posed a formidable challenge. Early in his career, Lincoln had championed "internal improvements"—economic development, as we call it today—advocating government investment to build canals and railroads. By 1860, thanks to ever-expanding rail lines, the original colonies were linked to the American West more tightly than ever. But it still took a passenger several numbing days to get from the prairies to the ocean, traveling mostly in upright chairs on unheated, soot-filled cars that rocked and pitched their way at barely twenty miles an hour. Each state, sometimes each county, imposed its own "standard" track gauge, as a result of which cross-country passengers were forced to change trains, and railroad lines, constantly.

Lincoln had done his share of traveling. He had gone all the way to Washington eleven years earlier, his family in tow, to take his seat for his one term in Congress. As he knew, such a trip required major investments in time and discomfort. For the opportunity to seize a prestigious rostrum in the East, however, Lincoln proved willing to make both.

Lincoln's old Illinois friend Ward Hill Lamon recalled that the telegram from New York "enchanted him," adding: "No event of his life had given him more heartfelt pleasure."[10]

The future president's longtime law partner William H. Herndon, so close to the senior attorney that the opposition press nicknamed him "Lincoln's man Friday," also testified to Lincoln's undisguised excitement on the Monday he returned to work, telegram in hand. Lincoln "looked much pleased . . . not to say tickled" when he rushed into the office around nine o'clock that morning. Over the years, Herndon would employ many a vivid word to describe Lincoln's topsy-turvy emotions. But only this once did he characterize his partner as "tickled."[11]

Still, Lincoln could not help toying with his junior associate that day, coyly announcing: "Billy, I am invited or solicited to deliver a lecture in New York. Should I go?"[12]

Herndon, who, whenever possible, liked to highlight his own influence on Lincoln, would recall that he helped to make history by replying: "By all means . . . and it is a good opening, too."

"If you were in my fix what subject would you choose?" Lincoln went on to inquire.

"Why a political one," answered Herndon, "that's your forte." As

Herndon put it: "I advised Mr. Lincoln I thought it would help open the way to the Presidency—thought I could see the meaning of the move by the New York men—*thought* it was a move against Seward—thought Greeley had something to do with it—think so yet—*have no evidence*. The result . . . was a profound one, as I think."

Herndon certainly sensed the dissident New Yorkers' "move against" pre-convention favorite Seward (although he did write his recollections with the benefit of nearly thirty years of hindsight). And he also detected the calculating hand of *New York Tribune* editor Horace Greeley, whom he had been dispatched to visit only a year earlier to make sure his influential Republican newspaper did not waver in its support for Abraham Lincoln in his Senate race against Stephen A. Douglas (in fact, Greeley had been sorely tempted to break ranks and back Douglas).[13]

By 1860, a number of Republicans in New York were indeed looking elsewhere for a national standard-bearer who could win not only, *their* state that fall, but enough *Northern* states to win the presidency. Seward's controversial earlier statements about the nobility of the anti-slavery movement and the inevitability of sectional discord—he had advocated a "higher law" than the Constitution and predicted an "irre-pressible conflict" between North and South—continued to haunt him. To some, he seemed vulnerable among Republican delegates in his quest for the nomination, and worse, beatable in a popular election if nominated. If Herndon is to be believed, Lincoln was thus encouraged to imagine from the very outset that a trip to New York could stoke the "little engine" of ambition that, as Herndon so vividly expressed it, "knew no rest." That engine barely needed such a spark for its owner to contemplate the highest political office in the country.[14]

Many historians persistently contend that Lincoln went east the following February harboring only the vaguest notion that he might emerge from the trip as a viable national candidate. These scholars argue that, at most, Lincoln undertook his trip aspiring no higher than the vice presidency, an office for which he had received some unexpected, but flattering, delegate support at the Republican convention back in 1856—though nowhere near enough to secure the nomination.

But the top job, the presidency, and the movement to deny Seward the nomination, was apparently on Herndon's mind from the first day Briggs's telegram arrived. If so, the prize could not have been far from Lincoln's thoughts, either.[15]

As Herndon recalled it for publication in his Lincoln biography, published thirty years later, on the morning that Lincoln came to work with the Briggs telegram in hand, he asked his partner and "other friends" not if he *should* go east, but only about "the subject and character of his address," as if his acceptance was already a foregone conclusion.[16]

The parameters of the invitation seemed almost boundless. Lincoln's talk was to be part of a series called the Plymouth Lecture Course. Briggs, who wired the initial feeler to Lincoln on behalf of an organizing committee composed of Joseph H. Richards of the New York newspaper the *Independent*, advertising agent J. M. Pettengill, and S. W. Tubbs, receiving teller of New York's Park Bank, had been asked by the three to take charge of inviting speakers for the lyceum-type appearances. Although they had never met, Plymouth Church minister Henry Ward Beecher was well known to Lincoln. The preacher was not only a prominent antislavery crusader, but also part of a famous family that boasted a sister who had written the most influential antislavery book of the age. Harriet Beecher Stowe's novel *Uncle Tom's Cabin*, first published in 1852, was already well on its way to becoming the best-selling book of the nineteenth century.[17]

"My acquaintance with Lincoln could hardly be called an acquaintance," Henry Ward Beecher later admitted. But he did consider himself "an observer" of Lincoln's career, explaining: "I followed him as I did every public character during the antislavery conflict." Beecher had already taken note of the "ability" Lincoln manifested in "his speeches parallel with Douglas in Illinois" in 1858. He no doubt looked forward to hearing him from his own pulpit by the time Briggs proposed that Lincoln lecture there in 1859.[18]

To get the church series in motion, Richards, Pettengill, and Tubbs had called on Briggs in October at his William Street office in Manhattan and asked him to draft invitations not only to Lincoln, but also to a famous orator, Senator Thomas Corwin of Ohio. Each speaker would be offered two hundred dollars, Briggs remembered, to appear in "a course of lectures these young gentlemen proposed for the winter." Briggs further recalled that "the proposition to lecture was accepted" by both men. But only Senator Corwin, on his way through New York to Washington for the next session of Congress, found it convenient to deliver his talk at Beecher's Church as originally proposed.[19]

Lincoln, on the other hand, managed to postpone his own lecture by nearly three months, while his hosts, without his knowledge, moved its location from Brooklyn across the East River to Manhattan. The changes would give Lincoln more time to prepare his speech, and offer him an even grander stage.

Pettengill seems to have understood from the first that Lincoln would be the more difficult speaker to pin down. The same day Briggs forwarded the original telegram—October 12—Pettengill wrote to William H. Bailhache, editor of the *Illinois State Journal*, to describe the lecture series at Beecher's Church, and lobby Lincoln's home-town supporter about the November 29 invitation. "Abe Lincoln . . . must come," Pettengill pleaded. "We want to hear a speech from him, such a one as he delivered in Cincinnati [a month earlier] would be perfectly satisfactory. He may speak on any subject . . . the utmost latitude may be observed."[20]

But much as Lincoln was enthused by the prospect of securing a forum in the East—not to mention the hefty two-hundred-dollar honorarium—he was from the first reluctant to commit to the proposed date. The text of his reply to the October 12 telegram has never been found, but it is apparent from Briggs's response to it less than three weeks later that Lincoln agreed to come east providing he could have more time to prepare his talk—ideally until the end of February 1860.

Time to prepare may have been only one of the factors behind Lincoln's request for a postponement. Ever the shrewd politician, Lincoln likely calculated, too, that a later appearance would make more of a splash in the Republican newspapers, if it could be scheduled as close as possible to the presidential nominating convention. As Lincoln undoubtedly saw it, an early 1860 lecture would have far more impact than one calculated to fit into an 1859 lyceum series. So Lincoln asked for a postponement. Instead, he got an offer to make a second speech—a portent of the invitation that would finally evolve.

Responding to Lincoln's counter-proposal, the obliging Briggs advised on November 1, 1859:

> I handed it over to the Committee, & they will accept your Compromise. And you may Lecture the time you mention, & will pay you $200. I think they will arrange for a lecture in N.Y. also. And will pay you $200 for that, with your consent. Then you may kill two birds with one stone.
>
> I understand the time between the 20th and last of February. Let me know about the week or so before the day fixed upon for the first Lecture.

If there was any doubt remaining that the summons had been inspired by anti-Seward forces within the Republican party, Briggs helpfully added a dig at his own senator. New York's "political coalition" was hard at work on its own local election campaigns, he reported to Lincoln, and he had "no doubt of the success of Republicans in this State." But Seward was thus far absent from the fray, and Briggs hastened to complain: "I think it is a mistake that Senator Seward is not on his own battlefield." Piling it on, Briggs wistfully told Lincoln: "Would that we would have the pleasure of listening to you, before the campaign closes."[21]

The campaign was over, and Lincoln was again on the road, when Briggs's new letter caught up with him. He had gone to Mechanicsburg, Illinois, to deliver a speech on November 4, traveled to Chicago on the tenth, and by the thirteenth arrived in Danville to help prosecute a murder case. Among all the nearby towns that he visited regularly to practice law, Danville always made Lincoln feel particularly welcome. Not long before, the town had named its new theater "Lincoln Opera Hall." Lincoln was reportedly "a little embarrassed by the honor," lamely joking that the last time someone had named a dog for him, the dog went on to lose every fight he subsequently undertook.[22]

Jokes aside, Lincoln knew all too well that after his painful 1858 defeat at the hands of Douglas he could not afford to lose more fights himself. The revised East Coast invitation must be answered, the opportunity seized. So there in Danville, he sat down to reply to Briggs on the stationery of the M'Cormack House hotel. His letter suggests that he was pleased about the postponement, but understandably confused about the unexpected new offer to deliver what would amount to a second two-hundred-dollar lecture in Manhattan.

> Yours of the 1st. closing with my proposition for compromise, was duly received. I will be on hand; and in due time, will notify you of the exact day. I believe, after all, I shall make a political speech of it. You have no objection?
>
> I would like to know, in advance, whether I am also to speak, or lecture, in New-York.
>
> Very—very—glad your election went right.[23]

WHETHER HE TOOK HERNDON'S advice or reached the same conclusion by following his own instincts, Lincoln made clear in this acceptance letter that his East Coast debut would be a "political speech," or more precisely, a political lecture.

He was no stranger to that medium. By the 1850s, Lincoln had evolved into a peripatetic, if inconsistent, figure on the Illinois lecture circuit. Lectures offered Lincoln the opportunity to speak on a wide variety of topics, demonstrate intellectual breadth, attract new audiences, travel to places where he could enlist new political allies, and earn additional money in the bargain. In a way, lecturing was Lincoln's third career—after politics and the law.[24]

Reformer Josiah Holbrook is credited with founding the American lyceum movement in 1826. Within a few years, lecture halls sprang up in cities and towns around the country, all vying to attract educated speakers to impart knowledge on a variety of subjects that might foster social unity through self-improvement.[25]

By the time Lincoln took the platform at the Young Men's Lyceum for his first major lecture in Springfield twelve years later, the country boasted more than three thousand local lyceums. Lincoln's 1838 effort was a grandiloquent but compelling discourse entitled "The Perpetuation of Our Political Institutions." Appalled by a recent wave of antiabolitionist violence in Illinois, Lincoln pleaded for "cold calculating reason" and "reverence for the laws." It was a theme to which he was destined to return.[26]

Over the years, Lincoln lectured on subjects as varied as temperance and agriculture. But his favorite effort, given on several occasions in 1858 and 1859, was a long, disjointed talk on discoveries and inventions. His dismay over its mixed reception may have actually fired his determination to accept the lecture challenge proffered by New York.[27]

Lincoln hit on—or maybe decided to borrow—the idea for the discoveries and inventions talk while riding the Illinois judicial circuit in the fall of 1855. Attorneys took turns on that trip reading aloud from historian George Bancroft's recently published lecture on *The Necessity, the Reality, and the Promise of the Progress of the Human Race*. Impressed, Lincoln determined to tackle the same esoteric subject himself—to "review man," as fellow lawyer Henry Clay Whitney recalled, "from his earliest primeval state to his present high development."[28]

The result proved less than successful. A pro-Douglas Democrat who earlier saw, and admired, Lincoln during the 1858 debates now complained: "He is a 'Big Gun' in the political world but—I think the people generally were disappointed in his lecture as it was on no particular subject and not well connected. He was, I thought, decidedly inferior to many a lecturer I have heard." The writer was quick to add, "but had he talked on his favorite theme—that of Politics, I have no doubt he would have done justice to his subject." It was as if the observer were predicting Lincoln's response to his upcoming East Coast lecture opportunity.[29]

Yet Lincoln persevered, delivering his flawed "discoveries and inventions" lecture several more times. As word spread that he remained willing to take his talk to new venues, however, he found himself besieged with invitations that he proved unable or unwilling to accept.[30]

Lincoln turned down one such request with a rare display of frankness on the subject. "I am not a professional lecturer—have never got up but one lecture; and that, I think, rather a poor one," he conceded. "Besides, what time I can spare from my own business this season, I shall be compelled to give to politics."[31]

Within his inner circle, there were few regrets. As Henry Clay Whitney bluntly put it, Lincoln "made a sorry failure in his attempt to invade the lecture field." And Ward Hill Lamon harbored similarly negative memories of Lincoln's "discoveries and inventions" talk. In Lamon's view, "Part of the lecture was humorous; a very small part of it actually witty; and the rest of it so commonplace that it was a genuine mortification to his friends."[32]

Billy Herndon did not disagree. The "discoveries and inventions" talk, he remembered, "was so poor that it was a failure—utter failure." Herndon thought he knew why:

> Mr. Lincoln had not the *fire*—taste—reading—eloquence &c., which would make him a lecturer—had no imagination—no fancy—no taste—no emotion, and no readings in that particular line. . . . He would, in the absence of a friend's opinion, as soon take up the Beautiful as any other subject for a lecture when he had no sense of it. Lincoln had poor judgments of the fitness and appropriateness of things.[33]

Still, as Herndon readily conceded of his partner, Lincoln also had an unquenchable tenacity of purpose: "The man who thinks Lincoln calmly sat down and gathered his robes about him, waiting for the people to call him, has a very erroneous knowledge of Lincoln. He was always calculating, and always planning ahead." Lincoln hardly needed Billy Herndon to advise him of the wisdom of going off to lecture on politics in the East. But he did understand that he would have to craft the lecture of his life. And as both of the law partners knew, lecturing was not as easy as it appeared. (Herndon, too, tried his hand at the Springfield lecture circuit, but with no success.) Whatever the risk of similar failure, Lincoln regarded the lecture invitation to Brooklyn as a challenge he could not refuse.[34]

• • •

LINCOLN HAD YET another good reason to accept the summons to go east in 1860. His oldest son, Robert, was enrolled at the Phillips Academy in distant Exeter, New Hampshire, and his father had not seen him for several months. Earlier, Robert had failed his Harvard entrance examinations miserably, flunking fifteen of sixteen subjects. His parents decided to send him off to preparatory school for a year of formal education until he could take the college admission tests again.

Lincoln was eager for his son's success, determined that Bob, as his mother and father called him, should enjoy the educational opportunities he had lacked himself. Robert later told at least one person that his father desired him to go to Harvard, and went so far as to ask his opponent Stephen A. Douglas to write a recommendation, convinced—correctly, as it turned out—that no one at the college would recognize the name "Lincoln."[35]

Abraham Lincoln painfully remembered his own meager education. The subject embarrassed him; he had been taught only "by littles" at primitive ABC schools on the prairie. Writing about himself in the third person, he later calculated that "the aggregate of all his schooling did not amount to one year," adding wistfully: "He was never in a college or Academy as a student; and never inside of a college or academy building since till he had a law-license. What he has in the way of education, he has picked up." Robert would be given the chance—indeed, would be expected—to do more than "pick up" an education.[36]

But contrary to one of the most stubbornly enduring of Cooper Union legends, Lincoln did not seize the chance to speak in the East just to get a free cross-country trip to see his boy. The future publisher George Haven Putnam, who would witness the Cooper Union address, later fueled that myth in a 1909 Lincoln biography that pointed to Robert himself as the source of the story.

"I heard from Robert Lincoln," insisted Putnam, "that his father had in January been planning to make a trip Eastward to see the boy . . ." but had postponed it when a client failed to pay the fee he needed to pay for the trip. Then came further word: "'Some men in New York' he said, 'have asked me to come to speak to them and have sent me money for the trip. I can manage the rest of the way.'"[37]

Robert Lincoln was alive and well when Putnam introduced this fantastic tale, and the fact that Robert did not move quickly to correct it, as he often did when writers misrepresented his father, suggests that he rather enjoyed believing it himself. However, it is not true. His father had already accepted and scheduled his trip east well before January. As for the money, as early as October, he had been assured that he would earn two hundred dollars for his speech, and the honorarium had been reconfirmed in November. Lincoln was hardly dependent on a legal fee to finance a trip to New York.[38]

There is no doubt that Robert Lincoln's parents missed their son. Mary wrote such a long letter to the boy on August 28, 1859, that she had to apologize to one of her regular correspondents later that day for writing her but a short one. By October, Mary was already dreaming of joining Bob the following summer, predicting they would become "somewhat of travellers" and see New Hampshire's White Mountains together. Whether Lincoln, too, corresponded with the boy is not known for sure. Robert took pains later in life to destroy his father's correspondence to him, but it would come as no surprise if his father sent him endearing and encouraging letters of his own. Parents and child had never really been separated before.[39]

Still, it strains credulity to imagine that Lincoln would have forgone "business," as he liked to call it—legal as well as political—to devote the time required for an eastern trip, merely to check up on his son, who had only been gone since late summer. By late 1859, several factors were indeed coalescing to beckon him east: his growing prospects for the presidency and the chance to introduce himself as a serious lecturer of the political kind in an area of the country where he had never before been seen or heard. Happily for father and son alike, they would enjoy a reunion in the bargain.

As 1859 wound down and the critical election year of 1860 began, arrangements for Lincoln's journey to the east bogged down in details as sticky as Springfield's notoriously muddy streets. "There was some confusion in the arrangements," conceded Richard C. McCormick, a member of the committee that ultimately took charge of the event. To say the least, this was something of an understatement.[40]

First came Lincoln's way a perplexing October 26, 1859, invitation from the Republican Central Committee of New York, inviting him to speak there on November 3 "preparatory to our state election." Chairman D. D. T. Marshall and his committee wrote that they "would be much gratified if you could make it convenient to be with us."[41]

Was this the promised invitation to deliver a second two-hundred-dollar lecture in New York City? No, but not until Lincoln wrote back to James A. Briggs a week later was the mystery solved. The Central Committee's unexpected invitation was entirely separate and uncoordinated. Lincoln learned that one had nothing to do with the other, and, after making sure he would not jeopardize the original Plymouth Church request by declining it, said no.

But his procrastination was meanwhile taking its toll on his Brooklyn hosts. By early 1860, James A. Briggs began feeling that it was growing "rather late in the season for a lecture, and the young gentlemen who were responsible were doubtful about its success, as the expenses were large." For reasons that can only be conjectured, the venue was moved. (Historians have occasionally suggested—incorrectly—that Lincoln's talk was moved because organizers needed a bigger hall, but in fact, the old Plymouth Church held more people than Cooper Union. Today's church docents suggest to modern visitors that organizers fretted that New Yorkers would have feared crossing the ice-filled East River to get to Brooklyn in the dark of a February night—as reasonable a suggestion as any other that has ever been advanced. Probably the best explanation is that the church's revenue-generating lecture season had simply ended.)[42]

In an inspiration, Briggs hit upon the idea of moving the talk to Cooper Union in Manhattan. Its auditorium was the largest in town (though, lacking a balcony, smaller than that at Plymouth Church). Other leading Republicans had scheduled speeches there, and a full house paying twenty-five cents apiece at Cooper Union would easily offset the honorarium and travel expenses Briggs had promised Lincoln. Initially, however, Briggs's skeptical associates did not endorse the idea.

Even with a large house at Cooper Union, the committee was "fearful it would not pay expenses—$350" including travel costs. Briggs was more confident. "I thought it would," he insisted. So "in order to relieve Messrs. Richards, Pettingill [sic], and Tubbs of all responsibility," Briggs next called on "some of the officers" of the Young Men's Republican Union and "proposed that they should take Mr. Lincoln, and that the lecture should be delivered under their auspices." But "they respectfully declined" too. Lincoln learned nothing of these problems.

Now Briggs grew worried. The "Young Men's Republican Club of New York *refused* to have *any thing* to do with it," he asserted. In desperation, he asked Simeon Draper, head of "The Draper Republican Union Club of New York," if he would "take Mr. Lincoln and the lecture, and assume the responsibility of the expenses." But Draper also said no. Lincoln, as Briggs put it, was now "left in the hands of the 'original Jacobs.'"[43]

With nowhere else to turn, Briggs told his Plymouth Church lyceum committee that it must take responsibility for finding a solution. After "considerable discussion," Briggs recounted, the four of them—Briggs, Pettengill, Richards, and Tubbs—agreed to assume the role of impresarios. They would personally underwrite Lincoln's trip, pay him the promised honorarium, take all the financial risks, and keep any and all profits for themselves. Not that they expected to profit much. In fact, Briggs had to pledge "to share one-fourth of the expenses, if the sale of the tickets (25 cents) for the lecture did not meet the outlay." The group even wooed the Young Men's Republican Union back into the sponsorship role once Briggs assured them that there would be no financial exposure.

Somehow, inexplicably, they failed to notify Lincoln in advance that his lecture would be relocated to Manhattan. This, amazingly, the speaker did not learn until he set foot in New York City in late February.

The group calling itself the Young Men's Central Republican Union had originally organized in June 1856 as the "Fremont & Dayton Central

Union" to rally support for John C. Frémont and William L. Dayton, the candidates for president and vice president, respectively, on the first-ever Republican national ticket. Now renamed, the club, under the leadership of chairman Cephas Brainerd, and a roster of senior "advisors" that included William Cullen Bryant and Horace Greeley, was determined to play an active role in the upcoming 1860 presidential campaign. Within the complex tapestry of New York politics, the group was not to be confused with the similarly named Young Men's National Union Club, not to mention the Young Men's Republican Committee—both of which now planned to hold meetings of their own around the same time Lincoln was destined to appear in the city: the last week of February 1860.[44]

A precocious teenager on the scene, George Haven Putnam, remembered the decisive meeting of the Young Men's Republican Union in editor William Cullen Bryant's office at the *Evening Post*. Someone suggested "that a cheque for expenses had better be sent to Springfield" as a down payment to guarantee Lincoln's visit, since "lawyers in the West did not always have money in their pockets." There was a "row," recalled the young lawyer Charles C. Nott, a member of the executive committee of the Young Men's Republican Union. "Everybody except myself was opposed to such a precedent and said we paid much less to more able and eminent men."[45]

The old poet Bryant spoke up in Lincoln's behalf. "I can but think," he declared, "that Mr. Lincoln has shown a better understanding of the policy and spirit of the Republican Party and of the conditions under which is to be made the coming Presidential fight, than has been shown by any other political leader in the country, not excepting even our own Seward." With this newest swipe at the New York senator, the mood of the gathering abruptly changed and the committee enthusiastically endorsed the invitation to the man from Illinois.[46]

In support of their own event, the leaders of the Young Men's Central Republican Union now sprang into action. Cephas Brainerd became the "bill sticker," hanging posters around town promoting the lecture. Richard C. McCormick assumed responsibility for public relations; he would make sure that Republican newspapers such as the *Tribune* and

Evening Post, and even the pro-Seward *Times,* reported the lecture in advance. Charles C. Nott, along with Benjamin F. Manierre, Charles H. Cooper, P. G. Degraw, James H. Welsh, E. C. Johnson, and Lewis M. Peck, all members of Brainerd's executive committee, no doubt pledged to work in their own ways to generate a crowd at Cooper Union.[47]

Perhaps overwhelmed by its sudden new responsibilities, not until February 9, 1860—barely two weeks before Lincoln's scheduled departure for New York—did the group dispatch a final, formal invitation out to Springfield over Charles C. Nott's signature. Now it was the committee, not the speaker, that wanted a delay. To "Abram" Lincoln (this time the writer failed to spell his guest's given name correctly!), the young Republican candidate for judge of common pleas proposed that Lincoln lecture in March as part of a new series featuring western Republicans. Neglecting only to report the change of venue, he wrote:

> The "Young Mens Central Republican Union" of this city very earnestly desire that you should deliver—what I may term—a *political lecture* during the ensuing month. The peculiarities of the case are these—A series of lectures has been determined upon. The first was delivered by Mr. Blair of St Louis a short time ago—the second will be in a few days by Mr C M. Clay, and the third we would prefer to have from you, rather than from any other person. Of the audience I should add that it is not that of an ordinary political meeting. These lectures have been *contrived* to call out our better, but busier citizens, who never attend political meetings. A large part of the audience would also consist of ladies[.] The time we should prefer, would be about the middle of March, but if any earlier or later day will be more convenient for you we would alter our arrangements.
>
> Allow me to hope that we shall have the pleasure of welcoming you to New York. You are, I believe an entire stranger to your Republican brethren here, but they have, for you, the highest esteem, and your celebrated contest with Judge Douglas, awoke their warmest sympathy & admiration. Those of us who are "in

the ranks" would regard your presence as very material aid; and as an honor & pleasure which I cannot sufficiently express.[48]

By this time, Lincoln had fixed on February 27 for his appearance. Probably he had promised his son a visit at Exeter. A mid-March lecture would not work. So he quickly wrote to New York to request that his own final choice of speaking date be honored. Not long thereafter, on February 15—three days after Lincoln's fifty-first birthday—Briggs wrote him to confirm the schedule, adding a none-too-subtle alert about the orator who was scheduled to precede Lincoln to the rostrum in the Young Republicans' new lecture series:

> Your letter was duly recd. The Committee will advertise you for the Evening of the 27th Inst. Hope you will be in good health & spirits, as you will meet here in this great Commercial Metropolis a right cordial welcome.
> The noble Clay speaks here to-night. The good Cause goes on.[49]

The group's message was clear: As Charles C. Nott had written a few days earlier, Lincoln was an "entire stranger" to the East, and this would be no "ordinary political meeting." Something more than an ordinary political speech would be required. Now Briggs reported that Francis Preston Blair had successfully opened the lecture series, and Cassius Marcellus Clay would likely be attracting another large crowd, and setting a high bar.

By this time, Abraham Lincoln was meticulously preparing his own lecture: reading, researching, making notes, drafting, and rewriting. As if not only "the Cause," but his own political life, depended on it.

Chapter Two

⊰ "So Much Labor as This" ⊱

N O FORMER EFFORT in the line of speech-making," remembered William H. Herndon, "had cost Lincoln so much time and
thought as this one."

Determined to suppress "the pyrotechnics of stump oratory" for
which he was famous, and substitute something new and unique in
political discourse, Lincoln devoted an enormous amount of time
between his acceptance and departure "in careful preparation" of his
eastern lecture. But he was more than merely "careful." Herndon
recalled that Lincoln devoted more time and energy preparing the lecture than to any speech he had ever made during his career: "He
searched through the dusty volumes of congressional proceedings in the
State library, and dug deeply into political history. He was painstaking
and thorough in the study of his subject."[1]

The subject would be slavery, the issue that had been roiling the
country with a growing ferocity since 1854.

That landmark year, Senator Stephen A. Douglas authored, and
masterminded congressional passage of, the Kansas-Nebraska Act. The
law overturned the 1820 Missouri Compromise, which had kept a pre-
carious lid on America's slavery caldron for more than three decades by

restricting the "peculiar institution" to the South. The Kansas-Nebraska law now offered settlers of new western territories the right to vote for themselves on whether to admit slaves within their borders. Douglas called the new principle "popular sovereignty," arguing that it would democratically advance national expansion and dramatically ease slavery tensions.

It did neither. To opponents, the Douglas doctrine, better described as "squatter sovereignty," was part of an insidious plot to spread slavery nationwide by encouraging slaveholders to migrate north and west and vote to import slaves. Within two years Kansas territory erupted in bloody violence between pro- and antislavery settlers.

Then in 1857 the Supreme Court intensified the crisis by issuing its controversial Dred Scott decision. In its ruling, the Court held that blacks could never be U.S. citizens, and pronounced any remaining vestige of the Missouri Compromise illegal, meaning that slavery could constitutionally be extended anywhere.

Abraham Lincoln had been more or less out of politics since reluctantly retiring from Congress in 1850 under a prearranged rotation agreement in which a series of prominent local Whigs consented to serve only one term each in the House. Now Lincoln was "thunderstruck" by the Kansas-Nebraska legislation and "aroused" back into the national debate by popular sovereignty and Dred Scott. He immediately denounced the doctrine as "sophistry," the "grossest violation yet" of the "sacred right of self-government," and an insidious scheme to establish slavery "by slow degrees, little by little," before territories were fully settled. Besides, he argued, "if the negro . . . is a man, then there is not even the shadow of popular sovereignty in allowing the first settlers upon such soil to decide whether it shall be right in all future time to hold men in bondage there."[2]

By the time he took the rostrum in the Hall of Representatives of the Illinois State Capitol on June 16, 1858, to accept the Republican nomination to oppose Douglas for the Senate, Lincoln was speaking for countless outraged Northerners who agreed that these events were part of a "conspiracy" to make slavery "perpetual, national, and universal."

As Lincoln warned that day in his "House Divided" address: "Either the *opponents* of slavery, will arrest the further spread of it, and place it where the public mind shall rest in the belief that it is in course of ultimate extinction; or its *advocates* will push it forward, till it shall become alike lawful in *all* the States, *old* as well as *new*—*North* as well as *South*."[3]

Throughout the summer and fall of 1858, in their widely publicized debates across Illinois, Lincoln and Douglas clashed repeatedly over popular sovereignty, the Dred Scott decision, the extension of slavery, and one issue that the Democrat repeatedly introduced, and the Republican consistently deflected: equal rights for blacks.

For Lincoln and the vast majority of his fellow Republicans, slavery, though morally degrading, was an issue that principally concerned white people. Black slavery was tolerable, if hateful, where it had long existed, below the Mason-Dixon Line. But expanded into the new territories, it threatened to limit opportunity for free white labor in a growing nation. Knowing they could not appeal to mainstream white voters by inviting sympathy for oppressed blacks—at a time when even freedmen generally lacked the right to vote for themselves—progressive Republicans like Lincoln often expressed their opposition to slavery by stressing that it poisoned white culture. Yet, as he had warned in a reply to Douglas four years earlier, the "greedy chase to make profit of the negro" could " 'cancel and tear to pieces' even the white man's charter of freedom."[4] Slavery's effect on the enslaved was never primary, although to his credit Lincoln did insist, throughout his debates with Douglas, that blacks were inalienably entitled to life, liberty, and the pursuit of happiness.

As Lincoln put it during the first debate at Ottawa: "I have no purpose to introduce political and social equality between the white and black races." This sentiment placed him squarely within prevailing white sensibilities of the day, however regressive they may sound in the twenty-first century. What elevated Lincoln above the prejudices of most of his contemporaries was his insistence, which he also declared of the black man that day at Ottawa: "But in the right to eat the bread, without leave of anybody else, which his own hand earns, *he is my equal and the equal of Judge Douglas, and the equal of every living man*."[5]

Throughout his seven outdoor "joint meetings" with Douglas, Lincoln protested the idea that such a basic moral principle could ever be subjected to a popular vote. For in the end, as he had asserted earlier, the "injustice" of slavery "deprives our republican example of its just influence in the world," encouraging "the enemies of free institutions, with plausibility, to taunt us as hypocrites." Besides, as Lincoln insisted, "If the negro is a man, is it not . . . a total destruction of self-government, to say that he too shall not govern *himself*?" In short, there could be "no moral right," he claimed, "in connection with one man's making a slave of another." Unfortunately, the Lincoln-Douglas debates failed to settle the volatile issue. Instead, they added yet more combustion to the growing crisis.[6]

SUCH WAS THE BITTER political history informing Abraham Lincoln's visit to the East. But from the moment he was asked to speak at Beecher's Church in Brooklyn, Lincoln determined that his address there would be a "lecture," not another campaign speech. He would prove historically what he had long argued politically: that the extension of slavery was wrong. He would show that recent efforts to nationalize slavery, like the Dred Scott decision, were, as he first suggested in 1857, "based on assumed historical facts which were not really true."[7] He had explored the history of American slavery once before at Peoria in 1854, but had focused his attention on nineteenth-century attempts at compromise. Now he would look back further into the past—to the record left by the founders.

To construct his address as a historical and political lecture kept faith with the spirit of the invitation and the sacredness of the church venue. It also promised the chance to exhume, and perhaps crown, Lincoln's bumpy career as a professional lecturer. And it offered Lincoln the opportunity to approach the wrenching slavery issue from a fresh perspective: by citing the lessons and precedents of the American past.

No one knows precisely when the idea for a political history lecture first gripped him, but once he settled on it, Lincoln realized that he would have to devote an enormous amount of labor to the project if he was to unearth the sources to support his case. He employed no researchers to check references, and no speechwriters to compose drafts. Lincoln wrote all of his speeches himself, pen to paper, word by word.

His time-consuming preparation apparently irked Herndon more than he was willing to admit in his own writings. Lincoln had long functioned as the "front man" in their partnership, publicly representing clients before judges and juries, earning newspaper attention for his legal and political efforts alike. Meanwhile, Herndon toiled away at the tedious paperwork that accumulated in the office. As much as the younger lawyer idolized his partner, the routine surely irritated Herndon from time to time, especially as Lincoln's renown soared. Lincoln's meticulous preparation for Cooper Union apparently proved such an occasion.

A self-proclaimed witness to those tense days of research and writing was Henry Bascom Rankin, who claimed to have served as a young clerk in the Lincoln-Herndon law office. Rankin recalled that "Herndon's patience was tried sorely at times" as Lincoln progressed "very slowly" on the speech, "loitering and cutting, as he thought, too laboriously."[8]

Rankin's observations must be carefully weighed. Census records show that he was actually employed in early 1860 as a farmhand in nearby Petersburg, but it is certainly possible that he saw Lincoln in the capital from time to time, or heard about his Cooper Union preparations then, or later, from people on the scene. Besides, it does not strain credulity to imagine Herndon, offended that he was not being asked to help with the most important speech of Lincoln's life, complaining to more than one office visitor about the slight.

For three or four months, or so Rankin testified, Lincoln worked assiduously at "writing and revising this great speech." He "spent most of this time, at first, in the study and arrangement of the historical facts he decided to use. These he collected or verified at the State Library." Lincoln also liked to talk and read aloud from his writings to gauge the reaction of potential audiences (he often drove Herndon to distraction reading newspapers aloud), and supposedly there were "frequent" discussions with Herndon "as to the historical facts and the arrangements of these in the speech." From time to time, Lincoln might have stepped into the adjacent office of a fellow lawyer to go over one detail or another. Rankin was certain that Lincoln "devoted more time" to the speech "than any he ever delivered." No one, not even verifiable eyewitnesses, ever contradicted him.[9]

Rankin was certainly correct about one thing: Lincoln's meticulous preparation revealed not only "the great grasp he had acquired in the discussion of political events," but "his peculiar originality in moulding sentences and paragraphs."[10]

It is easy to imagine Lincoln hard at work on his Cooper Union address—bent over a table, pen in hand, squinting in the gaslight as he sat before piles of large old volumes inside the handsome law library situated on the first floor of the state house across the square from his law office.[11]

Here, his head characteristically resting on his thumb, his index finger curved across his lips and up the side of his nose, his other three fingers tightly clenched, Lincoln pored over law and history books with intense concentration. When writing, whether at his small desk in his bedroom at home, in the law library, or in his noisy office, he would set his elbow on the table, place his chin in his hand, and "maintain this position as immovable as a statue" for up to half an hour at a time, lost in thought. As Rankin remembered with awe, when Lincoln was so poised in concentration he was simply "oblivious to all else."[12]

EARLIER IN 1859, the *Rockford*, Illinois, *Republican* proposed Abraham Lincoln to its readers as a worthy candidate to become the party's 1860 standard-bearer—as vice president. Reprinting the item in its "personal" column, however, *The New York Times* went further, acknowledging: "It is said, that some of 'Old Abe's' friends look still higher for him."[13]

"Old Abe" himself may already have been among them. In April he protested, "I must, in candor, say I do not think myself fit for the presidency," hastening to add that he was "flattered, and gratified, that some partial friends think of me in that connection." But such declarations of indifference to high honor were expected of politicians of the day. Ambition was fine, as long as it was not overtly expressed.[14]

The true measure of Lincoln's ambitions can be taken from his official schedule. Office seekers, then as now, even those merely "testing the waters," did so on the speaking circuit. For Lincoln, the milieu of the political stump offered both ego-massaging affirmation of his popularity and the useful opportunity to keep his name alive among the Republican faithful in the crucial months before the next national convention. Tellingly, in 1859 Lincoln crowded his schedule with speaking events.

As a result, he did not—could not—write the Cooper Union address in isolation, or in a vacuum: He was forced to compose it between political commitments, not to mention court dates, that kept him busy throughout late 1859 and into early 1860.

For example, he appeared at a trial in Urbana in late October, attended to numerous local legal matters throughout November and December, and the following month appeared before both the state supreme court and the U.S. circuit court in Springfield. In one crowded week late in January, he was at work every single day with court appearances, legal filings, declarations, and affidavits. He made his final appearance before the federal court on February 14—just eleven days before departing for New York—and might conceivably have appeared again had the court term not ended that day. Two days later he was still occupied with the redrafting of legal papers for yet another client.[15]

Then there was the siren call of politics. Although he had declined an invitation to address a Jefferson's birthday festival in Boston in April 1859, he did compose and send a long, inspired letter meant to be read aloud at the event, calculated to elicit nearly the same effect as a personal appearance. In it he declared: "Those who deny freedom to others, deserve it not for themselves; and, under a just God, can not long retain it." The letter was widely reproduced in party newspapers, irking Democrats who believed the author of the Declaration of Independence to be their perpetual political property. It was not the first attempt by

Lincoln to retrospectively recruit the founding fathers, including those who had owned slaves, to the antislavery cause. Nor would it be the last. He would do so again at Cooper Union.[16]

Within a few months, he was back on the road. Wisely, Lincoln clung when he could to Stephen A. Douglas's publicity-generating coattails. In their only direct electoral confrontation, the 1858 Senate race, Lincoln had won the popular vote, only to lose in the back rooms and legislative chambers. He undoubtedly sensed that his best hope of keeping his name alive was to continue his 1858 debates with the Little Giant as if nothing had really been decided, and whenever possible to extend them beyond the borders of Illinois—all the while clinging to the propriety-driven notion that he was not really a candidate for the White House.[17]

WHILE LINCOLN WAS pondering his, and his arch-rival's, next moves, Douglas traveled to New York first, in the summer of 1859, where he secretly negotiated to publish a definitive defense of popular sovereignty in the most prestigious literary journal of the day, *Harper's New Monthly Magazine*. The initiative was the senator's. After weighing the idea, publisher Fletcher Harper concluded that "the subject was of such paramount interest that our readers would be glad" to have access to such a manifesto. So began what deserves to be recognized as the final round of the Lincoln-Douglas debates: *Harper's* vs. Cooper Union.[18]

Devoting himself to his project with an intensity—and a passion for historical research—that Lincoln would soon replicate in preparing his Cooper Union address, Douglas consulted *Blackstone's Commentaries*, the Articles of Confederation, the Constitution, and *The Federalist Papers*, as well as a *History of the United States* written by George Bancroft, the author whose lecture on discoveries had earlier inspired Lincoln. Douglas also consulted *Elliot's Debates* for the transcribed proceedings of the state-by-state ratification of the United States Constitution, the very volumes to which Lincoln would soon turn to support his own interpretation of the history of slavery legislation for Cooper Union.

Unlike Lincoln, who was out of office and compelled to work independently, Douglas had help. His private secretary was assigned to delve back deeply into Colonial history, and found useful precedents in Queen Elizabeth's charter to Walter Raleigh. George Bancroft himself, a Douglas admirer, dispatched copies of documents from the Colonial era. As for the supporting arguments from the 1787 Northwest Ordinance—another document to which Lincoln would soon turn for his own research—they were recommended by none other than Ninian W. Edwards of Springfield, Lincoln's own, and very Democratic, brother-in-law.[19]

Douglas's lengthy screed, "The Dividing Line Between Federal and Local Authority: Popular Sovereignty in the Territories," appeared in the September 1859 issue of *Harper's*.

Filling nearly nineteen pages of the magazine, yielding finally to the latest installment of Thackeray's newest novel, Douglas's article caused a considerable stir, not only among Republicans but also within his own party. While fellow Northern Democrats hailed it, Southern Democrats who opposed any restrictions at all on the spread of slavery, including popular sovereignty, attacked it vigorously. The Alabama newspaper *Southern Era* went so far as to insist of Douglas that "the infection of his heresy" be expunged, explaining: "A leprous limb may corrupt the whole body; but let the offending member be amputated and the whole system may be restored to health."[20]

Lincoln must have been gratified, at least, that Douglas's article included a repudiation of the "house divided" warnings "advocated and defended" the year before "by the distinguished Republican standard bearer" in the 1858 senate race. Any reference to Lincoln in such a well-read and hotly argued piece would be useful. But Douglas also placed his argument squarely in opposition to William H. Seward's warnings of an "irrepressible conflict," characterizing Lincoln's future eastern Republican rival, not Lincoln, as "the most eminent and authoritative expounder" of Republican "political faith."[21]

Seward and Lincoln alike, Douglas charged, were equally guilty of foreseeing "no truce in the sectional strife" because they stubbornly refused to accept the Union as the founders had created it: "divided into free and slave States, with the right on the part of each to retain slavery so long as it chooses, and to abolish it whenever it pleases." As Douglas insisted, the federal government had no right to ban slavery in new territories; that right belonged exclusively to local authorities. To suggest otherwise was to cross "the dividing line between Federal and Local authority . . . familiar to the framers of the Constitution," and to violate "the great principle of self-government in the Territories." The true Jeffersonian ideal, Douglas argued, as if repudiating Lincoln's recent Boston letter, recognized the people of each territory "as the true source of all legitimate power in respect to their internal polity."[22]

Less convincingly, Senator Douglas also made reference to the controversial Dred Scott decision. Chief Justice Roger B. Taney's opinion that slaves were subject to perpetual bondage no matter where their masters carried them threatened to take the slavery question out of the hands of Congress and, by extension, out of the hands of the federal territories and their residents, where Douglas argued such decisions belonged. Now he twisted the record to suggest that the decision did no such thing, liberally employing ellipses and at one point transposing lines in order to bolster his argument.[23]

Douglas's article was quickly reprinted in other newspapers, although its reproduction was restricted under terms of the *Harper's* copyright, which inspired almost as much press commentary as did its contents. Eerily presaging a controversy that would arise over Lincoln's honorarium for Cooper Union, anti-Douglas journals now railed against the ban on cost-free access to the *Harper's* article. Douglas, the *New York Herald* charged, had "sold his brains to the Harpers, just as any plebeian contributor to their magazine would have done," as if to make certain that "even if defeated for the Presidency" he might "gather up a few dollars for [his] pains." The *Herald* sarcastically predicted a day when a future, incendiary speech by William H. Seward might cost $250 to reproduce, "deducting for insurance against spontaneous combustion." But Douglas was happy when he was stirring controversy. While some supporters urged him to lie low, he reveled in the attention.[24]

Political momentum at his back, Douglas next marched into neighboring Ohio to make speeches on behalf of local Democratic candidates. As the senator began promoting what he called the "great principle" of popular sovereignty, worried Ohio Republicans begged Lincoln "to head off the little gentleman" or risk losing the state to the Democrats. Angered when Douglas, at Columbus, sought justification for popular sovereignty from the "fathers who framed the government under which we live"—a phrase Lincoln would mock relentlessly at Cooper Union—he agreed to come.[25]

Still smarting from defeat in their Senate race, Lincoln may have inferred a more direct and personal challenge from Douglas's recent writings than the senator intended. To Lincoln, Douglas's *Harper's* article was a direct attack on Republicans who opposed the extension of slavery, himself included. Others were convinced that the piece was primarily a response to the Southern element within Douglas's own party. They believed the article represented not so much the renewal of his debates with Lincoln as the latest parry in his more recent debate with Senator Albert G. Brown of Mississippi. Along with that state's other senator, Jefferson Davis, Brown had recently attacked the Illinois Democrat for advocating a policy that entertained any restrictions at all on the spread of slavery. Like Lincoln, Douglas was looking ahead to his party's upcoming presidential convention. To secure the Democratic nomination, Douglas needed to make certain that his own house was not divided.

Not surprisingly, Lincoln preferred to view the *Harper's* article as a new debate opportunity. For Lincoln, as his old law associate Ward Hill Lamon explained, "The habit of combating" the Little Giant "was hard to break." His friends at the Chicago *Daily Press and Tribune* were delighted that Lincoln prepared to rise to the challenge. "In casting about for some proper person to reply to Mr. Douglas," the paper declared, "the Republicans of Ohio have selected the right man for the right place. Douglas' Popular Sovereignty will not be worth the cost of getting out the patient once ventilated by Lincoln."[26]

Now their combat shifted to the Buckeye State. Teasingly acknowledging that "the Giant himself has been here recently," Lincoln spoke at Columbus on September 16. With repeated jabs at Douglas's "copyright essay" in *Harper's*, Lincoln pointed to the "two main objects" in the piece with which he took issue:

> One was to show, if possible, that the men of our revolutionary times were in favor of his popular sovereignty; and the other was to show that the Dred Scott Decision had not entirely squelched out this popular sovereignty. I do not propose, in regard to this argument drawn from the history of former times, to enter into a detailed examination of the historical statements he has made. I have the impression that they are inaccurate in a great many instances.[27]

Lincoln was setting the stage for just such a "detailed examination" in the future, but he was not yet ready; he had yet to do the research that would be required for Cooper Union. For now, he would leap over the fence "at a bound," as he drawled to one of his Ohio crowds, rather than occupy his time pondering whether he could "crawl through a crack." A western political audience, he reckoned, preferred to hear him say things like: "The Judge, I think, comes very near kicking his own fat into the fire." Wisely, he would attempt no such homespun jargon in New York.[28]

Then it was on to Dayton and Cincinnati, where he continued his Lincoln-Douglas debate revival to the delight of his wife, who, along for the political trip, found the experience "charming." Obligingly, Douglas demanded to know in Cincinnati on the ninth: "Did you ever hear a Republican that dissented" from Lincoln's warnings of a "house divided"?[29]

Lincoln replied on the seventeenth. "We want, and must have, a national policy, as to slavery, which deals with it as being a wrong." Then came eleven paragraphs on the Northwest Ordinance of 1787, carefully repudiating Douglas's own interpretation of that milestone restriction in *Harper's*. To Lincoln, his opponent's contention that the Ordinance "never had a tendency to make a Free State, is a fallacy—a proposition without the shadow or substance of truth about it."[30]

Addressing one section of his speech directly to the South, Lincoln insisted: "We mean to treat you as near as we possibly can, like Washington, Jefferson and Madison treated you." Here was a technique—and an argument—he would soon bring to perfect pitch at Cooper Union.[31]

Lincoln had yet more to say about the Northwest Ordinance on a swing through Indiana a few days later. At Indianapolis, he reminded his audience that, plainly and simply, it "prohibited the taking of slavery into the North-western territory," pointing out: "Our fathers who made the government, made the ordinance of 1787." Douglas's *great principle* of 'Popular Sovereignty,'" he mocked for good measure, defied the ordinance—ran counter to the will of the founders. Slowly, carefully, with more conviction on each successive occasion, Lincoln was nursing along arguments that he would crystallize with unprecedented clarity and power a few months later in New York City.[32]

Even after renewing his debate with Douglas, Lincoln found he was far from being considered a leading presidential contender. Back home in Springfield at last, he found waiting on his desk an October 24 letter from a Pennsylvania Republican, irritatingly seeking his support for that state's favorite son, Simon Cameron, at the 1860 national convention. By then, Lincoln had already accepted the invitation to Brooklyn. Lincoln's refusal to endorse a potential rival for the nomination was coy; he had no intention of choosing sides as long as he had a chance at the prize himself: "For my single self, I have enlisted for the permanent success of the Republican cause; and, for this object, I shall faithfully labor in the ranks, unless, as I think not probable, the judgment of the party shall assign me a different position."[33]

For now, he was busily making notes, determined at long last to "crawl through the cracks" in that metaphorical fence surrounding Douglas's popular sovereignty arguments. Harking back to a phrase that Douglas had introduced in *Harper's*—a reference to "our fathers who framed the government under which we live"—soon to be repeated more than a dozen times at Cooper Union, Lincoln jotted down this fragment:

The effort to prove that our fathers who framed the government under which we live, understood that a proper division of local from federal authority, and some provision of the constitution, both forbid the federal government to control slavery in the federal territories, is as if, when a man stands before you, so that you see him, and lay your hand upon him, you should go about examining his tracks, and insisting therefrom, that he is not present, but somewhere else. They *did*, through the federal government, control slavery in the federal territories. They did the identical thing which D[ouglas]. insists they understood they ought not to do.[34]

Lincoln was certainly not for Negro equality ("How long, in the government of a God, great enough to make and maintain this Universe, shall there continue knaves to vend, and fools to gulp, so low a piece of demagougeism [sic] as this," he lamented to himself that fall).[35] Nor, however, was he prepared to let residents in the federal territories vote themselves to introduce slavery. Douglas might be entwined in new confrontations with other combatants, but for Lincoln it was still a competition with the Democrat from Illinois, still a perpetual debate for the final listener, the final reader, the final vote, in the next election. In anticipation came still more notes for speeches—furious jottings railing against "D.P.S."—Douglas Popular Sovereignty—including:

How D.P.S. is dangerous
    Re-open Slave trade
    Deludes and debaches [sic]—
Conclusion
    Must treat as a "*wrong*."
    Not to, yields all
U.S. not redeem all wrongs; but
S[lavery]. impairs & endangers general welfare.
Thou who do not think &c
We must think for selves—

S[lavery]. where it is

Forgotten law

But must *prevent*—

Have to employ *Means*.

Must be true to purpose.

If not, what.

Our principles will triumph.[36]

Even as Lincoln armed himself for further confrontation, Douglas sensed political danger elsewhere, debating not with Lincoln on the left, but with President Buchanan's attorney general, Jeremiah Black, on the right, while arranging for newspaper reprints and separately published pamphlets of his latest speeches and writings. Then he was forced to confront the serious illness of his wife. Divided and distracted, he may not have seen the threat approaching at Cooper Union. But first would come another blow to the dwindling hopes for sectional reconciliation.[37]

JOHN BROWN STRUCK on October 16, 1859—the very day after Lincoln read the telegram summoning him east. That night, leading a band of twenty-one guerrillas, black and white, the abolitionist renegade who had cut a violent path through Kansas launched a surprise attack against the federal arsenal at Harpers Ferry, Virginia. There he hoped to arouse and arm slaves into open rebellion against their white masters. But Brown never communicated his plans to slaves at nearby homes or plantations.

Thirty-six hours later, he was captured inside the arsenal by federal marines under the command of future Confederate general Robert E. Lee. Promptly tried and convicted, he was hanged in Charles Town, Virginia, on December 2. Brown's raid inspired some, angered others, and frightened many. Southerners gave voice to their fears of slave insurrections, charging the so-called "Black Republicans" of the North with encouraging dangerous revolutionaries. Northern Republicans, meanwhile, worried that Brown's highly publicized exercise in futility would radicalize the party's image, dooming its chances in the upcoming 1860 election, repudiated him. One thing was beyond dispute: John Brown's raid dramatically changed the dynamic of the slavery debate.

Lincoln's preparation for Cooper Union is seldom viewed within the context of the John Brown drama. All through Brown's widely reported trial in Virginia, Lincoln labored away on his lecture, unable to avoid taking into account the dangerous new turn of events at Harpers Ferry and Charles Town. Lincoln had every reason to fear that the Democrats would use the Harpers Ferry affair to paint all Republicans as radicals whose rhetoric fomented slave insurrection. He had to answer. Conveniently, he found an audience on which to practice his evolving response.

The day before Brown was hanged, Lincoln arrived in Kansas for another series of political speeches, this time in the territory where the doomed revolutionary had first gained public attention with a series of bloody raids on local proslavery settlers back in 1856. In the little town of Elwood, Lincoln declared the "Harper's Ferry affair" wrong for two reasons: "It was a violation of law and it was, as all such attacks must be, futile as far as any effect it might have on the extinction of a great evil."[38]

"Old John Brown has just been executed for treason against a state," Lincoln went on to acknowledge a few days later at Leavenworth. "We cannot object, even though he agreed with us in thinking slavery wrong. That cannot excuse violence, bloodshed, and treason. It could avail him nothing that he might think himself right." But here in Kansas, whose application for statehood had inspired the Kansas-Nebraska Act that, in turn, let the slavery genie out of the bottle, Lincoln was not ready to shrink from the main issue, or cede the high ground to the Democrats. Ending with a warning to those who would break apart the country rather than live under a future Republican administration, he turned the tables on fearful Southerners by warning: "So, if constitutionally, we elect a President, and therefore you undertake to destroy the Union, it will be our duty to deal with you as old John Brown has been dealt with."[39]

Not even Lincoln's distracting rhetoric could sweep the Harpers Ferry episode under the rug. John Brown would remain very much on the public mind through the time of Lincoln's visit to New York. As Lincoln surely understood during his trip to Kansas, he would have to deal with the issue again in the East. For now, he refused to be put on the defensive.

Instead he introduced, as if in rehearsal, the ideas he was contemplating for his Eastern lecture. At Elwood he asserted that the "Fathers of the Republic believed Slavery must soon disappear." At Leavenworth came the claim that Republicans were sectional only because they "get no votes in the South," along with an insistence that his party represented "true conservatism." Lincoln closed that address by claiming that modern Republicans "harmonized with the teachings of those by whom the Government was founded." All these thoughts were being honed, tested now, for Cooper Union.[40]

Before he left Leavenworth, Lincoln found time to inscribe his host's daughter's autograph album. Playfully, but perhaps still worrying about his fast-approaching trip east, he wrote: "Ere long some younger man will be more happy to confer *his* name upon *you*. Don't allow it, Mary, until fully assured that he is worthy of the happiness. A. Lincoln." Lincoln too was determined to prove himself worthy.[41]

EVENTS WOULD SIMPLY NOT ALLOW Lincoln to focus exclusively on his Cooper Union address. High on his list of priorities as he returned home and resumed work on his eastern lecture was another important project destined to advance his political standing: proper publication of the 1858 Lincoln-Douglas debates.

Ever since his Senate loss the year before, Lincoln had been "desirous of preserving in some permanent form, the late joint discussions between Douglas and myself." In other words, he wanted them published as a book. To facilitate such a project, he personally collected, and pasted into an oversized scrapbook, a complete run of debate transcripts: the pro-Republican *Chicago Press and Tribune* reprints of his own remarks, and the pro-Democratic *Chicago Daily Times* reports of Douglas's. "In my own speeches I have corrected only a few small typographical errors," he wrote a prospective publisher. He was perfectly willing to allow Douglas, in turn, "the right to correct typographical errors in his, if he desired."[42]

As early as Christmas 1858, Lincoln was convinced that "my Scrapbook will be reprinted," and by the following March several publishers were indeed expressing interest. But Lincoln was oddly reluctant to let the scrapbook out of his possession, and the proposal stalled. Not until he stumped Ohio for the Republicans in September 1859 was the project reinvigorated—and then, by chance. One day during his campaign tour, he inadvertently left his scrapbook behind in a hotel room. In frantically sending out the word that he wanted its safe return, he alerted local Republicans to its existence; they, in turn, took up the idea that it should be reproduced. Before long, the Columbus publishers Follett, Foster & Co. made plans to bring out an edition the following spring, to include Lincoln's Ohio speeches as well.[43]

On December 19, he sent John G. Nicolay, a young Republican officeholder who would later serve Lincoln as his White House secretary, to Columbus with the precious scrapbook, unwilling to "risk their loss by any public conveyance."[44]

With all the projects vying for his attention, Lincoln somehow also found time to respond to an intriguing request from a Pennsylvania newspaper for an autobiographical sketch. He had never written a word about his life before. After constructing a brief account of it now, he confessed in a cover letter: "There is not much of it, for the reason, I suppose, that there is not much of me." Then he added: "Of course it must not appear to have been written by myself." Victorian-era sensibilities still inhibited self-promotion.

About to write the most important speech of his life, laboring diligently to research it, and no doubt still weary from the political campaigns just ended, this is how Abraham Lincoln saw fit to describe himself on December 20, 1859, emphasizing his early struggles but saying almost nothing about his life since his rivalry with Douglas began in earnest, and nothing at all about his wife or children. It was as if it—and he—constituted a political work in progress, its conclusion as yet unknowable.

I was born Feb. 12, 1809, in Hardin County, Kentucky. My parents were both born in Virginia, of undistinguished families—second families, perhaps I should say. My mother, who died in my tenth year, was of a family of the name of Hanks, some of whom now reside in Adams, and others in Macon counties, Illinois. My paternal grandfather, Abraham Lincoln, emigrated from Rockingham County, Virginia, to Kentucky, about 1781 or 2, where, a year or two later, he was killed by indians, not in battle, but by stealth, when he was laboring to open a farm in the forest. His ancestors, who were quakers, went to Virginia from Berks County, Pennsylvania. An effort to identify them with the New-England family of the same name ended in nothing more definite, than a similarity of Christian names in both families, such as Enoch, Levi, Mordecai, Solomon, Abraham, and the like.

My father, at the death of his father, was but six years of age; and he grew up, literally without education. He removed from Kentucky to what is now Spencer county, Indiana, in my eighth year. We reached our new home about the same time the State came into the Union. It was a wild region, with many bears and other wild animals still in the woods. There I grew up. There were some schools, so called; but no qualification was ever required of a teacher, beyond *"readin, writin, and cipherin,"* to the Rule of Three. If a stranger supposed to understand latin, happened to sojourn in the neighborhood, he was looked upon as a wizzard. There was absolutely nothing to excite ambition for education. Of course when I came of age I did not know much. Still somehow, I could read, write, and cipher to the Rule of Three; but that was all. I have not been to school since. The little advance I now have upon this store of education, I have picked up from time to time under the pressure of necessity.

I was raised to farm work, which I continued till I was twenty two. At twenty one I came to Illinois, and passed the first year in Illinois—Macon county. Then I got to New-Salem, (at that time in Sangamon, now in Menard county, where I remained a year as a sort of Clerk in a store. Then came the Black-Hawk war; and I was elected a Captain of Volunteers—a success which gave me more pleasure than any I have had since. I went [into] the campaign, was elated, ran for the Legislature the same year (1832) and was beaten—the only time I have been beaten by the people. The next, and three succeeding biennial elections, I was elected to the Legislature. I was not a candidate afterwards. During this Legislative period I had studied law, and removed to Springfield to practice it. In 1846 I was once elected to the lower House of Congress. Was not a candidate for re-election. From 1849 to 1854, both inclusive, practiced law more assiduously than ever before. Always a whig in politics, and generally on the whig electoral tickets, making active canvasses. I was losing interest in politics, when the repeal of the Missouri Compromise aroused me again. What I have done since then is pretty well known.

If any personal description of me is thought desirable, it may be said, I am, in height, six feet, four inches, nearly; lean in flesh, weighing, on an average, one hundred and eighty pounds; dark complexion, with coarse black hair, and grey eyes—no other marks or brands recollected.[45]

ONE MORE DISTRACTION plagued Lincoln during the time he expected to devote his full attention to preparing his lecture: a bitter "family" squabble involving two important Illinois Republicans, Chicago newspaper publisher and mayor "Long John" Wentworth and Norman B. Judd, state senator, national committeeman, and chairman of the state Republican party.

It was Judd whom Lincoln had asked personally to deliver his 1858 letter to Stephen A. Douglas challenging the senator to debate. Few doubted that Judd was a loyal Lincoln man. But in 1859, just as Lincoln was starting his Cooper Union research in earnest, Mayor Wentworth ignited a political feud by accusing Judd of doing a miserable job for Lincoln during that Senate campaign, and of deserting him back in 1855 as well, when Lincoln had also been a contender for U.S. senator.

When Judd declared his candidacy for governor of Illinois in 1859, Wentworth's paper launched relentless attacks on him, accusing him of everything from misusing party funds, to improper land speculation, to promoting another Illinois Republican for the presidency. A furious Judd responded by suing Wentworth for one hundred thousand dollars for libel. As if this was not upsetting enough, Wentworth then asked Lincoln to defend him against the lawsuit. Judd, meanwhile, fumed that Lincoln "ought not to stand idly by and see me charged with foul wrong to you when you know it is unjust." Wentworth and his friends, Judd raged, ought to be "kicked in the kennel with the rest of the curs."[46] The affair was complicated further when, in late 1859, Wentworth declared for another term as mayor of Chicago.

Now Lincoln was facing open rebellion within a statewide political party that was supposed to be unified behind his presidential ambitions. The donnybrook threatened to weaken the organization at just the time he was also hoping that his state's Republicans could persuade the National Committee to stage the 1860 presidential convention in Illinois. If the rift was not quickly healed, either Judd's or Wentworth's friends could turn against him. Lincoln could not afford to choose sides.

The ugly fight dragged on for months. On December 9, Lincoln assured Judd: "The vague charge that you played me false last year, I believe to be false and outrageous." Five days later he sent off a letter to three prominent Chicago Republicans reiterating his "confidence" in Judd, and noting that "of all of the avowed friends I had in the canvass of last year, I do not suspect any of having acted treacherously to me, or to our cause." He could not help adding: "I dislike to appear before the public, in this matter."[47]

When Lincoln offered to step in to negotiate a compromise between the two protagonists, under which Judd would drop his lawsuit and

Wentworth recant his accusations, Wentworth sent Lincoln a bitter letter demanding "an immediate and *final* settlement," explaining caustically: "You may die, & then what?" That same day, February 9, 1860, Lincoln was compelled to interrupt the final preparations for his lecture to write lengthy letters to both men.[48]

To Wentworth, Lincoln made clear, "I am anxious to have that difficulty settled, so that both you and he can pull square in the cause & not be expending your strength in fighting oneanother [sic]." And to Judd, Lincoln sent a reminder that, feud or not, he needed the anti-Wentworth *Press and Tribune* to declare its support for his own political aspirations, before Judd's enemies began deserting to Seward or Edward Bates, "squeezing me out in the middle with nothing." "I am not in a position where it would hurt much for me not to be nominated on the national ticket," he explained, "but I am where it would hurt some for me to not get the Illinois delegates. . . . Can you not help me a little in this matter, in your end of the vineyard?"[49]

The Wentworth-Judd feud generated one positive result: It motivated Judd to show his friend that he could produce the newspaper endorsement for which Lincoln yearned. On February 16, the influential *Chicago Press and Tribune* published an extravagant editorial praising Lincoln as "a man of great breadth and great acuteness of intellect," even "executive capacity" (though he had never been called upon to demonstrate any), and urging "the nomination of Lincoln for the first place on the National Republican ticket." An exultant Norman Judd wrote a few days later to boast: "You saw what the Tribune said about you. Was it satisfactory?"[50]

Appearing in print a week before his departure for New York, it was more than satisfactory, even if it had come at the cost of much valuable time and energy. Just a day later came the final invitation to the East from Charles C. Nott and the Young Men's Central Republican Union. It was a good week. But Lincoln still worried about his role as intermediary. "There may be men who wish the breach between you and Judd to be widened," he warned Wentworth, "and if there be, they will naturally look with an evil eye at any one who tries to heal it."[51]

Although by then a final Judd-Wentworth settlement was close, Lincoln would depart for the East before the Illinois political mess was fully resolved. Judd was destined to lose his bid for the Republican nomination for governor, but Wentworth seemed well on his way to winning the party's endorsement for another term as mayor. Apparently oblivious to Lincoln's schedule, "Long John" wired Lincoln on Washington's birthday, February 22, with a request that he address a meeting in Chicago on Saturday the twenty-fifth—when, of course, Lincoln expected to be in New York. Added the mayor: "dont disappoint me."[52]

At least Lincoln had a legitimate excuse for refusing, although not all his friends were pleased. "I am sorry you will be so far from Wentworth & Judd," his close political associate David Davis worried on the eve of Lincoln's departure, making clear that his own political priorities were local, not national. "You ought to have instructed me what hotel you stopped at New York." Lincoln was probably delighted to escape. He left no word about where he could be reached.[53]

LINCOLN COMPOSED his speeches slowly, meticulously, laboriously. Over the years, a contemporary noticed, he grew "more and more in the habit of revising all he had written down to the latest hour possible before delivery" of his formal talks. Striving for simplicity, his speeches became "more eloquent," observed Herndon, as Lincoln worked to forgo "gaudy ornamentation . . . dropping gradually the alliteration and rosy metaphor of youth."[54]

Ward Hill Lamon remembered, "When Mr. Lincoln had a speech to write . . . he would put down each thought, as it occurred to him, on a small strip of paper, and, having accumulated a number of these, generally carried them in his hat or his pockets until he had the whole speech composed in this odd way." Only then would he "sit down at his table, connect the fragments, and then write out the whole speech on consecutive sheets in a plain, legible handwriting."[55]

Where Cooper Union was concerned, first came the research—more than he had ever undertaken to write a political address.

"My father, of course, had some books at home. I remember well a large bookcase full of them," Robert Lincoln testified as an old man. ". . . After my mother's death, when I rounded up such things as well as I could, I found myself in possession of twenty odd books, which I now have . . . among them . . . a book called 'Lives of the Signers,' which I have no doubt my father used in preparing his Cooper Institute speech."[56]

The book to which Robert referred was undoubtedly John Sanderson's *Biography of the Signers to the Declaration of Independence*. Although Lincoln did not own the original five-volume edition, he did possess the one-volume abridged version edited by Robert Taylor Conrad in 1847. Lincoln turned to it now for further insight into the lives and opinions of the founders. Douglas had insisted in *Harper's* that the heroes of the Revolution had reserved to the states the right to decide the future of slavery. Now Lincoln sought an avenue for rebuttal. What did these founders really think—both before and after the constitutional convention? Did they ever publish their later views? More to the point, did they ever have the opportunity, the responsibility, to vote on the issue? And if so, how did they come down?[57]

Here Lincoln found his opening theme: How had the framers voted on subsequent matters related to the slavery question? If they had sided with federal authority, as Lincoln increasingly suspected, he would have the perfect antidote to Douglas's own arguments in *Harper's New Monthly Magazine*.

As Lincoln knew, "the scenes of the revolution . . . like every thing else . . . must fade upon the memory of the world, and grow more and more dim by the lapse of time." To refresh his recollection, Lincoln began with Jonathan Elliott's *The Debates in the Several State Conventions on the Adoption of the Federal Constitution as Recommended by the General Constitution at Philadelphia, in 1787*, his own sheepskin-bound two-volume set of the original multivolume edition published in 1836. (He eventually gave his copy to his law partner Herndon, who years later sold it at auction.)[58]

Conveniently, the Lincoln-Herndon law firm owned the four volumes of James Kent's *Commentaries on The Constitution*. Page by page, in these and other books, Lincoln studied the words of the men whose names were now "transferred to counties and cities, and rivers and mountains," as he had noted in his lyceum lecture twenty-four years earlier, "revered and sung, and toasted for all time."[59]

Patrick Henry, for example, he found had once declared that "it would rejoice my very soul that every one of my fellow-beings was emancipated." Unfortunately, Henry also thought, as Douglas now did, that slavery was "a local matter, and I can see no propriety in subjecting it to Congress." But here in *Elliott* was evidence that at least two signers of the Constitution, William Blount and William Few, had later voted to prohibit slavery in the Northwest Territories. Others had cast similar votes. The more Lincoln searched, the more framers he discovered to have been opposed to the extension of slavery, or at least aware of federal authority to govern extension. By the time he finished, he had determined that of the thirty-nine signers of the Constitution who had gone on to express themselves on the issue, twenty-three had registered votes that showed that they believed the federal government had the power to regulate slavery.[60]

For up-to-date statistics he used his 1859 edition of Charles Lanman's *Dictionary of the United States Congress*. He had purchased it new, he later told its author, and found it "both interesting and valuable." Lincoln also read Hinton Rowan Helper's new book, *The Impending Crisis of The South*, to which his Cooper Union speech would refer. The explosive volume, which infuriated Southerners, called slavery "a great moral, social, civil, and political evil—a dire enemy to true. . . national greatness."[61]

The law library at the state capitol boasted a number of crucial books that Lincoln did not own: copies of Jefferson's autobiography, *The Letters of George Washington*, *The Papers of James Madison*, and the *Debates in the Federal Convention of 1787*. In these volumes he found more evidence for his theory, as well as powerful, agonized denunciations of slavery from the leaders of the previous century. As Washington himself had convincingly admitted, "There is no man living who wishes more sincerely than I do to see a plan adopted for the abolition of it." What was more, Washington had foreseen that slavery could indeed be controlled "by legislative authority," just as Lincoln would argue now.[62]

Lincoln searched scrupulously, too, through the dust-filled *Annals of Congress* and *Congressional Globe*—the early versions of what today is called the *Congressional Record*—for the texts of every relevant slavery debate and vote.

He probably consulted, too, a life of the Marquis de Lafayette, and likely examined the works of Alexander Hamilton. He reread Benjamin Franklin's petition against slavery. He looked through accounts of the great slave uprisings, including Nat Turner's insurrection in 1831. And he studied back issues of the Chicago and Springfield newspapers, along with the weekly national editions of the *New York Tribune*, in search of fresh evidence of Douglas's moral indifference to slavery. He read and reread Douglas's *Harper's* article, and reviewed the newspaper reprints of his own speeches, including the 1858 debates.

Working to develop arguments that would connect this newly assembled mountain of facts into a coherent narrative, Lincoln hit upon a novel device. The best way to record the fruits of his research was to make the facts themselves the core of his speech. A political demagogue like Douglas, he believed, might try to convince the public that the federal government had no right to control slavery in the federal territories. "But he has no right," Lincoln now wrote in his draft, "to mislead others" who have less access to history, and less leisure to study it, into the false belief that the founders believed any such thing. He would incorporate that sentiment into his manuscript. It was a prelude to his famous comment to Congress two years later: "Fellow citizens, *we* cannot escape history."[63]

With no researchers to assist him, no professional scholars to feed him documents, no secretary to take dictation, Lincoln sought his own "access to history," and, amidst the pressures of law and politics, the "leisure to study it." And now, armed with history, he was ready to answer Stephen A. Douglas one last time.

Although he apparently, inexplicably told sculptor Leonard Wells

Volk a few months later a fantastic story—that he "arranged and composed this speech in his mind while going on the cars from Camden to Jersey City" on the final leg of his journey to New York—the truth was that never in his life did Lincoln labor over an address so diligently, over such an extended period of time, and in the face of such wrenching distractions.[64]

As one of the young men who invited him would later observe, Lincoln produced "the most carefully prepared, the most elaborately investigated and demonstrated and verified of all the work of his life." Yet notwithstanding all his labors, "When at last he left for New York," Herndon remembered, "we had many misgivings—and he not a few himself—of his success in the great metropolis."[65]

"What effect the unpretentious western lawyer would have on the wealthy and fashionable society of the great city," admitted Herndon, "could only be conjectured."[66]

Chapter Three

⊰ "Some Confusion in the Arrangements" ⊱

No one in Springfield appreciated the significance of Lincoln's journey, or its risk, more than Lincoln himself. His research now behind him, his facts arranged, his arguments developed, he had already written and rewritten his draft, polishing the work further every time and everywhere he had the chance to work: at his law office, in the law library, or at night, by candlelight, at the little desk in the corner of his bedroom at home. To familiarize himself with the speech, he took to reciting passages aloud as he walked the streets of Springfield, occasionally with a giggling neighbor boy balanced atop his soaring shoulders.

Lincoln knew the stakes, the public expectations from his admirers, and recognized that they were getting higher. On February 5, the newly elected postmaster of the House of Representatives wrote from Washington to assure him that he would return home for the upcoming "presidential canvass to work I hope for A. Lincoln for President of the U. States." A few weeks earlier, an especially hopeful admirer had written to recommend a candidate for attorney general in a future Lincoln administration.[1]

Then, twelve days before he was scheduled to leave, he received the

long-anticipated news from Chicago: "Do not be surprised if the *Press &
Tribune* breaks ground for you in a few days." Just as promised, six days
later, the state's most influential Republican newspaper endorsed Lincoln for president, vastly expanding the stakes—and the pressure—facing Lincoln as his departure date grew nearer. He was no longer just a
possible candidate for the nomination; he was at last in the race, though
by no means yet a favorite.[2]

"Well may Illinois be proud of her Lincoln," cheered the Springfield
Journal. "No wonder that the West claims his nomination at Chicago."
Oddly, the *Tribune* had listed among Lincoln's virtues its confident
belief that he was "not learned, in a bookish sense." But the paper at
least acknowledged that he was also "laboriously attentive to detail,
industrious and conscientious." None of his friends at the *Tribune* could
have imagined how many books Lincoln had studied to prepare for his
"learned" eastern debut.[3]

The newly anointed Illinois favorite son did not consider his speech
finished until past mid-February. And even thereafter, a contemporary
observed, every subsequent day "until it was placed in his travelling
satchel, he took out the sheets and carefully went over the pages, making notations here and there, and even writing whole pages over again."
An eyewitness who glimpsed the final manuscript noted that it "was
written upon blue foolscap"—the standardized, ruled writing paper of
the day, each sheet about thirteen by sixteen inches—"all in his own
hand, and with few interlineations." William Herndon, for weeks critical of Lincoln's endless fussing, now pronounced the finished effort
"well worth the time devoted to it," later admitting "it would be the
crowning effort of Lincoln's life." At last, Lincoln was ready.[4]

First, last-minute matters required his attention at home. On January
30, Lincoln sent ten dollars off to Robert at Phillips Academy (the fourth
expense check he had been compelled to dispatch to his son in only six
weeks; perhaps he would talk to Bob about his spending habits when he
met him later on at school in New Hampshire). On February 1, Lincoln
deposited $539.95 into his account at the Springfield Marine and Fire
Insurance Company, more than enough to sustain even the free-spending

Mary Lincoln and their two younger boys during his absence. Then he made out a check for one hundred dollars to the local Springfield tailors George W. Woods and Jasen C. H. Henckle, whose shop stood on the west side of the public square, to pay for the brand-new black suit he had ordered for his New York trip. To go with it, he purchased a new pair of boots as well, blithely unconcerned that when he tried them on, they pinched his large feet.[5]

With no secretary to perform such tasks on his behalf, Lincoln presumably made all his own travel arrangements—rail tickets, hotel reservations, and the like. The night before his departure, he packed his own suitcase, but not the old leather valise or worn carpetbag he usually took on the judicial circuit. Worried that his New York hosts would think ill of her husband if he arrived with such shabby luggage, Mary insisted that he take her trunk instead.

She herself would not be making the trip. The last time Lincoln traveled to New York, on legal business two and a half years before, he had taken Mary with him. They had stopped at romantic Niagara Falls, "most pleasantly," she reported. But Mary came to regard New York City as a gateway, not a destination, much less an opportunity. Viewing the ships crowding the river on that 1857 trip, she could only think of traveling even farther. "How I long to go to Europe," she confided to her half-sister after observing "the large steamers at the New York landing, ready for their European voyage." Even on that blissful trip east, Mary could not help but feel "in my heart . . . that poverty was my portion" in life. She laughingly told Lincoln "that I am determined my next Husband *shall be rich*." She even boasted that she said so "often." Perhaps Lincoln did not share her amusement. His return visit to New York in 1860 would be undertaken without her.[6]

As departure day neared, there was yet more grinding legal work to complete—offers of new cases to consider, letters about old ones to write—as well as political correspondence to read and answer. He was surely cheered when his friend Abraham Jonas of neighboring Quincy, Illinois, wrote to predict jubilantly that "with proper exertions and judicious selections [at the forthcoming national convention] . . . we shall be able to carry the day and in November *proclaim victory to all the world*."[7]

As a public speaker, Lincoln was more in demand than ever. A week before departure day, Horace White, the friendly *Chicago Press and Tribune* correspondent who had covered the 1858 Lincoln-Douglas debates, forwarded a note from a Wisconsin Republican inviting Lincoln to make a speech there on February 28. White made no secret of his enthusiasm for the prospect. "You must get yourself in training for the Presidency," he urged, adding: "Go by all means." "It so happens that I am engaged to be at Brooklyn on the evening of the 27th.," Lincoln replied with just a hint of pride, "so that, of course, I can not be in Wisconsin, on the 28th."[8]

On Wednesday morning, February 22, half a continent from Lincoln's hometown, New Yorkers marched through torrential rain, gale winds, and slush to celebrate George Washington's birthday, most of them unaware that Illinois' new favorite son was about to depart for their city. That same day, as Springfield's military and fire brigades paraded through muddy streets in a Washington tribute of their own, the town's pro-Republican *Journal* carried a brief item:

> We understand Mr. Lincoln leaves home today for New York city [sic]. He is under an engagement to deliver an address before the Young Men's Association of Brooklyn, on the 27th inst.[9]

UNBEKNOWNST TO Lincoln, the *New York Evening Post* also reported that same day that "The Hon. Abram Lincoln of Illinois" would be coming to town to speak—not in Brooklyn, but at the Cooper Institute in Manhattan. "The Republicans of New York," it predicted, "will give him a cordial welcome."

Early that holiday morning, Lincoln withdrew one hundred dollars—fifty dollars in cash, and a fifty-dollar draft—to cover his traveling expenses. Then, at 11:15 A.M., as the Washington's birthday celebrations began massing in the center of town, he boarded a train at the depot a few blocks from his house. No friends accompanied him. There was no grand send-off. He left "as quietly," a contemporary marveled, "as if going out to attend some one of the courts of the Eighth District."[10]

As his train steamed out of town, Lincoln may have harbored doubts as formidable as the doubts facing New Yorkers buying tickets to hear him. Cooper Union would bring him into the Republican front-runner's front yard, testing his nerve more than any venture of his career. His entire political future was yoked to his ability to charm and impress an audience more sophisticated than any he had ever faced. But what Lincoln lacked in refined manners of the Eastern sort, he possessed abundantly in self-confidence.

The last word on his journey belonged to the opposition. The morning after his departure, Springfield's pro-Democratic sheet, the *Illinois State Register*, issued a wicked, tongue-in-cheek announcement of Lincoln's trip:

> SIGNIFICANT—The Honorable Abraham Lincoln departs today for Brooklyn under an engagement to deliver a lecture before the Young Men's Association of that city, in Beecher's Church. Subject, not known. Consideration, $200 and expenses. Object, presidential capital. Effect, disappointment.[11]

YEARS LATER, Joseph H. Medill, the pro-Republican editor of the *Chicago Press and Tribune*, testified that when Lincoln arrived in Chicago en route to New York in February 1860, he gave advance copies of his speech "to quite a number of us, requesting that we study it carefully and make such corrections and suggestions as we saw fit."

According to Medill, when Lincoln showed up at the newspaper's offices the following morning, "We handed him our numerous notes with the reference places carefully marked on the margins of the pages where each emendation was to be inserted. We turned over the address to him with a self-satisfied feeling that we had considerably bettered the document and enabled it to pass the critical ordeal more triumphantly than otherwise it would. Lincoln thanked us cordially for our trouble, glanced at our notes, told us a funny story or two of which the circumstances reminded him, and took his leave."

Yet "when the speech was finally delivered" in New York, Medill was shocked to discover, "it was exactly word for word with the original copy which Lincoln gave us. Not a change suggested had been adopted. I never knew whether Lincoln intended to play a joke on us, or whether he really believed that the alterations were not effective. I never mentioned the matter to him, and he said nothing more to me. To tell the truth, I was not exactly proud of the part I played in the matter."[12]

It is a good story. It has a Lincolnian ring of authenticity to it, and it was long accepted without dissent. One can easily imagine Lincoln arriving in town and heading straight for the office of the local Republican newspaper, there to swap stories and seek advice on his upcoming speech in the East. After all, Lincoln had the habit of auditioning his major addresses in front of friends and allies. He had done so before delivering his House Divided speech in 1858. Medill and his fellow *Tribune* journalists were especially loyal, longtime supporters, and they had just endorsed him for president. Lincoln trusted no newspapermen more.

But in this case, it is another of those seemingly indelible Cooper Union myths. Lincoln did not leave his manuscript with Medill in Chicago for the simple reason that he did not travel to Chicago to begin with. After he left Springfield on February 22, Lincoln proceeded northeast toward Indiana, reaching the junction known as State Line six hours later at 4:30 P.M. There he switched to a Toledo, Wabash & Western Railway train destined for Fort Wayne. Arriving in that city seventy-five minutes late in the early hours of Thursday morning, February 23, he barely had time to catch the 1:12 A.M. connecting train east from the newly built Pittsburgh, Fort Wayne and Chicago railway line station a block away. That train took Lincoln four hundred miles to Pittsburgh, where he arrived at 2:20 A.M. the following day, Friday, February 24. He never came close to Chicago.[13]

In all likelihood, Medill did not intentionally fabricate his Chicago story. He may simply have confused the details. Perhaps Lincoln sent copies of the finished speech for Medill's review when he was polishing it later for publication. Only then, of course, would Lincoln have had "copies" to share with the *Tribune* men.

From Pittsburgh, Lincoln's train chugged on to Philadelphia—arriving fourteen hours late at 1:00 A.M. on Saturday, February 25. The undoubtedly exhausted traveler from Springfield did not reach New York until later that same day. His journey—probably made without the comforts of sleeping or dining cars, which were rarities—took three all but unendurable days.[14]

For most of the trip, at least, he did not suffer alone. According to a five-line Fort Wayne newspaper item on February 23, "Hon. Abe Lincoln and wife came from the west this morning at 1 o'clock on the T. W. & W. R. R., and changing cars at this city, went east. 'Old Abe' looked like as if his pattern had been a mighty ugly one."[15]

Had the reporters questioned Abe's "wife" that morning, she would have replied that her name, in fact, was "Mrs. Smith," which might have sounded suspiciously like the cover-up for a potential scandal. This Mrs. Smith, however, was Mrs. Elizabeth Dorlan Smith of Springfield, who liked to refer to herself as a relative of Lincoln's "by marriage." They were certainly close.

Mrs. Smith's brother, like Lincoln, was married to one of the formidable Todd sisters. And Elizabeth's husband had, until the previous week, been a partner in the Springfield dry goods store founded by his brother (Lincoln's brother-in-law) Clark Moulton Smith. What was more, Stephen at one time boarded in the Lincoln home, where Lincoln grew fond of the Smiths' little boy, Dudley, born around the time the Lincoln-Douglas debates commenced in August 1858.[16]

When her husband decided to explore business opportunities in nearby Bloomington in early 1860, Mrs. Smith made arrangements to take her toddler on a visit to her relatives near Philadelphia. Once the Lincolns learned that she too was heading east, someone suggested that she schedule her journey so it would coincide with Mr. Lincoln's. Not only would he provide a welcome escort for Elizabeth, he apparently promised to "help take care" of little Dudley as well. In return, Mrs.

Smith claimed that she provided reassurance for Lincoln, who "never having been east, feeling timid about making the journey alone, wanted me to wait till he was ready to go to deliver his Cooper Institute speech." Here, Mrs. Smith exaggerated her importance a bit; Lincoln had of course been east several times before. But Mary Lincoln, for one, seemed uncharacteristically delighted with the arrangement, considering that it excluded her, and obligingly packed baskets of food for their journey. She even made sure her husband also had a "knitted woolen cap for use in the cars, particularly at night."[17]

"We traveled three days and three nights to reach Philadelphia," Elizabeth Smith remembered in a memoir penned thirty-five years later. "There were no arrangements in those days to accommodate the traveling public in the matter of eating and sleeping. We relied upon our lunch baskets for meals and sat up in a very crowded car all the way and obtained very little sleep." Picnicking was still better than gulping down bad food at railside eateries, watching nervously for the signals to reboard.[18]

Mrs. Smith further recalled that by the time they reached Ohio, delegations of local politicians alerted to Lincoln's movements began to board the train at each of its frequent stops to greet Illinois' new favorite son "and ride along and talk with Mr. Lincoln." Elizabeth even claimed seeing "a large crowd" at each station, insisting that Lincoln would "frequently . . . address these assemblies from the car platform." It is entirely possible that admirers recognized Lincoln along the way, but if so, no newspaper report or corroborating reminiscence has ever surfaced to support the story that he greeted them with impromptu oratory. It is far more likely that Mrs. Smith confused the 1860 trip with President-elect Lincoln's well-publicized inaugural journey from Springfield to Washington a year later, during which he was indeed called on to deliver a number of extemporaneous speeches en route.[19]

All along this exhausting, cold, jarring trip toward New York, Mrs. Smith remembered her famous escort worrying incessantly, if good-humoredly, about the fate of his stored luggage. "We used trunk checks in those days," she explained, "but it was necessary for the owner of a trunk to pick it out and identify it before the baggageman would deliver it." While he knew he could recognize his own trunk "anywhere he would see it," Lincoln feigned concern that he would not be able to recognize his wife's. "His remarks were frequent and often very droll and amusing as the uncertainty of his being able to recognize Mrs. Lincoln's trunk recurred to his mind when he should reach the end of the journey."[20]

The end finally came in the early hours of Saturday, February 25. Reaching Philadelphia, Lincoln probably saw Mrs. Smith to a carriage and made his farewells to the mother and child. It could not have been an easy journey for Elizabeth Smith or her son, not to mention Lincoln: The Smiths' constant company over some sixty-two hours probably meant that he enjoyed little or no time en route to review the manuscript for his lecture.

Nor did he seize the chance to do so in the city that had given birth, as Lincoln later put it, to "the institutions under which we live." Lincoln had a bit of time to spare between trains in Philadelphia, but rather than sit alone in the depot, he headed to the Girard House, a local hotel, where he expected to meet with two of Pennsylvania's most prominent Republicans: Congressman David Wilmot and Senator Simon Cameron. The two politicians had left a card or message for Lincoln at the Philadelphia station inviting him for a visit.[21]

Cameron, a onetime newspaper editor who became a wealthy construction magnate and, later, an elected official perpetually stamped with the taint of corruption, was emerging as Pennsylvania's first choice for the Republican presidential nomination—in other words, a formidable Lincoln rival. Wilmot, on the other hand, was a figure with more claim to the past than to the future. Back in 1846, he had introduced a famous amendment to a federal appropriations bill that would have forbidden slavery in any of the new territory acquired in the Mexican War. The amendment never passed, but the "Wilmot Proviso" earned Lincoln's admiration and support; he later reckoned that during his only term in the House of Representatives, he voted for it more than forty times.[22]

No one knows why Lincoln agreed to meet the two Pennsylvanians in the first place: to size them up, seek clues about how he might turn one against the other at the convention, or simply out of respect, in response to their cordial (or perhaps devious) invitation.[23] Whatever the reason, the meeting never took place. The late hour notwithstanding, Cameron and Wilmot were not in their rooms at the Girard House when Lincoln called on them. Later, after reaching New York, Lincoln dashed off two letters of explanation and sent them back to Philadelphia. The note that survives went to Cameron. It contained what proved to be the last words Lincoln is known to have written before taking the stage at Cooper Union on February 27:

I write this to say the card of yourself, and Hon. David Wilmot, was handed me yesterday at Philadelphia, just as I was leaving for this city. I barely had time to step over to the Girard, where I learned that you and he were not at your rooms. I regret that being so near, we did not meet; but hope we may yet meet before a great while.[24]

Back underway, the final leg of Lincoln's long journey east took just a few more hours. Probably, he used the time to study his speech, free at last of the squirming Dudley Smith. Perhaps he focused on his manuscript with particular intensity north of Camden—the recollection of which might have confused sculptor Leonard Wells Volk a few months later as he took Lincoln's life mask in Chicago and imagined hearing that his sitter had composed the entire speech during this brief leg of the voyage.

All in all, Lincoln took no fewer than five different trains to travel the nearly twelve hundred miles from Springfield. On three consecutive nights, he had been obliged to endure fatiguing, middle-of-the-night transfers. He had raced for some trains, and waited endlessly for others. Such frustrations were all too typical in a country where "the cars" were less than reliable, and local time ruled, meaning that Pittsburgh, for example, stubbornly and inexplicably remained twelve minutes behind

Philadelphia. Now, at long last, Lincoln found himself at the end of the line, inside the crowded, cavernous Jersey City terminal. There he claimed his trunk and made his way alone to the nearby docks for a trip across the Hudson River on the typically thronged Paulus Street ferry, operated by the Pennsylvania Railroad between Exchange Place in Jersey City and Cortlandt Street in New York. Probably forced to stand for the brief ride across the waterway, he would have shared cramped space with fellow passengers, carriages, and animals alike.[25]

Looming nearer as the ferry headed east was the towering skyline of New York—row after row of brick buildings as tall as five or six stories, and church spires rising even higher toward the winter sky, that of Trinity Church at Wall Street the tallest in town—281 feet high, or the equivalent of twenty-seven stories—and especially identifiable on the horizon. A flotilla of ships of all sizes and flags steamed and sailed around them, or rocked gently in their moorings on the Manhattan side, lined up, one after the other, their masts looking like rows of stacked bayonets. Ships just arrived in port from Virginia, Delaware, Rhode Island, South Carolina, and England were busily unloading their cargo onto the docks. The *Kangaroo* prepared to sail for Liverpool, and the *Quaker City* took on supplies for its imminent trip to Havana.[26]

Here, near what is now the North Cove Yacht Harbor, he finally stepped ashore. No one waited at the pier to welcome him.

Likely taking care to avoid the notorious "wharf rat" sneak thieves who prowled the docks, and for whom, the chief of police warned the public, "the cutting of a throat is no worse a crime than the stealing of a cup of coffee," Lincoln probably headed eastward on foot from the river along Cortlandt Street, hauling his trunk himself.

He passed near shanties, row houses, and sheds along streets that one day in the distant future would lie in the shadow of the twin towers of the World Trade Center. Reaching the broad, bustling thoroughfare of Broadway, lined with strolling pedestrians and packed with noisy horse-drawn streetcars, he turned north and walked to the grand, six-story hotel that dominated the boulevard between Vesey and Barclay streets, and where he and Mary had stayed in 1857: the Astor House.

There, Lincoln learned to his astonishment for the first time that he would be speaking two days later not at Beecher's Church in Brooklyn, but at Cooper Union in New York.

"THE FIRST IMPRESSION of a stranger entering New York," the *Daily News* reported a few days after Lincoln's arrival, "is that it was built the night before."[27]

What was not under construction seemed about to be torn down. Everything—and everyone—appeared to be in perpetual motion. "It is a big village . . . without boundaries," explained a French visitor who got his first glimpse of New York a few years later, "eating up the countryside as it needs room for more houses and stores." Like many tourists, the writer also found the city "mean and repellent," marred by "the broken pavement, the muddy streets, the parks full of weeds and briars, the horse-drawn omnibuses—clumsy wagons that roll on iron tracks—the irregularly placed houses, mottled with enormous posters," all of it exuding "the neglected ugliness of an open-air bazaar."[28]

The last time that Lincoln had booked rooms in New York, the Astor House was still considered the premier hotel in town. Here, as Lincoln knew, both Daniel Webster and Henry Clay had years before spoken in its public rooms. Now, as the city's frontier expanded ever northward, the Astor had been relegated to the south end of the "hotel belt," ceding a bit of its preeminence to the newer Fifth Avenue Hotel, the St. Nicholas, and the gleaming Metropolitan, where the "first hop" of the city's elite social season had been held just a few weeks earlier. But commercial establishments still crowded the Astor's ground floor, and the lobby and dining rooms teemed with activity. In 1860, guests consumed fifteen thousand oysters daily at the leading hotels alone.[29]

From the Astor House, Lincoln could clearly see a number of familiar landmarks. Just across the street to the south was George Washington's church, St. Paul's, erected back in 1764—ancient by Manhattan standards.

Just to the north stood the forty-nine-year-old City Hall, that handsome combination of Renaissance façade and Federal-style detailing that the noted architect Benjamin Latrobe had undeservedly ridiculed as a "vile heterogeneous composition." Inside reigned Mayor Fernando Wood, a pro-Southern Democrat whose powerful political organization, Mozart Hall, vied with the larger Tammany Hall for the loyalty of the growing Irish vote. Wood's 1859 re-election had been lauded by the *Richmond Enquirer*, which was not surprising since the mayor had made clear: "The South is our best customer."[30]

Southeast across City Hall Park, huddled around newspaper row, fifty dailies and weeklies massed inside imposing brick towers. This was the opinion-making capital of the country, where a line or two of press coverage in one of the powerful papers meant instant recognition among tens of thousands of voting readers. The *Tribune* alone claimed a national readership approaching two hundred thousand, the *Sun* as many as sixty-five thousand, and the *Times*, describing itself as "the youngest of the daily newspapers of the City," boasted on the very day that Lincoln arrived in town that it had quickly equaled its strongest rivals in readership and "become one of the most widely known and most firmly established daily journals of the United States."[31]

There was "a great deal of 'blowing' among the rival papers as to circulation," a Washington reporter observed. But the *Tribune* alone published an eight-page national weekly edition, featuring political news and "instructive entertainment," at two dollars a year for subscriptions.[32]

James Gordon Bennett's *Herald* tilted Democratic, as did the *News*, whose editor was the mayor's own brother. These papers did not much matter to Abraham Lincoln. Their hostility was to be expected.

And the *Times*, as the voracious newspaper reader from Illinois surely knew, had just reiterated its unwavering support for New York senator Seward for president, warning on February 22 that "the Republican party can only be defeated by defeating the nomination of William H. Seward" at the national convention. As for the *Tribune's* Horace Greeley, although he had met Lincoln back in 1847 he recalled him as "unremarkable," except for his height. Greeley had already "bolted" from the Seward camp and was waxing "hot and heavy," a rival newspaper reported, for Missouri's sixty-six-year-old conservative, Edward Bates. Greeley's support gave Bates every reason to believe, as he ponderously confided to his diary on February 26, that "the signs indicating my nomination are growing, in number and strength every day." Still, "knowing the fickleness of popular favor," the Missourian promised himself "not to set my heart upon the glittering bauble, as to be mortified . . . by a failure."[33]

New York's newspapers did not offer the only avenue to nationwide public attention. Just a few blocks away on Nassau Street, the prosperous lithography firm run by Nathaniel Currier and James Merritt Ives was busy churning out hand-tinted popular prints. For sale for as little as ten cents each in shops, from street vendors, and by catalogue, these primitive "pictures for the people" treated every imaginable subject from "abbeys" and "aborigines" to "Zachary Taylor" and the "steamship *Zaandam*." In a matter of months, Currier & Ives would begin issuing portraits of Lincoln, quickly helping to transform his unknown face into one of the most familiar in the country.[34]

For now, Lincoln walked through the streets of New York entirely unrecognized. If he strolled up Broadway he would have passed in rapid succession Fellow's Opera House, the Coliseum Theatre, the Minerva Rooms, and Mechanics Hall—the sites of nightly lectures, minstrel shows, and revues in a city that appeared incapable of resting, even in 1860. He would likely have marveled, as another visitor of the period did, at the hordes of passersby, "all dressed alike" in their Sunday best, characterized by "the quickness of their walk, their ungraceful and untiring activity," and on work days, their tireless attention to business. He would have passed by a hodgepodge of billboards, banners, and signs beckoning prospective customers to haberdashers, jewelers, photography salons, carpeters, and hatters.[35]

And Lincoln might have noticed, too, the policemen who appeared "to devote their energies to preserving Broadway from being utterly hammed up by carts, and to escorting ladies across that most treacherous of thoroughfares." Surely Lincoln watched in horror as pedestrians scurried to get out of the way of the city's speeding horsecars, whose drivers were notorious for racing their vehicles through the crowded streets with no concern for the dangers to passersby.[36]

No one could avoid noticing the vulgar behemoth of a pleasure palace sitting southeast across Broadway from the Astor House at the corner of Ann Street. "The temple of art in New York is the Barnum Museum," pronounced one tourist after seeing it for the first time, "where Icelandic giants, Patagonian women, dwarves, sea-serpents, albinos, and heaven only knows what else are being shown, and where the open-mouthed visitors are being taught the great art of mystification."[37]

This "ideal model of democratic taste" could attract political zealots as well as thrill-seeking gawkers, for New York was a town as consumed with politics as with commerce and spectacle. The recent, racially provocative debut of the allegedly African sideshow hoax, the "What Is It," for example, was promptly regaled by one witty New Yorker as "neither white man nor monkey, therefore Black Republican." That the freak show was likely inspired by the recent publication of *Origin of Species* was not lost on New York diarist George Templeton Strong, who called the "fearfully simian" attraction "a great fact for Darwin." Meanwhile, the press rushed to assure readers that "this most wonderful specimen of Brute Humanity" was "entirely docile" and, what was more, could "be seen at all ordinary hours without extra charge" alongside a living kangaroo, a baby anaconda, and a wax statue of John Brown. In New York, politics had a place even in the milieu of the sideshow.[38]

At least Barnum's was a step above the city's other "museums," most of which were dime-store attractions crowding around the Bowery, and frequented by prostitutes who were "continually on the go . . . accosting the men." Two years earlier, a Charity Hospital study had estimated that as many as 5% of Manhattan's unmarried females were engaged in sex for hire.[39]

Other local problems were unavoidable. An expensively dressed pedestrian such as Lincoln, making his way through Manhattan streets in winter, might find himself "knee deep with mud," even on supposedly glamorous Broadway. But the most skeptical visitor had to admit that "there is no other street in the world like it, even in its present unfinished condition." From the Battery to Union Square—a length of just two and a half miles—sixty-seven white marble buildings, eleven structures made of iron, twenty-one hotels, six churches, five theaters, two fountains, one park, one hospital, and fifteen banks all greeted the visitor. "Broadway," summarized one overwhelmed Englishman, "is the only street in America that can boast of a European reputation." But in response, an embarrassed local reporter, finding himself "bespattered with mud, from head to foot" after a brief Broadway stroll, wondered: "How can it be expected that any besotted European should believe in a system of government that fails in so simple a function as street cleaning?"[40]

Far worse than the dirt and discomfort, truly appalling poverty abounded in New York, too, practically at Lincoln's doorstep. Directly behind his hotel, the luxurious Astor House, groups of "wretched middle-aged women" habitually lay in wait for the trash to be hauled out back, then to hungrily "plunge their arms, up to their shoulders, if necessary, into the exposed receptacles, which are filled with the refuse from the plates of the guests of the house, feathers, bits of fat, bones, and the entrails of fowls . . . a moist and fast-corrupting mass of offal."[41]

Northeast of City Hall was the mother of all slums, the infamous Five Points, a confluence of squalid streets and decaying, overcrowded buildings erected on fetid swampland, and now occupied by impoverished Irish immigrants, destitute African-Americans, violent thieves, and prostitutes. Boston lawyer Richard Henry Dana, Jr., had described it as a "sink of iniquity & filth," but like other visitors before him, including Charles Dickens, he had been strangely attracted to its horrors. As curious as the others, Lincoln would soon follow them there.[42]

All of New York, well-to-do and destitute alike, was expanding rapidly—too rapidly, some feared. Over the past ten years, the population had swelled from 515,547 to 805,658; the city now housed 2.5% of the entire population of the United States and was home to more people than all but twelve of the other thirty-four states. More than three hundred thousand of its inhabitants were foreign-born—more than half of these were immigrants from Ireland—and most were working for minuscule wages at unskilled jobs, if they were working at all. In politics, New York leaned Democratic; in regional sympathies, Southern. Lucrative trade with the slave-holding states, seasoned with intractable racism, combined to make much of the city hostile to Republicans and reformers alike, not to mention radical abolitionists. Free blacks in New York, by and large, strove to remain invisible, the safer from recent European immigrants competing for menial jobs. As one Englishman noted, the African-Americans constituted "a race apart, never walking in company with white persons, except as servants."[43]

Moreover, by 1860, Northern banks had extended some $200 million in loans and credit to Southerners, and New York City, the financial capital of the country, had dispatched so much of the exported capital that the city could reasonably be seen by one observer as "a prolongation of the South." It was even rumored that some Broadway entrepreneurs owned slaves of their own—though slavery had long been illegal in New York. Certainly no one could deny, as President Buchanan's secretary of war, Virginian John B. Floyd, boasted to a group of New York merchants, that "the great staples of the South are the chief means by which your commerce is fostered, and your mechanics and artisans kept constantly at work." As the antislavery New York Evening Post complained, "The City of New York belongs almost as much to the South as to the North."[44]

The New York that Lincoln encountered on February 25, 1860, was nothing like Springfield, nothing like Chicago, and already different from the New York he had first discovered back in 1857. This thriving, suffering metropolis now boasted thirteen hospitals, fifteen libraries, a staggering 284 known churches, and an equally breathtaking 174 newspapers: not just the superpower dailies, but specialty publications ranging from the humorous Comic Monthly and Phunny Phellow, to religious periodicals like the Christian Intelligencer and the Jewish Messenger, to foreign-language papers like L'Eco D'Italia and the New Yorker Abend Zeitung, to the illustrated weeklies like Harper's, Frank Leslie's, and The New York Illustrated News.[45]

Competitive, brawling, noisy, dirty, frightening, expensive, awe-inspiring, revolting: New York in 1860 was simply the best place in America to get published, get rich, get lost, or get noticed. Arriving at the Astor House, the stone palace famous for its interior courtyard and indoor plumbing, Lincoln checked into a small room on the "office," or ground, floor along the south corridor. It probably rented at a cost of two dollars or two fifty a night on the American plan, meals included. Like many hotels in town, the Astor House was packed with guests—few of whom however, would have sympathized with Lincoln. The "season of Southern spring trade" had begun in New York, and cotton merchants from Virginia, Georgia, and the Carolinas were everywhere. In town to make new friends, Lincoln would ironically find himself living among future enemies.[46]

"WHEN I REACHED NEW YORK, I for the first [time] learned that the speech was changed to 'Cooper Institute,'" Lincoln later insisted. Picking up a copy of the Saturday *New York Tribune* he discovered, to his understandable concern, the following notice on page four:

> ABRAHAM LINCOLN of Illinois will, for the first time, speak in this Emporium, at Cooper Institute, on Monday evening. He will speak in exposition and defense of the Republican faith; and we urge earnest Republicans to induce their friends and neighbors of adverse views to accompany them, to this lecture.[47]

Horace Greeley's paper, which had given wide coverage to the Lincoln-Douglas debates back in 1858, now added a two-column life story of the speaker. The biographical sketch extolled Lincoln for "hard work and plenty of it, the rugged experiences of aspiring poverty . . . the education born of the log-cabin," all of which had combined to make him ". . . the man he has since proved himself." He had evolved, noted the *Tribune*, from "a most effective and convincing" Whig to the "remarkable" Republican who had outpolled Stephen A. Douglas in the Illinois canvass two years earlier.

"Such is ABRAHAM LINCOLN of Illinois," concluded the *Tribune* biography: "emphatically a man of the People, a champion of Free Labor, of diversified and prosperous Industry, and of that policy which leads through peaceful progress to universal intelligence, virtue and freedom. The distinguishing characteristics of his political addresses are clearness and candor of statement, a chivalrous courtesy to opponents, and a broad genial humor. Let us crowd the Cooper Institute to hear him on Monday night."

As Lincoln later admitted, "Commendation in newspapers . . . is all that a vain man could wish." What concerned him now was the sudden, unexpected revelation that he was not to speak at the Plymouth Church in Brooklyn after all, but in the new Manhattan auditorium opened in 1859: the Great Hall of Cooper Union.[48]

Richard C. McCormick, a member of the executive committee of the Young Men's Republican Union, acknowledged that "when Mr. Lincoln came to New York City, there was some confusion in the arrangements." Now, having learned "in the public prints" that he was to speak at Cooper Union, Lincoln informed McCormick that he "must review his address if it was to be delivered in New York."

"What he had prepared for Mr. Beecher's church-folks," Lincoln worriedly told McCormick, "might not be altogether appropriate to a miscellaneous political audience." And so, the rest of "Saturday was spent in a review of the speech."[49]

Knocking on the hotel room door also came George B. Lincoln—no relation to Abraham—who had met his "western namesake" as early as 1857 on a pilgrimage to Springfield, where he claimed that he told Abraham Lincoln he would win the next Republican nomination for the presidency. "Oh, they all want Seward," Lincoln had said at the time, laughingly. Now, "presuming that he would come to the Astor," George hurried over from his nearby office at 326 Broadway and found that the famous Mr. Lincoln "had just arrived."

"He greeted me cordially, as was his custom, and then told me that he was in a *fix*."

"He had accepted (he said) an invitation from the Plymouth

Ch[urch]. committee and had prepared his address with reference to its delivery" there.

"I must *re-write* my address in the main," Lincoln confided to his visitor. George Lincoln noticed that "his manuscript lay upon the table, he having been already at work with the re-writing before my arrival."

George sensed that the *Tribune* story would attract other callers "and interfere with his necessary work." So he offered to spend the day keeping him company in his room, and doing "what I could to entertain the callers, while he pursued his work."

"Sure enough," George Lincoln recalled, "the callers *abounded*." McCormick was among the first, joined by his fellow committee member Cephas Brainerd, along with George P. Edgar and Frank Ballard. Abraham ended up introducing George, and the visitors understandably inquired if the smaller Mr. Lincoln might be the lecturer's brother. "No," Abraham Lincoln graciously replied, "but I wish he was!"

Between interruptions, Lincoln struggled to revise his manuscript. Not until nightfall did George announce that he must return to his home in Brooklyn. Just before he left he asked Lincoln "if he would like to go over to Brooklyn and listen to a sermon from Mr. *Beecher* in the morning."

Lincoln was delighted. "Oh, yes," he exclaimed. "My wife told me that I must go and hear *Beecher* while in New York."[50]

Not surprisingly, George B. Lincoln was not the only one to claim credit for luring Lincoln to Henry Ward Beecher's church in Brooklyn. Nor was George the only New Yorker who boasted later of meeting and assisting Abraham Lincoln on Saturday, February 25, 1860.

The other, and more credible, claimant was Henry C. Bowen, editor of the *New York Independent*, an influential antislavery, Congregationalist weekly to which the Lincolns enthusiastically subscribed back in Springfield. The *Independent* boasted regular contributions from luminaries such as John Greenleaf Whittier and James Russell Lowell. But it was leaning at the time to William H. Seward for president, arguing that he "embodied in his speeches the moral protest of an enlightened and Christian public sentiment against the iniquity of slavery." The paper claimed a circulation of fifty thousand, but admitted in its editorial pages that it was having trouble getting local news dealers to offer it for sale.[51]

Bowen was alone, working late at his Ann Street office that Saturday afternoon. Otherwise, the rooms were deserted. The editor was completely absorbed in his paperwork when, suddenly, he heard a rapping at the door. Believing it was only a tardy messenger, he barked, "Come in," without lifting his head from "the affairs at his desk."[52]

He heard the door open and close—then silence—followed by a voice.

"Is this Mr. Henry C. Bowen?"

Yes, Bowen replied, still not turning to greet his visitor.

"I am Abraham Lincoln."

With that, Bowen spun around in his revolving chair and came face to face with the astounding-looking guest whose visit he had helped to arrange.

"I faced a very tall man wearing a high hat and carrying an old-fashioned, comical-looking carpet-bag," Bowen recalled. "My heart went into my boots as I greeted the tall stranger. His clothes were travel-stained and he looked tired and woe-begone, and there was nothing in my first hasty view of the man that was at all prepossessing. On the contrary, in this first view of him, there came to me the disheartening and appalling thought of the great throng which I had been so instrumental in inducing to come and hear Lincoln the following Monday night at Cooper Institute.

"For an instant I felt sick at heart over the prospect, and could not greet my visitor with any warmth of manner, although I tried very hard to suppress any manifestation of my thoughts. Lincoln himself eased my tension of dismay and surprise by speaking in a most kindly and genial voice."

"'Mr. Bowen,'" said he, "'I am just in from Springfield, Illinois, and I am very tired. If you have no objection I will lie down on your lounge here and you can tell me about the arrangements for Monday night.'

"There was such a blend of dignity and gentleness in the stranger's voice and words, such absence of self-consciousness, or embarrassment, that there came a degree of relief to the tension of my first disagreeable and disappointing impression."

Within minutes, Lincoln had won Bowen's "interested attention," and the editor's concerns were replaced by exultation "in prospect of a triumph when Lincoln greeted his audience."[53]

Lincoln "immediately made himself at home, completely covering the sofa, which was quite too small and short for his extended figure. I soon saw he was a talker. He bubbled over with stories and jokes, and speedily convinced me that I had made no mistake in recommending him as a lecturer."[54]

"Young Republican" Charles C. Nott, for one, would bristle at the hint that Bowen had recommended Lincoln for anything. Writing thirty-six years later, he angrily insisted: "Bowen of course had nothing to do with Mr. Lincolns [sic] coming. . . . If Bowen had anything to do with Briggs and his young men, so much the worse for Bowen, for they abandoned their Brooklyn plan for money. They feared that they would lose money by having the lecture (all it was then) in Brooklyn, and we bought them off by turning over to them the financial part of our Cooper Building Lecture, and they took charge of the ticket office, and collected the receipts, and pocketed the profits." By the end of the century, of course, everyone wanted a share of the credit for luring the future president to New York. Tellingly, Lincoln thought it important to seek out Bowen on his very first day in the city, exhausting journey notwithstanding. He was, after all, an influential editor, of the type Lincoln was accustomed to courting. By contrast, the young men of the Young Men's Republican Union sought out Lincoln.[55]

Bowen took credit, too, for inviting Lincoln to Plymouth Church the following morning, and this makes sense as well. Both Beecher and his sister Harriet Beecher Stowe were regular contributors to the *Independent*, and Bowen had served as a cofounder of Beecher's Church, helping to raise ninety-five hundred dollars to buy the land on which it was built. Lincoln declined an additional Bowen invitation to Saturday night dinner—he told the editor he would "have to give his whole time" to his lecture, "otherwise he was sure he would make a failure, in which case he would be very sorry for the young men who had invited him." But he was eager to worship at Plymouth Church the following morning. Now the recipient of at least one, perhaps two, invitations to cross the river to Brooklyn on Sunday, Lincoln returned to his quiet hotel room that night knowing he would soon be hearing one of the most famous orators of the age.[56]

Before he retired for the night, he may have picked up a copy of William Cullen Bryant's *New York Evening Post,* where he would have found yet another friendly notice of his arrival, another prediction that he would soon mesmerize his audience.

ABRAHAM LINCOLN IN NEW YORK.

We are to have an address from Abraham Lincoln, of Illinois, on Monday evening, at the Cooper Institute. Mr. Lincoln is the man who made the circuit of that state, in the last election of members of its legislature, speaking in opposition to Douglas, and who would have carried the state but for the unequal and unjust apportionment, by which a minority of the people choose a majority of the legislature. Mr. Lincoln is a native of Kentucky, who has of late years resided in Illinois, and is therefore a pro-slavery man by the best of titles—birth in a slave state, personal observation of the effects of slavery, and equal knowledge of the advantages of a state of society in which the laboring population is free. The subject of Mr. Lincoln's address will be the matters in controversy between the two great political parties of the country.[57]

PLYMOUTH CHURCH—the most famous antislavery church in America—first opened its doors in Brooklyn Heights in 1847. Beecher took over the pulpit that November (he would serve until 1887, through war and scandal), but the original building was destroyed by fire in 1849. The following year, a new, larger, red-brick Italianate structure was ready for occupancy on Orange Street, between Henry and Hicks streets. The huge new sanctuary proved more popular than ever. With Beecher's sermons appearing in print regularly in the *Independent,* the church became one of the most prestigious in the North, certainly the best known in Brooklyn, still a city in its own right, nearly four decades from its unification with Manhattan, and already boasting a population of 279,000. On most Sundays, a capacity crowd of twenty-eight hundred worshippers filled the pews of Plymouth Church, overflowing into nearby aisles as well.[58]

A longtime parishioner recalled that "travellers visited it, just as they went to Washington or Niagara. It was 'the thing' to hear Henry Ward Beecher in Plymouth Church." Among the "distinguished men" he recalled seeing at worship there "Sabbath after Sabbath"—including "famous editors, popular ministers, eminent statesmen, great generals" —were the Hungarian freedom fighter Louis Kossuth, Charles Dickens, the abolitionist "golden trumpet" Wendell Phillips, antislavery theologian Theodore Parker, who agreed with Lincoln about the moral dangers of popular sovereignty, antislavery editor William Lloyd Garrison, and on February 26, 1860, Abraham Lincoln. Such worshipers flocked to hear Beecher "because he had the faculty of stimulating the best there was in them, arousing their highest ambitions." The ambitious Lincoln, for one, probably needed no such arousal himself.[59]

Ferries to Brooklyn departed from the Fulton Street pier every seven minutes in 1860. Lincoln would have started his day with breakfast at the Astor House, then walked over to the East River to catch the boat to Atlantic Avenue on the Brooklyn side. The fare was two cents. Along the icy river, Lincoln saw what Walt Whitman had observed in "Crossing Brooklyn Ferry:" "The round masts, the swinging motion of the hulls, the slender serpentine penants,/the large and small steamers in motion."[60]

Henry Bowen was waiting in his pew, number 89, fourth row from the front, along the left-hand aisle, when Lincoln arrived just before services commenced around 10:00 A.M.[61]

The "members of the congregation," George B. Lincoln observed from his pew farther back, were immediately transfixed by "the sight of the singular looking" stranger, and, for the duration of the service, gawked at the odd giant whenever "he arose at prayer time, and stood *overlooking* the heads of the entire audience. He wore a turn down collar over a narrow cravat—showing his long, bony neck to the best advantage."[62]

Before the services began, Bowen introduced his guest to the worshipers in neighboring pews, and as one parishioner whispered to another, then another, news of Lincoln's presence spread through the church within minutes. Bowen also sent a note up to the pulpit inviting Reverend Beecher to meet Lincoln at the conclusion of the service.[63]

The minister, undoubtedly distracted by his wife's recent illness, nevertheless offered a typically spellbinding performance, and Lincoln listened in rapt silence. The sermon "seemed to interest him very much," Bowen recollected. No one thought to record precisely which sermon Lincoln heard, but if it was the oration printed five days later in the *Independent*, it must have offered particular comfort to the unfashionably attired visitor from Illinois. Preaching about what makes a man a gentleman, Beecher declared:

If a man is well-behaved and well clothed we say he looks like a gentleman. But a gentleman is a man that has truthfulness and honor, and is so trained in them that they govern him spontaneously, and are a second nature to him.[64]

When the service concluded, the minister stepped down to greet his famous guest, and "the interview seemed to attract the attention of the audience, who remained, almost in a body, to look at the distinguished stranger from Illinois." Hundreds of parishioners lined up for the chance to shake Lincoln's hand, too, until he finally said: "I think, Mr. Bowen, we have had enough of this show, and I will now go with you."[65]

Lincoln had agreed to take lunch with the Bowen family at their home on nearby Willow Street, but apparently thought better of it as he walked with the *Independent* editor as far as his front gate. There, Bowen's little boy remembered the tall visitor talking earnestly with his father, and then turning to leave.[66]

"Mr. Bowen," an agitated Lincoln abruptly announced when they reached the doorway, "I guess I will not go in."

"My good sir," Bowen protested, "we have arranged to have you dine with us, and we cannot excuse you."

But Lincoln was adamant. "Now, look here, Mr. Bowen, I am not going to make a failure at the Cooper Institute to-morrow night, if I can possibly help it. I am anxious to make a success of it on account of the young men who have so kindly invited me here. It is on my mind all the time, and I cannot be persuaded to accept your hospitality at this time. Please excuse me and let me go to my room at the hotel, lock the door, and there think about my lecture."[67]

And with that, Lincoln headed back to the Atlantic Avenue dock, where he caught the return ferry to Manhattan. He had before him the rest of Sunday, September 26, to finish transforming a Brooklyn church lecture into a political address for the Republican elite of New York.

At least he could enjoy the comforts of the Astor House, where "heat from furnace, light from gas, waiters at the touch of bell-spring, reading-room, smoking-room, hot water or cold, flowing as readily from the touch of every guest, as from the ancient rock at the touch of the prophet's wand," all awaited his return. "We shall next expect to hear," joked the *Times*, "of some mechanical contrivance for putting lazy folks to bed, and a crank mill through which they will be run in the morning, to come out washed, cravatted, brushed, and combed, ready for the breakfast table."[68]

With little time to spare, a deadline looming, and an important crowd anticipating his appearance, such an invention could have done Lincoln no harm.

Chapter Four

⊰ "Much the Best Portrait" ⊱

RICHARD C. McCORMICK, the volunteer advertising specialist for the Young Men's Central Republican Union, did his job
brilliantly. Monday's Republican newspapers abounded with notices
about Abraham Lincoln's speaking appearance that evening.

The appeal went beyond party politics. "Remember Abraham Lincoln's Address at the Cooper Institute to-night," urged the *Tribune*,
"and ask your friends who are not Republicans to accompany you to
hear it. It is not probable that Mr. Lincoln will be heard again in our
City this year if ever. Let us improve the present opportunity."

The *Evening Post* echoed: "Our readers will not forget that Abraham
Lincoln . . . will address the people of New York this evening, at the
Cooper Institute. . . . The public may expect a powerful assault upon the
policy and principles of the pro-slavery party, and an able vindication of
the Republican creed." And buried within the avalanche of amusement
notices in *The New York Times*, a small reminder appeared to prod those
who had yet to secure their places in the audience:

Hon. A. Lincoln, of Illinois,
will speak at the

> Cooper Institute,
> This (Monday) Evening, Feb. 27,
> to the
> Republicans of New-York.
> Tickets 25 cents.[1]

The paper that one Southern journal called a "vile Abolition sheet" described Lincoln as a "distinguished politician in Illinois, where he is exceedingly popular," and reminded readers that he was not only his state's "candidate for the Presidency," but "a man of unimpeachable character" and "an excellent speaker."[2]

If Lincoln did not realize it before—and it is hard to believe he did not—the newspapers of February 27 made it clear that he was to be auditioned that evening for the nation's highest office. Warning of "another Anti-Slavery Lecture Among Us," James Gordon Bennett's *New York Herald*, supporters of Democrat Stephen A. Douglas, said as much, bluntly reporting that "Mr. Lincoln . . . makes his bid for the nomination this evening." Somewhat less perceptively, the *Herald* added: "If Lincoln cannot succeed for himself, he hopes to contribute to the success of Seward, whose lieutenant he is." Of course, Lincoln's New York hosts wanted nothing to do with Seward. They had invited Lincoln—and, earlier, other prominent western speakers—to Cooper Union with the specific purpose of placing alternative Republicans on display in New York City, and reminding easterners that an eastern presidential candidate like Seward could not win the general election.[3]

The "Young Men," as Lincoln likely knew, tilted toward another western Republican, Salmon P. Chase of Ohio, for the nomination. Foolishly, Chase had rejected invitations from William Cullen Bryant and other New Yorkers to precede Lincoln to Cooper Union and deliver his own preconvention lecture "upon purely political subjects." Now, as Lincoln prepared to take the podium in a shower of publicity, Chase was quietly heading back home from Albany, his chance to pick up vital eastern media and political momentum evaporated. He would not even put in an appearance at Lincoln's talk on February 27, "as was hoped," the *Evening Post* announced with regret.[4]

Republican ex-congressman Francis Preston Blair, Jr., of Missouri had already appeared at Cooper Union before an enthusiastic audience described as "large, but not sufficient to fill the Hall." There, on January 25, he declared that "the whole history of the Republic from its foundation shows that Slavery was held to be a local institution, to be tolerated only in those States into which it had been thrust, and which were gradually to be relieved from the incubus as the growth of the white population renders the institution of free labor possible." A voracious newspaper reader, Lincoln would have seen and absorbed Blair's text before leaving for New York.[5]

Cassius M. Clay of Kentucky had been the next guest speaker imported by the Young Men's Central Republican Union, braving a storm that dumped eight inches of snow in the city to deny "that the recent raid of John Brown on Virginia was the effect of Republican principles." Then he turned his attention to Hinton Rowan Helper's controversial 1857 antislavery book, The Impending Crisis of the South. Helper, a Southerner, argued that slavery was corrupting his region and retarding national growth. The book agitated Southerners (Helper was forced to publish it in the North), but delighted Northerners who saw it as the first evidence that some whites in the slave-holding states recognized that slavery had to be contained and destroyed.

At Cooper Union on February 15, Clay had suggested that Southern criticism against Helper was inspired not by fears that his book might incite slave uprisings, as some maintained, but because it alerted the white masses "to the state of subjection in which they were held by the slaveholding interest." Clay's remarks, The New York Times reported, were "frequently interrupted by loud shouts of applause." Lincoln no doubt read reports of Clay's speech, too.[6]

Even the legendary sixty-five-year-old "Wagon Boy of Ohio," Thomas Corwin, had come to Cooper Union to speak in the Great Hall (unlike the others, full of praise for his Senate colleague, Seward). Corwin, who, like Lincoln, had originally been slated to speak only at Beecher's Church, had told a spellbound Cooper Union crowd on November 1, 1859, that the Ordinance of 1787 barring slavery in the new Northwest Territory had established an unimpeachable precedent for restricting its further spread. So many people crowded into the Great Hall to hear the famous orator that aisles, window sills, and even the stage were filled with listeners. The speaker did not disappoint them, shedding his coat, vest, and eventually his cravat as he warmed to his oration. As he had done in previous speeches in the vicinity, Corwin also cited "the opinion of the men who made the Constitution." Lincoln had done research on those same national founders.[7]

The pro-Douglas *New York Herald* proved the only newspaper in town to perceive a pattern to all this Cooper Union speechifying, complaining that "this lecture system is one of the means and appliances by which the republican party are working themselves into power. They announce lectures in large cities, which turn out to be nothing else than stump campaign speeches." Meanwhile, the paper fretted, "The democrats are quarreling with each other, instead of organizing a system of lectures or distributing documents as antidotes to the republican poison." By this time, Blair's speech was already out in pamphlet form.[8]

Not to leave the field entirely to antislavery Republicans, admirers of Virginia Senator Robert M. T. Hunter saw to the publication of his fire-eating January 1860 address on "Invasion of States." Though the presidential campaign season was still young, aspirants and would-be kingmakers made sure their speeches were put into print. In this sea of pamphleteering, Douglas and his popular sovereignty supporters seemed almost moderate, especially with the arrival in print of Hunter's angry insistence about the Negro that "the happiest relation which you can establish between that race and the white, is that of master and slave."[9]

HIRAM BARNEY, Richard C. McCormick, and several of their compatriots from the Young Men's Central Republican Union returned to the Astor House to call on their speaker on Monday morning, February 27.

"We found him in a suit of black, much wrinkled from its careless packing in a small valise," a horrified McCormick remembered. "He received us cordially, apologizing for the awkward and uncomfortable appearance he made in his new suit, and expressing himself surprised at being in New York." Lincoln was not quite prepared to let his youthful hosts forget that they had failed to communicate properly that night's arrangements in advance. But he also seemed genuinely mortified about the way he looked. "He felt uneasy in his new clothes and a strange place," he later told his friend Ward Hill Lamon. "His form and manner were indeed odd," McCormick admitted, "and we thought him the most unprepossessing public man we had ever met."[10]

That impression softened after McCormick summoned the boldness to ask permission to glance at Lincoln's manuscript. From then on, he "had no doubt that its delivery would create a marked sensation throughout the country."

McCormick published his recollections a few weeks after Lincoln's assassination in 1865, when readers were flush with Lincoln ardor and many writers proved eager to take some credit for the martyr's early successes. In McCormick's case, he could not claim authorship of Lincoln's lecture, but he could, and did, suggest that without him it would not have earned wide circulation or national fame.

As McCormick explained it: "I spoke to him of the manuscript of his forthcoming address, and suggested to him that it should be given to the press at his earliest convenience, that it might be published in full on the morning following its delivery. He appeared in much doubt as to whether any of the papers would care to print it, and it was only when I accompanied a reporter to his room and made a request for it, that he began to think his words were to be of interest to the metropolitan public. He seemed wholly ignorant of the custom of supplying slips to the different journals . . . and was charmingly innocent of the machinery so generally used, even by some of our most popular orators, to give success and *eclat* to their public efforts."

In truth, Lincoln was neither innocent nor ignorant about public relations in general, particularly when it came to stimulating newspaper reprints. If he seemed so to McCormick it was because, again, political aspirants of the day were trained to exude modesty, not ambition. In his years in the political spotlight, however, Lincoln had seen many of his speeches published in the newspapers. His recent talks in Ohio and

Kansas had all made the press. Earlier, he had encouraged the first on-the-scene stenographers to record his debates with Senator Douglas, the transcriptions of which appeared in newspapers throughout the country. Currently, he was awaiting their reappearance in a book whose publication he had personally arranged. And recently, he had written out an autobiography for the newspapers in Pennsylvania.

To believe in the face of all this experience that Lincoln did not intend his New York address to make the newspapers is absurd. Lincoln came to New York precisely to create a sensation in the national media.

For now, Lincoln charmed his young visitors by spinning engaging yarns about Douglas and their debates, "and in a very short time his frank, fluent conversation won our hearts and made his plain face pleasant to us all." He seemed "generous" and "kindly," even when discussing Douglas and the Democrats.

Making a surprise entrance at the Astor House at some point that day—there is disagreement over whether he preceded or followed the "Young Republican" delegation to Lincoln's room—was an old acquaintance from back home. Fellow railroad lawyer Mason Brayman had, like Lincoln, served as counsel for the Illinois Central. Years earlier, he had lived in the Lincolns' Springfield house when Lincoln went to Washington to serve in Congress. A native of Buffalo, he had recently returned to his home state after years in the West. Lincoln greeted him warmly.[11]

"Well, Brayman, how have you fared since you left Illinois?" Lincoln asked as they headed out to take their midday meal together.

"I have made one hundred thousand dollars and lost all; how is it with you Mr. Lincoln?"

"'Oh, very well,'" Lincoln replied "in his dry, good-natured way," explaining: "'I have the cottage at Springfield and about $8,000 in money. If they make me Vice-President with Seward, as some say they will, I hope I shall be able to increase it to $20,000, and that is as much as a man ought to want.'"[12]

Lincoln of course expected to earn much more in New York, but in political, not financial capital, and Brayman, a Democrat, seemed well aware of it. As he wrote to a friend:

I am at the Astor House. Mr. Lincoln is there, and we have spent much time together, but I am getting *crowded out*. While at Dinner to-day, he was waited upon by some admirers. He turned half round and talked "hoss" to them—introduced me as a Democrat, but one so good tempered that he and I could "eat out of the *same rack, without a pole between us*." After dinner we went to his room, then came a black republican to take him up Broadway "to show him the fine buildings."[13]

Brayman did seem duly impressed when a delegation from Paterson and Orange, New Jersey, arrived later in Lincoln's hotel room "begging him to go over and make speeches in those places" as well. "Thus you perceive, the fame of *Ancient Abraham*, has extended even into foreign lands. To these unsophisticated heathen he presented me, with a caution to be careful what they *said*, as I was a *Democrat*."

The crush of admirers proved too much for Brayman. Next "came a Young Men's Committee of five, whereupon I bolted for the door taking another man's coat in my haste." He called Lincoln outside long enough to say good-bye and teasingly "assure him that he was certainly become *an object of attention*, and he must have a *committee* of *reception* and a *private Secretary*." With that, Brayman made his "escape into the atmosphere of Wall Street, where my politicks [sic] would be estimated according to the value of my *collaterals*, instead of the company I was keeping."

"Mr. Lincoln speaks to-night at the Cooper Institute," Brayman wrote that day. "For the honor of Illinois we shall all turn out [to] hear him; and I anticipate a rousing crowd. He is in fine health and spirits, and will make a telling speech—perhaps his best."

First, McCormick and his "black republican" cohorts persuaded Lincoln he must get out of the hotel and do some sightseeing. Together, they proceeded to stroll up and down the city's great thoroughfare, joining the "hundreds and thousands in New York," as one observer joked, ". . . who cannot live out of Broadway . . . must breathe its air at least once a day, or they gasp or perish." The odd-looking group—three or four slightly built, well-dressed young New Yorkers dwarfed by the towering westerner in his "sleek and shiny," voluminous new suit—gawked at the churches, shops, and office buildings lining the street, along with the inescapable barrage of advertising signs and banners declaring in their emphatic variety: "Everything is for sale."[14]

"We accompanied him to several large establishments," McCormick reported, "with all of which he seemed much amused."[15]

EVENTUALLY, THEIR BROADWAY stroll took Lincoln and his young hosts as far north as the corner of Bleecker Street, where the celebrated photographer Mathew Brady had recently moved his operations.

No American camera artist had achieved more fame than Brady. He had snared prizes at international expositions, opened a satellite gallery in Washington, and forged reputation-enhancing alliances with painters, printmakers, and illustrated newspapers, all of whom competed for the right to reproduce his originals. A lithograph or woodcut of the day bearing the label "from a photograph by Brady" carried the assurance of accuracy and authenticity. To the *American Journal of Photography* Brady was, quite simply, "the prince of photographers."[16]

Recently, Brady had decided to escape from the gaggle of competitors who surrounded his studios downtown. He chose a new base of operations on Broadway and Tenth Street, but while it was being renovated, opened "Brady's Gallery of Photographs and Ambrotypes" at temporary quarters at 643 Broadway on the corner of Bleecker, only a few blocks from the new Cooper Union.[17]

Here, as in all of Brady's plush galleries, visitors arrived not only to have their pictures taken, but to view the vast display of framed portraits hanging on the walls, or leaning on banisters. Photography was still an infant medium, but during his career Brady had already captured likenesses of Dolley Madison, Chief Justice Roger B. Taney, Presidents Van Buren, Taylor, Polk, Pierce, and Buchanan, Commodore Matthew Calbraith Perry, Henry Clay, singer Jenny Lind, and many other celebrities, including most of the leading politicians of the late 1850s. Copies of these images were always on view to the public. On the day Lincoln arrived, one corner of Brady's "*haut* ensemble" featured the latest portrait of Stephen A. Douglas, looking to one viewer "somewhat fiery and slightly dogmatical." In another corner was a new image of William H. Seward. Few of the other visitors that afternoon would have doubted that these two senators would be squaring off for the White House later that year. They would have been wrong.[18]

Even in an interim studio that he would occupy for only nine more months, Brady spared no expense. He installed velvet curtains, satin wallpaper, cut-glass decorations, and highly polished marble and rosewood furniture. Amidst such "calm contentment," *Humphrey's Journal* advised, "the merchant, the physician, the lawyer, the manufacturer, even the restless politician" were likely to "forget their labors" and indulge themselves in "the cost of a portrait." Among them was lawyer-politician Abraham Lincoln. In order to update his celebrity gallery, Brady would have been as eager to photograph Lincoln as Lincoln was to be photographed by Brady.[19]

Lincoln was not entirely a stranger to the medium of photography. He had sat before cameras several times in his life, though few of the results contributed much to enhancing or expanding his image. As a congressman-elect, he had posed for the first time around 1846 at the rustic "daguerreotype miniature gallery" run by former druggist Nicholas H. Shepherd in Springfield. But Mary Lincoln hung the picture on the wall of her home; she did not attempt to have it copied and share it with others.

From time to time during the 1850s, other cameramen in nearby Illinois villages tempted Lincoln into their unadorned studios, where harsh light and primitive equipment invariably harshened the deep lines on his leathery face and highlighted his unattractive moles and warts. These prairie photographers did not think it their place to hand Lincoln a brush or straighten his tie before opening their shutters, so the pictures typically revealed too much neck and not enough *bon ton*. Mary Lincoln particularly objected to one profile taken in Chicago in 1857, owing, Lincoln admitted, to "the disordered condition of the hair."[20]

In recent years, perhaps by accident, more likely by design, Lincoln had managed to get his picture taken around the time of the great public events in his career. He had posed for an ambrotype in Beardstown, Illinois, on May 7, 1858, the day he won his most famous criminal case at the Duff Armstrong murder trial. Five days after the first Lincoln-Douglas debate, then six days after the fifth encounter, and again two days before the sixth, he sat for photographers as well. Purportedly, he was lured into a gallery in Columbus during his appearance there in September 1859, although the picture has never come to light. By the time he reached Brady's in New York, Lincoln at least associated major speeches with obligatory commemorative photography.[21]

Despite improvements in technology, photographs remained arduous to make, and difficult to reproduce. Camera equipment was primitive, and candid photography was yet unknown. A sitter who wanted his picture taken was compelled to visit a professional gallery, brace the back of his head against an iron clamp to help him hold still, and freeze motionless for the long exposure required to expose a plate. Subjects were discouraged from smiling, since it was difficult to maintain a happy expression over time; the mouth inevitably sagged downward. Thus rarely did a Victorian-era sitter look anything but grim and stiff.

The earliest photographs were printed on silverized copper plates, thick glass, or japanned metal, and framed behind brass mats in small leather or thermoplastic cases. These daguerreotypes, ambrotypes, and ferrotypes, as they were called, were designed as one-of-a-kind images, to be carried home by the sitters as keepsakes, seldom copied. At the time, photographs could not even be reproduced in the newspapers. So by the time Lincoln reached Mathew Brady's gallery on February 27, 1860, not one of his sixteen previous photographic portraits had ever been reproduced in multiple copies and broadly circulated. All that was about to change.

Lincoln had never met Brady, but he had almost certainly heard of him—perhaps seen his credit line on woodcuts of his celebrity portraits, or examined his *Gallery of Illustrious Americans*, a series of volumes featuring portraits of "our Great Men." Much as McCormick would like us to infer that he steered his unsuspecting guest toward the nearest available portraitist, it should be remembered that Lincoln was also asked to pose during his eastern trip by the little-known Beers & Mansfield of New Haven, but let the invitation slip his mind. By the time he remembered, he later explained, he was too busy to sit. Besides, by then he had been photographed by the great Mathew Brady. He had joined Brady's roster of "Great Men" and "illustrious Americans" himself.[22]

If Brady's new Bleecker Street studio looked anything like the galleries he had recently vacated, Lincoln was no doubt overwhelmed by his first glimpse of it. This was nothing like Shepherd's storefront operation back in Springfield. Lincoln and his hosts ascended a flight of stairs, entered through glazed, cut-glass doors, and came face to face with "the largest reception room in the city." As *Humphrey's Journal* had described the Brady headquarters a few years earlier:

> The floors are carpeted with superior velvet tapestry, highly colored and of a large and appropriate pattern. The walls are covered with . . . gold paper. The ceiling frescoed, and in the center is suspended a six-light gilt and enamelled chandelier, with prismatic drops that throw their enlivening colors in abundant profusion. The light through the windows is softened by passing the meshes of the most costly needle worked lace curtain, or intercepted, if occasion requires, by shades commensurate with the gayest of palaces, while the golden cornices, and festooned damask indicate that Art dictated their arrangement.[23]

Waiting his turn in the reception room, Lincoln unexpectedly came face to face with another patron, someone he knew by reputation and greatly admired, notwithstanding his known political sympathy for his archrival Douglas. It was the famous historian George Bancroft, whose lecture on mankind's great discoveries had inspired Lincoln's own unappreciated effort on the same topic.

Lincoln was promptly introduced to Bancroft, who graciously welcomed him to New York. The two chatted briefly. As Richard McCormick remembered the scene, "The contrast in the appearance of the men was most striking—the one courtly and precise in his every word and gesture, with the air of a trans-Atlantic statesman; the other bluff and awkward, his every utterance an apology for his ignorance of metropolitan manners and customs."[24]

At one point, Lincoln was overheard remarking to the famous author: "I am on my way to New Hampshire, where I have a son at school, who, if report be true, already knows much more than his father."[25]

Soon Lincoln was ushered upstairs to the "operating room," lighted by tinted overhead skylights, and crowded with furnishings and decorative objects fit for a mansion, waiting to be employed as props. Nearby stood the large reflectors ready to be aimed at the sitter to enhance the lighting. Brady's massive seventeen-by-twenty-one-inch wooden camera, its lens encased in gleaming brass, stood mounted on a pedestal.[26]

Here, the celebrated photographer greeted Lincoln and sized him up. The man who stood before him would not be easy to photograph in Brady's trademark formal style.

The German-born Republican Carl Schurz, who first met "Long Abraham" aboard a train steaming across the Illinois prairie, remembered that Lincoln was so tall that Schurz had to "throw his head backward in order to look into his eyes"—and Schurz, too, was over six feet tall. Studying him from the tips of his mammoth boots to his "battered" stovepipe hat, Schurz observed:

> His neck emerged, long and sinewy, from a white collar turned down over a thin black necktie. His lank, ungainly body was clad in a rusty black dress coat with sleeves that should have been longer; but his arms appeared so long that the sleeves of a "store" coat could hardly be expected to cover them all the way down to the wrists. His black trousers, too, permitted a very full view of his large feet.[27]

To his old friend Ward Hill Lamon, Lincoln looked "haggard and careworn" at this point in his life. He was only fifty-one years old, but he already exhibited "all the marks of protracted suffering." In Lamon's words, he was:

> Over six feet four inches in height, his legs out of all proportion to his body. His head was long and tall from the base of the brain to the eyebrow. His ears were large, his nose long and blunt, the tip of it rather ruddy, and slightly awry towards the right-hand side; his chin, projecting far and sharp, curved upward to meet a thick lower lip which hung downward; his cheeks were flabby, and the loose skin fell in wrinkles, or folds; there was a large mole on his right cheek and an uncommonly prominent Adam's apple on his throat."[28]

Brady responded to the challenge with an inspiration. He would not settle for a commonplace, close-up head-shot; in fact, he would move his camera as far away from this homely-looking man as possible. Instead he would emphasize, rather than disguise, his subject's greatest physical attribute: his soaring height. Lincoln would be asked, for the first time in his life, to pose before a camera standing up, not sitting down. To mask his narrow chest, Brady made certain that Lincoln opened his coat. This would make him appear broader. There was nothing Brady could do about Lincoln's right coat sleeve, however; it was just too short, and too much white shirt cuff peeked out from beneath it.

To add classical grandeur and the accouterments of statesmanship to the composition Brady added carefully chosen background props. He moved a *faux* pillar into the scene, and situated it behind Lincoln's right shoulder. At his left he placed a table piled with books. These would suggest intellectuality, and in the bargain help the long-limbed subject reach down and touch the little table that sat so far beneath his hand. Lincoln would now be surrounded by symbols of both public service and learning. In art, the pillar also represented suffering, selflessness, and strength: Christ had been bound to a pillar for the flagellation, and Samson hauled down the pillars of the Philistines' palace to punish them for their godlessness.[29]

Brady's assistants brought over the obligatory adjustable immobilizer, mounted on an iron tripod. But they found it too short for a man of Lincoln's stature; the clamp would not reach the subject's neck. The aides had to prop it up on a box or table to accommodate him. Someone must have brought a hairbrush and mirror. Lincoln did not want to appear in "disordered condition" again and incur his wife's disfavor. And the photographer no doubt wanted to make certain that Lincoln's hair, rather freshly barbered, at least covered the tops of those flapping ears.

Brady was still not satisfied with what he saw. "I had great trouble," he admitted, "in making a natural picture. When I got him before the camera I asked him if I might not arrange his collar, and with that he began to pull it up."

"Ah," said Lincoln, "I see you want to shorten my neck."

"That's just it," Brady replied, "and we both laughed."

And then, quickly, before Lincoln's shirt could again sink down to reveal that sinewy neck and throbbing Adam's apple, Brady's camera operator opened his lens and exposed the shot on a wet-plate glass negative—using the latest technological innovation in photography. From this, prints could endlessly be struck on thin emulsion paper, then affixed to stiff cardboard mounts. The result was a work of art. Abraham Lincoln's image was immortalized—in all its raw frontier vigor, refracted by the beguiling mystery of those dreamy eyes—just hours before he was to deliver the most important speech of his career.[30]

LEGEND TO THE CONTRARY, the picture, it must be said, made no immediate impact. Brady experimented with various styles of printing it, producing a three-quarter-length version with the words "Brady N.Y." boldly inscribed onto the pillar, and then published a vignetted bust portrait variant as well. For each, he painstakingly retouched Lincoln's face, softening the deep lines, erasing the dark circles above and beneath the eyes, correcting the roving left eyeball that disconcertingly roamed heavenward whenever he stared, and for one version went so far as to thin the subject's pendulous lower lip. However romanticized, there was simply no immediate public demand for the result.

Five weeks later, Lincoln was still unsure what had become of the Brady picture. When a Poughkeepsie, New York, admirer wrote to him asking for his latest photograph, Lincoln replied with a mixture of homespun and exasperation: "I have not a single one now at my control; but I think you can easily get one at New-York. While I was there I was taken to one of the places where they get up such things, and I suppose they got my shaddow [sic], and can multiply copies indefinitely. Any of the Republican Club men there can show you the place."[31]

Here was yet another, and not terribly convincing, example of the studied diffidence in which the presidential aspirant specialized. But it represented an accurate assessment of the situation as well. Lincoln still had no Brady pictures at his "control," nor was there any evidence that the portrait had been circulated in the East, where he was the least known, and it could do him the most good. It surely did not comfort Lincoln or his supporters that May when a Democratic newspaper in Boston hinted darkly that the newly crowned Republican nominee for president looked "very much like Ossawottamie [John] Brown, of Harper's Ferry notoriety."[32]

Brady finally came to the rescue later that same month. Once Lincoln triumphed at the Republican convention, stimulating public demand to know what he looked like, the photographer at last handed over his portrait for copying to *Harper's Weekly* and *Frank Leslie's Illustrated Newspaper*. Woodcut adaptations would soon grace both popular journals. Showing particular imagination, *Leslie's* added a window, bright sky, and large tree to the background, making the image seem fresh and almost candid. *Harper's* inserted a herd of buffalo roaming outside, a none-too-subtle reminder of the subject's western roots.[33]

Before long, Currier & Ives began churning out lithographic copies designed for display in the family parlor. But in an effort to find a market for the image even among Lincoln's foes, the self-proclaimed "Grand Central Depot for Cheap and Popular Pictures" also issued a slew of cartoons, laudatory and critical alike, usually depicting Lincoln as a bumpkin in a linsey-woolsey shirt, holding a rail-splitter's maul. His face, in all of them, was copied unmistakably from the Brady original. In one lampoon, he was a political tightrope walker balancing himself across treacherous waters; in another, a dangerous radical introducing Barnum's "African" novelty, the "What is It," to provocatively suggest "the superiority of the Colored over the Anglo Saxon race"; in yet another, a rail-splitter in frontier garb concealing the "negro issue" inside a woodpile made of his own split rails. Quickly, in rich, varied, and sometimes uproarious context, the Lincoln image was born, with Brady's Cooper Union portrait the endlessly adaptable standard model.[34]

Charles Dickens could not help noticing these pictures when he visited New York at the height of election season later that year. "Barefooted boys" and "lean fried up men," he reported, could be found hawking campaign medals from cigar boxes in "the luxurious marble-paved smoking rooms of the great hotels," and "through the long avenues of the railroad-cars." Up and down Broadway, Dickens observed, "The windows of the palatial shops are full of election caricatures." Cooper Union derivatives showing "Abe Lincoln spouting from a platform of rails, under which grins a half-concealed Nigger," and "a gaunt Abraham Lincoln trying to ford the Potomac and get into a very small 'White House'" did not escape the author's notice.[35]

Throughout this frenzied period, Brady's New York photograph inspired innumerable adaptations, both authorized and pirated, romanticized and caricatured, flattering and assaultive. Currier & Ives sold their handsome, richly colored lithographs at twenty cents apiece, six for a dollar, and black-and-white copies for even less. Currier & Ives's rivals, E. B. & E. C. Kellogg of Hartford, burnished one of their copies by adding a tasseled velvet curtain to the background and placing an official-looking document in Lincoln's clumsily redrawn hands. In one case, they unfortunately flopped the picture as well; the resulting print presented Lincoln's mole on the wrong cheek.[36]

To better effect, Currier & Ives issued one variation (another mirror image with the mole on the opposite side) showing Lincoln seated in a "chair of state" decorated with a stars-and-stripes crest, which provided a suggestive emblem of power and authority. Yet another head-and-shoulders version was so transformed it gave Lincoln a smirk. But at least it identified him as "Our Next President."[37]

For those who preferred steel engravings to lithographs, New York printmaker J. C. Buttre came out with handsome copies on both paper and silk. Buttre's "dime picture of Abraham Lincoln, beautifully engraved on steel and printed on the finest enamel card, about 4x6 inches in size," became a best seller thanks in part to an aggressive marketing campaign that stressed the appeal of the "little gem" to "Lincoln Clubs throughout the United States." An accompanying biography extolled the candidate as "a man of the People, raised by his own genius and integrity from the humblest to the highest position, having made an honored name, as a lawyer, an advocate, a popular orator, a statesman, and a man." Printed beneath the handsome likeness were the assuring words: "Photograph by M. B. Brady."[38]

During the rousing presidential race to come, in which candidate Lincoln never left home to campaign personally, the Brady Lincoln seemed to "appear" everywhere in his behalf, an ideal visual accompaniment to Lincoln's New York speech, by then itself in print. In tintype form, the image adorned a multitude of campaign pins and badges, and in crude woodcuts, it reappeared as well on illustrated mailing envelopes, some labeled "Honest Old Abe" or, in tribute to the candidate's temperance record, "The Cold Water Candidate." The pictorial weekly *Momus* placed it atop the muscled body of a rail-splitter cracking open a large log labeled "Democratic party."[39]

Dusting off an old engraver's plate bearing a full-figure portrait of the Republican presidential candidate of four years before, John C. Frémont, one printmaker adroitly burnished out the "Great Pathfinder's" face, and replaced it with Brady's image of the Rail-Splitter. The resulting composite showed the Cooper Union Lincoln sitting awkwardly atop Frémont's diminutive body, hand on hip, wearing a Prince Albert cutaway coat. However unrealistic, it seemed to represent Lincoln's emergence as Frémont's successor as Republican standard-bearer and apparently found an audience.[40]

Looking at the original photograph today, it is not at all difficult to understand why it inspired so many copies in so many media. Brady succeeded in making Lincoln look dignified, resolute, and powerful, all at the same time. None of the physical shortcomings all too apparent in the work of earlier photographers plague the Brady image: The wiry neck is concealed, the leathery skin softened, the perennially "disheveled" hair neat, the lantern jaws and elephantine ears minimized. What is left is not soft or fancy: It is the quintessential strong, self-made man. Clever lighting, deft retouching, and careful attention to props and details had even made Lincoln's badly tailored suit look handsome. Above all, the picture bore the prominent Brady imprint. That alone inspired artists to copy it. (It is not even hard to believe the traditional story that Brady made an ambrotype copy and presented it to Lincoln, and that Mary Lincoln later gave this copy to the minister who attended her husband at his deathbed.)[41]

As Mary alone might have sensed, some of the portrait's power was probably generated by an almost unnoticable flicker of mood. Lincoln, in holding his pose, had compressed his lips. Whether achieved by accident, design, or under instruction, the resulting taut expression—perhaps reflecting nothing more than impatience at the prolonged sitting—gave him a determined look unlike the passive and distracted expression he had worn in his previous photographs. The slight frown seemed to assure voters who had never seen or heard of Abraham Lincoln that he was up to the challenges that lay ahead. The person who knew him best would have agreed. As his wife later put it, whenever her husband "pressed or compressed his lips together—firmly . . . I fashioned myself accordingly and so did all others have to do sooner or later, and the world found out." That expression meant that Abraham Lincoln had made up his mind.[42]

By year's end, adaptations appeared around the country, and in France and England as well. Lithographer J. L. Magee issued a lithographed copy in Philadelphia. In London, *Vanity Fair* used a shaded Brady as the basis for an unflattering portrait of Lincoln as an African-American child dominating the cartoon *Et Tu, Greeley*, which lamented the Republican abandonment of Seward. The acerbic Frank Bellew, working for the New

York–based illustrated humor magazine, *Comic Monthly*, placed the Cooper Union visage on a scarecrow made of log rails and labeled the frightening result: "The Rail auld Western Gentleman." Most ironically of all, the portrait was used for an anti-Republican cartoon, *No Communion with Slaveholders*, that showed Lincoln praying at the Plymouth Church, with Beecher and Greeley, along with Seward, John Brown, and even George Washington, in attendance.[43]

Only with the introduction in late 1860 of the small *carte-de-visite*-size photograph, along with fancy leather albums to house them, was Brady finally able to capitalize fully on his own creation by churning out and selling mass-produced, three-by-four-inch card copies of his own.

By the time Lincoln headed east on another train from Springfield, almost a year later to the day—this time to assume the presidency—the man who in 1860 did not know where to procure copies of his most important image was not only fully aware of its ubiquity, but cheerfully handing out engraved copies to well-wishers along the way. To one such admirer, J. R. Drake, he presented a small copy published by the American Bank Note Company, first taking out a pencil and boldly signing below the image: "A. Lincoln." It was the only time he ever autographed a print.[44]

Lincoln looked nothing like the Cooper Union photograph by then. Inspired in part by a letter from a little girl in Westfield, New York, who wrote to complain that his clean-shaven face looked "too thin," Lincoln began to grow whiskers shortly after his election in November. It comes as no surprise to learn that his young correspondent had been inspired to write after seeing at the county fair a campaign poster featuring a crude engraved portrait based on Mathew Brady's ubiquitous photograph. Thus the picture that in effect introduced Lincoln's image to the public also played a part in changing it.[45]

It was appropriate, then, that once in the capital for his inauguration, though weary from yet another long journey by rail, Lincoln was nonetheless persuaded to visit Brady's Washington establishment to pose for the first studio portraits to show his luxuriant new beard fully grown.

This time, the camera operator was Alexander Gardner, destined soon to open a gallery of his own and eventually take more pictures of Lincoln than any other photographer. When a neighbor, painter George Henry Story, stopped by to witness the historic sitting, he found the president-elect nothing like the rustic boor he had read about. "In dress and appearance he was elegant," Story attested, "his clothes being made of the finest broadcloth." Times had changed. The man was living up to the image Brady helped create.

According to Story, Ward Hill Lamon, who had accompanied his old friend to the capital, stepped forward at the conclusion of the sitting and announced to the president-elect: "I have not introduced Mr. Brady."

Lincoln needed no such introduction. Supposedly, he "extended his hand and answered in his ready way, 'Brady and the Cooper Union speech made me President.'"

Had Lincoln really said so, no one by then would have disagreed—least of all Mathew Brady. But George Henry Story also added of the incoming president: "His hands and feet were small and shapely," casting doubt on everything else he remembered of that 1861 encounter, including the compliment to Brady.[46]

One thing is certain: Brady did not need Lincoln's approval to convince him of the impact his work had made. As New York artist Francis B. Carpenter later testified, "My friend Brady, the photographer, insisted that his photograph of Mr. Lincoln, taken the morning of the day he made his Cooper Institute speech in New York,—much the best portrait, by the way, in circulation of him during the campaign,—was the means of his election. That it helped largely to this end I do not doubt."

As Carpenter recognized: "The effect of such influences, though silent, is powerful."[47]

How LINCOLN SPENT the remainder of Monday, February 27, is not recorded. Myths abound—including one suggesting that he stopped in at McSorley's tavern for an ale. (Of course, as the *Chicago Press and Tribune* would soon report accurately, "He never drinks intoxicating liquors of any sort, not even a glass of wine," and certainly he would not have imbibed a few hours before making the most important speech of his career.) Most likely he simply went back to his hotel to rest. "From the gallery we returned to the Astor House," was all R. C. McCormick had to say on the subject, "and found that the arrangements for his appearance . . . had been completed."[48]

Lincoln had one final mission: Some time before leaving for his sightseeing tour and returning to his hotel, he found the time to make a purchase. At the Knox Great Hat and Cap Establishment at 212 Broadway, corner of Fulton Street, he bought a new top hat. Hats were important to Lincoln: They protected him against inclement weather, served as storage bins for the important papers he stuck inside their lining, and further accentuated his great height advantage over other men. Here in fashion-conscious New York, his suit was ill-fitting and creased, his stiff new boots cramped his feet, but at least he would look taller than any man in the city when he donned his new stovepipe topper and headed up to Cooper Union that evening.[49]

But would others head to Cooper Union, too? In 1860, just as now, New Yorkers and visitors alike could choose their evening "amusements" from a dizzying menu of local attractions. This February Monday was no different. Only a few blocks from Cooper Union, at the Academy of Music, the sensational sixteen-year-old soprano from Italy, Adelina Patti, was to make her debut in the opera *Martha*. For music lovers who preferred established stars, the legendary "Swedish Nightingale," Jenny Lind, was scheduled to sing at the Winter Garden.

Drama would tempt many New Yorkers as well. For a mere fifty cents, audiences could see English actress Laura Keene in *Jeannie Deans, or the Heart of Mid-Lothian*. The play had already attracted 109,000 spectators.[50]

For more prosaic tastes, the Palace Garden boasted the largest menagerie of elephants, pumas, hyenas, zebras, and vultures in the world. And warning that "the last week of the equestrian season" was at hand, Cooke's Royal Amphitheatre presented a troupe of performing ponies, "educated" horses, and famous riders. Niblo's Saloon featured George Christy's famous minstrel show, specializing in songs and farce performed in blackface, at twenty-five cents a ticket. And over at Barnum's wildly popular American Museum, five acts of multiple tableaux vivants were to unfold in "that surpassingly popular, touching, amusing, and beautiful picture of Southern life, Octoroon, or Life in Louisiana."[51]

Nor was Cooper Union the only hall in town presenting a lecturer on this winter evening. At Goldbeck's Music Hall on Broadway, J. H. Siddons was scheduled to enthrall with a talk on "the Great Domestic Obligation." The nearby Inebriate's Home offered a temperance lecture by Reverend Matthew Hale Smith. For self-help devotees, Reverend Theodore Cuyler was scheduled to ascend the podium at the Young Men's Christian Association on Broadway to orate on "The Intellect and How to Use It." And Dr. H. S. Gilbert was to launch a series of lectures on the lungs and digestive organs at the Hope Chapel.[52]

Whether the "masses" would fill Cooper Union that night for yet another "mass meeting," however, remained an open question for the host organization. The tickets seemed reasonably priced at twenty-five cents each (the same cost as an evening with Christy's Minstrels), but the unpredictable winter weather threatened to scare off the crowd. February had been a miserable month in the city. Snow accumulated so much that sewers clogged up, leaving streets awash in mud and muck and setting New Yorkers to anguish about diphtheria, rheumatism, chills, "and other bodily evils." A violent rainstorm on Washington's birthday disrupted traffic and tortured holiday marchers, but at least washed away "the dirty face which the City has lately worn," reported *The New York Times*. Then a dense fog rolled in, bringing traffic to a halt on both land and rivers. Within hours, Maylike breezes billowed into town, turning the city's streets into an "ice-cream mixture" of "mud" and "splosh."[53]

"What a climate is ours!" exclaimed the *New York Tribune*. "Fairyland, Bohemia, the realm of Dreams and Shadows—no mythic clime can equal its myriad variations of storm, sunshine, cloud, frost, rain, mist, hail, snow, and sunshine again—ever varying and intershifting, till the bewildered Manhattaner learns that all signs of the sky or air will afford his judgment no basis on which to predict the weather for a dozen hours ahead."[54]

Some eyewitnesses, and generations of historians since, reported that snow fell in New York that night ("The profits were so small . . . because the night was so stormy," recalled co-organizer Cephas Brainerd). Conceivably, contemporary Lincoln supporters said so later to help explain the hundreds of empty seats. But according to recently unearthed meteorological records, the weather remained clear and warm on the day of Lincoln's speech. By midafternoon, bathed by a mild southwestern breeze, the temperature in New York peaked at an unseasonably warm forty-four degrees. Not an ounce of precipitation was reported.[55]

Whether he walked, hailed a carriage, or jumped into a horse-drawn Broadway streetcar that evening, no one bothered to record. Accompanied by James A. Briggs, Lincoln found Cooper Union ablaze with light and humming with activity, just three and a half months into its first semester of free classes. Founder Peter Cooper had designed his experimental school, on which he lavished six hundred thousand dollars, to offer working men—and women—tuition-free night classes in engineering, chemistry, and art.

The sparkling, brownstone behemoth—officially named the Cooper Union for the Advancement of Science and Art—had opened the previous year on Seventh Street, between Third and Fourth avenues at the foot of the Bowery. Its entrance optimistically faced Astor Place and what was then the northern edge of Midtown Manhattan, as if pointed toward the city's inevitable future expansion. The school boasted its own museum (Cooper even purchased a stuffed white whale to display there), a roof garden, and a so-called "cosmorama." It included laboratories, classrooms, a paintings gallery, a "spacious" and "excellently well ventillated" reading room, and of course the "Great Underground Hall," where Cooper insisted that all political points of view be represented from its podium. Reportedly it had also been his idea that the auditorium be situated in the basement: Cooper was convinced that in the event of a fire or some other emergency, panicked crowds were less likely to trample themselves racing upstairs than down.[56]

Cooper's ambitious dreams had been realized. Both Republicans and

Democrats had already spoken from the stage. Classes were well underway and the library was filled with books and readers alike. *New York Evening Post* editor William Cullen Bryant had not been unrealistic, after all, in expressing the hope, a year earlier, that the "people's college" would be dedicated to "one of the noblest purposes which could be conceived of—moulding the human mind."[57]

Now Bryant himself was poised to preside over the February 27 meeting of the Young Men's Central Republican Union. Backstage, he perhaps tried to put the speaker at ease by reminding him that they had met once, very briefly, and long before. Nearly thirty years earlier, on a visit to Illinois, the poet had by chance encountered Captain Abraham Lincoln and his little company of volunteer soldiers on the march to fight Indians in the Black Hawk War (and finding their only enemy, Lincoln later admitted, to be the "musquetoes"). Bryant was "delighted" by the "tall, awkward, uncouth lad" and the "raciness and originality" of his conversation.[58]

As Lincoln later confided to young James A. Briggs, it was "worth a visit from Springfield, Illinois, to New York to make the acquaintance of such a man as William Cullen Bryant." Meanwhile, Lincoln was visibly nervous. "As he spoke to me before the meeting opened," the young, Harvard-educated attorney Joseph H. Choate recalled, "he seemed ill at ease, with that sort of apprehension that a young man might feel before facing a new and strange audience whose critical disposition he dreaded."[59]

Chapter Five

⊰ "Nothing Impressive About Him" ⊱

Out front, a "large and brilliant" audience filed into Cooper Union. Although as much as a fourth of the hall's eighteen hundred seats remained unfilled, co-organizer Henry C. Bowen seemed "astonished to see a crowded house." The young lawyer Joseph H. Choate, who would one day prosecute The Tweed Ring, was delighted to find himself in the presence of "all the noted men—all the learned and cultured of his party, editors, clergymen, lawyers, merchants, critics." Not since the days of Clay and Webster, rhapsodized the *Tribune*, had "a larger assemblage of the intellect and mental culture of our City" gathered to hear a political speaker. The crowd reflected, to another journalist, "the pick and flower of New York culture."[1]

Even Democrat Mason Brayman turned up. Lincoln had asked him to take a place in the rear of the hall. If he "did not speak loud enough," Brayman remembered Lincoln telling him, he was "to raise his high hat on a cane" as a signal.[2]

From overhead, the crowd could hear the constant hiss of the 168 gas burners feeding the auditorium's twenty-seven crystal chandeliers. The light fixtures in turn cast brilliant reflections against the mirrors lining the walls. No wonder *The New York Times* had declared that the

Great Hall could not be "equalled by any room of a similar nature in the city or the United States."[3]

The orator of the day would confront a vast, vertically arranged basement auditorium, furnished with swivel chairs lavishly upholstered in red leather. Row upon row of rounded, wrought-iron pillars—sixteen in all—supported a series of sandstone block arches that held aloft the chamber's high ceiling, creating the effect of a church nave. The architectural message was clear: This was a cathedral of knowledge and wisdom. The sole complaint was that, for some visitors, the pillars vexingly obstructed clear views of the stage.[4]

Shortly before eight o'clock, dignitaries began assembling on the elevated platform at the north end of the auditorium, assuming their special seats facing the audience, ready to welcome Lincoln. Here were "the Republican leaders of the city," including the event's young co-organizers Hiram Barney, Cephas Brainerd, Charles C. Nott, and James A. Briggs.

Joining them were the venerable Erastus Dean Culver, a judge in Brooklyn's municipal court; rising young attorney Abraham Jesse Dittenhoeffer; the Quaker abolitionist James Sloan Gibbons; former New York governor John Alsop King; Dr. S. Lounsberry; police commissioner James W. Nye; almshouse "governors" Washington Smith and Isaac J. Oliver; party leader Thomas B. Stillman; Samuel Sinclair of the *Tribune*; lawyer Edward Delafield Smith; and Theodore Tilton, a member of the editorial staff of the *Independent* who also served as superintendent of the Plymouth Church Sunday school. And here, too, was Horace Greeley, editor of the *Tribune* and determined mastermind of the dump Seward movement.

Eighteen men occupied the platform in all, and three more were about to make their entrance: *Evening Post* editor William Cullen Bryant, distinguished attorney David Dudley Field (whom Lincoln had debated thirteen years earlier at a River and Harbor Convention, also attended, as it happened, by Greeley); and of course the evening's star attraction, Abraham Lincoln.[5]

It probably remained unclear to many in the audience who the "young Republican" hosts really were: the sixty-seven-year-old Bryant, the forty-nine-year-old Greeley, or some of their equally venerable contemporaries scattered throughout the house. Not until the final annotated pamphlet version of the speech appeared did it become clear that the older men served as "senior advisors" to the younger. Seated out front that night, too, were many of the officers and advisors of the Young Men's Central Republican Union. In the latter category were stalwarts bearing such distinguished New York names as Jay, Fish, Drew, and Peabody.

At 8 P.M., a door opened and Bryant strode onstage. Then in quick order came the heavyset Field, and right behind him, at last, the towering Lincoln. The speaker's appearance stirred "loud and prolonged applause," and a few gasps as well. He was even taller than the crowd had expected. Lincoln sat down in the remaining empty seat on stage. It was clearly too small for him, because he could soon be seen twisting his long legs "around the rungs of the chair," looking "the picture of embarrassment."[6]

Before Lincoln could speak, there was formal business to conduct. Field stepped to the rostrum first, calling for and winning unanimous approval of Bryant as chairman of the meeting.

Then Bryant stood up, pronouncing it "a grateful office that I perform in introducing to you an eminent citizen of the West, hitherto known to you only by reputation, who has consented to address a New York assembly this evening." Bryant lauded the speaker as "a gallant soldier of the political campaign of 1858" and "great champion" of the Republican cause in Illinois.

"These children of the West, my friends," Bryant continued, "form a living bulwark against the advances of slavery, and from them, is recruited the vanguard of the armies of Liberty. One of them will appear before you this evening."

To secure the "profoundest attention" for the speaker, he concluded, "I have only, my friends, to pronounce the name of"—and here he likely paused for dramatic effect—"Abraham Lincoln of Illinois." With that the audience erupted with a burst of "prolonged applause."

"Impressed with the solemnity of the occasion . . . [Lincoln] got up very slowly"—so slowly, recalled George H. Putnam, that he worried for a moment that "the tall figure would never cease rising." To one alarmed onlooker, he appeared "rather unsteady" in his gait as he slowly shambled toward the front of the stage. At last Abraham Lincoln—all six feet four inches of him—stood at the velvet-covered, gold-tasseled, slant-top iron podium, "smiling graciously upon the audience," one observer noted, "and complacently awaited the termination of the cheering."[7]

Waiting for the rousing welcome to subside, Lincoln peered with his "bright . . . dreamy" eyes into row after row of spectators. With especially keen interest, he searched deep into the audience, past the empty red seats, for the friend he had planted in the very last row. Lincoln knew that the friend would signal him should the orator's unpredictable voice—sometimes shrill, sometimes "soft . . . as a girl's"—fail to carry to the back of the hall.[8]

With the cheering came renewed stares of disbelief.

"I would say that his clothes were cut somewhat in contrast to the prevailing style in New York and hung on him rather loosely." So eye-witness D. N. Foster, at age ninety, remembered distinctly, and tactfully, seven decades after he saw Abraham Lincoln appear onstage at Cooper Union.[9]

He need not have minced words. Others on the scene were far harsher in their recollections. The words "awkward" and "ungainly" punctuate half a dozen such reminiscences. Few on hand that night would ever forget their initial, startling glimpse of Abraham Lincoln.[10]

Standing before them was an ungainly, oddly dressed giant, dwarfing the other dignitaries on the stage even though he stooped forward as he walked. His wrinkled black suit ballooned out in the back. His withered, long, dark neck jutted upward from a comically loose collar that looked several sizes too big. Wiry black hair flew out in all directions, unable to hide enormous ears jutting akimbo from his leathery face. Massive hands clutched his manuscript.

Those who looked carefully noticed that his arms fell lower on his body than those of other men; that his feet seemed huge almost beyond belief; and that when he stepped on stage, he did not stride heel first, followed by toe, like most men, but with his whole foot raised and then lowered at once, step after step, like a large child who had just learned to walk. Those sitting close to the front could also detect that the speaker's face was badly pitted—"furrowed, wrinkled, and indented," in the words of a writer who later observed him closely, "as though it had been scarred by vitriol."[11]

"At first sight there was nothing impressive or imposing about him," echoed one young eyewitness. ". . . His clothes hung awkwardly on his gaunt and giant frame; his face was of a dark pallor, without the slightest tinge of color; his seamed and rugged features bore the furrows of hardship and struggle. His deep-set eyes looked sad and anxious." At best, the onlooker said, the speaker appeared decidedly "ill at ease."[12]

One eyewitness later reported to Maine-born journalist Noah Brooks—who had seen Lincoln speak four years earlier, in 1856, in the tiny town of Dixon, Illinois. Brooks had been as impressed by Lincoln's sledgehammer logic" as he was shocked by his "personal appearance."[13] Not much had changed. Brooks's informant turned a skeptical eye to the speaker at Cooper Union, and feeling nothing but "pity for so ungainly a man," thought to himself rather waspishly: "Old fellow, you won't do; it's all very well for the Wild West, but this will never go down in New York!"[14]

Organizer Charles C. Nott, however, saw nothing but virtue and character in the "ungainly man"—"unadorned, apparently unculti-vated, showing the awkwardness of unconscious rusticity. His dress that night before a New York audience was the most unbecoming that a fiend's ingenuity could have devised for a tall, gaunt man; a black frock coat ill-setting and too short for him in the body, skirt and arms, a rolling, low collar disclosing his long thin, shriveled throat, uncovered and exposed. No man in all New York appeared that night more simple, more unassuming, more modest, more unpretentious, more conscious of his own defects, than Abraham Lincoln."[15] As George Putnam recalled:

The first impression of the man from the West did nothing to contradict the expectation of something weird, rough, and uncultivated. The long, ungainly figure, upon which hung clothes that, while new for the trip, were evidently the work of an unskillful tailor; the large feet; the clumsy hands, of which, at the outset at least, the orator seemed to be unduly conscious; the long, gaunt head capped by a shock of hair that seemed not to have been thoroughly brushed out made a picture which did not fit in with New York's conception of a finished statesman.[16]

Watching from a ledge in the rear, Russell H. Conwell thought Lincoln seemed "an awkward specimen indeed," noting with amusement that "one of the legs of his trousers was up about two inches above his shoe; his hair was disheveled and stuck out like rooster's feathers; his coat was altogether too large for him in the back, his arms much longer than his sleeves." George H. Putnam, observing from the platform, worried that Lincoln's coat hung on him "like a gunny sack."[17]

To the *Tribune*'s correspondent: "He was tall, tall—oh how tall, and so angular and awkward that I had, for an instant, a feeling of pity for so ungainly a man. His clothes were black and ill-fitting, badly wrinkled— as if they had been jammed carelessly into a small trunk." Little did he know that they had been.[18]

As one of the co-owners of the *Evening Post* later sneered to a friend in London, Lincoln was not someone who would seem "a la mode at your splendid European courts." He might not even be safe from criticism "in our Atlantic drawing rooms."[19]

The speaker was not unaware of the audience reaction. For once in his life, Lincoln confessed to William H. Herndon when he got home, he was "greatly abashed over his personal appearance." Usually, Lincoln thought little about how he looked or dressed; he was not, Herndon admitted, "fastidious." In New York, however, "for a long time after he began his speech and before he became 'warmed up,' he imagined that the audience noticed the contract [sic] between his Western clothes and the neat-fitting suits of Mr. Bryant and others who sat on the platform. The collar of his coat on the right side had an unpleasant way of flying up whenever he raised his arm to gesticulate. He imagined the audience noticed that also."[20]

With his long, thick fingers Lincoln proceeded clumsily to unfold his sheath of manuscript pages. And then, in that harsh, "high-pitched" trumpet tone with which he unavoidably launched all of his orations, a timbre that seldom modulated until his vocal chords warmed and loosened, he uttered his very first public words in New York—in a discordant frontier twang that must have jolted every listener in the room:

"Mr. Cheerman . . . ."

At least "Mr. Chairman" is what some onlookers remembered hearing that night. The following morning, the authorized newspaper reprint of Abraham Lincoln's Cooper Union address instead suggested that he had begun his speech with the more formal salutation: "Mr. President and Fellow-Citizens of New York." If so, this opening was more all-embracing, and no doubt safer to articulate without too quickly revealing Lincoln's undisguisable Kentucky-Indiana accent.[21]

IN STYLE AS WELL as appearance, Lincoln was a unique public speaker. Unlike most of the famous orators of his age, he seldom gestured when he spoke—"never sawed the air," in William Herndon's words. He would typically begin his speeches with his hands behind his back, holding his left hand firmly with his right. A youngster who watched Lincoln debate Douglas agreed that "his gesticulations were few, though now and then his long index finger did valiant service."[22]

Nor did he roam the platform like so many of his contemporaries. "Mr. Lincoln planted himself squarely on his feet at the beginning of his speech with his hands clasped behind him," wrote a clergyman who witnessed one of his debates with Douglas, "and stood so motionless while he spoke that a silver dollar could have been laid on the platform between his feet at the beginning and Lincoln did not move enough during its continuance to touch it with either foot."[23]

Only after warming to his topic did Lincoln begin to relax and underscore his words with occasional gestures: not with his hands, however, but with his head, "throwing it with vim this way and that" like a "projectile," hair flying. With his eyes "aglow" and his heart "alive to the right," the effect of those quick movements was incandescent. As Herndon described that characteristic cocking of the head: "It some-times came with a quick jerk, as if throwing off electric sparks into com-bustible material." Even an opposition newspaper acknowledged "a remarkable mobility of his features, the frequent contortions of which excited the merriment" of the crowd at Cooper Union.[24]

When his subject was slavery—as it almost always was these days—he might once or twice in the course of a speech throw both arms upward or clench his fists, as if to "trample . . . the object of his hatred." But such moments were the exception, not the rule. On the platform, as Herndon described him:

> He always stood squarely on his feet, toe even with toe; that is, he never put one foot before the other. He neither touched nor leaned on anything for support. He made but few changes in his positions and attitudes. He never ranted, never walked backward and forward on the platform. . . . His little gray eyes flashed in a face aglow with the fire of his profound thoughts; and his uneasy movements and diffident manner sunk themselves beneath the wave of righteous indignation that came sweeping over him. Such was Lincoln the orator.[25]

His old Illinois friend Joseph Gillespie concurred: "He despised everything like ornament and display & confined himself to a dry and bold statement of his point and then worked away with sledge hammer logic at making out his case." In an age in which public oratory consti-tuted high entertainment, the best speakers were true performers—men, like Thomas Corwin, who could be counted on to roam the platform and discard their outer garments, one by one; or Lincoln's life-long rival Stephen A. Douglas, who was known for "clenching his fists, and stamping his feet." Lincoln was different. As Herndon summed it up: "He never acted for stage effect."[26]

Perhaps Lincoln adopted his lean, terse style to deflect from what one Ohio admirer regarded as an appearance "oddly different from any other man whom I had seen." Yet once he got more deeply into his talk, Lincoln inspired the eyewitness to conclude that "there was a certain artistic ability in him as a public speaker," a manner "quiet, chaste, and dignified . . . simple, direct, and almost religious . . . an indefinable something."[27]

But at first, to the audience at Cooper Union, as to most audiences, Lincoln sounded even worse than he looked.

Not for the first time, his voice, which could sound "shrill, piping, and unpleasant," betrayed him. It started out "thin" and "squeaky," according to one eyewitness named Tuttle, who later recalled: "It seemed to me pitched most uncomfortably high, and to come out with labor." One can almost see Mason Brayman frantically waving his hat on his cane from the back of the house, in a desperate effort to get Lincoln to pipe up. Taking note of his "involuntary comical awkwardness," the *New York Herald* correspondent on the scene reported that though "sharp and powerful," Lincoln's voice had "a frequent tendency to dwindle into a sharp and unpleasant sound." There was "not a trace," David Dudley Field's son observed from the platform, "of the smooth-tongued orator."[28]

"It took a moment or more . . . for the speaker to adjust his voice to the tone of the hall," admitted George Haven Putnam. But Putnam sensed that "as he progressed with his speech . . . these little matters were forgotten. The voice secured its proper intonation, and the hearers could not but be impressed with the solemnity of the speaker and with his absorption in his speech."[29]

Conceding that "Mr. Lincoln began his address . . . in a low, monotonous tone," the ever-hopeful Richard McCormick noticed with relief and amazement that "as he advanced, his quaint but clear voice rang out boldly and distinctly enough for all to hear. His manner was to a New York audience a very strange one, but it was captivating. He held the vast meeting spell-bound, and as one by one his oddly expressed but trenchant and convincing arguments confirmed the accuracy and irrefragability [*sic*] of his political conclusions, the house broke out in wild and prolonged enthusiasm. I think I never saw an audience more carried away by an orator."[30]

As Noah Brooks heard about it from another eyewitness: "He began in a very low tone of voice as if he were used to speaking out of doors and was afraid of speaking too loud. He said, 'Mr. *Cheerman*," instead of 'Mr. Chairman,' and employed many other words with an old-fashioned pronunciation. . . .

"But pretty soon, he began to get into his subject: he straightened up, made regular and graceful gestures; his face lighted as with an inward fire; the whole man was transfigured. I forgot his clothes, his personal appearance, and his individual peculiarities. Presently, forgetting myself, I was on my feet with the rest, yelling like a wild Indian, cheering this wonderful man. In the close parts of his arguments, you could hear the gentle sizzling of the gas burners. When he reached his climax, the thunders of applause were terrific."[31]

Summing up Abraham Lincoln's Cooper Union speech with undiminished enthusiasm more than forty years later, Joseph H. Choate remembered precisely the same metamorphosis: "When he spoke, he was transformed before us. His eye kindled, his voice rang, his face shone and seemed to light up the whole assembly as by electric flash. For an hour and more he held his audience in the hollow of his hand."[32]

LINCOLN'S FIRST FEW moments on stage at Cooper Union may have been the most awkward of his career. He had gotten through three pages of his manuscript when, according to an eyewitness named Russell H. Conwell, "he lost his place and then . . . began to tremble and stammer" as he "turned it over two or three times in search" of where he had left off. The crowd supposedly looked on in "silent derision."[33]

Even if Lincoln really lost his way in his text—and Conwell's recollection sounds suspiciously like an exaggeration—the speaker quickly recovered. Finding his place and regaining his bearings, Lincoln "let himself go," Conwell testified appreciatively. The "awkward arms and disheveled hair were lost sight of entirely in the wonderful beauty and lofty inspiration of that magnificent address." And when this "angel of oratory" quoted Frederick Douglass—"It is written in the sky of America that the slaves shall some day be free"—Conwell remembered with a thrill that "the applause was so great that the building trembled and I felt the windows shake behind me."

Unfortunately, Conwell "remembered" not only nonexistent windows, but a dramatic moment that never occurred, and so fostered yet another Cooper Union legend. There is no other record—not even a hint—that Lincoln quoted or even mentioned Frederick Douglass at Cooper Union. To have done so would have unwisely placed the speaker in the radical abolitionist wing of his party—precisely where he did *not* want to present himself to his hearing and reading audiences. What truly surprised his listeners that evening was that Lincoln barely mentioned another Douglas, *Stephen* Douglas, as nearly everyone in the audience had expected. But in time, Lincoln did get the crowd cheering just the same.[34]

Conscious of his "elite" audience in the New York auditorium, as well as the greater audience who would read his speech later in the press, Lincoln offered no customary, crowd-pleasing antislavery speech. Instead, in his long, ambitious lecture—some 7,715 words in all—he offered a laboriously researched, studiously legalistic, and dispassionately restrained antislavery treatise that hearkened back to the will of the founding fathers, preached political moderation and sectional harmony, yet at the same time bristled with barely contained indignation over the moral outrage of human slavery.

Lincoln believed that this unusual combination of approaches would not only play well in the Great Hall of Cooper Union, but impress newspaper readers around the country, and in the best of circumstances endure in campaign literature for the rest of this decisive year. At its core, the Cooper Union address was a subtle but unmistakable preconvention campaign speech, deftly crafted to thrust the speaker into the forefront of 1860 presidential politics.

To accomplish this goal, Lincoln drew from a vast arsenal of historical data, legalistic argumentation, and rhetorical flourish to offer three distinct speeches in one: an appeal to history, a criticism of (disguised as an appeal to) the South, and a rallying cry aimed at his natural constituency: Northern Republicans.

In the first section, he invoked the memory of the founding fathers, harnessing their unspoken endorsement for his antislavery position by offering a staggering mass of historical study to support the power of the federal government to restrict the spread of slavery—additionally, indirectly inviting an endorsement of Lincoln himself for mastering the nuances of the historical investigation.

In part two, while ostensibly asking Southerners for patience, peace, and understanding, he seasoned his conciliatory words with an implicit warning: if disaffection led to disunion, it would be the fault of a hostile South, not a tolerant North (especially if the country were led by moderates like Lincoln).

Then, in part three, Lincoln turned to his fellow Republicans and, in a majestic coda, urged them never to abandon the very principles that were unnerving Southerners in the first place.

"He was full of political history . . . analyzed everything, laid every statement bare, and by dint of his broad reasoning powers and manliness of admission inspired his hearers with deep conviction of his earnestness and honesty." So William H. Herndon described a typical Lincoln performance during his 1858 debates with Stephen A. Douglas. Herndon might as well have been describing Lincoln's approach to Cooper Union, for which he prepared his case with even more painstaking research. As Cooper Union eyewitness Richard McCormick remembered, "Its simple yet masterly style, its new and powerful logic, its mild and unanswerable disposition of the great agitating questions of the hour; its breadth of spirit and tender sincerity," all made its appeal both "opportune and forcible."[35]

How, precisely, did Lincoln bring it off? Most of the histories and biographies that mention Cooper Union cite Lincoln's painstaking preparation, tiring journey, and mesmerizing personal appeal, all of which are admittedly crucial to appreciating the speech. There can be no doubt that the political culture that made his invitation, and ultimate success, possible in the first place represents a major part of the story. But to dwell only on the emotional impact of Lincoln's appearance would be like admiring a great opera for its scenery. In the end, even the irresistible story of an awkward westerner charming an elite eastern audience fades in interest without parsing the speech itself: the words.[36]

Lincoln set several unspoken but ambitious goals for his first public words in New York.

First, as a western newcomer, he knew he must demonstrate his historical and legal acumen, along with a sophisticated self-assurance, to buttress his opposition to slavery expansion and, perhaps just as important, show that he was a thoughtful statesman, not just a frontier speechmaker.

Second, he must perform on the platform more persuasively, more convincingly, and more dramatically than either of the two formidable westerners who had preceded him to the Cooper Union podium, Cassius Clay and Frank Blair.

Third, he must present himself as the principal Republican alternative to New Yorker William H. Seward, by distancing himself from his own "house divided" sentiments of 1858, and by making it clear that he was unwilling to embrace Seward's vision (soon to be discarded by *its* author as well) that the country faced an "irrepressible conflict" over the slavery issue (true enough, as it turned out).[37]

Lincoln must separate himself from both Seward's negative fatalism and John Brown's dangerous radicalism. He must demonstrate that he was no threat to existing institutions in the South, even the repugnant institution of slavery. This would require him to present himself as more electable than Seward, and more moderate than the "house divided" Lincoln of 1858. And he must do so without offending the liberal Republican base whose enthusiastic loyalty any nominee would need to retain in order to win the general election.

Fourth, then, even as he preached reconciliation, Lincoln must also strongly reaffirm his devotion to the antislavery cause, and emphasize the moral superiority of the Republican position in the national dialogue on popular sovereignty. To Americans of his generation, moral absolutes were as important as logic, history, and politics. Even a conservative preaching tolerance of an overt evil (slavery) in order to prevent an even greater evil (destruction of the American experiment) must cling to the moral high ground. Lincoln knew he must not endanger his antislavery Republican base in a potential general election.

Fifth, he must again, and more convincingly than ever, "debate" Stephen Douglas in absentia, exposing Douglas's "popular sovereignty" doctrine as a ploy to nationalize slavery by convincing local majorities to endorse it in sparsely settled new territories. He must again tie Douglas firmly to proslavery Chief Justice Roger B. Taney, whose 1857 Dred Scott decision portended the same result. He must show that both Douglas and Taney perverted the intentions of the nation's founders. Lincoln had labored to connect Douglas to Taney throughout the Senate debates in Illinois. Now he must do so one more time, more convincingly than ever. He must make Cooper Union the eighth and final "Lincoln-Douglas debate," and win it as well.

In sum, Lincoln's mission at Cooper Union was symbolically, peremptorily, to "defeat" two formidable potential opponents at the same time: Seward, the prevailing favorite for the Republican presidential nomination, and Douglas, the presumptive Democratic nominee in the general election. Somehow, Lincoln must conquer them both in one evening's work.

And one only. Aside from reiterations of this speech over the days that would follow in New England, Lincoln likely knew that if he succeeded—and went on to win the nomination at the Republican national convention—he would never deliver another major political address. The prevailing political culture required that presidential candidates maintain aloof silence. If he failed in New York, he might remain a valuable soldier in the army of antislavery orators, but one with little chance for personal political advancement. If he succeeded, Cooper Union could triumphantly become his last such speech, by launching a national candidacy. To become so, it also had to be his best speech.

Chapter Six

⊰ "The Strength of Absolute Simplicity" ⊱

The facts with which I shall deal this evening are mainly old and familiar; nor is there anything new in the general use I shall make of them. If there shall be any novelty, it will be in the mode of presenting the facts, and the inferences and observations following that presentation.

THE FIRST TWO WORDS in Lincoln's Cooper Union Address are "the facts." He thereby immediately informs his audience that his speech will be an appeal to the head, not the heart. It will be an examination of right and wrong, not a call to emotionalism, not unlike the thrust of his Lyceum lecture, twenty-two years earlier, in which he had advocated "cold, calculating reason" above the "enemy" of "passion." Then, for emphasis at Cooper Union, Lincoln immediately repeats the phrase. "If there shall be any novelty, it will be in the mode of presenting *the facts*."[1]

Lincoln goes on to announce that what he will report is "old and familiar," not "anything new." Then another warning: there will be no "novelty" in what he says. Twice he says he will present only facts; three times he promises nothing fresh. It is almost an anti-introduction, an intriguing caveat emptor. Toying with his audience, craftily diminishing expectations (the easier to dazzle with what follows), Lincoln seems to be saying: Do not expect a major address. Of course, beguiled by his apparent self-effacement, and transfixed by his joltingly awkward style, the audience is riveted. Intellectually, this is Lincoln's shrewd way of asserting immediately that everything he says at Cooper Union will be incontrovertible: beyond reproach, beyond partisanship, beyond criticism.

It is no wonder that these peculiar, unadorned opening sentences sound dry to some listeners. But then, without fanfare, without even a transition, Lincoln proceeds immediately to quote Stephen A. Douglas and lay out his central expository theme with a phrase that—unbeknownst to the audience—will echo like mortar fire, repeatedly and relentlessly, throughout the Cooper Union address:

> In his speech last autumn, at Columbus, Ohio, as reported in "The New-York Times" [citing the *Times* was Lincoln's wise way of connecting his western oratory to his eastern audience], Senator Douglas said:
>
> *"Our fathers, when they framed the Government under which we live, understood this question just as well, and even better, than we do now."*

The "question," of course, is the extension of slavery. But if his listeners expect Lincoln to launch immediately into a direct attack on Douglas's assertion, they are due for another surprise. "I fully indorse this," Lincoln announces instead. And for good measure, he declares: "I adopt it as a text for this discourse." It "furnishes a precise and an agreed starting point for a discussion between Republicans and that wing of the Democracy headed by Senator Douglas." Lincoln thus proclaims unexpectedly that on this one crucial point, he agrees entirely with Douglas: He is willing for the great, divisive issue of the day to be left to the founders, because they understood it better than does the bitterly divided electorate of 1860.

By now the audience probably expects the name of Douglas to reverberate through the hall with stump-style rebuke throughout the speech. Again, the listeners will be surprised. Lincoln will mention Douglas by name only three more times in the next hour and a half. All together, he will identify or refer to him just five times in his entire address. And yet the fact that the "Little Giant" is the object of the onslaught that ensues will be clear to everyone in the hall.

Over the next ninety minutes, the audience will instead hear a panoply of other names: those of the founding fathers. Some are familiar and revered, others obscure—but all provide testimony across time, since Douglas had earlier introduced them as "expert witnesses" in establishing historical precedent on slavery. As Lincoln now reminds his listeners, Douglas argued that the founders believed that the Constitution limited the federal government's future jurisdiction over the expansion of slavery. Could Douglas be right?

In rebuttal, Lincoln will "cross-examine" the signers of that document, one by one. He will recite their history of votes on slavery extension and related issues from the days of the early Republic. He will pronounce their names no fewer than thirty-nine times. In the manner of dogged lawyerly rebuttal, he will repeat many of the more remote names over and over, reintroducing them to a new generation in a bravura combination of legal brief and history lesson.

He will cite George Washington eight times, Thomas Jefferson twice, and even manage to include Alexander Hamilton and Benjamin Franklin once each, though he concedes that they never recorded a single official vote against slavery during their lifetimes (but were, he asserts, known to be antislavery). And he will report the pre- and post-Constitution sentiments of other signers, pro- and antislavery, ultimately tallying their votes as if he is somehow conducting a final, decisive, irrefutable poll in the realm of historical memory. Having identified thirty-nine framers whose slavery votes cry out for analysis, he will repeat the number "thirty-nine" for emphasis twenty separate times in a parallel burst of reiteration for effect.

The rhetorical spine around which Lincoln will hang his proof— and the oration's rhetorical delight as well—will be constructed out of the repetition of the phrase that Douglas had uttered in Columbus. The senator had employed it as well, Lincoln knew, in his much-discussed recent article on "The Dividing Line" for *Harper's Magazine*: "Our fathers, when they framed the government under which we live, understood this question just as well, and even better, than we do now."

In a brilliant show of technique and argumentation, Lincoln will utter this exact phrase no fewer than fifteen times in his speech, and one can only imagine how he delights his audience each time he renews the refrain. Likely he alters the tone each time he pronounces the phrase, intoning it here with mock gravity, there with a sarcastic edge, and here again with a laugh of disbelief. By the time he is midway through his long presentation, the audience breathlessly awaits the next iteration of "our fathers, who framed the government"—eager to hear how Lincoln next pronounces it, and how he uses it to punctuate an argument, puncture a Democratic viewpoint, or implicitly pillory Douglas.

Lincoln carries his historical argument on two parallel courses, one positive, one negative. With one, he associates antislavery with the founders by repetition of their names and votes on slavery-related issues. At the same time, through similar thrusts of repetition, he mocks Stephen A. Douglas's contrary assertion that the Constitution bars congressionally imposed limits on slavery. Democrats, Lincoln demonstrates, misinterpret the founders—in short, they are guilty of tampering with America's most sacred secular heritage, the lessons of "our fathers." For "our fathers when they framed the government under which we live," as Lincoln reminds his audience again and again, understood the slavery issue better than Americans do in 1860. Thus Douglas and the Democrats, who claim to be true Conservatives, in fact deserve to be saddled with the mantle of radicalism far more than do the Republicans.

The phrase "our fathers," of course, carried a special resonance for Bible-reading Americans of 1860. The Scriptures mention "our fathers" more than fifty times. The Lord's Prayer begins with a form of the same two words. Americans took the phrase most seriously, and Lincoln could score additional points by suggesting that Douglas used it recklessly. In a subtle demonstration that he and his audience share this secret, Lincoln speaks of "our fathers" at least five times in his speech, and the "fathers" another nine—these in addition to the occasions on which he summons forth "our fathers who framed the government under which we live." Altogether, he mentions the nation's "fathers" thirty different times. The message is clear: the gods of America's secular heaven had ordained a limit to the spread of slavery with the hope and expectation of its eventual demise. And there could be no appeal to heaven. Douglas had misrepresented the intent of the fathers, and it was time to set the record straight, and expose the heretics.[2]

In Lincoln's widely reported speech accepting the U.S. Senate nomination two years earlier, the message—"a house divided against itself cannot stand"—was biblical. Lincoln had argued that slavery was doomed according to the word of God. Now, at Cooper Union, he would show that slavery was doomed according to the word of the secular gods of the American dream: the founding fathers.

Section One: The Fathers

To UNVEIL HIS HEROIC research, Lincoln first needed to identify "our fathers." Who were they? In response, he adopts an interpretation that will undergird his entire argument. He will rely on the men who signed the Constitution. "I suppose the 'thirty-nine' who signed the original instrument may be fairly called our fathers who framed that part of the present Government," he declares. Of course, had he chosen to inquire about the slavery sentiments of the signers of the Declaration of Independence, he might have been forced to a less satisfactory conclusion for his purposes.[3] But since Douglas had chosen to equate the "fathers" with the "government under which we live," Lincoln claims justification for basing his research on the framers of the document that created that government in the first place: the Constitution. Besides, Lincoln truly believed that freedom and equal opportunity were not only guaranteed by the Declaration, but attainable under the Constitution—which, after all, had never mentioned, much less endorsed, slavery by name, and never gave Americans the right, as Stephen Douglas insisted, to vote to deny freedom to other men, even black men.[4]

Now Lincoln is ready to demonstrate his mastery of the sources that so consumed him at the Springfield State Library. Had any of the "thirty-nine" ever acted, or voted, in such a way as to suggest that the government explicitly forbade or implicitly precluded federal restrictions on slavery? For more than twenty paragraphs he will now show, as he neatly seizes the high ground of the argument with a triplet of possessive pronouns, that:

our fathers

understood

our Federal Government and
our Federal Territories

Lincoln always strove for such rhetorical constructions, but at Cooper Union he is not yet at the stage of his narrative development that will elicit timeless triplet phrases like the "of the people, by the people, for the people" at Gettysburg. Instead, he uses a similar but not quite as demanding device, alternatively parallel and contradictory double phrasing—the device of antiphony—to neatly set up his audience for his arguments:

our Federal Government	*our* Federal Territories
our fathers understood	better than *we*
our former territorial acquisitions	*our* own states
we admit that it [slavery] is more prominent	*we* deny that we made it so
If you would have the peace of old times	readopt the precepts and principles of the old times
For this Republicans contend	with this . . . they will be content

Let us stand by our duty	Let us do our duty
Some of you delight	Some of you admit
You say we have made the slavery question more prominent.	You charge that we stir up insurrections among your slaves.

As to the founders, he urges that Americans:

speak as they spoke	act as they acted
As those fathers marked it [slavery]	let it be again marked

And, in a warning to those who would speak loosely about disunion, a caution to never:

Unsay what Washington said	undo what Washington did

Because:

Actions speak louder than words	actions, under such responsibility, speak still louder

Without fanfare or flourish, Lincoln poses the stark question that directed his research: "Does the proper division of local from federal authority, or anything in the Constitution, forbid *our Federal Government* to control as to slavery in *our Federal Territories?*" (The word "division" hearkens back to Douglas's screed on "the Dividing Line," and Lincoln will mockingly allude to the proper "line dividing" local and federal authority seven separate times in the speech.) As Lincoln reminds his listeners, Democrats believe the affirmative: that local governments or voters in new territories (via popular sovereignty) have the right to choose or reject slavery for themselves. Lincoln speaks for the Republicans in arguing for the negative: Nothing in the

Constitution prevents the federal government from restricting the spread of slavery.

In using negative proof, Lincoln acts the defense lawyer who needs only to show reasonable doubt. He does not attempt to prove that the Constitution authorizes Congress to legislate on slavery expansion; only that it does not *forbid* it to do so. The "burden of proof," he will proclaim, rests on the Democrats, not on the Republicans.

To settle the issue on these terms, Lincoln proposes to examine those occasions on which the "fathers" were called upon to cast votes on issues similar to those facing Americans in 1860. He chooses several, and introduces them slowly and thoroughly. Showing patience and attention to detail, he is continuing to surprise an audience that may have come to hear a slam-bang stump speech.

At the Congress of Confederation in 1784, he dryly recites, four "fathers"—future signers of the Constitution—were called on to vote on a measure to prohibit slavery in the emerging nation's vast Northwest Territory. Of these four, three—Roger Sherman, Thomas Mifflin, and Hugh Williamson—voted to ban slavery.

At the Congress of Confederation three years later, in 1787, two more future "framers" endorsed a similar prohibition for the Northwest Territory: William Blount and William Few.

Then, decisively, in 1789, at the first official session of the Congress of the United States, all sixteen "fathers" sitting—with George Washington himself concurring—voted unanimously on a bill to enforce the Ordinance of 1787, which included a ban on slavery in the Northwest Territory. Lincoln intones all sixteen names, some (like Sherman and Few) voting once again on the issue, and some, like James Madison, being heard for the first time.

For good measure, Lincoln points out that in 1789 Congress also took up an act to organize the Mississippi Territory. Slavery had long existed there, but the bill before Congress that year authorized restrictions on the importation of new slaves, and by voting on the final legislation, Lincoln argues, three more framers (John Langdon, George Read, and Abraham Baldwin) thus registered their belief, too, that the federal government had the right to regulate the institution.

Yet again in 1804, Lincoln reports, two framers were called on to consider similar restrictions in another region where slavery was already an established institution: the newly acquired Louisiana Territory. Again participating in a unanimous vote, the two "fathers" on hand (Baldwin and Jonathan Dayton) endorsed federal oversight. The overall legislation included a ban on the importation of new slaves from foreign shores, and all slaves who had entered the country after May 1, 1798, and banned any slaves who were brought into Louisiana except by owners who intended to use them to settle the territory.

And finally, in 1820, Congress met to consider the Missouri Compromise—the pacifying agreement, Lincoln's audience well knew, that had held the slavery debate in check until Douglas refired the caldron by introducing popular sovereignty thirty-four years later. On the Missouri bill, Lincoln reminds his audience, two surviving framers cast votes: Rufus King to ban slavery extension, Charles Pinckney to allow it.

Lincoln is now poised to unveil his final statistical tally, taking scrupulous care to avoid counting those framers who had voted on the issue more than once. Proceeding to calculate the result, he reports that twenty-three of the thirty-nine "fathers who framed the government under which we live" (a "clear majority," he argues) had enjoyed opportunities, both before and after acting on the "original instrument"—the Constitution—to express themselves on federal authority over slavery expansion. Of these, twenty-one of those who understood the question "better than we," or, as he quickly amplifies this judgment, "just as well, and even better than we do now," left an irrefutable record of their conviction that slavery should be prohibited in the territories.

And with a sly reference to Douglas's recent outpouring of rhetoric reaching the opposite conclusion, Lincoln points out: "As actions speak louder than words, so actions, under such responsibility, speak still louder." The Douglas interpretation, he argues, is not only "presumptuous" but "impudently absurd." And then Lincoln concludes his exegesis with a complex, sarcastic tautology directed against the Douglas Democrats who seek to pervert the intention of the founders. There can be no inconsistency in the fathers' votes, even if they appear to Douglas to be inconsistent with their recorded slavery sentiments on other occasions, simply because "those who did the . . . things, alleged to be inconsistent, understood whether they really were inconsistent better than we—better than he who affirms they are inconsistent." Lincoln has dazzled his audience with his repeated thrusts of barbed logic.

Now Lincoln is ready for his greatest historical leap, and he has laid out so many statistics, it will sound as logical as his earlier assertions: Of the sixteen who left no clear record, fifteen left behind significant hints that they would have sympathized with this viewpoint had they enjoyed the opportunity to register their votes. They included Benjamin Franklin, Alexander Hamilton, and Gouverneur Morris. Only one, Lincoln argues, South Carolina's John Rutledge, remained a firm proslavery man. And they all deserve to be counted in his definitive summary of "our fathers." And this is enough for Lincoln. In his final count, it is thirty-six to three in favor of restricting slavery, an overwhelming endorsement by "our fathers" of the very anti-slavery-expansion sentiments shared by the Republicans of 1860.

No one who carefully reads this opening section can doubt that Cooper Union proved much more than a demonstration of technique and style. It was clearly organized as a lecture by a "professor" who had mastered his history and was spilling over with facts and figures to buttress his position on founding principles. To youthful eyewitness Lyman Abbott, accustomed to "the dramatic and impassioned oratory of Henry Ward Beecher," here was something he recognized to be "as passionless, but also as convincing, as a demonstration in Euclid's Geometry, as clear and cogent, but also as absolutely without oratorical ornament of any description." So far. But as Lincoln's argument expanded, its logic irrefutable, Henry Field felt himself falling under the "merciless logic which no listener could escape, as he unfolded link after link in the iron chain of his argument."[5]

Lincoln had offered many of those arguments before, rehearsing and refining them across the West. Speaking at Indianapolis five months earlier, he had declared: "Our fathers who made the government, made the ordinance of 1787." In Kansas just two months before traveling to New York, he had asserted: "The Framers of the Organic Law believed that the Constitution would *outlast* Slavery." But not until Cooper Union did Lincoln prove the case so methodically, support it with so many facts, or present it with such sober diligence, reflecting what historian Jacques Barzun once described as his gifts of "infallible exposition" and "artistic detachment."[6]

At Cooper Union, Lincoln not only assails Douglas and the Democrats for promoting an unhistorical view of the nation's founders. He seeks audaciously to convert the founders themselves to the Republicans.

Lincoln crowns his historical inquiry with a clever defense for its infallibility. Closing his opening section, he suggests that from this day forward, anyone who wishes to say that the "fathers" believed there were no restrictions on the spread of slavery remains free to say so, but at the peril of being proven conclusively wrong. To make the point, Lincoln invents a prototypical stubborn Democrat and then batters him with logic. His deft series of propositions and rebuttals cuts the Democratic argument to shreds on the wings of a narrative whose decisive points flow like free verse:

If any man at this day sincerely believes [that slavery controls were prohibited by the founders]

he is right to say so

But he has no right to mislead others, who have less access to history, and less leisure to study it [unlike Lincoln the scholar-orator], into the false belief that "our fathers who framed the Government under which we live" were of the same opinion

If any man at this day sincerely believes "our fathers who framed the Government under which we live" [so believed]

he is right to say so

But he should, at the same time, brave the responsibility of declaring that, in his opinion, he understands their principles better than they did themselves . . .

and especially should he not shirk that responsibility by asserting
    that they "understood the question just as well, and even better,
    than we do now"

Provocatively, as if he is tallying the potential rebuttals he will
inevitably endure and wishes to reply in advance, he cautions "against
being misunderstood." He does not suggest that "we are bound to follow
implicitly in whatever our fathers did." Such blind allegiance to precedent, he cautions, "would be to discard all the lights of current experience—to reject all progress—all improvement." Lincoln is on record in
favor of, in awe of, human progress. So his beloved lecture on discoveries and inventions earnestly demonstrated, and Lincoln is not about to
back away from that belief in New York. But when it comes to the
"opinions and policy of our fathers," he maintains, we cannot supplant
their "great authority" without "conclusive" evidence and "clear" argument. Certainly not if Americans North and South, Republican and
Democrat, purport to believe that "they understood the question better
than we." The audience responds with laughter.

And then, suddenly, Lincoln brings his narrative drive to a halt:
"But enough!" he declares (the exclamation point is his), marking his
own impassioned dividing line between the first and second sections of
his speech, and effectively implying: There is no more room for debate
on this issue. With three more references to the "fathers" in a final volley of neat, catechistic couplets, he calls on all those who understand
the issue, and understand the intent of the framers on slavery, to:

speak as they spoke, and act as they acted upon it

This is all Republicans ask—all Republicans desire . . .

As those fathers marked it, so let it be again marked

For this Republicans contend

with this, so far as I know or believe, they will be content

Lincoln's brilliant conceit—accepting Douglas's contention that the "fathers" understood the future of slavery better than the men of 1860, then proving that the "fathers" actually wished slavery regulated, just as contemporary Republicans did—is offered in an almost entirely negative syntax, and with more complex rhetorical construction than Lincoln ever before offered in a major public address. He has shown himself a master of history, a self-confident logician, and a merciless debater, using repetition to crush and ridicule his absent opponents. In the end, however restrained, the message of his introductory section is perfectly clear: The Republicans, not the Democrats, are the true heirs to America's fathers. Therefore:

> As those fathers marked it [slavery], so let it be again marked, as an evil not to be extended, but to be tolerated and protected only because of and so far as its actual presence among us makes that toleration and protection a necessity.

Section Two: The Southerners

Lincoln begins his equally extraordinary second section by purporting to direct his remarks beyond his listening audience. Adopting the subjunctive tense, he issues an odd invitation:

> And now, if they would listen—as I suppose they will not—I would address a few words to the Southern people.

Here he employs another sophisticated rhetorical device, which the scholars of classical speech Michael C. Leff and Gerald P. Mohrmann have correctly identified as a *prosopopoeia*. Taken from the Greek word for "masked person," *prosopopoiia*, it defines personification, an argument directed against an absent person, or in the case of Lincoln at Cooper Union, to an entire absent section of the country: the South. He will say what he "*would* say to them [emphasis added]" if they could hear him, knowing full well they could not, and would not listen if they could.[7]

But Lincoln operates in this section on another level as well: having admitted that he knows the South will not "listen" to his words, what follows is an elaborate attempt to ingratiate himself with his Northern audiences by rallying them around rational, unifying sentiments that the South *should* entertain if only they were only reasonable on the issue of slavery, and believed what the "fathers" really intended. Thus what follows is what scholar David Zarefsky has called a "triangulation" of argumentation, in which Lincoln makes an offer to speak to the South, knowing that Southern newspapers do not print what he says, and immediately going above the heads of Southern audiences to direct his message to the North.[8]

The technique is subtle, but the arguments are forceful. Lincoln proceeds to pummel his imaginary Southern listeners with a series of charges and dares:

You consider yourselves a reasonable and a just people

You are not inferior to any other people

Still, when you speak of us Republicans

You do so only to denounce us as reptiles

You will grant a hearing to pirates or murderers but nothing like it to "Black Republicans"

Lincoln continues the colloquy with an equally riveting "You say we are sectional. We deny it" section. In a dazzling demonstration of *ad hominem* argumentation and *prosopopoeia* in which he fires out the word "you" twelve times, responding with "we" ten times; using "your" twelve times, and retorting with "our" or "ours" ten times, he fashions a perfectly harmonized imaginary dialogue in which he makes the case that the only reason Republicans get no support in the South is that Southerners refuse to allow Republicans to be heard, or contend for office, in their region. He is merely confirming the fact that Southerners, as he has reminded his New York audience, will likely not allow his words this night to reach them, either. Just as he has effectively "debated" the absent Douglas on the founders, now he debates the arrogant South on patriotism and the Union.

> You say we are sectional. We deny it. That makes an issue; and the burden of proof is upon you. You produce your proof; and what is it? Why, that our party has no existence in your section—gets no votes in your section. The fact is substantially true; but does it prove the issue? If it does, then in case we should, without change of principle, begin to get votes in your section, we should thereby cease to be sectional. You cannot escape this conclusion; and yet, are you willing to abide by it? If you are, you will probably soon find that we have ceased to be sectional, for we shall get votes in your section this very year.

Rebutting the standard Democratic charges of Republican sectionalism and extremism, he asks another series of questions of his imaginary accusers:

> What is it?
>
> Does it prove the issue?
>
> What is [your proof]?
>
> Are you willing to abide by it?
>
> Do you accept the challenge?

No, Lincoln concludes, Southerners are not willing to admit that their "proof does not touch the issue." Thereby, they show that they do not "indorse" the principles of "our fathers who framed the Government under which we live."

Who, then, taunts Lincoln, really bears responsibility for sectional discord? Who—North or South—has really violated Washington's farewell warning against sectional parties and the strife certain to follow? Lincoln wonders aloud (leaving little doubt what he believes): "Is that warning a weapon in your hands against us, or in our hands against you?" (Here is another concept Lincoln will explore in the future, when the new president answers his own Cooper Union question a year later by cautioning the South in his inaugural address: "In *your* hands, my dissatisfied fellow countrymen, and not in *mine*, is the momentous issue of civil war.")[9]

If it boils down to authentic conservatism—by which Lincoln means fealty to "our fathers" as a means to limit slavery, not to endorse conservatism for its own sake—then who is truly conservative, and who "revolutionary" and "destructive"? Here is the crux of his appeal to the absent audience in the South: the battle for the mantle of the fathers. To Lincoln, resistance to the spread of slavery qualifies as genuine conservatism ("the identical old policy . . . which was adopted by 'our fathers . . .' "); anything less so is revolutionary ("you . . . spit upon that old policy, and insist upon substituting something new").

This crucial section has misled some historians for generations, leading them to judge the entire Cooper Union address as conservative. In truth, there is nothing conservative about it by 1860 standards. It is implicitly anti-Radical, of course, because Lincoln is a mainstream Republican reaching out for national support, his ambition already fixed on the presidential nominating convention scheduled to begin in less than three months. But Lincoln emphasizes conservatism in this passage only to fend off Southern charges that Northerners are destructive. He is quick to point out that some Southerners are retrograde enough to advocate the return of the slave trade. That is not the kind of conservatism to which Lincoln aspires. And he also denies the conservatism of Douglas's "gur-reat pur-rinciple" of popular sovereignty, rolling his words in mockery of his rival's famous stentorian style to "renewed laughter and applause," because it is based on the idea that "'if one man would enslave another, no third man should object.'" Lincoln knows that many Southern conservatives believe just that. His idea of conservatism is to believe what the founders believed—to think as they thought, act as they acted—and based on those precious precedents, to curtail the spread of slavery.

The volley escalates. When Southerners "flaunt" George Washington's admonition against sectionalism, they conveniently ignore his support for prohibiting slavery in the Northwest Territories. When Southerners charge that Republicans are "revolutionary" and "destructive," they ignore the true meaning of conservatism: adherence to the "old and tried"—the lessons of those same "fathers who framed the Government under which we live," which, as Lincoln has just exhaustively demonstrated, lean decisively against slavery expansion.

Southerners say Republicans have made the slavery issue more prominent. But Lincoln insists that Southerners, not Republicans, have done so. Southerners blame Republicans for fomenting slave insurrections such as John Brown's. But Lincoln dares them to prove the "malicious slander." And then, unleashing another display of historical research, he shows that slave insurrections are "no more common now than they were before the Republican party was organized," citing as an example the 1831 uprising in Southampton County, Virginia, which was far bloodier than John Brown's raid at Harpers Ferry.[10]

Taking pains to distance himself from John Brown's brand of radicalism—not only for the benefit of the imagined Southern audience, but also for a Republican electorate wary of extremism—Lincoln pivots his argument further and charges that Southerners are attempting to use John Brown's "peculiar" escapade, and the appearance of Southerner Hinton Rowan Helper's scathing book on slavery, to blame, tarnish, and destroy an innocent Republican party. With barely masked pride, Lincoln reminds his audience that such tactics had failed in the 1859 state elections in which he had played such an important role. Now, to boisterous laughter and prolonged applause, he half-encourages the opposition to retain the strategy, predicting that appeals to fear are doomed to political failure again: "If you think you can, by slandering a woman, make her love you, or by vilifying a man make him vote with you, go on and try it."

Lincoln continues stonily: "But you will break up the Union rather than submit to a denial of your Constitutional rights"—rights, of course, that Lincoln has just proven are *not* guaranteed by the Constitution or the "fathers" who framed it. No, he charges, what you Southerners really want to do is "destroy the Government, unless you be allowed to construe and enforce the Constitution as you please, on all points in dispute between you and us. You will rule or ruin in all events." Historians who have maintained that the second section of Cooper Union is designed to conciliate either ignore or underestimate this heated charge. Lincoln's "words to the Southern people" here can only be meant to inspire, perhaps even incite, Republicans in the North.

And then Lincoln quickly moves to pre-empt one imagined Southern response: that the 1857 Dred Scott decision affirmed the right to hold slaves anywhere in the nation. In response, Lincoln reminds his audience that the bitterly contested ruling was issued by a divided court, with a bare majority, much unlike the overwhelming endorsement for slavery restrictions sanctified by "our fathers." It reflected "decision," Lincoln offers in a neat show of alliteration, "not dictum" (an authoritative pronouncement of a principle). Moreover, Dred Scott, Lincoln contends, "was mainly based upon a mistaken statement of fact—the statement in the opinion that 'the right of property in a slave is distinctly and expressly affirmed in the Constitution,'" which he rejects. Moreover, he predicts, when the Court realizes its error, the judges will "reconsider" their decision.

Besides, the same "fathers" who signed the Constitution had also crafted the Bill of Rights. They surely did not mean for the Taney Court to base a decision prohibiting Congress's right to regulate the expansion of slavery on an amendment—in this case the Fifth Amendment, which guarantees no person shall be deprived of life, liberty, or property without due process of law—of their own making. Surely the "fathers" who crafted the Bill of Rights would never have been guilty of creating amendments at odds with the original instrument.[11]

Thus, he tells "the South," and in so doing reminds the North as well, neither brand of extremism—neither John Brown's hopeless raid nor Roger B. Taney's audacious reconfiguration of the Constitution—can be taken as exemplary, or even meaningful. The former was an aberrant adventure destined for failure, the latter was a flawed ruling destined for correction. The rise of the Republican party certainly did not encourage John Brown. But the party is now honor-bound to dis-courage Dred Scott.

As was the case with the first section of his speech, the historical inquiry he had researched, then rehearsed at earlier venues, Lincoln's words to the South represented an elaboration, an improvement, on a rhetorical technique he had introduced at Kalamazoo, Michigan, four years earlier. There, he launched into an "appeal to the Democratic cit-izens here." The difference was that there really were Democrats in the crowd that day. At Cooper Union, Lincoln's *prosopopoeia* was more pro-nounced: There were probably no Southerners in his New York audi-ence on February 27, 1860 (the closest candidate may have been the anonymous New York correspondent for the *Richmond Enquirer*, who may well have been a New Yorker, not a Virginian). At Leavenworth, Kansas, less than three months before, Lincoln similarly spoke to absent Southerners: "You claim that you are conservative; and we are not. We deny it." The message is reintroduced in much the same fashion at Cooper Union.[12]

Now, Lincoln ends his "friendly" words to the South with a chilling warning: Do not for a moment believe that history will accept your seceding from the Union, and then blaming the election of a Republi-can president for disunion. "That is cool [by which he means marked by intentional effrontery]," Lincoln warns of such strained logic. It would be the same if, "A highwayman holds a pistol to my ear, and mutters through his teeth, 'Stand and deliver, or I shall kill you, and then you will be a murderer!'" It was no more sensible, or morally defensible, he concludes, to threaten "destruction to the Union, to extort my vote."

Southerners, he now makes clear, must be held wholly responsible for the potential destruction of the Union, not Northerners who simply advocate the founding fathers' brand of conservatism to limit the spread of slavery. And then Lincoln employs a rapid-fire series of warnings to argue that challenging the legitimacy of the Republican party was much the same as challenging the legitimacy of the Union itself. He leaves lit-tle doubt where the destructive spiral would lead.

And how much would it avail you, if you could . . . *break up*
[emphasis added] the Republican organization?

You cannot destroy that judgment and feeling—that sentiment—by
breaking up the political organization which rallies around it.

But you will *break up* the Union rather than submit to a denial of
your Constitutional rights.

You will destroy the Government, unless you be allowed to construe and enforce the Constitution as you please, on all points in
dispute between you and us.

You will rule or ruin in all events.

The colloquies continue. Southerners say Republicans make the
slavery question more prominent. "We deny it. We admit that it is more
prominent, but we deny that we made it so." Southerners charge that
Republicans "stir up" slave insurrections. "We deny it" (it is "malicious
slander"). Southerners hint that Republicans empowered John Brown.
"We do not believe it." ("True, we do, in common with 'Our fathers,
who framed the Government under which we live,' declare our belief
that slavery is wrong; but the slaves do not hear us declare even this"—
so how can Republicans incite them?) Southerners believe in a constitutional right to extend slavery. "We deny that such a right has any
existence in the Constitution, even by implication."

But within this series of dramatic denials, Lincoln issues the
strongest antislavery declaration of his address, masked though it is
within a defense of his political party, rather than a philanthropic sympathy for slaves. If the South were indeed listening, these words would
hardly have convinced them of Lincoln's conservatism. But they would
certainly have reminded them (and the Northern Republican audience
to whom he was really speaking) of his commitment to the eventual
destruction of slavery.[13]

Human action can be modified to some extent, but human
nature cannot be changed. There is a judgment and a feeling

against slavery in this nation, which cast at least a million and a half of votes. You cannot destroy that judgment and feeling— that sentiment—by breaking up the political organization which rallies around it.

The Republican party will survive and grow, Lincoln is saying, as long as slavery appears capable of spreading, not withering. Morality, sound judgment, and historical fealty require opposition.

Deftly, Lincoln manages in these initial two sections to win "debates" against two absent opponents. He has rejected Stephen A. Douglas's casuistical claim to alignment with the "fathers" in the first, and rejected Southern claims to conservatism, and the constitutional right to extend slavery, in the second. He has accomplished these goals without resorting to the passionate rhetoric characteristic of both Northern and Southern Democrats, of fire-eating slavery advocates or indignant abolitionists.

He has coolly, dispassionately proven federal authority to control slavery, and dismissed notions of Republican extremism. He has been conservative in tone, but liberal in message. And in successfully, dispassionately arguing each case, he has worked to establish himself as the best representative of principled Republican moderation. He has convincingly demonstrated: I am a western man who can appeal to the East; I am a Northern man who has shown Southern men that Southern men from the last century believed slavery should be placed on the course of ultimate extinction.[14]

Now his final challenge was to rally the Republicans directly.

Section Three: The Republicans

Lincoln concludes his remarkable, tightly controlled Cooper Union performance with "a few words now to Republicans"—eight paragraphs, the briefest of the three sections of the speech. They serve to summarize his historical arguments, define his political cause, and offer as his imperative a plea for unwavering support from the Republican rank and file.

Above all, he reiterates, he desires all parts of the country to remain "*at peace, and in harmony,*" and he urges fellow Republicans to "*do our part to have it so,*" even if "provoked." As he puts it, "Let us do nothing through passion and ill temper" (an echo of his 1838 Lyceum address). In that vein he urges Republicans to "calmly consider" the demands of Southerners, even of those who will not listen. Try to find common ground, he seems to be urging. Try to find ways to conciliate, pacify, even yield—as long as concessions do not subvert "our duty."

But Lincoln is again setting up an absent opponent for a calculated reply. This time he addresses Republicans who would compromise *too much*. Would the South be satisfied if the Territories were open to slavery? "We know they will not." Will the South be satisfied if Republicans pledge to "have nothing to do with invasions or insurrections? We know it will not." Note Lincoln now uses the future tense. He has invited the South to hear his words, "if they would listen," the subjunctive mood inviting their consideration. Now he employs an implied future tense to signal what will come of its refusal to listen to reason. Nothing will convince the South "that we do let them alone," Lincoln charges, except one unacceptable admission:

> This, and this only: cease to call slavery *wrong*, and join them in calling it *right*. And this must be done thoroughly—done in *acts* as well as in *words*. Silence will not be tolerated—we must place ourselves avowedly with them. Senator Douglas' new sedition law must be enacted and enforced, suppressing all declarations that slavery is wrong, whether made in politics, in presses, in pulpits, or in private. . . . We must pull down our Free State constitutions. The whole atmosphere must be disinfected from the taint of opposition to slavery, before they will cease to believe that all their troubles proceed from us.

Lincoln's message here is tantalizing, and again, elaborately indirect: He reaffirms his moderate belief that slavery can be tolerated where it exists, as long as it does not spread. But he nonetheless expresses indignation at its poisonous ramifications—its threat to freedom of speech and religion—if it does not cease ultimately to exist. He carefully posits as his main goal the preservation of the new Republican party, not the destruction of the institution that inspired its creation. But he admits that Republicans cannot convince the South that they mean them no harm unless they agree with the repugnant Southern belief "that slavery is morally right, and socially elevating."

This Lincoln is prepared to repudiate, though still couched in the indirect, parallel style of "we/they" argumentation he has maintained so rigorously throughout his address:

> If slavery is right, all words, acts, laws, and constitutions against it, are themselves wrong, and should be silenced, and swept away. If it is right, we cannot justly object to its nationality—its universality; if it is wrong, they cannot justly insist upon its extension—its enlargement. All they ask, we could readily grant, if we thought slavery right; all we ask, they could as readily grant, if they thought it wrong. . . . Can we cast our votes with their view, and against our own? In view of our moral, social, and political responsibilities, can we do this?

His litany of "right . . . wrong," "wrong . . . right" alternatives exhausted, Lincoln finally answers his own question: "If our sense of duty forbids this, then let us stand by our duty, fearlessly and effectively."

Lincoln now proceeds to one of the most complex, riveting conclusions he has ever constructed—highlighted by a dazzling, 110-word sentence in a penultimate paragraph that invokes the name of George Washington three times in forceful defense against the possibility of compromise on principle. He will invoke divine rule, and remind his listeners (and opponents) which of them are righteous, and which sinners. Having introduced the possibility of sectional harmony, he will now admonish Republicans against shedding principle to achieve it. There are few sentences in the Lincoln canon quite like it, and certainly he would attempt nothing quite so intricate again until offering his acknowledgment of divine retribution for slavery in his Second Inaugural Address. Here at Cooper Union he thunders:

Let us be diverted by none of those sophistical contrivances wherewith we are so industriously plied and belabored—contrivances such as groping for some middle ground between the right and the wrong [here he means popular sovereignty], vain as the search for a man who should be neither a living man nor a dead man—such as a policy of "don't care" on a question about which all true men do care—such as Union appeals beseeching true Union men to yield to Disunionists, reversing the divine rule, and calling, not the sinners, but the righteous to repentance—such as invocations to Washington, imploring men to unsay what Washington said, and undo what Washington did.

Once again, he has offered his alternatives in a dazzling show of parallel construction:

the right	and the wrong
neither a living man	nor a dead man
"don't care"	all true men do care
Union appeals	beseeching true Union men
Union men	Disunionists
not the sinners	but the righteous
unsay what Washington said	undo what Washington did

Lincoln mentions "duty" three times in his closing section—a harbinger of his peroration, in which Lincoln will align "duty" (mentioned two more times) with "faith," neatly tying up with an almost religious fervor the loose ends of an argument that began with a study of "our fathers."

Then comes the crescendo. After devoting so much time to negative argumentation, what is *wrong* with the pro-slavery-extension position, Lincoln will climax his speech by turning to what is *right* in the antislavery position. And in logical progression, he will insist that "right makes might."[14]

A year later, confronting secession, he will acknowledge in his First Inaugural Address that both North and South had "faith of being in the right." Four years after that, contemplating reunion without malice, delivering his Second Inaugural Address to a country battered by war, he will intone an eerie reprise about "firmness in the right, as God gives us to see the right." By then, his faith in right had been sorely tested, and, he believed, his hand guided by God.[15]

Tonight, on February 27, 1860, in New York, ninety minutes after he begins, Lincoln thunders out his moral outrage and intones a pledge to duty. As his future private secretary John G. Nicolay would observe, Lincoln thus brings his argument full cycle—from historical fact to emotional fever—and crafts for himself an entirely new image in the bargain, "yielding and accommodating in non-essentials . . . inflexibly firm in a principle or position deliberately taken."[16]

Neither let us be slandered from our duty by false accusations against us, nor frightened from it by menaces of destruction to the Government nor of dungeons to ourselves. LET US HAVE FAITH THAT RIGHT MAKES MIGHT, AND IN THAT FAITH, LET US, TO THE END, DARE TO DO OUR DUTY AS WE UNDERSTAND IT.

The capitalization of the last sentence was Lincoln's idea—at least he sanctioned it in reprints. Does its use mean that he shouted those words? Whether he did or not, he had concluded with perfect symmetry. The way had been shown by the fathers, embraced by Republicans, and misinterpreted by Southerners and Democrats. Destruction to the Union must be resisted. "Dungeons to ourselves"—a far more intriguing concept, suggesting the danger of facing the 1860 campaign without moral purpose—must be resisted with equal vigilance. "Right" and "duty" would henceforth be left to "we" and "us"—in other words, to Republicans—to understand, appreciate, and if necessary defend.

The perpetuation of slavery promised an end to popular government and personal liberty—destruction and dungeons. Freedom required moral vigilance, and duty could yet require might. The best course was unity: around Washington, his fellow founders, the "fathers," constitutional principle, sectional harmony. But principled Republicans had no choice but to accept that slave-holders would rebuff such appeals, and to reiterate their unwavering commitment to freedom.

At his Second Inaugural, Abraham Lincoln would appear as a tired warrior invoking the wrath of God to set the stage for a call for malice toward none. At Cooper Union, he was the vigorous antislavery man in conservative's clothing, invoking historical precedent and denying confrontationism to set the stage for a powerful call for resistance to immoral compromise. But the Second Inaugural was no more a call only for "charity for all" than the Cooper Union was merely a call for moderation.

Rather, the Cooper Union address was a magnificent anomaly, both lawyerly and impassioned; empirical and scholarly; a moderation of Lincoln's style and tone, accompanied by a stiffening reiteration of moral purpose; no "house divided" jeremiad, but instead a clear vision of national justice, animated by the confident expectation that it would prevail.

Abraham Lincoln folded his manuscript, removed his spectacles, and bathed in the applause that now engulfed him, having effectively drawn his own "dividing line" between right and wrong, between the past and the future—his country's and his own.

"THE SPEECH WAS MASTERLY, and fully sustained throughout; indeed a triumph," wrote Mason Brayman, the Springfield Democrat who had listened so obligingly from the very back of the hall, ". . . and the manner in which the speech was received, might justly awaken the pride of any living statesman. Without any preface of compliment; with scarcely a bow, he seized the strong points of the argument, and went straight through; not losing a link, not tripping, not wanting words, but speaking with studied precision and grammatical accuracy; and not even turning aside to tell a story, or provoke that mirth, which so often characterizes his more free and easy performances at home."[17]

"Solemnity . . . Precision and moderation." That was what impressed young George Haven Putnam about Abraham Lincoln's speech at Cooper Union, and, as he perceptively noticed, captivated the other listeners who crowded the Great Hall as well.

"His style of speech and manner of delivery were severely simple," came the similar opinion of an enthralled Joseph H. Choate. ". . . With no attempt at ornament or rhetoric, without pretence or parade, he spoke straight to the point. It was marvellous to see how this untutored man, by mere self-discipline and the chastening of his own spirit, had outgrown all meretricious arts and had found his own way to the grandeur and the strength of absolute simplicity."[18]

Mason Brayman was astounded at the transformation he saw in the Lincoln he knew from the Illinois stump:

It was . . . somewhat funny, to see a man who *at home*, talks along in so familiar a way, walking up and down, swaying about, swinging his arms, bobbing forward, telling droll stories and laughing at them himself, *here in New-York*, standing up stiff and straight, with his hands quiet, pronouncing sentence after sentence, in good telling english, with elaborate directness, though well condensed, and casting at each finished period, a timid, sidelong glance at the formidable array of Reporters who surrounded the table close at his elbow, as if conscious, that after all the *world* was his audience, on whose ear his words would fall from the thousand multiplying tongues of the Press.

Lincoln's one broad mockery of Douglas's "great principle" as a "gureat pur-rinciple" clearly enchanted listeners, but it allowed them only the briefest glimpse into the stump style, and the power to amuse with his wily repetitions, about which they had heard so much. As Brayman noticed, that once-defining attribute was kept in uncharacteristic check. "He presented point after point in such a fair, happy and telling way," *New York Independent* editor Henry Bowen noticed, "that he made an army of friends at once." Even Bowen's proslavery friends made sure to tell him, "I like that man, if I don't agree with him . . . He doesn't make you mad as [abolitionists William Lloyd] Garrison and [Wendell] Phillips do." Bowen believed that Lincoln made more Republican converts around town in twenty-four hours than had existed in all of New York the day before his speech.[19]

Not that Lincoln's appeal to logic—delivered in his "quaint" voice and "strange" manner—did not stir as much excitement as admiration. When Lincoln soared to his conclusion, asserting that "right makes might," the house "broke out in wild and prolonged enthusiasm," Richard C. McCormick remembered. ". . . The cheering was tumultuous." Horace Greeley's *New York Tribune* noticed the same effect: Lincoln's calm, sometimes humorous logic aroused the crowd into more of a frenzy than any sermon or vest-ripping diatribe ever had. "Mr. Lincoln is one of Nature's orators," an editorial proclaimed, "using his rare powers solely and effectively to elucidate and to convince, though their inevitable effect is to delight and electrify as well."[20]

"It was a great speech," an eyewitness told Noah Brooks. "When I came out of the hall, my face glowing with an excitement and my frame all aquiver, a friend, with his eyes aglow, asked me what I thought of Abe Lincoln, the rail-splitter. I said, 'He's the greatest man since St. Paul.' And I think so yet."[21]

IT IS DIFFICULT to imagine again a bygone political culture in which audiences subjected to a ninety-minute speech would respond to its conclusion not by racing for the exits, but by demanding more speeches. But that is exactly what happened at Cooper Union.

In the wave of cheering, the crowd called for further remarks. Editor Horace Greeley was called forward first, and as Lincoln looked on, the editor told the listeners that they had just heard "a specimen of what free labor and free expression of ideas could produce." Not content with so brief a tribute, the crowd next called for Police Commissioner Nye, who appeared reluctantly, and only to beg to be excused from marring "the effect of the address" by attempting to add anything new. (According to one newspaper, he proceeded to do so anyway.) Brooklyn's Judge

Culver was brought on, too, then David Dudley Field, and finally James A. Briggs, no doubt in acknowledgment of his role in bringing the orator from Illinois to New York.[22]

It was a proud moment for Briggs, but a delicate one, too. Briggs was, after all, still officially supporting Salmon P. Chase for president, and racing through his mind in the wake of Lincoln's triumph may have been the potential impact of Lincoln's speech on the candidate of his choice.

"Fellow citizens," he began, "one of three gentlemen will be our standard bearer in the canvass for President of the United States this year—the accomplished and eloquent Senator from New York, Mr. Seward, the late able Governor of Ohio, Mr. Chase, or the unknown knight who, on the prairies of Illinois in 1858, met the Bois Gilbert of the Democracy, Stephen A. Douglas, and unhorsed him, Abraham Lincoln." Time would soon tell, he declared, "whether the gallant son of Kentucky, who was reared in Illinois, and whom you have heard tonight, shall be the standard bearer in the fight."[23]

It was surely the first time Lincoln had ever heard his Illinois rival compared to the prosecutorial villain from *Ivanhoe* (the original Brian de Bois-Gilbert was the preceptor of the Knights Templar), but the crowd responded with cheers. More important, Lincoln heard Briggs's prediction with his own ears. For Lincoln, comparison to his better-known rivals, one a senator, the other a former governor, could be regarded as a milestone for the one-term congressman who had not held a major office in more than ten years. A dark horse candidate just twenty-four hours earlier, he was now, only moments after his New York debut, being touted in Seward's own state—and by a Chase man—as their equal.

A few weeks later, Briggs hastened to write his "dear friend" Chase to reassure him that, as far as he was concerned, "the contest for the Presidency is between yourself and Mr. Seward." By then, Senator Seward had delivered a conciliatory address of his own in Washington, and Briggs conceded that the New York senator's "late speech has improved his chances some." Of the once-unknown "knight," however, he said only: "Mr. Lincoln, of Ill. told me he had a very warm side towards you," admitting: "I was pleased with him, & paid him all the attention I could," as if doing so had required a special effort, and he had acted the enthusiastic host solely out of regard for the candidate from Ohio. The arrival of the letter must have reminded the politically savvy, self-absorbed Chase of what a foolish mistake he had made by declining to precede Lincoln to Cooper Union.[24]

Henry J. Raymond, the editor of *The New York Times*, was convinced that the "pre-eminent ability" Lincoln displayed at Cooper Union "compelled" easterners to acknowledge him as not only a leader among westerners, but a national figure. Overnight, he became the state's second choice for the presidential nomination, Raymond believed. Lurking so close to the front runner, Lincoln now posed a danger to Seward and Douglas alike. But he had made no "dungeon" to himself. For tonight, he had conquered New York.[25]

Chapter Seven

❧ "Such an Impression" ☙

H<small>IS PERFORMANCE TRIUMPHANTLY</small> accomplished, Lincoln went to dinner. His principal hosts counted their profits: all of $17, or $4.25 apiece. And the newspapers went to work. It was now their turn to make the most of the Cooper Union address. The next day, four of them—the *Tribune*, *Times*, *Herald*, and *Evening Post*—reprinted the entire speech, with all but one accompanying their reports with laudatory comments about the speaker. The battle for readers of the Cooper Union address was underway.

Circulation figures from the mid-nineteenth century are imprecise and inconsistent. They could as easily be inflated by publishing promoters as intentionally underestimated by competitive rivals. But it is surely safe to say that at least 170,000 copies of Lincoln's speech circulated in the press the day after its delivery at Cooper Union—easily a hundred times the number of people who sat in the Great Hall on the evening of the twenty-seventh. In an age in which newspapers represented the principal source of news, and politics constituted the overwhelming focus of the press, the coverage was gigantic.

An inescapable irony came in the fact that the most carefully prepared edition, that which appeared in the *New York Tribune*, probably never reached into Southern states, where Lincoln's "few words to the South" might have soothed their most important audience. By early 1860, the "black Republican" *Tribune* was already being routinely turned away at Southern post offices.

THE MECHANICS OF the overnight coverage remain something of a mystery. We cannot be certain precisely when Lincoln parted with his manuscript and handed it over to the typographers. Richard C. McCormick—who insisted that only when he ushered a reporter into Lincoln's room at the Astor House earlier that day did the "charmingly innocent" speaker begin "to think his words were to be of interest to the general public"—left no clue about when and how the process began. Nor, characteristically, did Lincoln, the cunning master of the newspaper reprint who seemed to enjoy making young McCormick believe he had never been so honored.[1]

There are two possibilities. One is that Lincoln gave his handwritten foolscap pages to a visiting reporter that morning, allowing the revised manuscript to be set in type while he left his hotel to tour the Broadway attractions, buy a new hat, and sit for his photograph at Brady's. The other is that he surrendered it that night at Cooper Union to a *Tribune* official, perhaps Horace Greeley himself, so that typesetting work could commence immediately after the event concluded in the Great Hall, probably around 10:00 P.M. Would this have left enough time for typographers to set and proofread a seven-thousand-word manuscript before the deadline for publication the following morning? Perhaps—but, as it turned out, the *Tribune* was not the only newspaper in town preparing to publish the speech on Tuesday, February 28. Three others managed to do so, too. It stands to reason, then, that Lincoln allowed his one and only manuscript copy out of his control for several hours on the morning or afternoon of the twenty-seventh; had he not, the other papers would not have been able to present their own fairly accurate reprints concurrently.[2]

Only if Lincoln handed over his manuscript early in the day would there likely have been sufficient time for the *Tribune* to set it in type and send proofs to the other newspapers so they too could begin the work of preparing it for publication. If this is the way the undertaking was managed, it is even conceivable that Lincoln ended up delivering his speech that evening from a typeset proof, not his original manuscript. Given similar opportunities at both his first and second inaugurations, he would do precisely this. (Lincoln's was a legible handwriting, but it was always easier to read from printed type.) Unfortunately, we have no hard evidence that he did this at Cooper Union—it is only speculation. We know that, by evening, Lincoln had some version of his lecture back in his possession, in time to carry it with him as he headed back up Broadway to Cooper Union and, by all accounts, hold it in his hand when he spoke. At the same time, four newspapers were busy setting it in type so it could appear on the streets in their morning editions.[3]

Inside the Great Hall, once the principal oration and postoration speeches concluded, Lincoln shook hands all around and accepted enthusiastic congratulations from many members of the audience. Then his hosts ushered him off to the Athenaeum Club on Fifth Avenue, near Seventeenth Street, for a celebratory supper. Hiram Barney and Charles C. Nott led the way, and once the party reached the club, they were joined by Richard McCormick, James A. Briggs, Benjamin F. Manierre, Charles W. Elliott, F. W. Ballard, and Charles T. Rodgers—most of them officers of the Young Men's Central Republican Union, and Rodgers its president.

Lincoln always enjoyed the company of admiring, politically savvy young men, and such young men were typically hypnotized by Lincoln. Tonight was no different. "All were delighted with the rude good humor of the guest," recalled McCormick of the festive meal, "who was in excellent spirits over his success at the institute." The supper was "as informal as anything could be," and the fare was simple. Lincoln added spice to the evening with his endless supply of stories. "His jokes were many and mirth provoking in the extreme," McCormick remembered. "At a late hour we parted, impressed with the originality and excellence of his character. There was a magnanimity of bearing, an exposure of heart and an irrepressible humor altogether refreshing."[4]

McCormick particularly remembered "bantering" with Lincoln—that night and throughout his New York visit—about the upcoming Republican convention and his guest's chances for the presidential nomination. Diplomatically, Lincoln suggested repeatedly that he thought the party still wanted Senator Seward as its nominee. But he "showed no anxiety in the matter," McCormick noted—especially in the afterglow of his speech at Cooper Union.

At one point over supper, Charles Elliott pressed the point. "Mr. Lincoln," he asked, "what candidate do you really think would be most likely to carry Illinois?" Lincoln's home state was crucial; without it, the Republicans could not hope to win the presidency in the fall. President James Buchanan, a Democrat, had won there four years earlier, and if Stephen A. Douglas secured the 1860 Democratic nomination, as expected, he would surely mount a strong native-son quest for its eleven electoral votes.

"Illinois is a peculiar State," came Lincoln's vague reply, "in three parts. In northern Illinois, Mr. Seward would have a larger majority than I could get. In middle Illinois, I think I could call out a larger vote than Mr. Seward. In southern Illinois, it would make no difference who was the candidate." Evidently, Lincoln was not quite ready to proclaim that he would be a superior vote-getter to Seward in the western states. Nor was he prepared, in the flush of his success, to deny it either. Elliott and his compatriots were left to wonder.[5]

Finally, the party at the Athenaeum Club broke up, and as the men donned their overcoats, they shook hands one more time with Lincoln and said good-bye. Then, realizing that they were about to abandon their guest of honor late at night in a strange city, someone volunteered: "Mr. Nott is going down town and he will show you the way to the Astor House."

The two men started down Broadway on foot, but after a block or two Nott noticed that the tall man in black was having pronounced difficulty walking. "Are you lame, Mr. Lincoln?" he asked.

To which Lincoln explained that he had new boots on his feet, and they were pinching painfully. Nott insisted they must take the next streetcar. The two men stepped aboard the first horse-drawn coach that appeared.

They sat there together silently until Nott, realizing he was nearing his home, rose first to exit the car. One more time he made his farewells to Lincoln and, assuring him that the streetcar would stop at the side entrance of his hotel, jumped off onto the pavement, leaving his guest to ride the rest of the way downtown alone.

Making his way to his house—and for years thereafter, over and over again—Nott wondered what thoughts occupied Lincoln's mind during the rest of his ride to the Astor House. Did he realize how brilliantly he had succeeded at Cooper Union? Did he feel abandoned in the teeming metropolis? Did he allow himself to ponder what might come next for him politically: competitiveness at the fast-approaching convention, a good chance for a Republican victory in the fall, a possible confrontation with Southern extremists following his election, and then . . . ? As Nott expressed it: "Did a faint shadow of the future rest upon his soul?"[6]

Nott's last glimpse of his guest, the only passenger left on the streetcar, gave the young man the impression that Lincoln was already adrift in melancholy thought. Nott would forever regret his decision not to ride with Lincoln all the way to the Astor House—"Not because he was a distinguished stranger," as he put it, "but because he seemed a sad and lonely man."[7]

It was near midnight by the time Lincoln left the horse-drawn car near City Hall. But late as it was, he did not return directly to the Astor House. Earlier in the evening, while at Cooper Union, he had asked Horace Greeley when he might be welcome to visit the *Tribune* office "to look at the proof slips" of his address before they were approved for publication. He knew from experience that newspapers had a way of mangling his speeches: His own words had been "shamefully and outrageously garbled" by the Democratic press during the Lincoln-Douglas debates, making him seem like "a booby," his supporters charged; Douglas, in turn, complained of much the same "mutilation" at the hands of the hostile Republican press. Lincoln was determined to protect himself from such "emasculation," whether intentional or accidental, at the hands of the newspapers.[8]

Now he walked southeast across City Hall Park to the *Tribune* building, then headed upstairs to the composing room, entering a large, noisy space cluttered with "an ample expanse of type-fonts, gas jets" and ". . . long tables covered with columns of bright, copper-faced type," as a onetime reporter described the scene. Determined as he was to personally oversee the publication of his address, Lincoln must have been exhausted from his long day, although speechmaking always seemed to exhilarate, not tire, him. "I can speak three or four hours at a time," he once told a fellow attorney, "without feeling weary." He would need a further burst of energy to see tonight's speech into print.[9]

The chief *Tribune* proofreader for this shift was Amos Jay Cummings—a future congressman—who, Lincoln learned, had just pulled a set of printed galleys from the press and was about to commence the task of comparing them against the original manuscript (inviting the unanswerable question: If Cummings already had the manuscript in his possession, when had Lincoln surrendered it, and what had he read from at Cooper Union?). "Drawing a chair up to the table," Cummings remembered, Lincoln "sat down beside" the proofreader, "adjusted his glasses, and in the glare of the gas light read each galley with scrupulous care. When these words were read and corrected, he waited until the revised proof was prepared and brought in, and these he read and made the corrections himself." His "manner," Cummings remembered, "was that of a man accustomed or indifferent" to the "midnight sights and sounds" of a newspaper office. With good reason: Lincoln had seen his speeches into print before.[10]

"After all the proofs were read," Cummings said, "Mr. Lincoln had a few pleasant words with me and then went out alone and passed through Printing House Square and City Hall Park to the Astor House where he was lodged."

Sadly, Lincoln was apparently not as careful with his original as he was with its adaptation. While reading proof, Cummings testified, Lincoln tossed his handwritten manuscript aside, page by page, whenever he was satisfied that each had been faithfully reproduced in type. The thought occurred to neither man to preserve the original. That night, so the old story goes, those now priceless pages were swept out with the trash, never to be seen again. So another Cooper Union legend maintains.[11]

Yet when he spoke the next evening in Rhode Island, and then later at Exeter, Woonsocket, New Haven, and other New England venues, Lincoln demonstrated that he had either memorized significant portions of the lengthy speech (unlikely); retained a useful proof sheet that was either given to him early on the twenty-seventh or handed him hours later at the *Tribune* composing room (possible); or perhaps saved that original handwritten manuscript himself after all (also possible).

None of Lincoln's major pre-presidential addresses survive in original handwritten form. All we have of his 1854 Peoria speech and the 1858 house divided address, for example, are newspaper reprints. Did Lincoln surrender each of those manuscripts to the local press for typesetting, too, never to claim them? Or is it conceivable that he retained all the originals, and at some point stored them back home at Springfield, keeping them there until his departure for the White House in 1861, when he may have discarded them—or left them with caretakers—rather than transport them to Washington? All that is certain is that the Cooper Union manuscript is missing. Whether it has vanished forever is a matter of conjecture.

When Lincoln awoke in his room at the Astor House early on Tuesday, February 28, he probably rushed directly to the hotel lobby, where news dealers were already hawking the morning dailies. Lincoln promptly found that three of them featured reports, along with transcripts, of his Cooper Union address.

Not surprisingly, the pro-Douglas *Herald* proved the least generous with editorial praise. Under the headline: "The Presidential Campaign. Another Republican Orator on the Stump. Speech of the Hon. Abraham Lincoln of Illinois," James Gordon Bennett's widely read paper ran the entire address (an unexpected bonus for Lincoln), including crowd interruptions and reactions (the only journal to do so). As if to explain the enthusiastic audience response, the paper revealed that "a peculiar characteristic" of Lincoln's delivery "was a remarkable mobility of his features, the frequent contortions of which excited the merriment which his words alone could not well have produced." Nor could the *Herald* resist reporting that the hall had been only "three quarters filled" for the occasion. As the paper remarked, sounding a theme that would soon resonate in other pro-Democratic newspapers: "The tax of twenty-five cents per capita did not—as it very frequently does—act as a preventative on the visitors." All together, the *Herald* report occupied two long, prominent columns on page two. Such coverage was worth far more than a full house in the Great Hall of Cooper Union.[12]

Even better, *The New York Times* devoted three of its prime page-one columns to Lincoln's speech. "When MR. LINCOLN had concluded his address," it reported, "during the delivery of which he was frequently applauded, three rousing cheers were given for the orator and the sentiments to which he had given utterance." As was increasingly the case on the pages of the comparatively understated *Times*, editorial encomia in the news columns were otherwise absent.

The most enthusiastic morning coverage appeared in Greeley's *Tribune*. "The Speech of ABRAHAM LINCOLN at the Cooper Institute last evening was one of the happiest and most convincing political arguments ever made in this City, and was addressed to a crowded and most appreciating audience," the page-two story began. And then came an acknowledgment that even the paper's own complete and authorized transcript would not be adequate to do justice to the memorable presentation. As the paper introduced its coverage:

We present herewith a very full and accurate report of this Speech; yet the tones, the gestures, the kindling eye and the mirth-provoking look, defy the reporter's skill. The vast assemblage frequently rang with cheers and shouts of applause, which were prolonged and intensified at the close.

Then the *Tribune* crowned its report with an extraordinary assessment of Lincoln's debut, the most widely quoted appraisal of the speech that made Lincoln president: "No man ever before made such an impression on his first appeal to a New-York audience." The transcript of Lincoln's address occupied a good part of page six.[13]

Out in Brooklyn, the *Daily Times* found room for only a brief page-three notice: "Hon. Abraham Lincoln, of Illinois, delivered at the Cooper Institute, yesterday evening, an able address on the power of Congress to legislate on slavery in the Territories." No mention was made of the fact that the address had originally been intended for that city. Other Brooklyn papers were altogether silent. But the avalanche of press attention was just beginning.[14]

Late that afternoon, William Cullen Bryant's *New York Evening Post* weighed in with the most extensive and flattering coverage yet. Two columns on page one, and another two columns on page four, were devoted to the speech. The front-page headline left no doubt that, in Bryant's view, Lincoln had triumphed:

The Framers of the Constitution in
Favor of Slavery Prohibition.

THE REPUBLICAN PARTY VINDICATED.

THE DEMANDS OF THE SOUTH EXPLAINED.

Great Speech of Hon. Abraham Lincoln,
of Illinois, at Cooper Institute.

The *Evening Post* soon followed with an editorial, entitled "Mr. Lincoln's Speech," which sought to justify its extraordinary allocation of space in a world "growing almost too busy and too mischievous for the newspapers to keep pace with it." But, as the *Post* made clear: "When we have such a speech as that of Abraham Lincoln, of Illinois, delivered at the Cooper Institute last evening to a crowded, deeply interested and enthusiastic audience, we are tempted to wish that our columns were indefinitely elastic. . . . We have made room for Mr. Lincoln's speech, notwithstanding the pressure of other matters, and our readers will see that it was well worthy of the deep attention with which it has been heard. That part of it in which the speaker places the Republican party on the very ground occupied by the framers of our constitution and fathers of our republic, strikes us as particularly forcible.

"All this may not be new," the paper conceded, "but it is most logically and convincingly stated in the speech—and it is wonderful how much a truth gains by a certain mastery of clear and impressive statement." Readers seemed to agree. One wrote to the paper simply to "thank you for publishing the speech of Abe. Lincoln, before the 'Young Men's Republican Club.'"[15]

Abraham Lincoln did not get the chance to read the *Post* that heady day; in fact, he would not enjoy the opportunity to examine Bryant's notices for nearly two weeks. By the time its first edition hit the streets, he had already made his way to Manhattan's New Haven Depot on Twenty-seventh Street and Fourth Avenue, and was aboard the 8:00 A.M. express steaming toward New England for his next speech, and a reunion with his son Robert. In New Haven, he changed trains at the Chapel Street station for a shore line express to New London. And there, he switched cars again, this time to the New York, Providence & Boston Railroad (also known as the Stonington Line) bound for Rhode Island. All told, the trip took eight hours. There would be no time to rest now.

BEFORE HE LEFT NEW YORK, so one contemporary later recalled, Lincoln had received one more important visitor in his Astor House room: Erastus Corning, the formidable president of the New York Central Railroad. Its network of tracks by then extended from Buffalo to Albany along the east-west corridor once dominated by the Erie Canal. Corning had heard Lincoln's speech at Cooper Union, and, hugely impressed, determined on the spot to offer Lincoln a lucrative legal retainer. He decided to call on him the following day and invite him to become the principal attorney for his company.

The story that has come down in history about Corning's alleged visit has been repeated in the Lincoln literature for more than a century. But it is so unlikely a tale that it is hard to imagine how it escaped discrediting for so long, unless it is because it is such a compelling yarn. It certainly offers an object lesson in myth-making, and demonstrates that Lincoln's appearance in the big city was important early enough to stimulate its share of legends. As Herndon put it, Lincoln fully "captured the Metropolis." Even its population of craven merchants supposedly beat down Lincoln's door to woo him from politics.[16]

According to the story, early on Tuesday morning Corning rushed down to the Astor House, where by chance he encountered his cousin James B. Merwin—an acquaintance of Lincoln's—in the crowded lobby. Corning blurted out the news of his mission and asked how he might get an audience with last night's orator.

"He's the easiest man in the world to see," Merwin replied, and led the way to Lincoln's room. There, Corning spilled out his breathtaking offer.

"Mr. Lincoln, I understand that in Illinois you win all your lawsuits."

"Oh, no, Mr. Corning, that is not true," Lincoln laughed, "but I do make it a rule to refuse unless I am convinced the litigant's cause is just."

"Would you entertain an offer from the New York Central Railroad, Mr. Lincoln," Corning suddenly ventured, "to become its General Counsel at a salary of $10,000 a year?"

Lincoln was caught by surprise. The money was fantastic. It was any lawyer's dream come true—except perhaps for a lawyer now poised on the brink of serious consideration for the presidency.

After a long silence, Lincoln supposedly replied with a smile: "Why, Mr. Corning, what could I do with $10,000 a year? It would ruin my family to have that much income. I don't believe that I had better consider it."

But Corning would not take this jest for a final answer. "You don't have to decide till you get a letter from me," he said as he prepared to take his leave. "I'm going to get our directors together and advise them to engage you at $10,000 per year." And with that, the tycoon left Lincoln and Merwin together and departed.

"Of course, you'll accept?" Merwin inquired once they were alone.

"No, Merwin, I don't think I shall."

"Why, man alive, of course you'll accept! Why debate about it?" But Lincoln said nothing more. He merely shook his head in silence.

Merwin claimed that he subsequently went along with Lincoln on his journey to New England, then accompanied him all the way back to Illinois, during which time he repeatedly raised the issue of the Corning job offer. Supposedly, the two discussed the pros and cons endlessly on the train. But no final resolution was reached.

Calling on his friend again soon after he settled in back home at Springfield, Merwin was shocked to find Lincoln looking "as if he had been up all night, and . . . fearfully depressed."

In response to Merwin's expressions of concern, Lincoln explained that he had spent the morning wandering through a quiet grove near Springfield where he often retreated to deliberate thorny problems. "There he had literally wrestled with the question of leaving Springfield and becoming a New York corporation lawyer," Merwin contended.

"Of course, you'll accept Corning's offer?" Merwin finally asked.

"No, Merwin, I have decided to decline it," Lincoln announced. "I've got his letter offering the place and am going to answer it to-day, in the negative."

With that, James B. Merwin asserted, Lincoln resisted the last temptation keeping him from an all-out run for president.[17]

There may possibly be a grain or two of truth to this elaborate, melodramatic recollection, which has been repeated over the years in a number of books. But not much more. For one thing, Corning and Merwin would have had to call on Lincoln near dawn on the twenty-eighth to find him before he checked out and departed for the depot. There is no surviving testimony to corroborate Merwin's claim that he accompanied Lincoln on the rest of his journey. Finally, no job offer from Corning or his railroad survives in the Lincoln Papers.

Years later, a New York journalist named Charles T. White admitted that he had first written down the tale many years after the alleged incident occurred. It was dictated by Merwin when he was an old man. But having heard it from his lips many times before, White was satisfied that the story of the Corning offer "was substantially true." Later, however, when another writer, John W. Starr, Jr., probed the New York Central archives in the late 1920s in preparation for a book on Lincoln and the railroads, he could find no record of any written offer from the company. Needless to say, no formal reply in Lincoln's hand could be found, either. Besides, as Starr further learned, Erastus Corning had in fact been serving only as a director of the line at the time, not as its president. The railroad's sitting corporate secretary also reminded Starr that the type of offer Merwin described would not have been tendered by a member of the board, but by a chief executive officer.

Journalist White still insisted that there was a reasonable explanation for the absence of surviving proof. Corning, he pointed out, went on to become a leader of the antiwar "Copperhead" Democrats during Lincoln's presidency. In 1863, he chaired an Albany meeting that bitterly denounced the Lincoln administration for violating civil liberties, to which Lincoln replied with a famous letter defending suspension of the writ of habeas corpus. White's theory was that Corning was so mortified by the thought that he had once nearly enlisted the despised Lincoln for his business interests that he destroyed every shred of evidence that he had ever made him an offer.[18]

That explanation seems too convenient to be true. More to the point, by 1860—both before, and certainly after, his speech at Cooper Union—there is scant possibility that the once-ambitious railroad lawyer would for a moment have entertained an entreaty that he drop politics and devote himself anew to what he liked to call "business." He had come too far as a leader of the Republican party, and the "cause" required too much of his energies for him to consider retreating to private life. The biggest prize of all now loomed within his grasp. And it did not await him at the New York Central.

Besides which, cinematic though the tale must have seemed when introduced to a 1920s-era audience enthralled by the new art of movies, Lincoln did not have a favorite Springfield "grove" where he walked off his uncertainties. But even if he had, it is unlikely that he would have taken himself there to agitate over a no-brainer like the alleged Corning offer. The presidency, it might be noted, paid twenty-five thousand dollars per year—two and a half times what the New York Central allegedly had in mind for him.

The last word on the subject belongs, appropriately, to Robert T. Lincoln, in whose direction Lincoln now headed on Tuesday, February 28. Robert would himself go on to a lucrative career as a railroad executive, and he surely would have made it his business to find out the truth about the Merwin allegations. When asked about it, Robert replied firmly: "I never before heard of the alleged offer by Mr. Corning to my father, after he had made his speech at the Cooper Institute, and I do not for a moment believe there is any foundation for the statement."[19]

THERE IS NO RECORD of the formal invitation that convinced Lincoln to stop in Providence, Rhode Island, and there give another long speech en route to see Robert at Exeter. But within days—hours, perhaps—of his New York visit, requests began pouring in from cities and towns across New England and New York State. Even before his Cooper Union success was fully reported, Lincoln was already being beseeched to speak at political gatherings nearby. The appearance of his speech in the New York dailies intensified the pressure.

Further stoking the growing Cooper Union fever, the *Tribune* meanwhile announced plans to republish Lincoln's address as a separate pamphlet "for cheap circulation." Newspapers across the country turned their attention as well to Lincoln's New York debut.[20]

Slow to catch up with the news from the distant East Coast, Lincoln's hometown Republican paper, Springfield's *Illinois Daily State Journal*, took until March 1 to give prominence to the preoration biographical sketch that had appeared in the *New York Tribune* a week earlier. (Late as it appeared, this article offered the locals their first hint that Lincoln had spoken not in Brooklyn but in New York; Mary Lincoln must have been surprised to learn that unexpected bit of information about her husband.) That same day, the equally pro-Lincoln *Chicago Press and Tribune* belatedly reported not only that "'Old Abe' speaks to-night at Cooper Institute, before the Republicans of New York City," but that "the Republican State Committee of Connecticut have induced him to agree to make a few speeches in that State." The *Chicago Daily Evening Journal*, reporting that "Hon. 'Old Abe' made his debut before a New York audience at Cooper's Institute," accurately explained that he had proceeded to New England "at the urgent solicitation of the Republicans of Rhode Island and Connecticut."[21]

The following day, February 29, the *Chicago Press and Tribune* reprinted the *New York Tribune*'s editorial commendation of Lincoln's address. "I must say," its Washington correspondent reported around the same time, "I hear the name of Lincoln mentioned for President in Washington circles, ten times as often as it was one month ago. The more politicians look over the field in search of an *available* candidate, the more often they are convinced that 'Old Abe' is the man to run the race with."

To the *Tribune*'s man in Washington, Lincoln's path to the nomination now seemed obvious and attainable. "If the States of the Northwest shall unite upon him, and present his name to the Chicago Convention, there is a strong probability that he will receive the nomination, and as certain as he is nominated he will be President." Before long, the paper also published the full Cooper Union address. The Chicago *Daily Journal* added its enthusiastic report that "Hon. 'Old Abe' made his debut before a New York audience at the Cooper's Institute" before a "large audience." Born in Chicago, nurtured in New York, and now attracting renewed attention back in Chicago, the Lincoln presidential boom was quickly gaining momentum.[22]

Not all the Cooper Union coverage was positive, of course. In the South, to which Lincoln had so theatrically "directed" an entire section of his speech, the influential *Richmond Enquirer* published an emphatic denunciation by its New York correspondent. Warning ominously that "the Black Republicans are active," the paper reported: "They invite Cassius M. Clay, Giddings, F. P. Blair, and Abram [sic] Lincoln to repeat their Western stump speeches at the Cooper Institute, under the name of lectures." Lincoln was singled out for condemnation, "having delivered himself of a stale speech . . . which was concocted in his contest with Douglas in Illinois." Against such an onslaught, the paper worried:

> The Democrats sit still; without a word to say. No reply is circulated against Helper's blasphemous treason; no answer is made to the lying black Republican lecturers and orators of Cooper's Institute, and so far as they are concerned, you would think that Rome (the country) was doomed, and given over to "Cataline conspirators," to spoliation, and to the destruction of Union and Liberty. Against such demonical demonstrations, the South is divided.[23]

In the North, predictably, editorial response ran strictly according to party lines, with the Democratic press either silent or as critical as the barrage from Richmond, and with some pro-Seward Republican journals stubbornly holding back the praise. The negative articles, most of them unseen and unread since they first appeared in 1860, are worth re-examining in detail, because they offer valuable clues to how public opinion was shaped in pre–Civil War America. In the generations before the introduction of broadcast journalism, these party-aligned newspapers offered readers their only window onto current events. Their coverage was unremittingly biased, and where the political opposition was concerned, frequently vicious. But it helped fuel mass participation in the electoral process at a rate unimaginable in modern America.

New York's anti-Republican *Daily News*, for example, charged that Lincoln, the "great gun of the occasion" at Cooper Union, had simply not convinced the paper "that Congress has the power to legislate on the subject of slavery in the Territories." Lincoln "and his confreres," it argued, "have no weight nor influence against the simple fact that 'the

Constitution does not give the power to Congress.' Is not this enough for some sound, right-minded, honest men?"[24]

The *Herald* assailed Lincoln for trying to attach himself to the founders. "It is idle to quote the fathers of the Republic, including Washington and Jefferson in favor of the present Republican crusade against slavery," James Gordon Bennett argued in an editorial. "It is true that Jefferson for a time became tainted with the French revolutionary levelling notions about negro slavery, and other things; but he afterwards changed these opinions."[25]

In Springfield, a week after Cooper Union, the steadfastly pro-Democratic *Illinois State Register* finally carried its own highly critical report on the New York speech of "our own 'Abe Lincoln,' of this city." Lincoln, it first reminded its readers, could always be expected to "lay down false premises and draw false conclusions—to misstate the position of his adversary, and by special pleading and sophistical reasoning to lead the mind of his hearer and reader from the true facts in the controversy." Sounding wounded, or at least defensive, the *Register* insisted of Lincoln: "No man professes greater fairness in his public harangues, and no man is less scrupulous in his arguments. When Mr. Lincoln denies that the republican party is sectional, he denies a fact that is as self-evident as his own existence. . . .

"This speech of Mr. Lincoln is a more maturely conceived effort than any of his speeches during the Douglas campaign," the paper conceded. "It is more jesuitical, abounds with more sophistry and special pleading, and withal is more ingeniously constructed than any of his previous speeches that we have ever heard or read. It is admirably calculated to mislead the unsuspecting and unreflecting mind; but it will not bear the test of criticism, either of its positions or arguments."[26]

And the paper was not yet finished with Cooper Union. Three days later, insisting it had no purpose "to review Mr. Lincoln's speech at the Cooper Institute, at length," the *State Register* did precisely that, presenting a long, assaultive piece describing it as "a speech characterized throughout with perversions of history and facts, with unfair and illogical arguments and with false premises and false conclusions."

"Therefore, in reply to Mr. Lincoln's question, 'can we, while our votes will prevent it, allow it to spread in the national territories, and to overrun us here in those free states,'" the *Register* taunted, "we would ask him, where does he find the power to prevent the extension of slavery into a free territory, except in the people of the territory themselves?" To suggest otherwise, the strongly pro–popular sovereignty *Register* insisted, showed Lincoln's "reckless disregard for facts."

"Such is the mode of discussion pursued by Mr. Lincoln in his speech at Cooper Institute," concluded the opposition paper. ". . . The unsuspecting superficial reader may be misled by it, but every intelligent, investigating, impartial mind will pronounce it an undignified specimen of demagogism, wholly unworthy [of] the character of a statesman, and that would be discreditable to a third rate political pettifogger."[27]

Springfield's rival pro-Republican *Journal* entered the fray around the same time. Having first printed the text of the speech "to the exclusion of much other matter," the paper made clear its admiration for the "masterly production" by printing a letter it had received from an eyewitness to Lincoln's "great triumph" at Cooper Union:

> It was heard by a most intelligent and decorous audience—the rabble element being absent—and the manner in which the speech was received *might justly awaken the pride of any living Statesman*. The speech is reported in the *Tribune* very accurately as spoken. It will probably have a wide circulation and be more generally read than any of his speeches yet published.[28]

In that prediction, the *Journal* proved correct.

THE STAGE, HOWEVER, would not belong to Lincoln alone. On February 29, only hours after Lincoln took the rostrum in Providence to reiterate the sentiments of his Cooper Union address, the front runner for the Republican presidential nomination, William H. Seward, rose on the floor of the United States Senate in Washington to make a major speech of his own. The atmosphere was charged with partisan tension, the audience sensing that history was being made. Stephen A. Douglas and the future president of the Confederacy, Jefferson Davis, were among the colleagues looking on in the ornate chamber at the Capitol. Among all the Democrats in the Senate, only Douglas had crossed the aisle to greet Seward when the session began the month before.[29]

Lincoln's future commissioner of public buildings, Benjamin B. French, who found a place in the thronged Senate galleries that day, observed: "Hundreds who came to listen had to go away." French "listened for nearly an hour and a half" to Seward's conciliatory oration. He reported in his diary: "It was a great speech. Let the N. Y. Herald and other papers of that genus say what they please against it—I say it was a great speech, and will tell."[30]

Had Seward read the Cooper Union speech the day before? The question remains intriguing, if unanswerable. Much as Lincoln had done in New York, Seward focused part of his Senate argument on what "our fathers undertook . . . to erect a free empire" in eighteenth-century America. Much like Lincoln, he assailed John Brown's raid on Harpers Ferry, and made clear that such acts of terrorism were neither encouraged nor approved by true Republicans. Much like Lincoln, he pledged that Republicans had no plan to interfere with slavery where it already existed. And much like Lincoln, he warned against disunion.

The Republican party, the gruff-sounding senator pledged, "will take up the word Union, which others are so willing to renounce, and, combining it with that other glorious thought, Liberty, which has been its inspiration so long, it will move firmly onward, with the motto inscribed on its banner, 'Union and Liberty,' come what may, in victory or in defeat, in power as out of power, now and forever." Echoing with those strains from Daniel Webster, the speech carried no mention of Seward's controversial old calls for a "higher law" or an "irrepressible conflict," just as Lincoln's Cooper Union speech had studiously avoided his old notion of a "house divided against itself."[31]

Seward went so far as to predict that though "the pillars of the noble fabric that protects us" seemed to be "trembling before our eyes . . . the appointed end of this agitation comes at last . . . the country becomes calm once more." In Seward's view, the conflict was no longer irrepressible; it was over.[32]

Seward's fustian appeal for calm did not lack for its share of admirers. Seemingly forgetting its superlatives about Lincoln's Cooper Union address only two days before, the New York Tribune now reported that "the whole spectacle was much more striking than any witnessed this Winter"—presumably including Lincoln's "first appeal" to a New York audience. In a whirlwind season of competing political speeches and breathless newspaper reporting, pre-eminence proved all too brief, and suddenly Lincoln's Cooper Union triumph seemed already to be facing the threat of premature oblivion.[33]

Bryant's Evening Post, just days after effusively praising Lincoln, now hailed Seward's oration as "distinguished for its insight, its ability, its manliness, its comprehensive and statesmanlike views, and a certain noble impassiveness, which shows the author is as superior to his opponents in moral nature as he is in intellectual." Declaring that the country should be "flooded with this noble vindication of the principles of the Republican party," the Tribune quickly offered reprinted copies at a cost of a dollar per hundred, and eight dollars per thousand. Lincoln's would not be the only speech in print. "All honor to Seward," gushed the New York Sun. Neither Seward nor the Republican papers, it was clear, were yet ready to cede the presidential field to the man from Illinois. Clearly, the cause of antislavery remained far bigger than its two most eloquent proponents.[34]

In response, Lincoln had little choice but to enlarge his speaking schedule once Seward's Senate oration bumped him from the headlines. Even among Republicans seeking attention in Republican organs, the competition for newspaper space was fierce, and Lincoln was wise enough to realize that two days of eastern press attention for his New York debut would constitute an end or a beginning. For it to become the latter, he needed to continue making news. If he did not, Seward might end the winter more buoyed by his Senate address than Lincoln had been by Cooper Union.

Further reminders that politics still ruled the newspaper business came when readers of the Republican daily of Albany, New York, were not even informed when Lincoln proceeded from their state to New England. Its editor was the controversial, crafty political veteran Thurlow Weed, the Republican boss who functioned as Seward's chief backer, and in the view of many party faithful offended by Weed's tactics and ethics, his chief liability as well. Weed was nonetheless determined to promote his candidate and, when he could, ignore his potential challengers.[35]

Now, no doubt at Weed's direction, rather than report on the progress of Seward's rival through Rhode Island, New Hampshire, and Connecticut, the *Evening Journal* peppered its pages with praise that Seward's Washington performance had elicited from an assortment of Yankee journals. A New Bedford, Massachusetts, paper was quoted as declaring: "Mr. Seward . . . has no superior in his peculiar view of logical disquisition." The *Burlington*, Vermont, *Daily Times* was reported to have concluded of the senator's latest oration: "The hour and the man are both come." Meanwhile, upstate New York's most important Republican newspaper ignored Lincoln's Cooper Union appearance altogether and instead printed a speech by a Westchester County assemblyman about an obscure railroad bill currently before the state legislature.[36]

Only when Lincoln won the presidential nomination that May did the pro-Seward newspaper in New York's state capital finally relent and issue reprinted copies of the Cooper Union address at the standard price of a dollar per hundred, eight dollars per thousand. But the *Evening Journal* would stubbornly continue to offer, as well, copies of Seward's old "irrepressible conflict" address—the radical speech that had ironically helped doom his chances at the convention—as well as copies of his February 29 speech in the Senate. It "would be idle," Thurlow Weed's paper frankly admitted once Seward lost to Lincoln, "to attempt to disguise disappointment at the failure of the Chicago Convention" to nominate their favorite son.[37]

The week after both Lincoln and Seward made their strikingly similar—but in style, wholly different—pleas for principled moderation on slavery, the widely read *New York Tribune Weekly* published both men's addresses in the same edition. Tellingly, even the Seward-hating Greeley gave Seward's speech the prime position; it occupied six columns on the front page. Lincoln's Cooper Union address took up six columns on pages two and three.[38]

However squeezed by Seward, Lincoln could not have been dissatisfied with these early reprints. They constituted superb coverage for a westerner's first New York speech. But there could be little doubt who remained the putative Republican front runner that winter. It was not Abraham Lincoln. Cooper Union may have thrust Lincoln into the Republican pantheon, but it did not by any means obliterate rival voices in the Republican press, nor escape vigorous condemnation in the newspapers controlled by Northern Democrats or Southerners. The long-held, long-cherished myth that the speech catapulted Lincoln to the pinnacle of party prominence, muted other presidential contenders, and attracted the press's unwavering praise, washes away in the wake of the evidence. Cooper Union did not mark the end of Lincoln's rise; it represented the beginning.

NOR, IT IS WORTH remembering, were Lincoln and Seward the only prominent public speakers to tackle the slavery issue with major addresses in the winter of 1860. Half a world away, on March 26, the impassioned African-American ex-slave, orator, and editor Frederick Douglass ascended a platform in distant Glasgow, Scotland, to offer his own views on what the United States Constitution was capable of authorizing in regard to slavery.

His speech was of course bolder, more radical—and understandably angrier—than those of either Seward or Lincoln, both of whom were trying hard at the time not to appeal to passion but to suppress it. Not surprisingly, Douglass's speech made less impact than either. For one thing, it was delivered far from the locus of the American slavery debate. And of course, its author was a black man, not a mainstream

THE DAY OF THE COOPER UNION ADDRESS

Mathew Brady took this iconic photograph of Abraham Lincoln in New York on February 27, 1860, just hours before he was due at Cooper Union. Nearly as much as the speech itself, the picture helped transform Lincoln's image from rural curiosity to dignified sophisticate. (LIBRARY OF CONGRESS)

INVITED TO SPEAK

The original telegram inviting Lincoln to speak in the East, this history-altering message actually offered him an engagement not in New York, but at the Plymouth Church in Brooklyn. (LIBRARY OF CONGRESS)

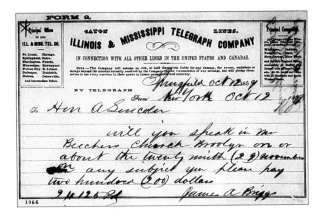

LIFELONG RIVAL

Stephen A. Douglas, the Democrat who debated and defeated Abraham Lincoln for the U.S. Senate in 1858, was Lincoln's lifelong political rival. At Cooper Union, Lincoln would reply to Douglas's latest published defense of Popular Sovereignty. This photograph by the Jesse Whitehurst Gallery in Washington was taken around the same time as Lincoln posed in New York for Brady. (GEORGE BUSS COLLECTION)

NEW YORK IN 1860

The sights Lincoln saw when he reached New York. (Top) Bustling Broadway, with the Astor House, at right, where he stayed, and, at left, Barnum's Museum, which he avoided. (Bottom) Cooper Union, the tallest building in this scene, as it looked a few months after Lincoln's visit. In the foreground are horse-drawn streetcars of the type the speaker rode back to his hotel after the dinner that followed his speech. (MUSEUM OF THE CITY OF NEW YORK, HARRY T. PETERS COLLECTION; HAROLD HOLZER)

Four men who figured prominently in Lincoln's trip to New York. (Clockwise from top left) Editor Horace Greeley, whose *New York Tribune* published the speech; Senator William H. Seward, whose dominance of New York Republican politics Lincoln sought to topple (the two had met in Boston in 1848); Robert T. Lincoln, the teenaged son Lincoln went on to visit in New Hampshire; and Rev. Henry Ward Beecher, abolitionist Brooklyn minister whose Sabbath services Lincoln twice attended during his trip East. (NEW YORK STATE MUSEUM—GREELEY; ALL OTHERS THE LINCOLN MUSEUM, FORT WAYNE, INDIANA, #83, 3789, 4028)

There is no known photograph of Lincoln delivering his Cooper Union speech, but this period drawing comes closest to showing what the scene looked like. The speaker stands before a wrought-iron podium on the elevated stage of the Great Hall. Reporters take notes from the front row of the auditorium, and the audience is sprinkled with women, as contemporary reports attested. But this sketch shows Lincoln looking rather handsome. Eyewitnesses were in fact stunned at first by his grotesque appearance. (COOPER UNION COLLECTION)

Believed to be the only surviving ticket to the Cooper Institute address, this recently discovered green-colored card is one of 1,500 used that night. (COURTESY OF CHARLES MCSORLEY)

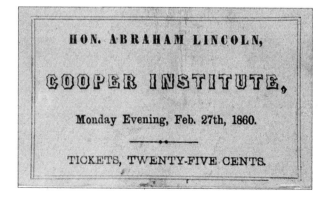

HON. ABRAHAM LINCOLN,

COOPER INSTITUTE,

Monday Evening, Feb. 27th, 1860.

TICKETS, TWENTY-FIVE CENTS.

SEEKING SYMPATHY FROM HIS WIFE

Six days after delivering his lecture at Cooper Union, and still on the road, Lincoln paused to write this letter to his wife, Mary. Cooper Union, he modestly reported, "went off passably well." But his subsequent "little speech-making tour" through New England, he complained, exhausted him. He had been "unable to escape this toil," and had he foreseen it, he admitted, "I think I would not have come East at all." (LIBRARY OF CONGRESS)

CONVENTION COMPETITORS

Three months after the Cooper Union address—and on the eve of the Republican national convention—*Harper's Weekly* published this engraved group portrait of the leading contenders for the party's presidential nomination. Seward, pictured in the center, largest in size, retained his long-held status as heavy favorite. Still a dark horse, Lincoln was relegated to the bottom row, second from the left, but at least casting his eyes directly on the White House. This May 12 print may have been the first to copy Brady's Cooper Union photograph. (THE LINCOLN MUSEUM, #4579)

PROMINENT CANDIDATES FOR THE REPUBLICAN PRESIDENTIAL NOMINATION AT CHICAGO.—[FROM PHOTOGRAPHS BY BRADY.]

NEWLY ANOINTED CANDIDATE

On November 10, 1860, a few days after Lincoln won the presidential election, *Harper's Weekly* published this retooled, mirror-image engraving of Brady's nine-month-old photograph. Although Brady's original showed the subject as dignified enough to appeal to urban voters, many artists now took up the postconvention emphasis on Lincoln's inspiring frontier roots. This engraver added a window and bucolic setting visible outdoors, complete with roaming buffalo outside the window in the distance, to remind readers of the candidate's rural origins. (HAROLD HOLZER)

A "COOPER UNION" BADGE

During the summer and fall of 1860, Brady's Cooper Union pose re-emerged on prints, broadsides, banners, buttons, badges, and other campaign ephemera. This brass-framed ambrotype—a photo on glass—was issued in Boston and, as the surviving label on the reverse shows, was designed to be worn by supporters of the "Hon. Abraham Lincoln" for president. The hole in the top of the frame indicates it was once worn suspended from a ribbon or string. (STANLEY KING COLLECTION)

LINCOLN THROUGH THE MAILS

A quaint staple of nineteenth-century politics was the illustrated mailing envelope, designed to testify pictorially to a correspondent's political beliefs. These 1860 examples reproduced Brady's Cooper Union pose within flag-festooned decorative borders. The envelope at top, published in New York, reminded buyers that Lincoln had started life as a prairie rail-splitter. The Hartford-made example at bottom crowned the portrait with a Liberty Cap, suggesting "Old Abe" would fight to end slavery. (HAROLD HOLZER)

" Constitution and the Union—Harmony and Prosperity to all."—LINCOLN.

" Old Abe" the Man for the Times.

Lincoln by Currier & Ives

The "Cooper Union" Lincoln was copied—and modified—in at least four different 1860 prints by Currier & Ives. (Clockwise from top left) A handsome bust portrait; a variant with ears and mouth reduced in size; another with eyes and suit lightened; and a revised version with ludicrous beard added to update the pose once Lincoln grew whiskers. (MUSEUM OF THE CITY OF NEW YORK; THE OLD PRINT SHOP, INC.; THE LINCOLN MUSEUM, #1987, 1988)

LINCOLN IN CARTOON
AND CARICATURE

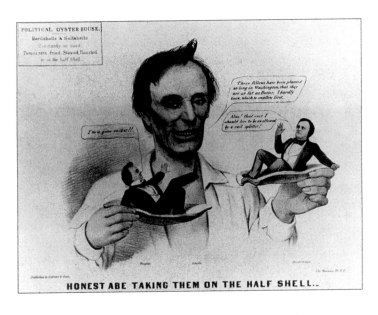

HONEST ABE TAKING THEM ON THE HALF SHELL..

"ET TU, GREELEY?"

The Cooper Union pose inspired much campaign caricature. (Top) Clad in a frontiersman's open shirt by Currier & Ives, Brady's Lincoln smiles almost grotesquely as he prepares to devour two of his presidential opponents, Democrats Stephen A. Douglas and John C. Breckinridge. (Bottom) Another Cooper Union–inspired Lincoln is shown as a miniature witness to the drama of the Republican party's "assassination" of Caesar-like front runner William H. Seward. Like some prints of the period, this engraving in *Vanity Fair* portrayed the antislavery Lincoln as black. (LIBRARY OF CONGRESS; HAROLD HOLZER)

Brady's photo also served as a model for anti-Lincoln caricature, often issued by the same commercially minded publishers who produced the flattering ones. Such cartoons typically warned that Lincoln favored racial equality. In one example, Currier & Ives turned its retrograde portrayal of the Barnum sideshow attraction, the "What Is It" (left), into a vicious campaign cartoon, *An Heir to the Throne* (bottom). It hinted that "this intellectual and noble creature" would be Lincoln's successor in Republican politics. (MUSEUM OF THE CITY OF NEW YORK, THE GERALD LE VINO COLLECTION; THE LINCOLN MUSEUM, #431)

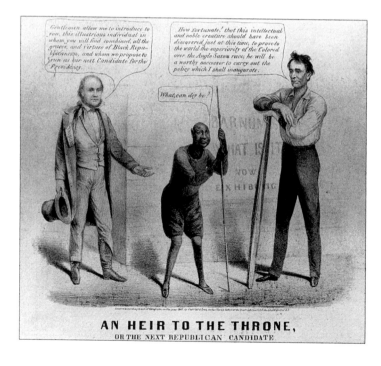

CAMPAIGN BIOGRAPHIES FEATURE COOPER UNION

Several 1860 Lincoln biographies reprinted the Cooper Union address, one calling it "a brilliant close to this period of his life, and a fitting prelude to that on which he is believed to be about to enter." One of the earliest of these influential "campaign lives," this June 1860 effort by New York journalist D. W. Bartlett also featured a crude N. Orr woodcut of Brady's Cooper Union photograph on its cover. (FRANK AND VIRGINIA WILLIAMS COLLECTION)

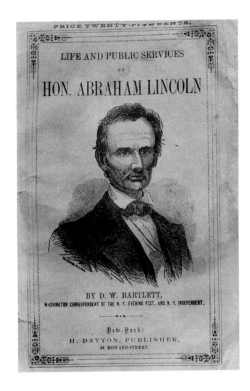

LINCOLN "REAPPEARS" IN EUROPE

Although Lincoln never traveled overseas, Brady's Cooper Union photo was often adapted by European printmakers. This retouched adaptation was engraved and published in London, and made Lincoln—rouge-cheeked and thin-lipped—look like an English dandy. (HAROLD HOLZER)

This September 6, 1860, letter to Abraham Lincoln accompanied delivery of the first of 250 "author's copies" of this final, annotated version of the Cooper Union address—the title page of which is reproduced here. It was published just in time for maximum impact during the presidential campaign. (LIBRARY OF CONGRESS; COOPER UNION COLLECTION—PHOTOGRAPH BY DON POLLARD)

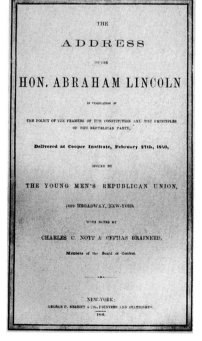

LINCOLN MOURNED, COOPER UNION REMEMBERED

As president, Lincoln went on to deliver more acclaimed speeches, but even at the time of his death in 1865, the Cooper Union address was not forgotten. On the day of his funeral in Washington, State Department employees wore this badge (left), which featured, surrounded by black borders, the still-famous final exclamation from Lincoln's New York debut: "RIGHT MAKES MIGHT." In 1901, William Cullen Bryant's old paper, the *New York Evening Post*, celebrated its centennial by publishing a woodcut of Lincoln delivering the Cooper Union address (right)—a bearded Bryant seated at right, arms folded. But forty-one years after Lincoln's appearance, the paper apparently forgot that the speaker had been clean-shaven when he came to New York. (JAMES SWANSON COLLECTION, PHOTO COURTESY OF THE ABRAHAM LINCOLN BOOK SHOP, CHICAGO; NEW YORK POST)

white politician. But it did consider the same issues. Like Seward's Senate speech, it has never been considered within the context of Lincoln's presidency-making address at Cooper Union. It deserves to be.

Exploring the very same theme that Lincoln had—the Constitution as it applied to slavery—Douglass insisted at Glasgow: "The Constitution declares that no person shall be deprived of life, liberty, or property, without due process of law." On this point, Lincoln would not have disagreed. But then Douglass went on to deny "that the Constitution guarantees the right to hold property in man" anywhere, asserting that the document "leans to freedom, not to slavery." Lincoln, on the other hand, had been careful at Cooper Union to assure the South that he had no interest in interfering with slavery where it existed, protected by the Constitution. Looking ahead in a different way toward the presidential election fast approaching back at home, Douglass insisted: "I . . . believe the way to abolish slavery in America is to vote such men into power as will use their power for the Abolition of slavery." But such men—of the electable variety, anyway—were not to be found in New York, Illinois, or Washington. At this point, both Lincoln and Seward were taking pains to *deny* that they were abolitionists. It would take secession and civil war to merge the aspirations of all three orators.[39]

Under different circumstances, in a less racist society, Lincoln's and Douglass's orations might have been judged, perhaps even printed, side by side. As early as 1841, a dazzled New Hampshire editor had proclaimed that as a public speaker, Douglass had "few equals." Now, in his full magnificence at Glasgow, Douglass summed up his outrage against slavery by thundering: "Let the freemen of the North, who have the power in their own hands, and who can make the American Government just what they think fit, resolve to blot out for ever the foul and haggard crime, which is the blight and mildew, the curse and the disgrace of the whole United States."[40]

Douglass likely did not realize that day that both Abraham Lincoln and William H. Seward—two of the Republicans who might yet give voters the opportunity to elect an antislavery man to the White House—had examined remarkably similar questions in their own speeches a few weeks earlier. News did not carry quickly across the Atlantic in 1860. So we cannot justly view Douglass's Glasgow speech as a response to either Seward or Lincoln. But it surely revealed their differences. In Douglass's view, the Constitution not only permitted the restriction of slavery in the territories; it could be used to destroy slavery where it already existed. Neither Lincoln nor Seward had dared to so suggest in their own speeches. To even hint at such "radical" abolitionist beliefs would have outraged the vast majority of white voters and doomed either man's chances of winning the presidency.[41]

Nor did Lincoln learn of Douglass's speech—if he ever learned about it at all—until months thereafter. He might have been surprised to know that, just as one of Stephen A. Douglas's speeches had inspired his own Cooper Union address, Frederick Douglass, too, had risen in Glasgow to reply to an earlier oration, in this case a speech delivered by English abolitionist George Thompson at City Hall in Glasgow on February 27, 1860—coincidentally, the very same day Lincoln rose to speak at Cooper Union in New York. Both Lincoln's and Douglass's speeches, then, were in essence rebuttals, not declarations. In reputation, over time, Lincoln's at least has become something more.[42]

Frederick Douglass would speak at Cooper Union himself one day. And he would come to know Abraham Lincoln as a "big brother" and "the first great man that I talked with . . . who in no single instance reminded me of the difference between himself and myself, of the difference of color." For now, his memories of New York City were dominated by recollections of his first visit years before. He could vividly remember reaching New York on his flight to freedom, and then "walking amid the hurrying throng, and gazing upon the dazzling wonders of Broadway"—much as the white visitor from Springfield did when he followed Douglass to town as an invited guest, not a runaway, in 1860.[43]

Now, a month after Lincoln rose to speak at New York's Cooper Union, Frederick Douglass also delivered a major address on slavery and the Constitution—but as an exile. Unlike Lincoln and Seward, Douglass would find no mainstream New York newspaper willing to print and circulate his remarks. Such opportunities were seldom afforded to

black men, even famous ones like Douglass. Douglass would ultimately
manage to get his Glasgow address published as a pamphlet, but its distribution in America was severely limited. The best printer he could
enlist was based in remote Halifax, Canada.[44]

As far as Lincoln's admirers (and Seward's detractors) in New York
City were concerned, the press coverage of Cooper Union proved almost
too good to be true. All it lacked, they seemed to feel, was adequate
appreciation for Lincoln's hypnotic manner: his power to amuse and
enthrall with a jolt of the head or the flash of an eye. Something beyond
words.

So Lincoln was quickly given to understand. Soon after he left New
York, a letter from Hiram Barney, member of the advisory board of the
Young Men's Central Republican Union, caught up with the peripatetic
lecturer in New England. There could be no doubt that enthusiasm for
Lincoln had not yet dampened. Wrote the exultant Barney:

> The Tribune has a good report of the words of your speech. What
> a pity that it cannot give the manner of it! It was a rare treat last
> night that the republicans of New York enjoyed. My son, who is
> a graduate of Harvard University & a student of the law school
> there, said this morning—"It was the best speech I ever heard."[45]

Lincoln's success could also inspire envy—another sign of his surg-
ing influence. Back in Brooklyn, a frustrated Republican loyalist signing
himself "Kings County" reacted to Lincoln's appearance across the river
by calling on his city's own antislavery faithful to organize themselves
for the November election—before it was too late.

"While the Republicans of New York are laboring in a creditable and
worthy manner by . . . inviting men like Cassius M. Clay, Abraham Lincoln, and others, to speak to them, to encourage them, and inspire them
with the true Republican spirit, the Republicans of King's county are
lying in a dormant state," he complained. Could not some party luminary,

like "Kentucky's noble son"—it was not clear here whether the pleader meant Clay or Lincoln, both of whom could claim roots in the Bluegrass State—"be sent over to awaken them from their lethargy?"[46]

But by then, as it happened, both of Kentucky's sons, Lincoln and Clay alike, were already on the campaign trail in New England.

The man who signed himself "Kings County" probably did not even realize that Lincoln had originally been invited to speak in his own city of Brooklyn. If he did, he surely regretted that Lincoln had not appeared there as planned.

Within days, readers of the *Evening Post*—not just across the river in Manhattan, but across the country—were leaving little doubt that Lincoln's speech had made a seismic impact. One wrote to thank the paper just for publishing the speech. And another stated plainly what few had taken seriously only a few days earlier: "We of the West want Abraham Lincoln nominated at the Chicago Convention."[47]

Chapter Eight

⊰ "Unable to Escape This Toil" ⊱

SENSING—PERHAPS HOPING—that his preferred candidate for president would take maximum advantage of his presence in the East, Horace White of the *Chicago Press and Tribune* wired Lincoln on February 25: "How long do you remain in New York & which way do you go next?" The answer would have surprised and pleased even Lincoln's most ardent Illinois supporters.[1]

Over the next eleven days, with but one Sabbath to rest, Lincoln would deliver eleven more speeches in three New England states, appearing before thousands of additional Republican voters in person, and reaching tens of thousands more in "the prints." For each occasion, he would recycle the core of his Cooper Union address, ending nearly every oration with a variation on the climactic rallying cry that had provoked a standing ovation in New York—the reassurance that the cause of freedom, even restrained by patience, was destined to prevail: "Let us have faith that right makes might."

If Lincoln harbored any hope (as some legends suggest) that Cooper Union represented the sole challenge of his eastern trip, or that a quiet reunion with his son would follow immediately thereafter, he quickly learned otherwise. John Eddy, a prominent Rhode Island attorney, cornered him in New York and urged him to speak the very day after Cooper Union in Providence. Lincoln seized the opportunity.[2]

After spending two years retreating from the fatalistic radicalism of his "house divided" address, his two weeks in New England gave Lincoln the chance to reiterate the new phrase he had introduced to take its place. "Right makes might" evocatively summed up his maturing, presidential-year attitude on slavery. He was no longer preaching the inevitability of a national conflagration. He was urging forbearance, summoning the original intent of the founding fathers in order to justify placing slavery on the "course of ultimate extinction" by curtailing its spread.

He was now a gradualist—with faith that there was strength in justice, and justice in strength; in the "patient confidence in the ultimate justice of the people," as he would express it a year later at his first inaugural. He had revived, and felicitously rephrased, the themes of his first public lecture at the Springfield Lyceum back in 1838. He still believed in "unimpassioned reason" and "a reverence for the constitution and laws." "Let us do nothing," he had said at Cooper Union, "Through passion and ill temper," no matter how convinced Republicans remained that slavery was "wrong."[3]

Following his physically demanding journey across the country to New York, his New England tour brought Lincoln to the brink of exhaustion. Words like "toil" and "worn" crept into his correspondence. The schedule would have been grueling even had it been well planned, but Lincoln's haphazard route saw him zigzag first north, then south, then north again, and finally south one more time—going wherever audiences demanded his presence. Intercity travel was laborious in the best of circumstances in 1860, and Lincoln's crazy-quilt itinerary proved especially draining. But he was willing to endure the most taxing discomfort to appear before Republican audiences, especially in response to invitations that took him to three state capitals and two university towns. His schedule ended up requiring more concentrated travel—not to mention four more speeches—than even the Lincoln-Douglas debates:

Monday, February 27	New York (Cooper Union)
Tuesday, February 28	Providence, R.I. (Railroad Hall)
Wednesday, February 29	Travel (eight hours)
Thursday, March 1	Afternoon: Concord, N.H. (Phenix Hall)
	Evening: Manchester, N.H. (Smyth's Hall)
Friday, March 2	Dover, N.H. (City Hall)
Saturday, March 3	Exeter, N.H. (Town Hall)
Sunday, March 4	Rest, worship
Monday, March 5	Hartford, Conn. (City Hall)
Tuesday, March 6	New Haven Conn. (Union Hall)
Wednesday, March 7	Meriden, Conn. (Town Hall)
Thursday, March 8	Woonsocket, R.I. (Harris Hall)
Friday, March 9	Norwich, Conn. (Town Hall)
Saturday, March 10	Bridgeport, Conn. (Washington Hall)
Sunday, March 11	New York (worship and sightseeing)

Yet another resilient Cooper Union myth—holding that the weary Lincoln accepted his Rhode Island, New Hampshire, and Connecticut speaking invitations only to oblige local supporters, not to advance his own political fortunes—deserves to be as firmly punctured as the legend of the alleged temptations of the New York Central Railroad.

The otherwise reliable Robert Lincoln fed this particular myth himself, arguing for fifty years that his father's "unanticipated speeches" in New England were all made "without thought" of "the effect which was being made upon his future career. . . ." To his dying day, Robert believed the addresses "would not have been made but for his visit to a school boy." Perhaps not, though to deny that Lincoln immediately sensed their impact on his political career reflects the näiveté of the "school-boy," not the perceptiveness of the older man. At one of his appearances, after all, Lincoln was introduced as an ideal candidate for vice president on a ticket with local favorite Seward; at another he was overtly hailed as the next Republican nominee for the presidency. Lincoln was not deaf. With each speech, his fame grew, and his chances improved.[4]

Lincoln agreed to deliver speeches in eleven New England cities at first blush to aid his party regionally. His hosts believed his appearances would help Republicans win closely contested local springtime elections. He, in turn, realized that, if successful, local Republicans would feel an obligation to his presidential candidacy—especially if Seward faltered at the convention. In New Hampshire, moreover, Lincoln might be able to convert to Republicanism the state's old "Know-Nothings"—veterans of the fading American party who for years had worked to build a national movement to oppose immigration.[5]

"I am not a Know-Nothing," Lincoln had confided to a friend five years earlier. Prejudice against foreigners was nothing but "degeneracy." "How can any one who abhors the oppression of negroes, be in favor of degrading classes of white people?" Yet these "degenerate" nativists also opposed the extension of slavery, and by 1860 Lincoln believed that the new Republican party needed to welcome old Know-Nothings into its ranks in order to build a coalition broad enough to defeat the Democrats.[6]

Sensing that Cooper Union had improved his own chance to become the enlarged party's presidential nominee, Lincoln knew from the outset that New England successes could only improve his political prospects. If Lincoln the westerner prevailed at the national convention, it stood to reason that he would fare well in the West in November's popular vote. That is precisely why so many easterners, like Greeley, were wary of nominating one of their own: They worried that New Yorker Seward could not win enough western states to offset expected losses in Southern and border states, where no Republican would likely even be listed on the presidential ballot.

Unlike Seward (and the 1856 Republican nominee, the celebrity Pathfinder of the West, John C. Frémont), however, the unknown Lincoln needed to prove himself acceptable to eastern Republicans, for whom Seward was the logical, if not universally embraced, presidential choice. The historian who claimed in 1929 that "there was not more than a secondary thought of self in his New England stumping" underestimated Lincoln's political ambition—and his political acumen.[7]

There was another compelling reason for Lincoln to undertake a rigorous speaking tour in New England. Probably realizing, even then, that if he succeeded at the convention he would not speak publicly until Election Day, Lincoln understood that these days might offer him his final opportunity to "campaign" personally for the White House. So he subjected himself to a pace more like the schedule of a modern presidential primary candidate than that of a nineteenth-century "available" man. He had once confided to journalist Noah Brooks his contempt for "the wicked doctrine of availability, which would ruin any party." He believed that to be successful in 1860, a Republican nominee had to demonstrate himself actively as "an exponent of the principles of the party." He was now prepared to expound those principles in new geographic areas and with new energy—to rise, as far as the political culture would tolerate, beyond mere "availability."[8]

At least he had in hand a stock speech, although it had already been widely reproduced. Never before in his career, not even in Ohio and Kansas, had Lincoln taken an oration "on the road" and reintroduced it almost daily to new audiences. But he realized, correctly, that the Cooper Union address, in successively modified form, would play well everywhere he toured. Motivated by all these factors, and bueyed along his route by audience enthusiasm, Lincoln was on a mission. As William Wilkinson of Poughkeepsie, New York, put it in a letter dated February 25, and possibly forwarded to Lincoln while he was on tour: "I see by our Republican Journals that the citizens of New York are to be favored with an address by you. . . . I am rejoiced to see one of our most eminent champions, so nobly engaged in so hopeful a field of (political) missionary labor."[9]

Lincoln's "missionary labor" in New England deserves to be understood as a calculated follow-up to his acclaimed eastern political debut. His son Robert merely occupied the path of success.[10]

ON THE SAME DAY that he spoke in New York, February 27, the *Providence Journal* broke the news "with the greatest satisfaction" that Lincoln would speak the following evening, "at a place to be hereafter announced." With barely a day to go before his appearance, no venue had been secured for the speech. Yet with perfect confidence, the paper added: "We need not ask for him an audience. No hall in this city will hold the earnest Republicans who will flock to hear this noble and eloquent defender of their principles and their cause." And Lincoln had yet to utter a word at Cooper Union.[11]

Lincoln's subsequent New England appearances actually represented his second political visit to the heart of Yankee America. Back in 1848, then-congressman Lincoln had delivered ten well-received speeches in Massachusetts on behalf of Whig presidential candidate Zachary Taylor. But twelve years had passed since, and it is unlikely that many people in the neighboring New England states remembered those appearances.[12]

Once again, Lincoln would be following Cassius Marcellus Clay into a region of political contention—just as he had done at New York. That "magical . . . noble" Kentuckian had just attracted a large crowd to Touro Hall in Hartford for a well-received two-and-a-half-hour oration on February 25. The pressure on Lincoln to surpass Clay mounted, especially in Hartford, at the tail end of what would become his eleven-city swing.

A few days before that, quite by chance, Lincoln encountered Clay aboard a train near New Haven. It was his "first opportunity to take him by the hand." Proceeding along the way together, the two shared conversation—then, a grotesque observation: The passenger sitting in the row in front of them, as they could not help noticing, was plagued by an unsightly growth on his neck.

Perhaps revolted, Clay never mentioned the subject. But Lincoln brought it up publicly only a few days later during one of his New England speeches, demonstrating that he was the superior of Clay, and most other orators of the day, in finding vivid ways to illustrate his arguments. To Lincoln, the afflicted man offered a sign—a vision—justifying his willingness to allow slavery to survive where it existed in anticipation of its eventual, certain demise:

There was an old gentleman in the car, seated in front of us, whose coat collar was turned far down upon the shoulders. I saw directly that he had a large wen on his neck. I said to Mr. Clay,

That wen represents slavery; it bears the same relation to that man that slavery does to the country. That wen is a great evil; the man that bears it will say so. But he does not dare to cut it out. He bleeds to death if he does, directly. If he does *not* cut it out, it will shorten his life materially.

If the "wen" spread, of course, it meant death, too. That obvious fact remained unspoken. Lincoln had made his point. Yet Lincoln could not help confiding to Clay his "homely" personal reasons for believing slavery wrong: "I have always thought that the man who made the corn should eat the corn."[13]

BY FEBRUARY 28, the Providence organizers had booked Railroad Hall for Lincoln. The capacious auditorium occupied the second floor of the city's twin-spired Union Passenger Depot. In an effort to build a crowd, the Republican press reported on the morning of his scheduled appearance that Lincoln's New York speech had been "greeted with an audience large in numbers and enthusiastic in feeling."[14]

Lincoln lived up to the advance publicity. According to the pro-Republican *Journal*, his address, unambiguously touted as an event "to open the campaign of 1860," proved another triumph. The hall was "filled to overflowing" with fifteen hundred enthusiasts. Arriving there following dinner at John Eddy's nearby home, Lincoln was cheered from the moment he appeared at the doorway of the auditorium, and earned another burst of loud applause when the evening's chairman offered "stirring" words to introduce "the orator of the occasion."[15]

Once again, onlookers were at first "disappointed" by the "long, lank figure" in "his loose frock coat," but typically admitted that "as he proceeded with his speech our solicitude disappeared." One young Brown University student named Amasa Eaton was particularly horrified when the "grotesque and uncouth" speaker engaged in a debate with a heckler. "He made faces at the audience and set them laughing," Eaton sniffed. But Eaton was one of the few whom Lincoln did not charm.[16]

Sadly, the *Journal*, owned by Rhode Island Republican senator Henry B. Anthony, failed to record the speech. It noted only that, "with characteristic humor," Lincoln "began by alluding good-naturedly" to an attack on him in the local Democratic paper, "which he had read on his way hither in the cars." Then he launched into his familiar, defensive justification for his old house divided address. This time, however, he defused its message by showing "that he occupied only the ground which was taken by the founders of our government, and triumphantly vindicated himself and the Republican party against the false charges which are so unscrupulously brought against them." It was the Cooper Union research, recycled.[17]

Supposedly the editor of the city's Democratic sheet, the *Daily Post*, confided that he thought the speech "the finest constitutional argument for a popular audience that I have ever heard." But officially, his paper sneered: "We think the Illinois orator would do well to revise his statistics on slavery and the Constitution before he addresses another abolition audience in the North lest his teachings drive them to let slavery alone as our Fathers did."[18]

Just as in New York, the Republican press praised Lincoln's fresh style. "He abounds in good humor and pleasant satire, and often gives a witty thrust that cuts like a Damascus blade," the *Journal* noted. "But he does not aim chiefly at fun. He strives rather to show the plain, simple, cogent reasoning that his positions are impregnable, and he carries his audience with him, as he deserves to."[19]

Once again, the evening did not end before local Republicans took to the platform to call for a motion to thank Lincoln formally "for his eloquent effort," to which the crowd responded with "three rousing cheers." The "distinguished orator" did not get to make his exit until he personally greeted a throng of admirers, and promised two of them, banker Lattimer W. Ballou and merchant Edward Harris, that he would deliver a speech in Woonsocket, Rhode Island, the following week.[20]

Only then did Lincoln get some rest at John Eddy's house where, his host's four-year-old son later remembered, the odd-looking visitor "gave me a few red gumdrops, probably intended for his own use." After an overnight stay (on reasonably comfortable furniture built to accommodate his six-foot-two host), Lincoln probably boarded a 10:40 A.M. train to Exeter. Nearly six hours later, at 4:27 P.M. on Wednesday, February 29, he arrived in the New Hampshire village where Robert, if he was liberated from his classes in time, surely greeted his father at the platform. But it was not to be an exclusively private reunion. Before he even left the depot, Lincoln was surrounded by a group of local Republicans wondering if he would deliver additional speeches in nearby Concord, Manchester, and Dover. Certainly he would.[21]

The day before, he had received an urgent telegram from New Hampshire Republicans: "Will you speak to the Republicans of Exeter when you arrive here. And what night. Please answer by telegraph." By then he knew that his New Hampshire trip would be more political than personal.[22]

With its five electoral votes, New Hampshire was hardly the prize that New York, with seven times the electors, represented. But in 1856, just four years after the election to the presidency of her favorite son, Democrat Franklin Pierce, the state had gone for Republican Frémont, and Lincoln, or any 1860 Republican nominee, could reasonably expect to be competitive there in November. So could Lincoln's son.

After failing to gain admission to Harvard—based on the rigorous entrance tests that Robert's hometown education ill-prepared him to take, much less pass—the sixteen-year-old boy was showing real promise in his studies at the Phillips Exeter Academy. Surviving records of his test scores, which have never before been published, show that at the time of his father's visit, he was earning 8s and 9s in Latin, 7s and 8s in Greek, and mostly 9s in math, on a scale of one to ten. (The grades were based on recitation, composition, declamation, and scholarship.)

Robert would end his first term with an impressive 8.9 average—significantly higher than the 6.5 earned by his best friend at school, George Clayton Latham (his pal since their days together back at the Springfield Academy). By his second and third terms, Robert was destined to improve to 9s and 10s in all the courses in his demanding curriculum. That summer, he would go on to pass his Harvard entrance examinations and move on to Cambridge. Lincoln was pleased to learn of Robert's success; after all, he was paying all of twenty-four dollars per year for the boy's education, not counting two dollars weekly for room and board (lights and fuel twenty five cents extra).[23]

Like many Exeter students, Robert and George were allowed to live off campus as long as they honored the school's 7:00 P.M. curfew. They roomed together at Mr. and Mrs. Samuel B. Clarke's brick residence on Hemlock Square. But during his visit Lincoln probably lodged elsewhere. He did not, however (despite what some local histories report), get to enjoy a reunion with local Republican leader Amos Tuck, who had served with Lincoln in Congress years before, and in 1856 had cast his vote for him for vice president at the Republican National Convention in Philadelphia. Tuck's own correspondence shows that he was out of town for the visit, and was irritated to learn that Lincoln did not even bother to call on his family.[24]

Early the next morning, March 1, Lincoln boarded the seven o'clock train for nearby Concord, New Hampshire (via Lawrence, Massachusetts), where he spoke at 1:30 P.M. at Phenix Hall. This time, at least, Robert got to go with him, as did George Latham. Then it was off to Manchester for his second speech of the day before an "immense gathering" at Smyth Hall. That night, Lincoln stayed at Manchester's City Hotel. March 1860 was dawning as frenzied as February had ended.[25]

No FULL REPORT has been found of his afternoon address at Concord, but fifty years after the appearance, the town's onetime mayor could still remember the "peculiar facial and lingual expressions" of the orator. A few days later, the local Republican paper editorialized that the source of Lincoln's appeal was his "irresistible logical force and power." The peroration (probably the same as at Cooper Union), the *Concord Statesman* added, "brought his audience to their feet. . . . At the conclusion nine roof-raising cheers were given." For pharmacist E. H. Rollins, it was enough to win him over to the Republicans. That day, he abandoned the Know-Nothings and became a Lincoln man.[26]

From Concord, Lincoln raced off to catch the train for Manchester, which, according to a snide report in the Democratic press (a precursor to an impending political controversy over Lincoln's supposed greed), had won a bidding war for his services after nearby Nashua offered only half the one-hundred-dollar fee the speaker allegedly demanded. Before speaking, Lincoln had time to tour the Amoskeag Mill, the largest cotton mill in the country, to see firsthand where slave-harvested cotton went to market.[27]

According to a fragmentary newspaper account of his speech, Lincoln told the large crowd that assembled despite a rainstorm to hear him at Smyth's Hall that Republicans rejected charges that their party was sectional. Again he noted that George Washington "approved and signed an act of Congress, enforcing the prohibition of slavery in the North Western Territory." Once more, he suggested that national agitation over slavery was being fomented not by Republicans, but by Democrats "who taunt the Republicans as being radical and sectional." And again he insisted that popular sovereignty advocates could find no "precedent or . . . advocate in the century within which our government originated." Then, as the newspaper report concluded: "The speaker said, let us not be slandered from our duty by the false accusations against us, nor frightened from it by menaces of destruction to the Government, nor of dungeons to ourselves"—all straight out of his Cooper Union address.[28]

"He indulges in no flowers of rhetoric, no eloquent passages," observed the *New Hampshire Mirror*. ". . . For the first half-hour, his opponents would agree with every word he uttered and from that part he began to lead them off, little by little, cunningly, till he seems to have gotten them all in the fold. He displays more shrewdness, more knowledge of the masses of mankind than any other public speaker we have heard."[29]

His two-speech day completed, Lincoln returned to his hotel for some desperately needed rest, then headed off by rail the following morning, Friday, March 2, for his next engagement. He spent four hours between trains in Lawrence, Massachusetts, where the Pemberton Mill had collapsed in January, burying in a smoldering ruin dozens of employees, many of them women and girls. Lincoln may have visited the site of the catastrophe; he would write home about it later. From Lawrence, Lincoln proceeded through Exeter (where he deposited Robert and George), and on to Dover, a town hugging the Maine border about eighteen miles to the north. Here, Lincoln had been officially invited by the town's Republican chairman, George W. Benn, who had dispatched a letter to Robert at Exeter "to ascertain whether it is possible that he can be persuaded to deliver an address upon political topics before the citizens of this city previous to our State election, March 13." Robert very properly replied that he would give his father the letter "as he arrives and he will answer it for himself, though I have no doubt he will be happy to comply with your kind invitation should his time permit."[30]

Reaching Dover, Lincoln stopped to take supper at the handsome home of a local businessman named George Mathewson, who then escorted him to City Hall, where an astounding crowd of between fifteen hundred and two thousand, from all across the countryside, heard an address echoing with highlights from Cooper Union. "That is cool," Lincoln laughed at one point, repeating the joke he had introduced in New York about the highwayman "who holds a pistol to my ear, with 'stand and deliver, or I shall kill you, and then you will be a murderer.'" And then, after again urging Republicans to reject the "'don't care' policy of Douglas . . . which was reversing the divine rule, and calling, not the sinners but the righteous to repentance," he closed with his new trademark peroration—"having faith that right makes might, let us to the end, dare to do our duty." In all, "Mr. Lincoln spoke nearly two hours," reported the *Dover Intelligencer*, "and we believe he would have held his audience had he spoken all night."[31]

Lincoln slept that night at the Mathewson house, then left the next day, Saturday, March 3, for the one-hour train ride back to Exeter. After three New Hampshire engagements, he was ready to face his son's classmates and teachers—not to mention Robert himself. The boy had last heard Lincoln speak in public at the final Lincoln-Douglas debate at Alton, Illinois, back on October 15, 1858.[32]

This time, as a local band serenaded arrivals from the town's mud-soaked streets, the crowd grew so thick outside Town Hall that even

Robert had to push his way into the building. When Lincoln finally entered the hall from the rear, one of Robert's school friends, Robert Atkins, took one look at the guest of honor and thought: "What a darned fool I've been to walk up here through the mud to hear *that* man speak." Within ten minutes, he remembered, "I was glad I was there."[33]

Eighteen-year-old Warren James Prescott, who braved the thick mud all the way from his farm at Hampton Falls, was similarly horrified at first, then captivated. "He sat all hunched up, legs crossed, and honestly I think his foot was as long as the end of the little table on the platform," Prescott recalled. When Lincoln rose to speak, Prescott said to himself: "I wish I was at home." But again, within ten minutes, he felt he "wouldn't have been anywhere else but in that hall." When Lincoln finished the talk, Atkins said, "the cheers nearly raised the roof."[34]

Marshall Snow, Exeter class of 1861, also attended Lincoln's talk that night. Like most of his classmates, he liked "Bob" Lincoln, regarding him as a gentleman and a "very good dresser" and was curious to see what his famous father looked like. When the speaker arrived on stage and "succeeded in arranging his long legs under or about" his chair, it was clear that the younger Lincoln had not inherited his sartorial sensibilities from his father. As Snow remembered: "His hair was rumpled, his neckwear was all awry, he sat somewhat bent in the chair, and altogether presented a very remarkable, and, to us, disappointing appearance."

"We sat and stared at Mr. Lincoln. We whispered to each other: 'Isn't it too bad Bob's father is so homely? Don't you feel sorry for him?'"

But when Lincoln "untangled those long legs from their contact with the rounds of the chair," drew himself up to his full height and launched into his speech, "not ten minutes had passed"—that transformative moment somehow always seemed to occur ten minutes into Lincoln's presentations—"before his uncouth appearance was absolutely forgotten by us boys. . . . His face lighted up and the man was changed; it seemed absolutely like another person speaking to us. . . . There was no more pity for our friend Bob; we were proud of his father."[35]

Again, no record was made of the speech. Another eyewitness, Albert Blair, a student from Illinois, insisted with amusement that Lincoln "occasionally put a question to his audience," and once, hearing no reply, drawled: "You people here don't jaw back at a fellow as they do out West." But the listener also thought that "in boldly meeting the imperious legalism of the South," Lincoln "did not fail to impress every hearer."[36]

Yet his work was not done. On this interminable Saturday, March 3, Lincoln faced yet another daunting task: catching up with correspondence that had been forwarded to Exeter, including still more entreaties that he extend his tour and deliver additional speeches.

The day before, the Republican City Committee of Portland, Maine, sent a hand-delivered request "to visit our City, at any time, that may suit your convenience, within a few weeks, and address our citizens on political questions." Also by hand, the New Hampshire Republican State Committee dispatched urgent advice that Lincoln avoid Massachusetts but go instead to Connecticut, whose "people need you more & have the more right to claim you." Cooper Union had launched a phenomenon.[37]

And then from Isaac Pomeroy, head of the Young Men's Republican Working Club of Newark, New Jersey, came a plea to "secure you (if possible) to address us." Explained Pomeroy: "We came over to New York this morning early but we were not able to find you. . . . [L]et me assure you that we would be most happy to greet you . . . as I verily believe in a field where your peculiar abilities and experiences in handling the sophistries of Douglassism [sic] would be better appreciated and productive of more political good than any where else, that I know of in the Union." But though Pomeroy vowed "a welcome worthy of the man and of the cause," even Lincoln had a limit, and it proved to be New Jersey. As Lincoln replied to Pomeroy on March 3:

Owing to my great itineracy in this region, yours of the 28th. ult has just reached me. I have already spoken five times, and am engaged to speak five more. By the time these engagements shall be fulfilled, I shall be so far worn down, and also will be carried so far beyond my allotted time, that an immediate return home will be a necessity with me. At this very sitting I am declining invitations to go to Philadelphia, Reading, and Pittsburgh in Pa.

You perceive I treat you no worse than I do others. The near approach of the elections in N. H. Conn. and R.I. has been the means of their getting me so deeply in here. I hope I may yet be able to visit New-Jersey and Pa. before the fall elections. While at New-York a Mr. William Silvey got a promise from me that I would write him whether I could visit, & speak at New-Ark. Will you please show him this?[38]

Lincoln was true to his word. He rejected two separate entreaties that he lecture at the Harrison Literary Institute in Philadelphia. He refused to fill in for Horace Greeley in Ohio, or make an exception after yet another plea from "doubtful" New Jersey that he speak in Orange. He said no to an invitation to Reading, Pennsylvania. He could not be everywhere. But he did resolutely accept confirmation that he would arrive in short order in Hartford, Meriden, and New Haven. His hosts were named, his lodgings arranged. "Do not fail," warned the summons, "for the sake of Connecticut."[39]

ON SUNDAY HE RESTED, received his New York honorarium, and complained.

Exhausted, overwhelmed by offers he could not possibly accept if he ever wanted to get home, annoyed by the absence of letters from his wife, and worried by news that his younger boys had come down with an illness back in Springfield, Lincoln sat down on March 3 to write a long, self-indulgent letter to Mary. It was the second letter he sent home during his trip, but the only one that survives. Here was the only appraisal he ever left—and a typically modest one, at that—of his performance at Cooper Union.

It had, he admitted, his pride showing just a bit, "gone off passably well." Where it would propel him he was almost afraid to speculate. He had been required to travel endlessly, and rework his Cooper Union masterpiece for audiences who had likely read it in the press. He wanted Mary to appreciate his labor, and share his triumph. For a man not given to confiding his personal feelings through the mail, even to Mary, this letter was nothing less than an *épanchement de cœur*.

Dear Wife: Exeter, N. H. March 4. 1860

When I wrote you before I was just starting out on a little speech-making tour, taking the boys [Robert Lincoln and George Latham] with me. On Thursday they went with me to Concord, where I spoke in day-light. and back to Manchester where I spoke at night. Friday we came down to Lawrence—the place of the Pemberton Mill tragedy—where we remained four hours awaiting the train back to Exeter. When it came, we went upon it to Exeter where the boys got off, and I went on to Dover and spoke there Friday evening. Saturday I came back to Exeter, reaching here about noon, and finding the boys all right, having caught up with their lessons. Bob had a letter from you saying Willie and Taddy were very sick the Saturday after I left. Having no despatch from you, and having one from Springfield, of Wednesday, from Mr. [Harrison G.] Fitzhugh, saying nothing about our family, I trust the dear little fellows are well again.

This is Sunday morning; and according to Bob's orders, I am to go to church once to-day. Tomorrow I bid farewell to the boys, go to Hartford, Conn. and speak there in the evening; Tuesday at Meriden, Wednesday at New-Haven—and Thursday at Woonsocket R. I. Then I start home, and I think I will not stop. I may be delayed in New-York City an hour or two. I have been unable to escape this toil. If I had foreseen it I think I would not have come East at all. The speech at New-York, being within my calculation before I started, went off passably well, and gave me no trouble whatever. The difficulty was to make nine others, before reading audiences, who have already seen all my ideas in print.

If the trains do not lie over Sunday, of which I do not know, I hope to be home to-morrow week. Once started I shall come as quick as possible.

Kiss the dear boys for Father

Affectionately   A. Lincoln[40]

The only satisfaction the weary politician found that day—aside from the constant reminders that he was still very much in demand—came with the receipt of a letter sent "care of Robert T. Lincoln, Exeter Academy" by his Cooper Union host James A. Briggs. Inside was a check for two hundred dollars, Lincoln's honorarium and expenses for his New York visit—a payment that would soon come back to haunt him. Predictably, it was accompanied by a request that he make still more speeches. He would not, and he seemed almost gleeful at another opportunity to recite the names of the towns he had conquered, one by one.

"Since I left New York," he wrote to Briggs before heading off to church with his son, "I have spoken at Providence R. I. and at Concord, Manchester, Dover, & Exeter, in this state; and I still am to speak at Hartford, Meriden, and New Haven, in Conn. and at Woonsocket in R.I. Then I close and start for home. . . . Much as I appreciate your kindness allow me to beg that you will make no arrangements to detain me. Having overstaid my allotted time so greatly, I must hurry home." He would escape "this toil," after all.[41]

Then, as Robert had "ordered," it was off to the worship services at the Second Congregational Church, where Reverend Orpheus T. Lanpheer delivered the sermon, and for the rest of the Sabbath, quiet time at last with his boy. That evening, some of Bob's friends came to call at his lodgings to meet his famous father, among them a young man named Robert Cluskey.[42]

"Cluskey plays the banjo," Bob suddenly announced that night.

"Does he?" Lincoln replied enthusiastically. "Where is the banjo?"

"It is at my room," Cluskey answered.

"Can't you get it?"

"Oh, I don't think you would care for it, Mr. Lincoln."

"Oh, yes."

So Cluskey went home and got his banjo, returned, and played a few tunes for Bob's delighted father. At one point, Lincoln impulsively turned to his son and declared: "Robert, you ought to have one." One report holds he even tried the instrument himself.[43]

No one knows how long the impromptu concert continued, or how late father and son stayed awake that Sunday night. But at seven the next morning, Lincoln made his farewells and dutifully dragged himself to the Exeter depot for the train that would take him to Connecticut—and more speeches. The next time he saw Robert he was the Republican candidate for the presidency.

HARTFORD CITY HALL was "full . . . pressed down, shaken together, and running over" on Monday, March 5, for Lincoln's 7:30 P.M. speech. Lincoln again rose to the occasion, reminding his audience that the "old fathers" had believed in the idea of an "irrepressible conflict," adding, "Jefferson said it; Washington said it. Before Seward said it, the same statement was made by Pryor of Virginia in his Richmond *Enquirer*, the leading paper of his State." Here was a "cool" way of impressing listeners with his thorough Cooper Union research on the founders, while slyly reminding them of his chief rival's obnoxious warnings about the inevitability of conflict. "We stick to the policy of our Fathers," he declared at one point. Indeed, they had served him well on this tour.[44]

Unexpectedly, Lincoln turned his attention as well that night to the local news of the hour, the Massachusetts shoe-workers' strike. At one point he affected a hilarious regional accent to mimic a local Democrat who had characterized the labor unrest as "onforchunit wahfar brought aboat boy this sucktional controvussy!." Lincoln's answer: "I am glad to know that there is a system of labor where the laborer can strike if he wants to! I would to God that such a system prevailed all over the world." Then came a new variation on the rousing old conclusion: "Let us not be slandered or intimidated to turn from our duty. Eternal right makes might—as we understand our duty, let us do it!"[45]

Again, no handwritten text survives. Souvenir hunters rummaging on stage after Lincoln's departure, however, found a page of notes the speaker had left behind on a table. Here, at least, was a clue, albeit a somewhat perplexing one, on how Lincoln reached his standard "right makes might" conclusion at Hartford:

. . . We must deal with it.

Magnitude of question.

What prevents just now?

Right—wrong—indifference

Indifference unphilosophical

    Because nobody is indifferent

    Must be converted to

    Can be, or can not be done.

    I suppose can not.

    But if can, what result?

Indifference, then, must be rejected.

And what supported?

Sectionalism

Conservatism

John Brown

    Conclusion[46]

After the speech, a brand-new local Young Republican Club calling itself the "Wide-Awakes" marched Lincoln back to his hotel to the strains of music from the Hartford Cornet Band. Their demonstration marked the birth of a new political movement. Within months, "Wide-Awake" chapters would spring up in cities all over the North, their members sporting slick hats and capes to protect themselves from the hot oil that dripped from the burning torches they carried aloft in their processions. By summer, the exuberant Wide-Awake groups would go national, emerging as the most excitement-generating element of the street campaigns across the North for Lincoln.

Hartford's Democratic paper promptly labeled Lincoln's oration there "an abolition harangue," claiming that "Mr. Lincoln apologised for the slovenliness of his personal appearance, and for not having changed his linen" before going on "to enlighten the people in New England with regard to the superiority of the African race over that of the Anglo-Saxon." Implementing Lincoln's interpretation of the founders' intentions, it warned, would guarantee the Union's split into separate chunks of a mosaic, "baffling the skill of our modern Republican artists to combine again."[47]

But the city's Republican journal reported "tremendous enthusiasm" for the speaker's "quaint allusions" and "forcible arguments." "The effect of last night's meeting will long be felt," it predicted, "and whenever hereafter we see the name of *Lincoln*, warm remembrances will be awakened in the hearts of thousands."[48]

To eyewitness Daniel Bidwell, who later became editor of the *Hartford Post*, "Mr. Lincoln's speech was meaty, logical, convincing." His "gaunt, homely figure, unpretending manner, conversational air, careless clothing and dry humor made him at once a favorite with the audience, who felt that he was indeed a man of the people." That evening, the mayor gave a champagne reception for Lincoln. The guest of honor, author of an old temperance lecture, of course did not imbibe.[49]

Before he left town, however, Lincoln did find time to take a long walk and visit a bookstore on Main Street, where he encountered one of the town's leading citizens, ex-Democrat Gideon Welles. The white-bearded, blonde-wigged politician-editor loathed Seward, convinced that the senator controlled New York politics through a "profligate system of legislative grants, bounties, and favors." As Lincoln surely knew, the influential Welles was searching for a presidential alternative. And Welles, in turn, admired Lincoln's "sturdy intellectual independence" and thought him "an effective speaker . . . earnest, strong, honest, simple in style and clear as crystal in his logic." At the May convention Welles would ultimately support Chase. But in 1861, perhaps remembering their meeting and his obligation to New England, Lincoln would name Welles his secretary of the navy.[50]

The next morning, Tuesday, March 6, Lincoln found himself rejecting one more speaking invitation. To F. A. Faulkner of Keene, New Hampshire, Lincoln promised only to find a substitute. He dashed off a note to James A. Briggs in New York, urging him to get "Mr. Greeley or Gen: Nye"—two of those who had heard him at Cooper Union—"or some good man, to go and speak at Keene, N. H. next Friday evening? I promised to have it done if possible; and I will be much obliged if it can be."[51]

That chore done, Lincoln left town and proceeded to New Haven, the second college town on his tour (Providence boasted Brown, and New Haven, Yale), where he was ushered to the home of his host, James F. Babcock, editor of the pro-Republican *New Haven Daily Palladium*. Newspaper stories and quickly printed "dodgers"—leaflets—heralded his arrival. In the evening, Babcock led him to Union Hall, where he beguiled another huge throng, many of whom stood "closely wedged" throughout the two-hour talk best remembered for Lincoln's metaphorical explanation for why slavery should be left alone where it existed. It was precisely the kind of frontier-style homily that Lincoln had studiously avoided presenting at Cooper Union:[52]

If I saw a venomous snake crawling in the road, any man would say I might seize the nearest stick and kill it; but if I found that snake in bed with my children, that would be another question. [*Laughter.*] I might hurt the children more than the snake, and it might bite them. [*Applause.*] Much more, if I found it in bed with my neighbor's children, and I had bound myself by a solemn compact not to meddle with his children under any circumstances, it would become me to let that particular mode of getting rid of the gentleman alone. [*Great laughter.*] But if there was a bed newly made up, to which the children were to be taken, and it was proposed to take a batch of young snakes and put them there with them, I take it no man would say there was any question how I ought to decide! [*Prolonged applause and cheers.*]

That is just the case! The new Territories are the newly made bed to which our children are to go, and it lies with the nation to say whether they shall have snakes mixed up with them or not. It does not seem as if there could be much hesitation what our policy should be! [*Applause.*][53]

This homey new allusion forcefully made, Lincoln returned to his proven themes: the Constitution, Washington's Farewell Address, John Brown's raid, and the shoe-makers' strike ("I *like* the system which lets a man quit when he wants to, and wish it might prevail everywhere.") In contrast, he held that slavery was "a great moral, social and political evil," that slaves were "*men*, not property," and that both God and the Declaration of Independence required that slavery "ought to be treated as a wrong." He had taken his legalistically grounded New York speech a giant moral step forward.

Otherwise, the speech proved, a Yale student on the scene testified, "practically a repetition of the ... famous Cooper Institute speech." As Lincoln "warmed to his subject," the observer recalled, "his eyes glistened with the fervor of his own enthusiasm, the lines of his homely face disappeared."[54]

The eyewitness was right to notice the echoes of Cooper Union as Lincoln repeated: "Wrong as we think Slavery is, we can yet afford to let it alone where it is." Finally, after urging his audience, "let us stand by our duty, fearlessly and effectively," and exhorting against "some middle ground between the right and the wrong, vain as the search for a man who should be neither a living man nor a dead man," Lincoln issued the familiar warnings against calling the "righteous," not the "sinners" to repentance, "imploring men to unsay what Washington did."[55]

At the climax of the speech, it was the Cooper Union address verbatim. By now he had committed its demanding syntax to memory:

Neither let us be slandered from our duty by false accusations against us, nor frightened from it by menaces of destruction to the Government, nor of dungeons to ourselves. Let us have faith that right makes might; and in that faith, let us, to the end, dare to do our duty, as we understand it.[56]

At those words, Babcock's paper reported, "There was witnessed the wildest scene of enthusiasm and excitement that has been seen in New Haven for years." When it subsided, a marching band paraded Lincoln back to Babcock's home, where a thousand well-wishers gathered and shouted for him to appear until he reluctantly emerged to say "a few eloquent words" of farewell.[57]

"As he stood there in the glare of the torchlights," another onlooker remembered, "we took in mental retrospect the impression the evening had made upon us, the greatness of the theme, the convincing logic, the intense earnestness, the rugged honesty of purpose, and the magnetic wit of the man, and above the conviction that encompassed and abode with us, that there was one who would continue the fight for a lifetime."[58]

The next afternoon, Wednesday, March 7, as New Haven's Democratic press stubbornly reported "general disappointment among those who heard him through," Lincoln joined three hundred exuberant local Republicans on a special train to Meriden (hundreds more crowding on board at North Haven, Wallingford, and Yalesville). News of his New England tour had spread, and Lincoln was no longer traveling in isolation. His trips had assumed the excitement of a political bandwagon in perpetual motion. A torchlight procession met the throng at Meriden and led the way to Town Hall. Here, Lincoln delivered yet another two-hour speech, then returned to the Meriden depot. Late as it was when he arrived back in New Haven, yet another brass band was on hand to escort him noisily to Babcock's home.[59]

Somehow, on Thursday, March 8, Lincoln managed to rise early enough to catch a 7:15 A.M. eastbound train for his return visit to Rhode Island. Stopping for another three-hour layover in New London, he took lunch at the City Hotel, then boarded a 1:30 P.M. train back to Providence. Arriving there at 4:15 P.M., he was greeted by four to five hundred "earnest Republicans," who joined the visitor aboard a 6:30 P.M. special up to Woonsocket, paying fifty cents apiece for the privilege of riding on the cars with Lincoln. Entertainment was provided by the local "Du Dah" Club band, which played "stirring campaign songs" all along the way.[60]

Between a thousand and fifteen hundred people crowded "spacious and elegant" Harris Hall for the "grand rally" on that warm, drizzly March 8 evening. Even the new auditorium, the second largest in the state, proved "incapable of accommodating the multitude which assembled." By this point in time, as his host declared in his introduction, Lincoln could appear in "no village or hamlet so retired, that his fame will not have preceded him as the champion of freedom." As the *Providence Journal* acknowledged, "the great champion of Illinois has become as much of a favorite in New England as he is in his own state."[61]

That night, a local manufacturer bluntly scribbled in his diary: "Presidential campaign for Republican party for 1860 opened in Woonsocket tonight by Honorable Abraham Lincoln of Illinois—a very tall spare man."[62]

Lincoln spent that night at "Oakley," his host Edward Harris's opulent Woonsocket mansion, and then at 8:25 the next morning, was back on the southbound "cars." Changing trains at Providence at 12:35 P.M., he proceeded to his next stop: Town Hall in Norwich, Connecticut, for yet another address before still another large crowd, where again his "wonderful eloquence . . . created the same impression that he had made elsewhere." The event was followed by a celebratory reception at the Wauregan House, where Lincoln booked to stay overnight, and where one observer spied him, past three in the morning, inexhaustible, sitting on his bed "half undressed," but still exchanging jocular stories with his new political friends.[63]

One admirer who had listened enraptured by the Norwich speech, but shunned the party afterward, was a local minister named John Gulliver. The next morning, he was surprised and delighted to find himself at the railroad depot where Lincoln himself was waiting with Norwich's mayor, peering down the tracks every few minutes, and "inquiring, half impatiently and half quizzically, 'Where's that "wagon" of yours? Why don't the "wagon" come along?'"[64]

When the mayor introduced the minister to the anxious visitor, Lincoln fixed his gaze on the stranger and remarked: "I have seen you before, sir!"

"I think not," Gulliver answered, "you must mistake me for some other person."

"No, I don't; I saw you at the Town Hall last evening."

"Is it possible, Mr. Lincoln, that you could observe individuals so closely in such a crowd?"

"Oh, yes! That is my way. I don't forget faces. Were you not there?"

"I was, sir," Reverend Gulliver admitted. ". . . I consider it one of the most extraordinary speeches I ever heard."

This interested Lincoln, and when they finally boarded their train, he invited Gulliver to sit with him. From there all the way to Bridgeport, the minister engaged the politician in one of the most astonishingly frank Lincoln conversations ever recorded—so highly personal that its reliability was later questioned by some biographers, starting with William H. Herndon.

Lincoln confided to self-proclaimed Democrat Gulliver that he was dazzled to learn that Yale's professor of rhetoric had heard him at New Haven and not only "gave a lecture on it to his class the next day," but proceeded to Meriden to hear him again "for the same purpose." This Lincoln found "very extraordinary."

"I have been sufficiently astonished at my success in the West," Lincoln confessed. ". . . But I had no thought of any marked success in the East, and least of all that I should draw out such commendations from literary and learned men." Now he wanted to know "what it was in my speech which you thought so remarkable, and what you suppose interested my friend, the professor, so much."

"The clearness of your statements, Mr. Lincoln," came Gulliver's reply, "the unanswerable style of your reasoning, and especially your illustrations, which were romance and pathos, and fun and logic all welded together." It could have as easily been a review of the Cooper Union address.

"I have been wishing for a long time to find some one who would make this analysis for me," Lincoln responded. "It throws light on a subject which has been dark to me. I can understand, very readily, how such a power as you have ascribed to me will account for the effect which seems to be produced by my speeches. I hope you have not been too flattering in your estimate. Certainly, I have had a most wonderful success, for a man of my limited education."

This led Gulliver to inquire about Lincoln's schooling, to which

Lincoln offered an unexpectedly revealing explanation of how he developed the simple, direct style of public oratory that had attracted such attention in New York and New England:

> I remember how, when a mere child, I used to get irritated when any body talked to me in a way I could not understand. I don't think I ever got angry at anything else in my life. . . . I can remember going to my little bedroom, after hearing the neighbors talk of an evening with my father, and spending no small part of the night walking up and down, and trying to make out what was the exact meaning of some of their, to me, dark sayings. I could not sleep, though I often tried to, when I got on such a hunt after an idea, until I had caught it; and when I thought I had got it, I was not satisfied until I had repeated it over and over, until I had put it in language plain enough, as I thought, for any boy I knew to comprehend. This was a kind of passion with me, and it has stuck by me; for I am never easy now, when I am handling a thought, till I have bounded it North, and bounded it South, and bounded it East, and bounded it West. Perhaps that accounts for the characteristic you observe in my speeches, though I never put the two things together before.

Herndon, the self-appointed guardian of Lincoln's life story, never doubted that Gulliver "possibly followed" Lincoln out of Norwich that day and "had a conversation" with him. But he pointed out "nine or ten mistakes" in the reminiscence, which was first published in the press in 1864. (For one thing, he correctly noted, the child Lincoln never had his own bedroom.) More to the point, his old law partner argued, it was Lincoln's "habit to play shut mouth." He was much too reticent and secretive by disposition to confide to a total stranger "the history of himself and his origin."[65]

But in the matter of Lincoln recollection, Lincoln always trumps Herndon as a source, even a "silent" source. What Herndon did not know is that shortly before publishing his story in the *New York Indepen-*

dent, Reverend Gulliver wrote directly to the president, enclosing advance proofs of the article that detailed the conversation that, its author admitted, "you have probably forgotten, which I had with you some years since.[66]

"I send it to you that if I have fallen into any important errors of fact, I may correct them and that if you judge it imprudent to publish it, it may be suppressed." Lincoln apparently found nothing worth suppressing. As far as we know, he either set Gulliver's letter aside without objection, or supplied the now-lost approval its writer sought. The reverend, whom Herndon acknowledged to be "a gentleman and a true Christian," would certainly not have allowed the piece to appear in print had the president objected.[67]

Rather, as he rose to speak at Bridgeport's Washington Hall on Saturday night, March 10, to reiterate the sum and substance of his Cooper Union–New Haven orations one final time, Lincoln could benefit, thanks to Gulliver, from discovering within his childhood memories a crucial secret of his oratorical success: his old yearning to understand. Symbolically, Lincoln was now helping eastern audiences to "walk the floor" until they too could unlock the "exact meanings" of the "dark sayings" threatening to destroy the Union.

Leaving his last New England audience on its feet cheering, Lincoln returned to the depot to board a night train to New York. His days of "toil"—terrible and exhilarating at the same time—were finally coming to an end. He had endured, and thrived, despite a crazy-quilt itinerary that a distant observer might easily have concluded had been concocted by a madman whose mission was to kill the candidate by exhausting him to death.

Back in Manhattan, where the press had avidly reported the "glorious reception" accorded "Abe Lincoln" on his tour, the *Tribune* marveled: "He has spoken once in New England for each secular day since his address in our City, two weeks ago. Mr. Lincoln has done a good work and made many warm friends during this visit."[68]

"Imperative" business now called him home to Springfield, but "in this quarter," the *Tribune* accurately predicted, "he will long be gratefully remembered."[69]

• • •

BUSINESS HAD TO WAIT a few more days. Arriving back at the Astor House on Saturday night, Lincoln planned a busy Sunday devoted to worship and charity.

First, as Lincoln told James A. Briggs as soon as he arrived, "I have seen what all the New York papers said about that thing of mine in the Cooper Institute, with the exception of the New York Evening Post, and I would like to know what Mr. Bryant thought of it." Briggs promptly sent over a copy of the paper so Lincoln could read Bryant's flattering account. There was no editor Lincoln respected more.[70]

And there was no minister he respected more than Henry Ward Beecher. As Lincoln later put it, "There was not upon record, in ancient or modern biography, so *productive a mind*." Beecher, for his part, felt that Lincoln's Cooper Union triumph had all but "settled" the search for a Republican candidate for president. On this Sunday morning, just as he had done two weeks before, Lincoln headed back to Brooklyn to hear Beecher preach again at Plymouth Church. This time, however, he arrived late. An onlooker remembered that the service had already reached the announcement of the text, "when the gallery door at the right of the organ-loft opened, and the tall figure of Mr. Lincoln entered, alone." The church was crowded, but an usher surrendered his seat in the balcony and then observed with astonishment the startling "effect of the sermon upon the western orator." Lincoln began making noises:

> As Mr. Beecher developed his line of argument, Mr. Lincoln's body swayed forward, his lips parted, and he seemed at length entirely unconscious of his surroundings,—frequently giving vent to his satisfaction, at a well-put point or illustration, with a kind of involuntary Indian exclamation,—"*ugh!*"—not audible beyond his immediate presence, but *very* expressive.[71]

Back in Manhattan later in the day, Lincoln met Hiram Barney and the two paid a visit to the Five Points, the horrific slum that *The New York*

Times declared, just a few days before Lincoln's Cooper Union address, had earned "the reproach and opprobrium of New-York." Here, "murder and lust, drunkenness and theft, the most abject poverty and the most beastly sensuality, joined hands." Yet the district had also emerged as a laboratory for charity work, not to mention a perverse tourist attraction that had even lured Charles Dickens to its "poverty, wretchedness, and vice" (from which he was protected by two policemen).[72]

Like many visiting celebrities, Lincoln wanted to see the Five Points for himself before he returned home. Reformers had opened a charity mission, the Five Points House of Industry, at its ironically named Paradise Square. It now gave hope to 150 abandoned and abused children, offering them a home in exchange for "honest toil." Lincoln's hosts wanted to show it to him.

Guided by Barney, who served as a trustee, and Reverend Samuel B. Halliday, one of the school's founders, Lincoln toured the six-story facility and looked in on a Sunday school class, where a teacher noticed the "tall, and remarkable-looking man enter the room, and take a seat among us":

> He listened with fixed attention to our exercises, and his countenance manifested such genuine interest, that I approached him and suggested that he might be willing to say something to the children. He accepted the invitation with evident pleasure, and coming forward began a simple address, which at once fascinated every little hearer, and hushed the room into silence. His language was strikingly beautiful, and his tones musical with intensest feeling. The little faces around would droop into sad conviction as he uttered sentences of warning, and would brighten into sunshine as he spoke cheerful words of promise. Once or twice he attempted to close his remarks, but the imperative shout of "Go on!" "Oh, do go on!" would compel him to resume. As I looked upon the gaunt and sinewy frame of the stranger, now touched into softness by the impressions of the moment, I felt an irrepressible curiosity to learn something more about him, and when he was quietly leaving the room, I begged

to know his name. He courteously replied, "It is Abra'm Lincoln, from Illinois!"[73]

A companion whispered appreciatively to Lincoln that his stories of his own childhood—of suffering from deprivation and cold back on the prairie—had clearly inspired the children.

"No, they are the ones who have inspired me," Lincoln insisted, "—given me courage. . . . I am glad we came—I shall never forget this as long as I live."

Before leaving, Lincoln accepted from Reverend Halliday the gift of a book about impoverished children, *The Lost and Found; or Life among the Poor.* Lincoln would carry the volume all the way home to Springfield, where Mary would read it "with much interest," and lend it to her friends. Her husband, she noted a few weeks after the 1860 election, retained "a lively recollection, of his visit to the Inst[it]ution, whilst in New York."[74]

In a sense, the Five Points was an ideal place to close Lincoln's visit to the East—the urban equivalent of the kind of hopeless, dirt-floor log cabin squalor that he had endured as a child on the prairie, and from which he had now fully emerged, the toast of the country's most sophisticated city, and a genuine candidate for president.

Here, speaking privately to the children of the House of Industry, he could stress his belief that anything was possible in a system of free labor—just as he insisted in his public speeches. Lincoln was now beginning to offer the same message of limitless opportunity to African-Americans, telling his audience in New Haven just hours before: "I want every man to have the chance—and I believe a black man is entitled to it—in which he *can* better his condition." At the Five Points, he was reaffirming it to European-Americans, even those living in degrading circumstances one step above that of caged animals. He was also reaffirming the message to his political hosts. And perhaps to himself.[75]

Later in the day, Barney took Lincoln back for tea at his home on Fourth Avenue near Union Square. Joining them at the table, Barney's sister-in-law marveled at their guest's "awkwardness of manner, homeliness of feature, and not over clean hands," the complete opposite of his host. Typically, she admitted, "I shortly forgot the disagreeable in admiration of his intelligence and heartiness and wit. He tells an excellent story and has, (what I like very much in any one) a genuine laugh.[76]

After tea, perhaps still thinking about his inspiriting visit to the Five Points, Lincoln decided to go to church again, this time to an evening service at the Church of Divine Unity on Broadway between Prince and Spring streets, to hear another well-regarded pulpit orator, the Universalist preacher Edwin Hubbell Chapin.[77]

Sometime between worship services on this long and eventful New York Sunday, Lincoln strolled with James A. Briggs past the city's main post office, where Briggs blurted out: "Mr. Lincoln, I wish you would take particular notice of what a dark and dismal place we have here for a postoffice, and I do it for this reason: I think your chance for being the next President is equal to that of any man in the country. When you are President, will you recommend an appropriation of a million dollars for a suitable location for a postoffice in this city?"

Making what Briggs recalled as a "significant gesture," Lincoln assured him: "I will make a note of that." He was no longer an unknown visitor. Now he was making promises for a future administration.

A few hours later, strolling up Broadway to the Church of Divine Unity, Lincoln suddenly turned to Briggs and declared appreciatively: "When I was East, several gentlemen made about the same remark to me that you did to-day about the Presidency; they thought my chances were about equal to the best."[78]

By the time he boarded his train for home the next morning, they were.

Chapter Nine

⊰ "Preserve It for Your Children" ⊱

W ITH CHEERS—and importunings for more speeches—resounding in his head, Abraham Lincoln finally headed home.

In a letter to his wife from Exeter he had assured Mary that he would be back in Springfield by Monday, March 12. In the end, he did not even depart New York until that morning, taking the Erie Railroad north and west for the slow, scenic ride across the snow-covered Southern Tier of New York State.

For Lincoln, it was not just a sightseeing experience. At one town along the way, Hancock, nestled along the Delaware River within sight of the northeastern fringe of Pennsylvania on the opposite shore, he was unexpectedly greeted by well-wishers and "stepped off the car to greet and shake hands with the natives." News of his arrival had reached the remote village in advance. Journalist Charles T. White claimed that the scene recurred at a few other towns along the way. Nothing like this had ever happened to Lincoln outside his region.[1]

The next day, Lincoln reached Toledo, Ohio, and changed to a Toledo, Wabash & Western line train, which pulled into Fort Wayne, Indiana, at 5:20 P.M. After another jostling, overnight ride into Illinois, the weary traveler finally reached Springfield at 6:50 A.M. on Wednesday, March 14, "in excellent health and in his usual spirits." His career-altering trip to New York and back had lasted exactly three weeks.[2]

To those who asked him about his adventure, Lincoln had nothing but good things to say. "Our down East friends did, indeed treat me with great kindness," he happily reported, "demonstrating what I before believed, that all good, intelligent people are very much alike." Especially, one presumes, if they cheered Abraham Lincoln. Adding to the exuberant mood, William Herndon and other friends showered him with "earnest congratulations" for his "dazzling success in the East." Herndon, for one, still believed that Seward remained the overwhelming favorite to win the Republican nod for the White House, but he noted that Lincoln returned from New York convinced "that the Presidential nomination was within his reach." There seemed to be something different about him; a new gravitas, stiffened by a new resolve.[3]

FOR A WHILE, it was back to the mountain of accumulated mail for Lincoln. The very day of his arrival home, the vigilant correspondent summoned the energy to apologize to the New Haven photographers who had asked him for a sitting during his brief visit to town March 6. "I beg you will believe me guilty of no intentional disrespect," he assured William A. Beers and Sereno Mansfield. To Alexander H. Harvey of Buffalo, he explained why he could not pause in that city, en route home, to there deliver yet another public address: "The appointments I had then already made carried me so far beyond my allotted time that I could not consistently add another."[4]

Such requests to pose and speak had become routine business by now. But there was something urgent and heartening in this latest correspondence: letters from supporters boldly talking about the upcoming presidential race, and from Lincoln, hints in return that he was at least interested, flirting more openly with the idea, confirming his availability, well aware of his improved standing. But he remained concerned that Douglas continued to spread what he termed the "infernal stereotypical lye"—perhaps a mere misspelling, perhaps his attempt to craft a corrosive-sounding homonym—suggesting Lincoln's belief in "negro equality." Ever cautious, ever ambitious, he wished to escape the outcast status to which out-and-out abolitionists were relegated in national politics. By his reasoning, he could still oppose both slavery and racial equality without inconsistency, or damage to his presidential prospects.[5]

He would not, however, "enter the ring on the money basis," first because it was "wrong," and second, because, as he confessed, "I have not, and can not get, the money" needed to underwrite a campaign. To one correspondent he declared: "I could not raise ten thousand dollars if it would save me from the fate of John Brown." But he did offer to send one supporter a hundred dollars to finance a trip to the convention in May, should he become a delegate. After all, he conceded, "for certain objects, in a political contest," the expenditure of some money was "both right, and indispensable."[6]

To another supporter, he daydreamed wistfully that if he needed suddenly to remake his life in an entirely new location, he might well head west and try Kansas—Leavenworth, maybe, where he had made his last major speech before traveling to New York or perhaps Atchison. These seemed like "fine growing places." But he knew he could not allow himself to think negative thoughts. This was no time for another bout of the periodic depression he called his "hypo." His energy must remain firmly focused on the upcoming Chicago convention, on a possible future not in Kansas, but in Washington.[7]

Within a week, however, Lincoln dutifully returned to his legal work in Springfield, immersed in "business," writing and filing demurrers and agreements, and by the twenty-third arrived in Chicago for the big "sand-bar" case in federal court, spending his spare time sitting for sculptor Leonard Wells Volk, the latest evidence of his growing reputation. Many politicians sat for photographs, but only statesmen posed for sculptures.[8] It was from Chicago that he penned his first known letter assessing his chances at the fast-approaching convention, glad to know he had "friends" willing to support him, and laying out a specific strategy for a come-from-behind success. "If I have any chance," he calculated, "it consists mainly in the fact that the *whole* opposition would vote for me if nominated. (I dont mean to include the pro-slavery opposition of the South, of course.) My name is new in the field; and I suppose I am not the *first* choice of a very great many. Our policy, then, is to give no offence to others—leave them in a mood to come to us, if they shall be compelled to give up their first love."[9]

His old friend Milton Hay, an Illinois lawyer whose nephew John later became President Lincoln's assistant secretary, responded with a formal declaration from the local Republican club. Acknowledging Lincoln's recent successes in New York and New England, Hay noted: "No inconsiderable portion of your fellow citizens in various parts of the country have expressed their preference to you as the candidate of the Republican Party for the next presidency."[10]

"I have never professed an indifference to the honors of official station," Lincoln had admitted privately in 1858, "and were I to do so now, I should only make myself ridiculous." But the sensibilities of the period required that presidential candidates be "drafted." Lincoln could provide nothing more than strong hints and subtle encouragement. "I feel myself disqualified to speak of myself in this matter," he advised an Ohio lawyer who was wondering whom to support, adding half-jokingly that "when not a very great man begins to be mentioned for a very great position, his head is very likely to be a little turned." And as he made clear to supporters in Bloomington, he intended for now to be less visible—certainly less vocal: "I very much prefer to make no more speeches soon." As he put it on another occasion: "Save me from the appearance of obtrusion."[11]

But there was no keeping Lincoln off the speaker's platform. Four days after affirming his vow of silence to his Bloomington friends, he was appearing there in spite of himself, arguing that congressional Democrats' recent support of an antipolygamy bill demonstrated their selective interpretation of the Constitution. By insisting on popular sovereignty on the slavery issue, but conceding Congress's right to outlaw multiple marriage, he charged, Douglas's party seemed willing to declare polygamy wrong, and slavery right. It was not a major campaign speech, but it earned some attention in the local press. A few days later, Lincoln tried one more time to make a success of his old, apolitical "Discoveries and Inventions" lecture in Springfield. It was as if public speaking were a drug, and Lincoln a hopeless addict; he could not give it up.[12]

Two weeks after that, in early April, the results came in from the springtime elections in Connecticut, and Lincoln was "gratified" to learn of Republican victories in the state where he had made five of his twelve eastern speeches. With "the fiery furnace" of those local contests cooling, his old New Haven host, James H. Babcock, was now free to ask Lincoln how he could help him in the presidential race. Lincoln, he pointed out gratefully, had helped bring out the largest Connecticut Republican turnout ever; now Babcock wanted to return the favor and bring Connecticut Republicans out for Lincoln.[13]

The candidate-in-waiting remained cautious, at times bafflingly so. "As to the Presidential nomination," Lincoln told Babcock, "claiming no greater exemption from selfishness than is common, I still feel that my whole aspiration should be, and therefore must be, to be placed anywhere, or nowhere, as may appear most likely to advance our cause." Despite a deadlock at the opposition party's convention in Charleston, South Carolina, he remained convinced that his perennial rival Douglas would win the Democratic nomination, creating the potential for a climactic final contest between them. But to only one old friend, Lyman Trumbull, who ironically was not enthusiastic about Lincoln's candidacy, was he entirely frank about the White House—and not until April 29. Just three weeks before the convention was scheduled to begin, Lincoln finally confided what many people already realized: "The taste *is* in my mouth a little."[14]

THE PUBLIC WAS HUNGRY, in turn, for Lincoln, and what it got was a banquet of Cooper Union publications. Within hours of his return home from the East, Lincoln learned that his Cooper Union speech would soon be published in pamphlet form by his hometown newspaper, and within days, under his "hasty supervising," the *Journal*'s fourteen-page reissue appeared for sale, entitled: *Speech of Hon. Abraham Lincoln in New York, in*

Vindication of the Policy of the Framers of the Constitution and the Principles of the Republican Party Delivered in the Cooper Institute, February 27, 1860. Even before Lincoln reached Springfield, the *Journal* was proudly touting the fact that its pamphlet edition of "Mr. Lincoln's Great New York Speech, printed with large type and on good paper," would be ready shortly—though it would also include Seward's recent address before the U.S. Senate. The price was fixed at twenty-five cents per dozen, and one dollar per hundred, with a penny extra for postage. The bulk orders were meant for Republican clubs across the country; they would, in turn, distribute the individual pamphlets to their members. In this way, such reprints constituted crucial ammunition for the information-starved, politically insatiable America of Lincoln's time.[15]

Even earlier, back in New York, Horace Greeley had rushed out the speech in pamphlet form as "Tribune Tract" Number 4, under the headline: *National Politics. Speech of Abraham Lincoln, of Illinois, Delivered at the Cooper Institute, Monday, Feb. 27, 1860.* The pamphlet was ready by March 6, while Lincoln was still traveling through Connecticut. When he returned to New York, he found it already available to the public.[16]

Greeley marketed the eleven-page *Tribune* edition aggressively. Copies were put up for sale at the paper's New York offices at a price of four cents a copy, twenty-five cents per dozen, $1.25 per hundred, and ten dollars per thousand (prices that were later reduced). As a bonus, the publication included Wisconsin Republican senator James Doolittle's February 24 speech attacking "the new doctrine of judicial infallibility," as did Lincoln's address at Cooper Union just three days later, and also, like Cooper Union, railing against "the headstrong zeal pursued by the other party to force slavery into Territories." Doolittle had even claimed that the principles of Jefferson were "identical with those of the Republican party of to-day."[17]

It was as if Republicans were now speaking with one voice: identifying with the founders, attacking the Dred Scott decision, rebuking John Brown, and drawing their own "dividing line" on slavery extension. Lincoln did not say it alone; but he said it best. Two of these pamphlet productions employed the word "vindication" in their titles, as if in acknowledgment of Lincoln's central role in confirming the Republican faith in conservative and constitutional opposition to slavery. The *Tribune* pamphlet focused clearly on the Cooper Union speech. "Mr. Lincoln's is probably the most systematic and complete defense yet made of the Republican position with regard to Slavery," the *Tribune* declared in its initial advertisement for the reprints. "We believe no speech has yet been made better calculated to win intelligent minds over to our standard. Will the friends of the Cause everywhere aid us to circulate it?"[18]

The answer was yes. The *Tribune Tract* edition proved enormously popular, going through at least five additional editions. Meanwhile, within days a new edition appeared in Washington entitled *The Republican Party Vindicated. The Demands of the South Explained,* and this publication, too, would be reprinted several times, as early runs sold out. The *Detroit Tribune* added an edition of its own shortly thereafter (at fifty cents per hundred, five dollars per thousand), and a one-penny *Chicago Press and Tribune* pamphlet hit the streets around the same time. Lincoln had made the Cooper Union Address with no help from others; now it was being remade by Republican journals eager for wider distribution and, of course, some extra revenue in the bargain.[19]

By April 6, Lincoln could playfully report to an admirer from Edwards County, near Illinois' southern border with Indiana: "Pamphlet copies of my late speech at Cooper Institute, N. Y., can be had at the office of the N. Y. Tribune; at the Republican Club Room at Washington, and at the office of the Illinois Journal at this place. At which place they are cheapest, I do not certainly know. " What he did know was that his New York oration was enjoying a new and sustained life in pamphlet form, and was being purchased, individually, and in bulk alike, by admirers and groups across the North.[20]

"We are by no means surprised that it called out the highest encomiums of the New York Republican press," commented the *Chicago Press and Tribune* in announcing its own edition, "or that it was at once determined to issue it in pamphlet form as a campaign document." As a campaign document! Seward, for one, understood all too well, if too late, the threat Lincoln posed to his candidacy. Furious at the Chicago paper for all of its efforts on his rival's behalf, he excoriated its editor for abandoning him in favor of "that prairie statesman."[21]

BEFORE LONG, SEWARD'S supporters struck back. Within days, they unleashed a series of attacks on Lincoln for allegedly demanding an honorarium to deliver his political speech in New York. The Lincoln men rushed to their candidate's defense. Charges flew back and forth in the newspapers.

Then, on the night of April 17, just a month before the convention was scheduled to convene in Chicago, New York's Central Republican Campaign Club—the regular party organization that remained pledged to Seward—met at Clinton Hall to vilify the "young men" who had invited Lincoln to their city two months earlier. Speaker after speaker rose to denounce both the western visitor and his eastern hosts. Their attacks did not focus on Lincoln's speech. They homed in on his purported avarice.

It was "disgraceful to the republican party," one Seward man named F. J. Young charged, "that a price should be charged to hear a republican speech." The next orator expressed himself as "filled with astonishment" to learn "that a distinguished republican, yes, gentlemen, a man whose name had been presented by one of the states of the Union as a candidate for the Presidency—charged and received two hundred dollars for a speech at Cooper Institute."[22]

That brought onlooker James A. Briggs angrily to his feet. The man who had helped lure Lincoln to New York insisted that his guest was "in no manner responsible for what occurred" when he reached town. Briggs went through the entire history of the Cooper Union engagement: its origins as a lecture for the Plymouth Church course in Brooklyn, its transfer to New York "where more people could hear it," and the organizers' decision to charge a fee to recoup expenses, which Briggs insisted was made entirely without Lincoln's approval or knowledge. Briggs would "not sit still and hear Mr. Lincoln arraigned, because he was innocent of any improper conduct."[23]

But the Seward men did not let up. C. S. Spencer replied acidly that he was sure "Lincoln was sorry that he ever received the $200." Another speaker offered a stinging resolution affirming that all future Republican meetings be held with "open doors." Someone proposed an amended version specifically condemning the Young Men's Central Republican Union. Yet another speaker called Briggs's group "shysters."

For weeks the contretemps percolated nationwide. From Washington came a venomous newspaper attack on Lincoln as "the two shilling candidate . . . who charged his own friends two-shillin' apiece to hear him talk about politics." And a Fort Wayne journal pointed out that Lincoln's supporters had appropriately been asked to fork over "the regular circus rate of twenty-five cents' admittance fee" to hear him.[24]

The situation irritated Lincoln enormously, especially when sympathetic newspapers felt they, too, must begin carrying reports of the dispute. Even before the Seward men rallied to denounce him in New York, the pro-Lincoln *Middleport, Illinois, Press* reluctantly published the story, prompting its worried editor, a Lincoln supporter named Cornelius F. McNeill, to send the clipping on to the candidate himself. Lincoln was horrified.

As far as the injured candidate was concerned, the honorarium libel had only emerged when a "drunken vagabond" in the Young Men's Central Republican Union, "having learned something about the $200, made the exhibition out of which *The Herald* manufactured" the original story that ignited the controversy. Conveniently ignored was the fact that the hometown *State Register* had first reported on the honorarium on the very day of Lincoln's departure for New York—indicating that the story was in the air in Springfield as early as February.

In the same indignant vein, garnished with an even rarer dose of disingenuousness, Lincoln determined to provide his own version, in exhaustive detail, of the history of his New York engagement. And then he insisted that no one ever repeat it: His opponents, he believed, wanted a controversy. They could have it only if he offered denials and explanations. As successful as Cooper Union was, few other speeches in his career had put him more perilously on the defensive. None made him so certain it had done him enough good that he could afford to turn the other cheek to his critics. As he insisted in a letter to the editor of The *Middleport*, Illinois, *Press* on April 6:

It is not true that I ever *charged* anything for a political speech in my life—but this much is true: Last October I was requested, by letter, to deliver some sort of speech in Mr. Beechers church, in Brooklyn, $200 being offered in the first letter. I wrote that I could do it in February, provided they would take a political speech, if I could find time to get up no other. They agreed, and subsequently I informed them the speech would have to be a political one. When I reached New York, I, for the first [time], learned that the place was changed to "Cooper Institute." I made the speech, and left for New Hampshire, where I have a son at school, neither asking for pay nor having any offered me. Three days after, a check for $200—was sent to me, at N. H., and I took it, *and did not know it was wrong*. My understanding now is, though I knew nothing of it at the time, that they did charge for admittance, at the Cooper Institute, and that they took in more than twice $200.[25]

Lincoln's uncharacteristically self-righteous letter was wrong on at least two obvious counts. He certainly expected a two hundred-dollar check for his speech, having received such an offer in the very first telegram inviting him to Brooklyn in late 1859. In addition, James A. Briggs had sent the two hundred dollars to him at Exeter, accompanied by the unforgettably flattering compliment, "I wish that it were $200,000 for you are worthy of it." Lincoln had deposited that amount and more (probably including some accumulated legal fees) in his bank account as soon as he returned to Springfield. How could he *not* know that the funds were raised through a door charge? Likely he knew, too, that the speech did not earn double the amount of his honorarium, or four hundred dollars, for the Young Men's Central Republican Union. Briggs later recalled that the profit after expenses amounted to only seventeen dollars (out of which he kept a fourth, $4.25, for himself). It is not unreasonable to imagine that he shared that information with Lincoln.[26]

Wisely, Lincoln chose not to argue the matter point by point. "I wish no explanation made to our enemies," he instructed editor McNeill. "What they want is a squabble and a fuss; and that they can have if we explain; and they can not have if we don't." His request was: "Give no denial, and no explanations."[27]

But some of his surrogates could not help themselves. In a letter to *The New York Times*, a correspondent signing himself only "B."— undoubtedly James A. Briggs—repeated in full detail the explanation he would provide the Seward club, to little avail, a few weeks later. About Lincoln's lecture, he insisted: "All who heard it were satisfied; they received more than they paid for. And before any gentlemen charge a man, who is the very soul of honor, and who is self-sacrificing to a fault, with 'meanness,' they should post themselves as to the *facts*."[28]

But by then, the "facts" were being twisted by the Democratic press as well as the Seward clubs. The matter never quite died. But it did not escalate into a full-blown scandal, either. In the end, the fuss was not nearly consequential enough to arrest Lincoln's momentum as the Republican National Convention approached.

SHORTLY BEFORE the Republicans were scheduled to meet for their national convention at Chicago, *Harper's Weekly* published a large engraving of the eleven leading candidates for the party's presidential nomination. Occupying the central place in the print, largest of all in size, and impressively surmounting a drawing of the city of Washington, was a portrait of the heavy favorite, William H. Seward.

As for the other contenders, they were made to appear all but suspended in Seward's powerful orbit, portrayed in smaller portraits placed above and below, to his left and right. Surrounding Seward were: Edward Bates of Missouri, Nathaniel Banks of Massachusetts, William

Pennington of New Jersey, Salmon P. Chase and John McLean of Ohio, Simon Cameron of Pennsylvania, John C. Frémont of California, John Bell of Tennessee, and Cassius M. Clay of Kentucky. Sharing the bottom row—along with fellow long-shots Frémont, Bell, and Clay—was Lincoln, his portrait modeled after Brady's strong Cooper Union photo, but otherwise looking to all the world like an also-ran. Like Seward, *Harper's Weekly* underestimated Abraham Lincoln.

The delegates commenced their voting on May 18 at the Wigwam, a massive temporary structure packed with wildly cheering Lincoln enthusiasts who had used counterfeit tickets to elbow out Seward men from the galleries. Lincoln stayed home in Springfield.

The first ballot gave Seward 173½ votes, Lincoln 102, Cameron 50½, Chase 49, and Bates 48. The twin shocks were Lincoln's strong showing and Seward's failure to get close to the 233 votes required for nomination. Lincoln had not only won the unanimous support of the Indiana and Illinois delegations, but also some surprising support from New Hampshire, where he had spent so much time in March. The state voted 7–1 for Lincoln over Seward. Connecticut gave 2 of its votes to Lincoln, and to Seward none.

On the second ballot, Seward gained only 11 votes, and Lincoln 79, aided by defections from New Hampshire, Rhode Island, Ohio, and Pennsylvania. The vote now stood at Seward 184½, Lincoln 181, but the momentum was all Lincoln's.

To frenzied shouts of "call the roll, call the roll," the third ballot got underway immediately, and more delegates from Rhode Island, Pennsylvania, and Maryland promptly switched over to Lincoln, too. Then, needing only 1½ votes to put the candidate from Illinois over the top, Ohio rushed to move four votes into his column, officially giving Lincoln the nomination as the "wildest enthusiasm" erupted inside the Wigwam. A few scattered hisses could be heard, probably from New York's stunned delegation. Its huge bloc of 70 convention votes had never left Seward's column, but in the end, they did not matter.[29]

As Lincoln's supporters triumphantly hoisted a life-size portrait of the newly anointed candidate to the platform (causing some delegates to stare in horror), a loyal supporter wired the new nominee in Springfield: "Abe we did it. Glory to God."[30]

ALMOST FROM the moment he became the Republican candidate for president, Lincoln decided "to make no speeches." This time he meant it. He would not "write or speak anything upon doctrinal points," no exceptions. Writing rather pompously from New York—"This wilderness of Humanity, and of concentrated selfishness," he called it—Cooper Union cohost James A. Briggs agreed, begging Lincoln to express no opinions "until the Jews are restored to Judea." Obligingly, one of the first tasks that Lincoln assigned to his newly hired private secretary, John G. Nicolay, was the drafting of a form letter to be sent in response to any and all requests for his political opinions. Emphasizing that "his positions were well known when he was nominated," the letter explained that the nominee "must not now embarrass the canvass by undertaking to shift or modify them." In other words, he would say nothing new because he would not risk saying anything inflammatory. The strategy had worked well enough to stifle the Cooper Union honorarium flap; it should work to stave off any political brushfire that might erupt during the rest of the campaign.[31]

For the next six months, Lincoln maintained his silence, to the point that Herndon observed: "He is bored, bored badly." He opened a temporary office at the State Capitol, where he tended to his mail, sat for artists, and stiffly greeted visitors. The public saw nothing of him, save for a solitary appearance, standing in his front doorway, dressed in a white coat, as a parade of supporters marched past his house. "The whole world and his wife was there," an old friend exclaimed. Lincoln posed that day for a photograph, and made his basement available as a darkroom. But he refused entreaties that he give a formal speech.[32]

To one correspondent who sought his views on reassuring the South, Lincoln insisted that "my published speeches" afforded more insight than "anything I would say in a short letter, if I were inclined now, as I am not, to define my position anew." In other words, he was saying: "Read the Cooper Union speech. Read the Lincoln-Douglas debates."[33]

By the time that letter was written, the long-awaited, book-length version of the Lincoln-Douglas debates had finally appeared in print. Though Douglas howled that the reprints did him an "injustice" by presenting inaccurate transcriptions of his speeches, the volume promptly became a major best seller. New printings were ordered, and sales eventually exceeded thirty thousand.[34]

WITHIN DAYS OF LINCOLN's nomination, the avalanche of Cooper Union reprints resumed. First the Republican Executive Congressional Committee issued an eight-page pamphlet version of the *Speech of Hon. Abraham Lincoln, of Illinois, at the Cooper Institute, New York City, February 27, 1860.* The reprints were offered in bulk rates of fifty cents per hundred. The *New York Herald* transcript was adopted, complete with notations of interruptions for applause. And the *Albany Evening Journal* edition began circulating in earnest, marketed to Republicans throughout the state at two cents per copy, twenty cents per dozen, and eight dollars per thousand. Lincoln could afford to remain a sphinx; such publications were effectively presenting his positions on history and politics.

The party depended heavily on German-born voters for support, so it is not surprising that two foreign-language pamphlets soon joined the ranks: The *New-Yorker Demokrat* issued one of the first, the nine-page *Die nationale Politik. Rede von Abraham Lincoln, von New-York. Gehalten im Cooper Institut . . .* and *Rechtfertigung der republikanischen Partei . . . Rede des Ehrb. Abraham Lincoln, von Illinois. Gehalten im Cooper-Institut in New-York am 27. Februar 1860.* Shortly thereafter came a Dutch-language version, *De Republikeinsche Party verdedigd enz. Redevoering von Abraham Lincoln, In het Cooper Institut.*[35]

The speech turned up, as well, in some of the special Republican campaign newspapers that now sprouted up across the North—a unique phenomenon of the "hurrah" campaign in which the chief campaigner did no campaigning. In Pennsylvania, for example, the town of Browns-ville's pro- Republican daily, the *Clipper*, became one of the first to pub-lish such a Lincoln weekly. Calling it *The Rail Mauler*, its publisher promoted it as "the spiciest little campaign sheet in the country." On August 10, *The Rail Mauler* featured the Cooper Union address in full, under the headline, "The Speech of the Age," bringing the text for the first time into that decisive battleground state. Devoting three of its pages to the reprint, the paper editorialized with a succinct explanation for Cooper Union's durability:

> We publish below one of the closest, most terse, and most logical speeches we have ever read in the English language. It is as remarkable for its beauty of expression and perspicuity of thought, as for the cogency of its reasoning and the invulnerable character of its arguments.
>
> Read this speech; and preserve it for your children, as a model production by a self-made man.[36]

By this time, Lincoln did not need another pamphlet or campaign paper to convince him of the growing impact, the astonishingly broad circulation, and the continuing political value of his Cooper Union speech. His personal correspondence was bringing him such reminders regularly. One admirer wrote from the Rocky Mountains to inform the candidate that "your interesting speech delivered in Newyork on the over whelming topics of the day has been by me at least delightfully and attendantly read," particularly its "liberal views and high toned liberty statements."[37]

Another correspondent, from Dobbs Ferry, New York, proudly informed Lincoln on July 18 that the Cooper Union speech had inspired his recent *New York Times* article attacking the Supreme Court's opinions on "Property in Man"—the Dred Scott decision. And from Edward L. Pierce of Boston came a letter two days later reporting that he "had read your Cooper Institute speech," and now had no doubt "you will be elected President, my friend—and . . . will be found equal to the responsibility." There was no longer any question, Pierce concluded, that Lincoln was "true" to the "anti-slavery cause."[38]

But no Cooper Union correspondence delighted Lincoln more than the letter he received just five days after he won the presidential nomination from one of the organizers of his New York speech, Charles C. Nott. Nott's letter informed him that the Young Men's Central Republican Union planned "to publish a new edition in larger type & better form, with such notes & references as will best attract readers seeking information." Nott enclosed for Lincoln's inspection a copy of one of the imperfect early pamphlet editions, which he had filled with proposed editorial changes, vowing to make his formal edition "as nearly perfect as may be." As Nott assured Lincoln: "Most of the emendations are trivial & do not affect the substance—all are merely suggested for your judgment." Lest the nominee object to any tampering at all, Nott hastened to acknowledge:

> You and your Western friends, I think, underrate this speech. It has produced a greater effect here than any other single speech. It is the real platform in the Eastern states, and must carry the conservative element in New York, New Jersey, and Pennsylvania. . . . I cannot help adding that this speech is an extraordinary example of condensed English. After some experience in criticising for Reviews, I find hardly anything to touch & nothing to omit. It is the only one I know of, which I cannot *shorten* and—like a good arch—moving one word tumbles a whole sentence down.

All Nott wanted now from Lincoln were the details of his research, asking: "Have you any memoranda of your investigations which you would approve of inserting?"[39]

Lincoln replied about a week later to confess that he "would not object to, but would be pleased rather, with a more perfect edition of that speech." But he gave Nott the bad news that he "did not preserve memoranda of my investigations," adding: "I could not now re-examine, and make notes, without an expenditure of time which I can not bestow upon it." Lincoln was not actively campaigning for the White House, but he was spending so much time explaining his silence that he hardly had the leisure to redo and record his research.[40]

With no other choice, Nott and his coeditor, Cephas Brainerd, went to work on their own back in New York to verify and record Lincoln's sources. To their dismay the process took them some three weeks of intensive labor. Each successive day of painstaking work magnified their awe for the speaker's extraordinary preparation. Nott and Brainerd "ransacked" all "the material available in the libraries in New York," yet still needed to seek guidance from antislavery advocate William Goodell, and historians George Bancroft (whom Lincoln had met at Brady's) and Richard Hildreth (author of the monumental six-volume *History of the United States*).[41]

While his young editors labored away on footnotes, Lincoln dashed through their proposed revisions to the text. "Some of your notes I do not understand," he reported of the marked copy Nott had provided. Others he did—and for the most part, he did not like them. In an extraordinarily detailed response, the busy candidate itemized his objections and corrections, demonstrating that he wished to maintain full control over the contents of his most important 1860 campaign address. This was the longest, most detailed letter Lincoln ever wrote about one of his speeches. Clearly, he continued to believe Cooper Union sufficiently important to require his scrupulous attention:[42]

So far as is intended merely to improve in grammar, and elegance of composition, I am quite agreed; but I do not wish the sense changed, or modified, to a hair's breadth. And you, not having studied the particular points so closely as I have, can not be quite sure that you do not change the sense when you do not intend it. For instance, in a note at bottom of first page, you proposed to substitute "Democrats" for "Douglas." But what I am saying there is *true* of Douglas, and is not true of "Democrats" generally; so that the proposed substitution would be a very considerable blunder.

Your proposed insertion of "residences" though it would do little or no harm, is not at all necessary to the sense I was trying to convey. On page 5 your proposed grammatical change would certainly do no harm. The *"impudently absurd"* I stick to. The striking out *"he"* and inserting *"we"* turns the sense exactly wrong. The striking out *"upon it"* leaves the sense too general and incomplete. The sense is "act as they acted *upon that question"*—not as they acted generally.

After considering your proposed changes on page 7, I do not think them material, but I am willing to defer to you in relation to them.

On page 9, striking out *"to us"* is probably right. The word *"lawyer's"* I wish retained. The word *"Courts"* struck out twice, I wish reduced to "Court" and retained. "Court" as a collection more properly governs the plural "have" as I understand. "The" preceding "Court," in the latter case, must also be retained. The words "quite," "as," and "or" on the same page, I wish retained. The italicising, and quotation marking, I have no objection to.

As to the note at bottom, I do not think any too much is admitted. What you propose on page 11 is right. I return your copy of the speech, together with one printed here, under my own hasty supervising. That at New York was printed without any supervision by me. If you conclude to publish a new edition, allow me to see the proof-sheets.[43]

Nott did exactly as he was asked, however disingenuous Lincoln's odd claim that he had played no role in supervising the first New York printing of his speech. The young man forwarded a set of proofs to Lincoln for his examination, promising to forward the revised galleys as well. Just as he had at the *Tribune* on the night of his speech, Lincoln wanted not one, but two chances to ensure the accuracy of the printed version.

But on August 28, Nott again wrote to Springfield to tell Lincoln that his publisher had insisted on proceeding with the printing of the pamphlet *"without waiting to send you the proofs"*—evidently referring to a second round of galleys. Nott hastened to assure Lincoln he had "made no alterations other than those you sanctioned," save for two. Inexplicably, three days later Nott forwarded the corrected proofs anyway, accompanied by the explanation that two thousand copies were to be printed immediately, followed by a mass-produced "stereotyped" edition that would definitely incorporate Lincoln's last-minute revisions.[44]

Ultimately, Nott did get to impose a few revisions of his own. He inserted a minor word change in a quotation from the Constitution. And he had spotted and corrected a more important error. The old Georgia congressman Abraham Baldwin, Nott insisted to Lincoln, had never voted for the Ordinance of 1787, as Lincoln had asserted in his New York address. In fact, Baldwin had not voted on the measure at all, as Nott discovered, having ceded his place in Congress that session to one William Pierce, who did vote for the Ordinance. Nott now proposed—unless Lincoln objected—to change from four to three the sentence "where you sum up the number of times he voted."[45]

Lincoln let Nott's change stand, though he blamed Greeley's *New York Weekly Tribune*, not himself, for the error. "I have looked over the sheets hastily," he reported on September 6, "and herewith return them. You perceive I have touched them only very lightly. The notes you add I have not attempted to compare with originals, leaving that entirely to you. I think the notes are exceedingly valuable." He referred to a separate letter on the Abraham Baldwin matter (which Nott never seems to have received), and renewed his thanks to the Young Men's Republican Union for "their exceeding kindness towards me in this matter."[46]

In retrospect, the editors did a brilliant job of recreating Lincoln's research—though not an absolutely perfect one. The edited version had a handful of errors in italicization; it is unlikely that anyone noticed.

A few weeks later, on September 17, Nott shipped off 250 copies of the newly published pamphlet to Lincoln, who replied with renewed words of gratitude even before the shipment arrived. "I am greatly obliged to you for what you have done, and what you propose to do."[47]

Lincoln was undoubtedly pleased by the production. The handsomely printed thirty-two-page edition, encased in a durable cover, featured thirty-five copious source notes, impressively detailing all of Lincoln's laborious historical investigations, reminding readers that he was a politician who reverenced, studied, and learned from history. He did not merely voice his opinions; he armed himself with facts, however difficult to obtain them. Understandably, the editors wanted their readers to know how much work the sourcing had required—both of Lincoln and of them. As their preface declared:

> No one who has not actually attempted to verify its details can understand the patient research and historical labor which it embodies. The history of our earlier politics is scattered through numerous journals, statutes, pamphlets, and letters; and these are defective in completeness and accuracy of statement, and in indices and tables of contents. Neither can any one who has not travelled over this precise ground, appreciate the accuracy of every trivial detail, or the self-denying impartiality with which Mr. Lincoln has turned from the testimony of "the fathers," on the general question of Slavery, to present the single question which he discusses. From the first line to the last—from his premises to his conclusion, he travels with a swift, unerring directness which no logician ever excelled—an argument complete and full, without the affectation of learning, and without the stiffness which usually accompanies dates and details.[48]

The result, the editors contended, was not just a pamphlet but a true "historical work—brief, complete, profound, impartial, truthful—which will survive the time and the occasion that called it forth, and be esteemed hereafter, no less for its intrinsic worth than its unpretending modesty."[49]

Like Lincoln's February 27 appearance at Cooper Union, the pamphlet version of his speech apparently did little to generate revenues for the Young Men's Central Republican Union, though it did not lose money either. Writing to the son of his old coeditor, Cephas Brainerd, forty-seven years later to express his delight about a planned reprint,

Nott commented: "The cost, or rather absence of cost . . . arouses my wonder and admiration, and makes me wish that you had been our financial manager in 1860."[50]

In political terms, however, the 1860 Nott-Brainerd edition profited Lincoln enormously. It multiplied the circulation of his most important campaign-year oration, and kept both its impressive research and its conciliatory spirit before the voting public. As Lincoln later confided to New York senator Ira Harris, perhaps after reminiscing one day about his trip to the city and its remarkable impact on his life, Cooper Union was the only one of his speeches that he ever saw handsomely published. "It seems sad that the author of the Gettysburg Address and the second inaugural should never have seen his wondrously chosen words decently printed," commented the editors who brought out the 1907 facsimile. "But it also seems appropriate that if but one thing of his writing was to be set before his eyes in fairly good type, it should be the speech that made him President."[51]

Charles C. Nott agreed that their endeavor gave Lincoln "one of the greatest pleasures of his life," constituting "the first time in his life where he had been treated as a scholarly man, as a thoughtful statesman" instead of as a "Western Stump Orator."[52]

As Nott saw it: "Notwithstanding the heat and bitterness of the time," the annotated Cooper Union pamphlet was "the most truthful and dignified campaign document that was ever issued." But Nott insisted that some of the credit belonged to its young editors. "Its truthfulness," he wrote, "it owed to Mr. Lincoln, its dignity to Mr. Brainerd and myself."[53]

Nott left no doubt what inspired the production. Writing more than fifty years after Lincoln took the stage at Cooper Union, he wrote: "We believed that it would make him President and ban slavery from the Territories, and we gave our best efforts to make it worthy of a great cause."[54]

THE COOPER UNION Address was to enjoy one more influential incarnation during the campaign of 1860: as a prominently featured appendix in a host of book-length campaign biographies that rolled off the presses that summer and fall, specifically designed to introduce the Republican presidential candidate to an electorate still largely unfamiliar with him. As many as two hundred thousand copies of various Lincoln biographies circulated during the 1860 contest. All extolled the candidate's inspiring rise from his log cabin birth to the threshold of the White House. All marveled at his self-education. All mentioned the Cooper Union address—the culmination of his prenomination career—with many reprinting it in full. And a good number of them included the other Cooper Union "masterpiece"—Brady's day-of-the-speech photograph—to illustrate their subject, making him look as presidential as his speech made him sound.[55]

The very first such campaign life, the so-called "Wigwam Edition" of *The Life, Speeches, and Public Services of Abram Lincoln*, may have gotten the nominee's given name wrong ("It seems as if the question of whether my first name is "Abraham" or "Abram" will never be settled," Lincoln complained around the same time. "It is *Abraham*"). But it did feature the Cooper Union photograph on its cover, and the entire Cooper Union Address inside.[56]

Similarly, a so-called "Wide Awake" edition of *The Life and Public Services of Hon. Abraham Lincoln, of Illinois, and Hon. Hannibal Hamlin, of Maine*—his vice-presidential running mate—displayed J. C. Buttre's engraved adaptation of the Brady photograph as a frontispiece, and devoted twenty-two pages to a reprint of the address. Calling it "perhaps one of the greatest speeches of his life," J. H. Barrett's best-selling *Life of Abraham Lincoln* printed highlights from the address, including the peroration, and called it "the last of the great speeches" of the pre-White House Lincoln. "It forms a brilliant close to this period of his life, and a fitting prelude to that on which he is believed to be about to enter."[57]

Perhaps the most fitting biographical tribute came from D. W. Bartlett, a political observer whose 1859 collection of life sketches of the likely presidential candidates for 1860 had not even included Lincoln—though it astonishingly featured Jefferson Davis as a possible contender for the Democratic nod. Lincoln's nomination belatedly inspired from Bartlett a full-length life story, along with a nineteen-page transcript of the Cooper Union Address, and a by-now-standard frontispiece engraving after the Brady photo.[58]

Bartlett's book presented not only the words of the address, but also an evocative description of Lincoln's style of delivery—a reminder of the engaging technique with which the speaker had captivated his New York audience back on February 27:

> His manner before a popular assembly is as he pleases to make it, being either superlatively ludicrous or very impressive. He employs but little gesticulation, but when he desires to make a point, produces a shrug of his shoulders, an elevation of his eyebrows, a depression of his mouth, and a general manifestation of countenance so comically awkward that it never fails to "bring down the house." His enunciation is slow and emphatic, and his voice, though sharp and powerful, at times has a frequent tendency to dwindle into a shrill and unpleasant sound; but as before stated, the peculiar characteristic of his delivery is the remarkable mobility of his features, the frequent contortions of which excite a merriment his words could not produce.[59]

Of all the 1860 campaign biographies, perhaps the most famous was the work of William Dean Howells, not only because it boasted the best-known author, but because Lincoln reviewed and commented on the text before it was published—including, we must assume, the laudatory description that Howells crafted to report his 1860 appearance in New York: "His speech at Cooper Institute, in the commercial and intellectual metropolis, was the most brilliant success in everything that makes such an effort successful. His audience was vast in numbers, and profoundly attentive. They found him, indeed, lank and angular in form, but of fine oratorical presence; lucid and simple in his style, vigorous in argument." Lincoln changed not a letter of this passage. This, we may conclude, is the way he wanted Cooper Union remembered.[60]

• • •

LATER THAT YEAR, the Democratic party split into Northern and Southern factions, making a Republican victory in the fall almost inevitable. Stephen A. Douglas proved in the end to be as unacceptable to the South as he was to the antislavery men in the North. Although he won the Democratic nomination in June, Southern delegates abandoned the convention in protest and went on to regroup and name John C. Breckinridge of Kentucky as their own nominee. Complicating matters was the emergence of a fourth candidate, John Bell, as standard bearer for a new group calling itself the Constitutional Union party. No one ruled out the possibility that the election might end with no candidate winning enough electoral votes to earn the presidency. In such an event, the House of Representatives would choose a president, and it was unlikely to be Abraham Lincoln.[61]

According to plan, Lincoln stuck close to home between May and November, content to let pamphlets, songsters, biographies, newspapers, tintype badges, and popular prints do the campaigning for him—abetted by the rousing "hullabaloo" enthusiasm of the Wide-Awake marching clubs. Douglas, on the other hand, broke with tradition and hit the campaign trail with a vengeance, ostensibly to visit his ailing mother in New England, but making sure to stop along the way to electioneer. His trip into the Northeast was as damaging as Lincoln's had been helpful. Douglas subjected himself to both physical exhaustion that wrecked his health and political ridicule that injured his prospects. The Douglas barnstorming did little to stem the Republican tide.

On November 7, 1860, nearly 4.7 million white American men went to the polls—a remarkable 80 percent of all eligible voters—to choose their president. Lincoln, whose name did not even appear on the ballots in ten Southern states, won less than 40% of the popular vote nationwide, meaning that six out of every ten voters cast their ballots for his opponents. But Lincoln still managed to capture an overwhelming majority of electoral votes: 180, to 72 for Breckinridge, 39 for Bell, and only 12—Missouri and New Jersey—for Douglas, even though the "Little Giant" captured the second-highest tally of popular votes.

In the states Lincoln had visited on his 1860 tour of New York and New England, Lincoln racked up nearly 55% of the vote:

State	Lincoln	Douglas	Bell	Breckinridge
New York	362,646 (54%)	312,510 (46%)	—	—
Connecticut	43,792 (57%)	15,522 (20%)	3,291 (4%)	14,641 (19%)
Rhode Island	12,244 (61%)	7,707 (39%)	—	—
New Hampshire	37,519 (57%)	25,881 (39%)	441 (0%)	2,112 (3%)
Totals	456,201 (55%)	361,620 (43%)	3,732 (0%)	16,753 (2%)

More important, to go along with his clear popular mandate in these four states, Lincoln secured all fifty electoral votes from the region. But in one of the great ironies of a presidential campaign that in a sense was born in New York City, the city itself—that is, Manhattan and the Bronx— gave him scant support on Election Day, 1860. Douglas received 62,482 votes to Lincoln's 33,290, a 65%–35% landslide. Lincoln went down to decisive defeat as well in Brooklyn (20,583 to 15,883), Queens (4,392 to 3,759), Staten Island (2,370 to 1,408) and Westchester County (8,081 to 6,771). Only a massive outpouring of Lincoln support in northern counties, where he had never uttered a public word, turned the state and its thirty-five electoral votes to the Republicans.

Cooper Union may have helped nominate and elect Lincoln by inspiring an influential outpouring of nationally circulated published transcripts and pamphlets, but in the overwhelmingly Democratic city where Lincoln had risen to deliver the actual speech, it had not produced anything close to victory.

In another sense, it likely did help diminish the anti-Lincoln vote enough to ensure statewide victory. Although Lincoln's vote in New York City amounted to only 35%, it represented a huge improvement over Republican John C. Frémont's tally against Democrat James Buchanan in the presidential election four years earlier. In that 1856 contest, Frémont, too, won New York State, but only because a vigorous third-party challenge by a New Yorker, former President Millard Fill-more, split the anti-Republican vote and threw the state into the Fré-mont column. In 1860, however, the splinter candidates—Breckinridge and Bell—drew scant support in the Empire State. The race boiled down to Lincoln vs. Douglas. Lincoln would still have eked out a statewide victory with no more citywide support than the pitiful vote Frémont had garnered four years earlier, but it would have meant a much closer statewide election, and with the slightest, unpredictable last-minute complication, might have gone the other way. On this score alone, Cooper Union made a tangible difference.

Year	County	Republican	Democratic	Other Parties
1856	New York	17,771 (22%)	41,913 (53%)	19,922 (25%)
1860	New York	33,290 (35%)	62,482 (65%)[62]	

James A. Briggs, Lincoln's Cooper Union cohost, was one of the first to send congratulations "upon your election by the people to the high-est office in the world." As Briggs saw it, picking up a theme from Lin-coln's New York speech: "The Constitution has been vindicated."[63]

That New York State, whoever it chose as president, remained bitterly divided on slavery and race issues—anti-Republican in its southernmost areas, pro-Republican to the north, mirroring the wrenching divisions then plaguing the entire nation—was confirmed by the results of a little-remembered referendum that Election Day: New York's vote on a state constitutional amendment designed to grant suffrage to free African-Americans. Even in a state where slavery had been illegal since 1827, the measure went down to overwhelming defeat, failing in Manhattan alone by more than fifty-five thousand votes, a staggering 86% to 14% affirma-tion of intractable white supremacy and inflexible racial intolerance.[64]

HAD ABRAHAM LINCOLN failed in New York, few would likely recog-nize his name or face today. We might not even recognize the country he went on to defend and rededicate. Without Cooper Union, Lincoln might have ended up, at best, as a historical footnote.

But Abraham Lincoln succeeded. He rose to the most arduous challenge of his career to that point. He delivered a speech that electrified an important audience that included two of the most prominent pro-Republican newspaper editors in the country, who made sure his words then reverberated in print until they reached tens of thousands of readers across the Northern states. Lincoln came to New York an aspiring politician who had endured more defeats than victories, and left politically reinvigorated, and ideally positioned for a political rebirth.

Cooper Union proved a unique confluence of political culture, rhetorical opportunity, technological innovation, and human genius, and it brought Abraham Lincoln to the center stage of American politics at precisely the right time and place, and with precisely the right message: that slavery was wrong, and ought to be confined to the areas where it already existed, and placed on the "course of ultimate extinction"; that the Union was sacred, and could never be rightfully destroyed by sectional discord.

A similar appearance, and a like message, merely a year earlier (thus before the introduction of mass-produced photography) could not have generated the same impact, could not have made Lincoln the principal icon of America's domestic altars. A year later (once the decisive 1860 election had been settled), Lincoln's visit either would not have occurred at all or would not have much mattered. Instead, time, place, and technology happily conspired to Lincoln's enormous benefit that winter—and it could only have happened in New York.

Still, it remains as crucial to understand what the Cooper Union address did *not* accomplish as it is to comprehend what it *did*. For generations, historians have given too much credit where it is *not* due, and paid insufficient attention where it *is*.

In the former category, the Cooper Union address did *not* make Abraham Lincoln a popular hero in New York City, nor translate into popularity among the city's voters, the majority of whom remained confirmed Democrats, eventually of the specifically anti-Lincoln variety.

Neither did the Cooper Union speech help the soon-active Lincoln presidential campaign to wrest New York delegates to their cause at the Republican National Convention that May.

Nor was Cooper Union just a happy accident—a chance meeting of man and audience yielding unexpected results. Rather, Lincoln's visit was a carefully staged act in a messy local political drama, organized to introduce New Yorkers to western Republicans in order to upstage and unhorse William H. Seward. Lincoln's was the last such address in the series, and turned out to be the most sensational, thanks to his meticulous preparation and riveting performance.

The Cooper Union address has been hailed—and in some instances criticized—by modern historians as a conservative speech, but it was not really conservative at all. This is yet another misconception. It was an ingenious attempt to make Republican principles *appear* unthreatening to moderate Northerners by identifying them with historical doctrine. But Lincoln's analysis did not make his message conservative; it merely invited conservatives to hew comfortably to his antislavery message.

Nor did the Cooper Union opportunity inspire from Lincoln a poetic masterpiece (at least until its peroration) on a rhetorical par with his great presidential addresses. This is precisely why the speech remains among the most frequently mentioned, yet least often quoted, of Lincoln's major pre-presidential addresses. For the most part, it was almost mordantly legalistic and historical, an appeal not to passion but to logic.

That is what the Cooper Union address was *not*. It did not win the hearts of New York City voters, New York State convention delegates, or students of great oratory. (Nor did New Yorkers brave a snowstorm to hear him.) And it was not a conservative speech.

Yet the Cooper Union address accomplished as much as any speech Abraham Lincoln ever delivered. Even though it barely created a ripple in New York City voting patterns, it unleashed a tidal wave of celebrity nationwide. And it did much more.

For one thing, it allowed Abraham Lincoln successfully to "campaign" for president of the United States on the North's most prestigious political stage, New York City, without violating mid-nineteenth-century taboos against personal campaigning. As a result, Lincoln there became a serious aspirant for the White House.

Cooper Union also gave Lincoln the chance to "debate" Stephen A. Douglas one last time, without facing the unsettling challenge of again meeting him face to face. Lincoln had never inspired as much press attention as he did in 1858 on the debate trail in Illinois. In New York he revived his long-standing public quarrel with Douglas on a far larger stage, shrewdly calculating that the approach would work even better in Douglas's absence, and earn the same outpouring of newspaper interest, as had the "joint meetings" for the Senate race.

In addition, Cooper Union gave Lincoln the opportunity to bury his lingering reputation as the radical doomsayer who had quoted the Bible in 1858 to warn that "a house divided against itself cannot stand," but then found himself on the defensive during the Lincoln-Douglas debates, repeatedly explaining and softening that position. In New York, Lincoln went on record, in the new political environment toxically charged by the recent John Brown raid at Harpers Ferry, as an unthreatening moderate (not a conservative), committed to accommodation with the evil of slavery, where it existed, if it would save the country. At the same time, he made it clear that he was unwilling to accept responsibility for the country's dissolution if Southern state rights radicals refused to listen to patriotic calls to reason. And he pointedly refused to call slavery right simply because Southern extremists demanded it.

And Cooper Union handed Lincoln, too, a powerful publicity tool with which to reach Republicans nationwide: the New York press. At Cooper Union, Lincoln managed to electrify the media in the media center of the nation.

The Cooper Union invitation also inspired Lincoln's most successful "standard" political speech—one that he successfully repeated and reiterated over the next few weeks with the same focus with which modern politicians take pains to stay "on message" during campaign news cycles.

Of equal significance, Cooper Union gave Lincoln the opportunity to prove his universal appeal beyond the confines of the western frontier that produced him. It demonstrated to the entire eastern region, through newspaper reprints and subsequent personal appearances, that he was a serious, learned, dignified public figure, far more civilized than the prairie-bred storyteller who had mesmerized rowdy crowds on the debate trail in 1858. Cooper Union helped cement Lincoln's reputation as a spellbinding orator while correcting the impression that he was merely a vulgar stump speaker and rustic comedian.

Lincoln's friend and biographer, Isaac N. Arnold, seemed to understand this point perfectly. He believed the "profound and exhaustive" Cooper Union address "surprised" and "delighted" its audience principally because it eschewed "rant, declamation . . . and witty points." It was precisely the opposite of what the crowd expected of a speaker of Lincoln's reputation. Instead, it was a "calm, clear, learned, dignified" brief from "an accurate and laborious student of history," so thoroughly researched and calmly argued, that it was no wonder that Lincoln "awoke the next morning to find himself famous." Arnold was not exaggerating when he pronounced that a speech of such learning, yet presented in such plain language, was simply "unparalleled" in the realm of political rhetoric. It should not surprise modern readers—especially those accustomed to style triumphing over substance—that it ignited so much attention, or spawned such a successful presidential boom. Of course, Lincoln's speech was substantive. But it was also a triumph of stylistic reinvention, illustrated, moreover, by what then constituted high-tech graphics. With one eye on the issues and the other on his image, and seemingly well aware of the power of the reprinted word and picture, Lincoln remade himself in New York on February 27, 1860. It is fair to say that never before or since in American history has a single speech so dramatically catapulted a candidate toward the White House.[65]

Offering restrained scholarship one moment, and pungent assurance the next, the Cooper Union address established Lincoln as both a credible witness to the past and an inspiring leader for the future. Just as the western man emerged in New York as the equal of any eastern sophisticate, the man of ambition transformed himself there into a man of mission, not only electable, but a potential instrument for both preserving the Union and expunging slavery. With America agonizing under the dread of division, Lincoln offered Cooper Union as an anchor: the opportunity, perhaps the final opportunity, to save what the founders had created, purified of the one blight that violated the promise of equality enshrined in the Declaration of Independence. He had expressed such sentiments on the hustings for six long years, articulating them with increasing skill at each successive venue. At Cooper Union, he reached his rhetorical zenith. Soon enough, burdened by the presidency and the war, he would surpass it. But for now, he had accomplished the great work of his career. Without it, his career might well have ended.

All in all, while Cooper Union did not produce significant new first-ballot support for Lincoln's candidacy at the forthcoming Republican convention, it won him enough prominence in the East to transform him into the favorite westerner in the race for the presidential nomination. It all but eclipsed the better-known Edward Bates of Missouri and Salmon P. Chase of Ohio, no mean feat. Lincoln arrived in New York as an ambitious pretender. He returned to Illinois as an intriguing second choice for the White House, deftly positioned to triumph at the convention if the front runner stumbled—which he did.

One can even reasonably speculate that Cooper Union did win Lincoln *enough* admiration, and enough support, among New York City Republicans to limit Democratic voting majorities there that November. Suppressing the opposition vote downstate helped Lincoln eke out an overall statewide victory and win the state's mother lode of electoral votes.

His trip also planted the seeds of popular support that would blossom for the Republicans that autumn in the bellwether states of Connecticut, New Hampshire, and Rhode Island. Lincoln's additional speeches there have never elicited quite the credit they deserve for further transforming the rail-splitter into presidential timber.

In a sense, the Cooper Union address qualifies to be remembered as Abraham Lincoln's first campaign speech for the presidency. What makes it crucially important is that—including the variations on the theme he proceeded to deliver in New England—it was also his *last* presidential campaign address. Bowing to tradition, he would say no more publicly until his election to the White House nine months later.[68]

He did not have to do so. Instead, he helped the speech endure through carefully controlled republication. In print, Lincoln's speech became a best seller. Its prolonged life as a campaign document helped it endure, and helped keep Lincoln's name alive before the voters while he remained at home until the election, unwilling to break precedent and campaign actively in his own behalf for the White House.

Cooper Union was not just a speech: It was a conquest—a public relations triumph, a political coup d'état within the Republican party, and an image transfiguration abetted by the press and illustrated by the most felicitous photo opportunity in American history.

In response to a crucial opportunity to make a national impact—or face an ignominious retreat to the prairie in the same anonymity with which he arrived in New York—Abraham Lincoln not only made a spectacular debut at Cooper Union, he also introduced a new political dialectic. It was characterized by a fresh, lean style of elocution, free of bombast, metaphor, and vituperation, instead constructed out of facts and reason, supported by history and national experience, and infused with moral certainty.

SIX WEEKS AFTER Election Day, on December 20, as Lincoln began contemplating the preparation of his first major speech since appearing at Cooper Union—his forthcoming inaugural address—South Carolina seceded from the Union. The long-dreaded crisis was now at hand, but Lincoln offered nothing new to calm the storm. As one newspaper reported, the president-elect's previously published "sentiments," including what he had "declared in his speech at the Cooper Institute . . . are referred to as embracing the principles and policy of his administration." The abolitionist newspaper the *Liberator* believed this was enough, reminding readers that at Cooper Union Lincoln had declared it "exceedingly desirable that all parts of this Confederacy shall be at peace, and in harmony, with one another." But as the *Liberator* now acknowledged, "utterly useless has all this billing and cooing proved on the part of Mr. Lincoln. The South are eager for his immolation."[66]

⊰ EPILOGUE ⊱

To THE VICTORS belonged the spoils. Abraham Lincoln's 1860 election ended eight years of Democratic party control of federal patronage, opening wide the doors of opportunity for Republicans hungry for jobs, spoils, and favors. Those who helped Lincoln arrange his triumph in the East earlier that year were not forgotten. Here was strong, if subtle, evidence that Lincoln tangibly appreciated Cooper Union's defining role in making him president.

Hiram Barney, the Cooper Union organizer who went on to raise thirty-five thousand dollars for the Lincoln campaign, was rewarded with one of the biggest prizes of all. Lincoln named him collector of the Port of New York, where he proceeded to earn a fortune through the long-prevailing, inherently corrupt system of commissions and fees. After a few years on the job, Barney became a political liability for the administration, and Lincoln reluctantly approved his ouster in 1864. By the following January, Lincoln's debt to his onetime New York host was apparently forgotten; Barney could not even gain access to the president's office after waiting "several hours in vain." In an act of sublime poetic justice, Barney's ouster had been engineered by the onetime presidential hopeful he had jilted back in 1860: William H. Seward.[1]

In September 1862, Lincoln appointed another Cooper Union organizer, Cephas Brainerd, to the post of arbitrator for the United States in the Treaty of England on Suppression of the African Slave

Trade. The post was not only prestigious, it required Brainerd to travel no farther than his own city of New York. The candidate whom Brainerd beat out for the position was none other than his Cooper Union coorganizer James A. Briggs. For a time, President Lincoln evidently could not decide which of them to reward with the plum assignment. In July 1862 he recommended Brainerd, then in August called Briggs "an excellent man," and the following month said he would be "very glad to appoint Briggs." In January 1863, however, the U.S. Senate confirmed Brainerd; Briggs apparently went unrewarded.[2]

A better fate awaited Henry C. Bowen. After boasting that he had "never asked a favor before," Bowen succumbed in 1862 and sought a patronage job from Lincoln as collector of revenue in Brooklyn. James W. Nye was named territorial governor of Nevada in 1862, and three years later became the new state's first United States senator. James F. Babcock, Lincoln's host in New Haven and editor of the city's pro-Republican newspaper, became collector of the Port of New Haven. And Amos Tuck, who kept a watchful eye on Lincoln's son Robert at Exeter, was appointed naval officer for the port of Boston.[3]

Charles C. Nott had a rougher time. When the Civil War broke out, the coeditor of the annotated Cooper Union pamphlet quickly enlisted, rising to the rank of colonel of the 176th New York Volunteers. But he was later captured and spent thirteen months as a prisoner of the Confederacy in Texas, later publishing a best-selling memoir, *The Cavalry Saddle and the Prison Camp*. In January 1865, President Lincoln belatedly rewarded Nott, appointing him a judge of the U.S. Court of Claims. He stayed on the bench for more than thirty years. At least Lincoln needed to do nothing directly to reward the eminent poet-editor William Cullen Bryant, who had introduced him at Cooper Union. But it is probably no coincidence that the president managed to name Bryant's barely literate brother, John, an Illinois Republican, as a collector of internal revenue in 1862.[4]

LINCOLN RETURNED TO New York in February 1861, now as president-elect, en route to Washington for his inauguration. For days, as his train moved slowly from Springfield east to Albany, then south to Manhattan, he maintained the official silence on policy matters that he had adopted shortly after returning home from New York nearly a year before. His often light-hearted impromptu remarks at stops along the way managed to worry, rather than reassure, the country.

Once again he booked rooms at the Astor House on Broadway, but this time, unlike his solitary disembarkation in 1860, his arrival did not escape public notice. As his carriage rolled down Broadway, large crowds gathered along the streets. But there was no eruption of the kind of cheering he had heard during his last visit at Cooper Union.

Walt Whitman was on the scene for his return, mortified by the absence of what he called "the glad exulting thunder-shouts of countless unloos'd throats of men." The *New York Herald* agreed that the chilly New York welcome lacked "human roar and magnetism." On the other hand, Whitman was grateful that no "outbreak or insult" occurred, for as he well knew, Cooper Union success notwithstanding, Lincoln "possess'd no personal popularity in New York and not much political." At least one admirer carried a banner that recalled Cooper Union: "Right Makes Might." That day, Lincoln attended a reception in his honor at City Hall, hosted by a mayor hard at work behind the scenes plotting to take New York—like the South—out of the Union. "I reckon," Lincoln is said to have responded when warned about the scheme, "that it will be some time before the front door sets up house-keeping on its own account."[5]

Formally addressing the mayor's reception, and then appearing on City Hall's balcony to greet a crowd below, Lincoln reiterated his position—more solemnly—in the last remarks he would ever deliver in New York. "There is nothing," he warned, "that can ever bring me willingly to consent to the destruction of this Union, under which not only the great commercial city of New York, but the whole country has acquired its greatness." Fully aware that New Yorkers "do not by a majority agree with me in political sentiments," he insisted that he nonetheless continued to find inspiration in "the renown of those great men who have stood here, and spoke here, and been heard here."[6]

●　●　●

IN RESPONSE TO his Cooper Union invitation, Lincoln traveled to New York City to deliver a speech designed, at least in part, to outflank favorite son William H. Seward. Eight months later, in what amounted to a reverse iteration of that journey, New Yorker Seward traveled to Lincoln's home town of Springfield, Illinois. But it was not to under-mine him. Still chafing from his defeat at the convention, the onetime Republican front runner nonetheless gamely delivered a rousing speech urging Lincoln's victory.

Once elected, Lincoln repaid Seward's loyalty—and also recognized his pre-eminence in the party—by naming him secretary of state. Still, Seward likely continued to agonize. Why had Lincoln been able to use Cooper Union to overcome his controversial "house divided" image, while Seward had failed to ameliorate his own "irrepressible conflict" message with his similarly conciliatory 1860 Senate oration? He may finally have discovered the explanation shortly before Lincoln's inaugu-ration: the new president's better instinct for the spoken word, and his vastly superior craftsmanship as a writer. Asked to review Lincoln's inaugural address, Seward suggested a new conclusion:

> I close. We are not we must not be aliens or enemies but fellow countrymen and brethren. Although passion has strained our bonds of affection too hardly they must not be broken. I am sure they will not be broken. The mystic chords which proceeding from so many battle fields and so many patriot graves pass through all the hearts and all the hearths in this broad conti-nent of ours will yet again harmonize in their ancient music when ["touched as they surely" crossed out] breathed upon by the ["better angel" crossed out] guardian angel of the nation.

Ever the masterful editor—as well as writer—Lincoln retained the idea but adroitly reworked the paragraph, and out of a sentimental trifle came poetry. With Lincoln's subtle, characteristic recrafting, it read:

> I am loth [sic] to close. We are not enemies, but friends. We must not be enemies. Though passion may have strained, it must not

break our bonds of affection. The mystic chords of memory, stretching from every battle-field, and patriot grave, to every living heart and hearthstone, all over this broad land, will yet swell the chorus of the Union, when again touched, as surely they will be, by the better angels of our nature.[7]

Seward served in the State Department throughout the Lincoln administration, surviving an attempted 1862 ouster backed by two of the foes who had shared the stage with Lincoln on the night of his Cooper Union speech: Horace Greeley and David Dudley Field. On the night of April 14, 1865, at practically the same moment as John Wilkes Booth stole into Ford's Theatre to shoot Abraham Lincoln, one of Booth's accomplices, Lewis Powell, forced his way into Seward's home near the White House, and repeatedly slashed at the secretary with a large knife. Badly scarred, he survived to resume his duties, and served in his post until 1869—what would have been the end of the second Lincoln administration.

BY THE TIME he arrived back in New York as president-elect, Lincoln looked little like the man who had visited the city to speak at Cooper Union the year before. "Tired, sunburned, adorned with huge whiskers," a reporter noticed earlier in his journey, he appeared quite "unlike the hale, smooth-shaven, red-cheeked individual who is represented upon the popular prints."[8]

Many of those prints had been based on, or blatantly copied from, the riveting Mathew Brady photograph for which Lincoln had posed the day of his Cooper Union speech. Now, thanks to Lincoln's unexpected, unannounced decision to change his appearance by growing a beard, the engraved and lithographed adaptations were suddenly obsolete.

So was Brady's original. But the tonsorial decision that doomed Brady's ability to further market his original photograph proved a bonanza for the derivative printmakers. They simply dusted off their outdated plates and stones and altered them, imposing whiskers whose length and thickness they could only at this point guess. However ludicrous, their products were eagerly purchased by a public eager for a glimpse of their new president's new look.

Thus the "Cooper Union Lincoln" survived for years—outliving the 1860 campaign, even the subject himself, copied in America and Europe alike, all but permanently disguised behind the famous whiskers that Lincoln did not wear when he sat at Brady's gallery.

COOPER UNION ITSELF remained a locus for political debate and patriotic expression during the 1860 campaign, throughout the Civil War—and after. Following on the heels of Lincoln's appearance, the American Anti-Slavery Society convened at the school in April, and both Republicans and Democrats staged "mass meetings" there in June. That October, the new Constitutional Union party hosted a "fusion" rally of its own at Cooper Union.[9]

Among the orators who followed Lincoln to its Great Hall was Frederick Douglass, who called for immediate emancipation there in February 1862. The following month, abolitionists unanimously passed a set of antislavery resolutions at Cooper Union. Organizers promptly sent the document, signed by forty-nine New Yorkers, on to the White House. In January 1863, with the Emancipation Proclamation now a reality, Douglass returned to Cooper Union to speak at a huge "Jubilee of Freedom."[10]

Lincoln himself never entered Cooper Union again, but not for lack of opportunity. In November 1863, barely a week after delivering the Gettysburg Address, the president was invited to address a mass meeting at Cooper Union organized to support his call for additional volunteers for the military. Organizers asked Lincoln to "Encourage by your voice the active efforts of the loyal men of this City in support of the Union Cause."[11]

"Nothing would be more grateful to my feelings, or [in] better accord with my judgment than to contribute, if I could, by my presence, or otherwise, to that eminently patriotic object," Lincoln replied. At the time, however, Congress was preparing to reconvene and Lincoln was suffering from a mild but debilitating case of smallpox. Tempting as it was to return to the scene of his great 1860 triumph, the president declined the summons, explaining that "the now early meeting of congress, together with a temporary illness, render my attendance impossible." But he did send a message to be read aloud, in which he declared: "Honor to the Soldier, and Sailor everywhere, who bravely bears his country's cause. Honor also to the citizen who cares for his brother in the field, and serves, as he best can, the same cause— honor to him, only less than to him, who braves, for the common good, the storms of heaven and the storms of battle." With that ringing sentiment, delivered by a substitute, Lincoln's second and last "Cooper Union address" ended.[12]

Less than two years later, organizers of an April 11, 1865, meeting to mark the anniversary of the attack on Fort Sumter tried one more time to lure the president back to Cooper Union. Again, Lincoln did not go. Had he traveled to New York that week, Lincoln would have been unable to go to Ford's Theatre on April 14. He would have eluded John Wilkes Booth's Good Friday plot to end his life.[13]

Future presidents did speak at the Great Hall, among them Ulysses S. Grant and William Howard Taft. Then in 1940, the Cooper Union inaugurated an annual Lincoln lecture. Twenty years later, on the centennial of Lincoln's Cooper Union address, Ralph McGill, editor of the *Atlanta Constitution*, used the occasion to call for a new national dialogue on race. A hundred years earlier, McGill reminded his audience, Lincoln had called for a similar dialogue, which the South had resisted, choosing secession and war. He worried that the region would be equally hostile to rapprochement now.[14]

Cooper Union's long reign as a political arena came to a bizarre climax during the bitter 1977 Democratic primary campaign for mayor of New York. One summer evening, as candidates Bella Abzug, Mario Cuomo, Percy Sutton, Herman Badillo, Edward Koch, and incumbent Abraham D. Beame sat on the stage of the Great Hall engaged in a televised debate, an intruder raced down the aisle of the auditorium and hurled a pie at the mayor. Reacting with lightning speed—worried, he explained later, that the prankster was hurling something more dangerous—Cuomo, a future New York governor, leaped off the high stage and tackled the pie-thrower. It was the last dramatic political news event in

Cooper Union's history—until 2003, when Democratic presidential candidate Howard Dean stood in the Great Hall to pledge "to bring white Americans and black Americans" together, and also to concede that he had been "clumsy" in offering to extend his appeal to Southerners who display the Confederate flag on their trucks.[15]

PERHAPS INSPIRED by his father's visit to Phillips Exeter Academy, Robert Todd Lincoln passed his grueling college entrance exams in late 1860, and went on to Harvard and Harvard Law School. He later served as secretary of war, ambassador to the Court of St. James, and president of the Pullman Company. Ironically, the success spawned by the trip to New York and New England—Lincoln's election to the presidency—doomed his relationship with his father. "Henceforth," he admitted, "any great intimacy between us became impossible." After the assassination, Robert lamented: "I scarcely even had ten minutes quiet talk with him during his Presidency, on account of his constant devotion to business."[16]

Robert's school friend George Clayton Latham, who accompanied Lincoln and Bob to the Concord and Manchester, New Hampshire, speaking engagements, did not fare quite as well. He subsequently failed the Harvard exams for a second time, in response to which a busy Abraham Lincoln took the time to write a now-famous letter of encouragement. "In your temporary failure there is no evidence that you may not yet be a better scholar, and a more successful man in the great struggle of life, than many others, who have entered college more easily," Lincoln advised George on July 23, 1860. "You are sure to succeed." Not long afterward, the new president's expectations were fulfilled. George Latham passed his college entrance exams—not for Harvard, but for Yale.[17]

MORE THAN THREE years after Lincoln visited their charity school, the impoverished boys of the Five Points House of Industry—boys with names like McCarty, Donague, Carey, Ryan, O'Neil, and Higgins—wrote a letter to the president. They wanted him to know that they still remembered "with pleasure your visit to our School on a Sunday afternoon, in the month of March, 1860." They had forgotten neither his message nor his example. And now he had consecrated his inspiring rise from poverty by issuing the Emancipation Proclamation. It is unlikely Lincoln ever prized a letter more. As the 118 signatories declared:

> We also remember that you then said the way was open to every boy present, if honest, industrious, and perserv[er]ing, to the attainment of a high and honorable position.
>
> We take the liberty herein to congratulate you, sir, that your own life history illustrates the truth of the words you then addressed to us; and that so soon thereafter your own countrymen should have set their seal to your honesty and trustworthiness by conferring upon you the highest honors in the gift of a free people.
>
> We pray God, the All-Wise Governor of the universe to have you in His care and guidance, to enlighten you by His wisdom, and to further honor you as His instrument in liberating a race, and in leading your countrymen through present troubles, to righteousness, peace, and prosperity. May He ever own and bless you and yours.[18]

ON FEBRUARY 27, 1860, Lincoln had concluded his Cooper Union address by declaring that "right makes might." On April 14, 1865, actor John Wilkes Booth sat down to write to his mother of his contrary belief that "might makes right." Hours later, Booth murdered the president in Washington.[19]

Henry Ward Beecher, whom Lincoln had heard preach twice during his visit east, now eulogized him. "Four years ago, O Illinois, we took from your midst an untried man, and from among the people; we return him to you as a mighty conqueror. Not thine any more, but the nation's; not ours, but the world's."[20]

William Cullen Bryant, the poet-editor who had introduced Lincoln at the Great Hall, was inspired to express his own sadness in verse:

> *In sorrow by thy bier we stand,*
> *Amid the awe that hushes all,*
> *And speak the anguish of a land*
> *That shook with horror at thy fall.*

Thy task is done; the bond are free;
We bear thee to an honored grave,
Whose proudest monument shall be
The broken fetters of a slave.[21]

At the funeral in Washington, Lincoln's rousing Cooper Union call was revived. Clerks of the State Department wore a special silk mourning ribbon, beneath whose portrait of the late president were the only slightly corrupted words: "Let us have faith that RIGHT MAKES MIGHT and in that faith unto the end dare to do our duty as we understand it." When Lincoln's remains reached New York, observers noted that "the Cooper Institute was decorated very neatly. On the front, over the arch and door, were streamers of black and white muslin, and in the centre a large star made of black and white crape, with the initials A. L."[22]

But New York remained a city of absurd as well as sublime expressions and exhibitions. Three months after the funeral, fire struck Barnum's Museum, that gaudy centerpiece of the Broadway that Lincoln had come to know. One of the few exhibits rescued from the flames was the wax figure of Jefferson Davis, Lincoln's Confederate counterpart. Still smarting from the long war and the assassination of the President, a mob of angry New Yorkers strung it up from a lamppost.[23]

Even that odd incident was more comprehensible than New York's bizarre vindication of Booth ally John H. Surratt. Surratt's mother Mary had been convicted and executed as a conspirator in the Lincoln assassination plot. John, himself a suspect, had been pursued halfway around the world for years. Finally captured in Egypt and brought home to stand trial for complicity in the president's murder, he somehow managed to escape conviction for any crime. And then, on December 9, 1870—more than five years after Lincoln's death, more than ten years after Lincoln's speech inside the Great Hall—John H. Surratt appeared on stage in New York to deliver a celebrated lecture on John Wilkes Booth and his plot to kidnap, then murder, the sixteenth president of the United States.[24]

The place was Cooper Union.

⊰ APPENDIX ⊱

Abraham Lincoln's Cooper Union Address
New York, February 27, 1860

THE FOLLOWING TEXT is an amalgam, but one that I hope provides a useful, even definitive, text of the speech that made Lincoln president.

Lincoln's Cooper Union address was initially published by four New York newspapers on February 28, 1860, the day after its delivery. Though he later denied doing so, Lincoln helped supervise its preparation in one of these journals, the *New York Tribune*, which may have shared the approved text with the others. Shortly thereafter, the paper issued the address in pamphlet form as a part of its *Tribune Tract* series.

The text that follows here faithfully recreates instead the formal, heavily annotated thirty-two-page edition that was subsequently prepared by Charles C. Nott and Cephas Brainerd of the Young Men's Republican Union of New York, Lincoln's Cooper Union hosts. It was published in September 1860, as a Lincoln presidential campaign document, by George F. Nesbitt Printers and Stationers of New York, and enjoyed wide distribution.

To aid in its creation as a postconvention campaign piece, Lincoln personally corrected the existing *Tribune* edition, then directed his young editors to the sources he had consulted when researching his oration back in Springfield. Lincoln maintained a robust correspondence with Nott, precisely detailing his editorial wishes, and ultimately proofread the galleys and footnotes. The result is this final, approved copy of the speech— the nearest thing to an "authorized" text of the Cooper Union address, since Lincoln did not preserve the original handwritten manuscript.

Surviving original copies of the 1860 "Young Republican" pamphlet are highly coveted today by Lincoln collectors, although an accurate reprint, complete with notes, can be found in *The Collected Works of Abraham Lincoln*, published in the 1950s.

I have incorporated within the Nott-Brainerd edition record of crowd interruptions for "applause" and "cheers." Although the *New York Tribune* reported that the "vast assemblage frequently rang with cheers and shouts of applause," it failed to indicate such reactions in its published text. Among the four February 28 newspaper reprints, in fact only the pro-Democratic *New York Herald* attempted to indicate what it called the "frequent and irrepressible applause." No other transcript corroborates these interruptions, and of course there is no way to know for certain whether its reporter accurately identified Lincoln's applause lines. Nevertheless, it is the only such transcript we know of, and for this reason alone, it deserves to be remembered.

The *Herald* text of the speech was considered definitive enough in its day. It was subsequently adapted for one of the earliest Lincoln campaign biographies, the "Wide-Awake Edition" of *The Life and Public Services of Hon. Abraham Lincoln, of Illinois, and Hon. Hannibal Hamlin, of Maine* (his running mate), published by Thayer & Eldridge of Boston in late May or early June, 1860. The book adopted interesting subheadings and paragraphing (superior to Lincoln's own way of re-presenting the speech, in my view) but they are not employed here.

Nor was the Thayer & Eldridge reprint by any means a perfect edition. Its text is at variance with other versions at several points in the address—some of which are noted on the following pages in editorial notes. Inexplicably, an entire section appearing in both the newspaper reports and the later authorized edition, beginning with "In the language of Mr. Jefferson (page 273) and ending with "human nature cannot be changed" (page 274)—was omitted from the Thayer & Eldridge reprint. It is included here, along with a wonderful little section, beginning with "You did not sweep New York" (page 271), which evidently delighted his listeners, and certainly merits inclusion.

By inserting the record of crowd response, moreover, it is possible for the first time to recreate the speech both as it was originally heard, and as Lincoln wanted it remembered. Thereby we come closer than we ever have before to the words Lincoln uttered at Cooper Union, together with the response of his New York audience.

Interestingly, as this transcript suggests, the applause and laughter from the audience occasionally erupted at unexpected moments—yet seldom in response to those crowd-pleasing rhetorical flourishes that a modern reader suspects might arouse a crowd. One newspaper reported that Lincoln's constant reiteration of phrases did elicit "audible grins," whatever those might be, but the *Herald* reprint did not so indicate, so we have no corroboration of this entirely believable testimony—only our assumption that it describes precisely the kind of reaction Lincoln anticipated, intended, and received.

The applause lines that *were* recorded, however, provide valuable insight into the New York political culture of 1860, and show how a dexterous western politician understood and appealed to it so well. Lincoln's mastery of history evokes tremendous appreciation. His famous "word to the South," on the other hand, surprisingly inspires what we may only surmise was a derisive howl of laughter. As for his palliating references to John Brown, they win neither applause nor shouts of disapproval—only laughter—as if the very idea that responsible Republicans could endorse Brown's radicalism is a joke. Did Lincoln expect he would get this kind of reaction? He certainly found out when he mentioned John Brown's name.

A final word: Occasional editorial notes have been inserted in both the text of the speech and the Nott-Brainerd footnotes to help the reader identify some of the more obscure references. The original "Young Republican" pamphlet listed the sources as "Note 1," Note 2," etc.; for purposes of this reproduction, the preferred modern footnoting style has been adopted.

Otherwise the text is as Lincoln approved it in 1860.

ADDRESS

MR. PRESIDENT AND FELLOW CITIZENS OF NEW-YORK:—

The facts with which I shall deal this evening are mainly old and familiar; nor is there anything new in the general use I shall make of them. If there shall be any novelty, it will be in the mode of presenting the facts, and the inferences and observations following that presentation.

In his speech last autumn, at Columbus, Ohio, as reported in "The New-York Times," Senator Douglas said:

"Our fathers, when they framed the Government under which we live, understood this question just as well, and even better, than we do now."

I fully indorse this, and I adopt it as a text for this discourse. [*Applause.*] I so adopt it because it furnishes a precise and an agreed starting point for a discussion between Republicans and that wing of the Democracy headed by Senator Douglas. It simply leaves the inquiry: *"What was the understanding those fathers had of the question mentioned?"*

What is the frame of government under which we live?

The answer must be: "The Constitution of the United States." That Constitution consists of the original, framed in 1787, (and under which the present government first went into operation,) and twelve subsequently framed amendments, the first ten of which were framed in 1789.[1]

Who were our fathers that framed the Constitution? I suppose the "thirty-nine" who signed the original instrument may be fairly called our fathers who framed that part of the present Government. It is almost exactly true to say they framed it, and it is altogether true to

---

1. The Constitution is attested September 17, 1787. It was ratified by all of the States, excepting North Carolina and Rhode Island, in 1788, and went into operation on the first Wednesday in January, 1789. The first Congress proposed, in 1789, ten articles of amendments, all of which were ratified. Article XI. of the amendments was prepared by the Third Congress, in 1794, and Article XII. by the Eighth Congress, in 1803. Another Article was proposed by the Eleventh Congress, prohibiting *citizens* from receiving titles of nobility, presents or offices, from foreign nations. Although this has been printed as one of the amendments, it was in fact never ratified, being approved by but twelve States. *Vide* Message of President Monroe, Feb. 4, 1818.

say they fairly represented the opinion and sentiment of the whole nation at that time. Their names, being familiar to nearly all, and accessible to quite all, need not now be repeated.[2]

I take these "thirty-nine," for the present, as being "our fathers who framed the Government under which we live."

What is the question which, according to the text, those fathers understood "just as well, and even better than we do now?"

It is this: Does the proper division of local from federal authority, or anything in the Constitution, forbid our Federal Government to control as to slavery in our Federal Territories?

Upon this, Senator Douglas holds the affirmative, and Republicans the negative. This affirmation and denial form an issue; and this issue—this question—is precisely what the text declares our fathers understood "better than we." [Cheers.]

Let us now inquire whether the "thirty-nine," or any of them, ever acted upon this question; and if they did, how they acted upon it—how they expressed that better understanding?

In 1784, three years before the Constitution—the United States then owning the Northwestern Territory, and no other,[3] the Congress of the Confederation had before them the question of prohibiting slavery in that Territory; and four of the "thirty-nine" who

---

2. The Convention consisted of sixty-five members. Of these ten did not attend the Convention, and sixteen did not sign the Constitution. Of these sixteen, six refused to sign, and published their reasons for so refusing, viz: Robert Yates and John Lansing, of New-York; Edmund Randolph and George Mason, of Virginia; Luther Martin, of Maryland, and Elbridge Gerry, of Mass. Alexander Hamilton alone subscribed for New-York, and Rhode Island was not represented in the Convention. The names of the "thirty-nine," and the States which they represented are subsequently given.

3. The cession of territory was authorized by New-York, Feb. 19, 1780; by Virginia, January 2, 1781, and again, (without certain conditions at first imposed,) "at their sessions, begun on the 20th day of October, 1783;" by Mass., Nov. 13, 1784; by Conn., May —, 1786; by S. Carolina, March 8, 1787; by N. Carolina, Dec.—, 1789; and by Georgia at some time prior to April, 1802.

The deeds of cession were executed by New-York, March 1, 1781; by Virginia, March 1, 1784; by Mass., April 19, 1785; by Conn., Sept. 13, 1786; by S. Carolina, August 9, 1787; by N. Carolina, Feb. 25, 1790; and by Georgia, April 24, 1802. Five of these grants were therefore made before the adoption of the Constitution, and one afterward; while the sixth (North Carolina) was authorized before, and consummated afterward. The cession of this State contains the express proviso "that no regulations made, or to be made by Congress, shall tend to emancipate slaves." The cession of Georgia conveys the Territory subject to the Ordinance of '87, except the provision prohibiting slavery.

(continued on next page)

afterward framed the Constitution, were in that Congress, and voted on that question. Of these, Roger Sherman, Thomas Mifflin, and Hugh Williamson voted for the prohibition,[4] thus showing that, in their understanding, no line dividing local from federal authority, nor anything else, properly forbade the Federal Government to control as to slavery in federal territory. The other of the four—James M'Henry—voted against the prohibition, showing that, for some cause, he thought it improper to vote for it.[5]

In 1787, still before the Constitution, but while the Convention was in session framing it, and while the Northwestern Territory still was the only territory owned by the United States, the same question of prohibiting slavery in the territory again came before the Congress of the Confederation; and two more of the "thirty-nine" who afterward signed the Constitution, were in that Congress, and voted on the question. They were William Blount and William Few;[6] and they both voted for the prohibition—thus showing that,

---

(*continued from previous page*) These dates are also interesting in connection with the extraordinary assertions of Chief Justice Taney, (19 How, page 434,) that the "example of Virginia was soon afterwards followed by other States," and that (p. 436) the power in the Constitution "to dispose of and make all needed rules and regulations respecting the Territory or other property belonging to the United States," was intended only "to transfer to the new Government the property then held in common," "and has no reference whatever to any Territory or other property, which the new sovereignty might afterwards itself acquire." On this subject, *vide* Federalist, No. 43, sub. 4 and 5.

4. Sherman was from Connecticut; Mifflin from Penn.; Williamson from North Carolina, and M'Henry from Maryland.

5. What Mr. M'Henry's views were, it seems impossible to ascertain. When the Ordinance of '87 was passed he was sitting in the Convention. He was afterward appointed Secretary of War [under Washington, appointed in 1796—ed.]; yet no record has thus far been discovered of his opinion. Mr. M'Henry also wrote a biography of La Fayette [he had been La Fayette's private secretary—ed.], which, however, cannot be found in any of the public libraries, among which may be mentioned the State Library at Albany, and the Astor, Society, and Historical Society Libraries at New-York.

   Hamilton says of him, in a letter to Washington (*Works*, vol. 6, p. 65): "M'Henry you know. He would give no strength to the Administration, but he would not disgrace the office; his views are good."

6. William Blount was from North Carolina, and William Few, from Georgia—the two States which afterward ceded their territory to the United States. In addition to these facts the following extract from the speech of Rufus King in the Senate, on the Missouri Bill, shows the entire unanimity with which the Southern States approved the prohibition:—

in their understanding, no line dividing local from federal authority, nor anything else, properly forbade the Federal Government to control as to slavery in federal territory. This time the prohibition became a law, being part of what is now well known as the Ordinance of '87.[7]

The question of federal control of slavery in the territories, seems not to have been directly before the Convention which framed the

---

"The State of Virginia, which ceded to the United States her claims to this Territory, consented, by her delegates in the old Congress, to this Ordinance. Not only Virginia, but North Carolina, South Carolina and Georgia, by unanimous votes of their delegates in the Old Congress, approved of the Ordinance of 1787, by which Slavery is forever abolished in the Territory northwest of the river Ohio. Without the votes of these States the Ordinance could not have been passed; and there is no recollection of an opposition from any of these States to the act of confirmation passed under the actual Constitution."

7. "The famous ordinance of Congress of the 13th July, 1787, which has ever since constituted, in most respects, the model of all our territorial governments, and is equally remarkable for the brevity and exactness of its text, and for its masterly display of the fundamental principles of civil and religious liberty."—*Justice Story*, 1 *Commentaries*, §1312.

"It is well known that the Ordinance of 1787 was drawn by the Hon. Nathan Dane, of Massachusetts, and adopted with scarcely a verbal alteration by Congress. It is a noble and imperishable monument to his fame."—*Id.* note.

The ordinance was reported by a committee, of which Wm. S. Johnson and Charles Pinckney were members. It recites that, "for extending the fundamental principles of civil and religious liberty, which form the basis whereon these republics, their laws and constitutions, are erected; to fix and establish those principles as the basis of all laws, constitutions and governments which forever hereafter shall be formed in the said Territory; to provide also for the establishment of States and permanent government, and for their admission to a share in the federal councils, on an equal footing with the original States, at as early periods as may be consistent with the general interest—

"It is hereby ordained and declared, by the authority aforesaid, that the following articles shall be considered as articles of compact between the original States and the people and States in the said Territory, and forever remain unalterable, unless by common consent, to wit:" *

"Art. 6. There shall be neither slavery nor involuntary servitude in the said Territory otherwise than in the punishment of crimes whereof the party shall have been duly convicted; provided always that any person escaping into the same, from whom labor or service is lawfully claimed in any of the original States, such fugitive may be lawfully reclaimed, and conveyed to the person claiming his or her labor or service."

On passing the ordinance, the ayes and nays were required by Judge Yates, of New-York, when it appeared *that his was the only vote in the negative.*

The ordinance of April 23, 1784, was a brief outline of that of '87. It was reported by a Committee, of which Mr. Jefferson was chairman, and the report contained a slavery prohibition intended to take effect in 1800. This was stricken out of the report,

(*continued on next page*)

original Constitution; and hence it is not recorded that the "thirty-nine," or any of them, while engaged on that instrument, expressed any opinion on that precise question.[8]

In 1789, by the first Congress which sat under the Constitution, an act was passed to enforce the Ordinance of '87, including the prohibition of slavery in the Northwestern Territory. The bill for this act was reported by one of the "thirty-nine," Thomas Fitzsimmons, then a member of the House of Representatives from

----

(*continued from previous page*) six States voting to retain it— three voting to strike out—one being divided (N.C.,) and the others not being represented. (The assent of nine States was necessary to retain any provision.) And this is the vote alluded to by Mr. Lincoln. But subsequently, March 16, 1785, a motion was made by Rufus King to commit a proposition "that there be neither slavery nor involuntary servitude" in any of the Territories; which was carried by the vote of eight States, including Maryland—*Journal Am. Congress,* vol. 4, pp. 373, 380, 481, 752.

When, therefore, the ordinance of '87 came before Congress, on its final passage, the subject of slavery prohibition had been "*agitated*" for nearly three years; and the deliberate and almost unanimous vote of that body upon that question leaves no room to doubt what the fathers believed, and how, in that belief, they acted.

8. It singularly and fortunately happens that one of the "thirty-nine," "while engaged on that instrument," viz., while advocating its ratification before the Pennsylvania Convention, did express an opinion upon this "precise question," which opinion was *never* disputed or doubted, in that or any other Convention, and was accepted by the opponents of the Constitution, as an indisputable fact. This was the celebrated James Wilson, of Pennsylvania. The opinion is as follows:—

MONDAY, *Dec.* 3, 1787.

"With respect to the clause restricting Congress from prohibiting the migration or importation of such persons as any one of the States now existing shall think proper to admit, prior to the year 1808: The Hon. gentleman says that this clause is not only dark, but intended to grant to Congress, for that time, the power to admit the importation of slaves. No such thing was intended; but I will tell you what was done, and it gives me high pleasure that so much was done. Under the present Confederation, the States may admit the importation of slaves as long as they please; but by this article, after the year 1808, the Congress will have the power to prohibit such importation, notwithstanding the disposition of any State to the contrary. I consider this as laying the foundation for banishing slavery out of this country; and though the period is more distant than I could wish, yet it will produce the same kind, gradual change which was pursued in Pennsylvania. It is with much satisfaction that I view this power in the general government, whereby they may lay an interdiction on this reproachful trade. But an immediate advantage is also obtained; for a tax or duty may be imposed on such importation, not exceeding $10 for each person; and this, sir, operates as a partial prohibition; it was all that could be obtained. I am sorry it was no more; but from this I think there is reason to hope that yet a few years, and it will be prohibited altogether. *And in the meantime, the new States which are to be formed under the control of Congress in this particular, and slaves will never be introduced amongst them.*"—2 *Elliott's Debates,* 423.

Pennsylvania. It went through all its stages without a word of opposition, and finally passed both branches without yeas and nays, which is equivalent to a unanimous passage.[9] [*Cheers.*] In this Congress there were sixteen of the thirty-nine fathers who framed the original Constitution. They were John Langdon, Nicholas Gilman, Wm. S. Johnson, Roger Sherman, Robert Morris, Thos. Fitzsimmons, William Few, Abraham Baldwin, Rufus

It was argued by Patrick Henry in the Convention in Virginia, as follows:

"May not Congress enact that every black man must fight? Did we not see a little of this in the last war? We were not so hard pushed as to make emancipation general. But acts of Assembly passed, that every slave who would go to the army should be free. Another thing will contribute to bring this event about. Slavery is detested. We feel its fatal effects. We deplore it with all the pity of humanity. Let all these considerations press with full force on the minds of Congress. Let that urbanity which, I trust, will distinguish America, and the necessity of national defence—let all these things operate on their minds, they will search that paper, and see if they have power of manumission. And have they not, sir? Have they not power to provide for the general defence and welfare? May they not think that these call for the abolition of slavery? May they not pronounce all slaves free, and will they not be warranted by that power? There is no ambiguous implication, no logical deduction. The paper speaks to the point; they have the power in clear, unequivocal terms, and will clearly and certainly exercise it."—3 *Elliott's Debates*, 534.

Edmund Randolph, one of the framers of the Constitution, replied to Mr. Henry, admitting the general force of the argument, but claiming that, because of other provisions, it had no application to the *States* where slavery *then* existed; thus conceding that power to exist in Congress as to all territory belonging to the United States

Dr. (David—ed.] Ramsay, a member of the Convention of South Carolina, in his history of the United States, vol. 3, pages 36, 37, says: "Under these liberal principles, Congress, in organizing *colonies*, bound themselves to impart to their inhabitants all the privileges of coequal States, as soon as they were capable of enjoying them. In their infancy, *government was administered for them* without any expense. As soon as they should have 60,000 inhabitants, they were authorized to call a convention, and, by common consent, to form their own constitution. This being done, they were entitled to representation in Congress, and every right attached to the original States. These privileges are not confined to any particular country or *complexion*. They are communicable to the emancipated slave, (for in the new State of Ohio, slavery is altogether prohibited), to the copper-colored native, and all other human beings who, after a competent residence and degree of civilization, are capable of enjoying the blessings of regular government."

9. The Act of 1789, as reported by the Committee, was received and read Thursday, July 16th. The second reading was on Friday, the 17th, when it was committed to the Committee of the whole house, "on Monday next." On Monday, July 20th, it was considered in Committee of the whole, and ordered to a third reading on the following day; on the 21st, it passed the House, and was sent to the Senate. In the Senate it had its first reading on the same day, and was ordered to a second reading the following day, (July 22d,) and on the 4th August it passed, and on the 7th was approved by the President.

King, William Paterson, George Clymer, Richard Bassett, George Read, Pierce Butler, Daniel Carroll, James Madison.[10]

This shows that, in their understanding, no line dividing local from federal authority, nor anything in the Constitution, properly forbade Congress to prohibit slavery in the federal territory; else both their fidelity to correct principle, and their oath to support the Constitution, would have constrained them to oppose the prohibition.

Again, George Washington, another of the "thirty-nine," was then President of the United States, and, as such approved and signed the bill; thus completing its validity as a law, and thus showing that, in his understanding, no line dividing local from federal authority, nor anything in the Constitution, forbade the Federal Government, to control as to slavery in federal territory. [*Loud applause.*]

No great while after the adoption of the original Constitution, North Carolina ceded to the Federal Government the country now constituting the State of Tennessee; and a few years later Georgia ceded that which now constitutes the States of Mississippi and Alabama. In both deeds of cession it was made a condition by the ceding States that the Federal Government should not prohibit slavery in the ceded country.[11] Besides this, slavery was then actually in the ceded country. Under these circumstances, Congress, on taking charge of these countries, did not absolutely prohibit slavery within them. But they did interfere with it—take control of it—even there, to a certain extent. In 1798, Congress organized the Territory of Mississippi. In the act of organization, they prohibited the bringing of slaves into the Territory, from any place without the United States, by fine, and giving freedom to slaves so brought.[12] This act passed both branches of Congress without yeas and nays. In that Congress were three of the "thirty-nine" who framed the original Constitution. They were John Langdon, George Read and Abraham Baldwin.[13]

---

10. The "sixteen" represented these States:—Langdon and Gilman, New Hampshire; Sherman and Johnson, Connecticut; Morris, Fitzsimmons, and Clymer, Pennsylvania; King, Massachusetts; Paterson, New Jersey; Few and Baldwin, Georgia; Bassett and Read, Delaware; Butler, South Carolina; Carroll, Maryland; and Madison, Virginia.

11. *Vide* note 3, *ante.*

12. Chap. 28, § 7, U.S. Statutes, 5th Congress, 2d Session.

13. Langdon was from New Hampshire, Read from Delaware, and Baldwin from Georgia.

They all, probably, voted for it. Certainly they would have placed their opposition to it upon record, if, in their understanding, any line dividing local from federal authority, or anything in the Constitution, properly forbade the Federal Government to control as to slavery in federal territory. [*Applause.*]

In 1803, the Federal Government purchased the Louisiana country. Our former territorial acquisitions came from certain of our own States; but this Louisiana country was acquired from a foreign nation. In 1804, Congress gave a territorial organization to that part of it which now constitutes the State of Louisiana. New Orleans, lying within that part, was an old and comparatively large city. There were other considerable towns and settlements, and slavery was extensively and thoroughly intermingled with the people. Congress did not, in the Territorial Act, prohibit slavery; but they did interfere with it—take control of it—in a more marked and extensive way than they did in the case of Mississippi. The substance of the provision therein made, in relation to slaves, was:

First. That no slave should be imported into the territory from foreign parts.

Second. That no slave should be carried into it who had been imported into the United States since the first day of May, 1798.

Third. That no slave should be carried into it, except by the owner, and for his own use as a settler; the penalty in all the cases being a fine upon the violator of the law, and freedom to the slave.[14] [*Prolonged cheers.*]

This act also was passed without yeas and nays. In the Congress which passed it, there were two of the "thirty-nine." They were Abraham Baldwin and Jonathan Dayton.[15] As stated in the case of Mississippi, it is probable they both voted for it. They would not have allowed it to pass without recording their opposition to it, if, in their understanding, it violated either the line properly dividing local from federal authority, or any provision of the Constitution.

In 1819–20, came and passed the Missouri question. Many votes were taken, by yeas and nays, in both branches of Congress, upon the various phases of the general question. Two of the "thirty-nine"—

14. Chap. 38, § 10, U.S. Statutes, 8th Congress, 1st Session.

15. Baldwin was from Georgia, and Dayton from New Jersey.

Rufus King and Charles Pinckney—were members of that Congress.[16] Mr. King steadily voted for slavery prohibition and against all compromises, while Mr. Pinckney as steadily voted against slavery prohibition and against all compromises. [*Cheers.*] By this, Mr. King showed that, in his understanding, no line dividing local from federal authority, nor anything in the Constitution, was violated by Congress prohibiting slavery in federal territory; while Mr. Pinckney, by his votes, showed that, in his understanding, there was some sufficient reason for opposing such prohibition in that case.[17]

The cases I have mentioned are the only acts of the "thirty-nine," or of any of them, upon the direct issue, which I have been able to discover.

To enumerate the persons who thus acted, as being four in 1784, two in 1787, seventeen in 1789, three in 1798, two in 1804, and two in 1819–20—there would be thirty of them. But this would be counting John Langdon, Roger Sherman, William Few, Rufus King,

---

16. Rufus King, who sat in the old Congress, and also in the Convention, was the representative of Massachusetts, removed to New-York and was sent by that State to the U.S. Senate of the first Congress. Charles Pinckney was in the House, as a representative of South Carolina.

17. Although Mr. Pinckney opposed the "slavery prohibition" in 1820, yet his views, with regard to the *powers* of the general government, may be better judged by his actions in the Convention:
    FRIDAY, *June 8th*, 1787.—"Mr. Pinckney moved 'that the National Legislature shall have the power of negativing all laws to be passed by the State Legislatures, which they may judge improper,' in the room of the clause as it stood reported.
    "He grounds his notion on the necessity of one supreme controlling power, and he considers this as the *corner-stone* of the present system; and hence, the necessity or retrenching the State authorities, in order to preserve the good government of the national council."—P. 400, *Elliott's Debates.*
    And again, THURSDAY, *August 23d*, 1787, Mr. Pinckney renewed the motion with some modifications.—P. 1409, *Madison Papers.*
    And although Mr. Pinckney, as correctly stated by Mr. Lincoln, "steadily voted against slavery prohibition, and against all compromises," he still regarded the passage of the Missouri Compromise as a great triumph of the South, which is apparent from the following letter:

    CONGRESS HALL, *March 2d*, 1820, 3 o'clock at night.
    DEAR SIR:—I hasten to inform you, that this moment WE have carried the question to admit Missouri, and all Louisiana to the southward of 36°30', free from the restriction of slavery, and give the South, in a short time, an addition of six, perhaps eight, members to the Senate of the United States. It is considered here by the slaveholding states, as a great triumph.
    The votes were close—ninety to eight-six—produced by the seceding and absence of a few moderate men from the North. To the north of 36°30', there is to be,

and George Read each twice, and Abraham Baldwin, three times [*Applause.*] [Lincoln said "four times," not three, at Cooper Union, as the press reported the next day, but evidently corrected this error for the final pamphlet—*ed.*; Thayer & Eldridge version had him adding: "He was a Georgian, too" to "great applause and laughter".] The true number of those of the "thirty-nine" whom I have shown to have acted upon the question, which, by the text, they understood better than we, is twenty-three, leaving sixteen not shown to have acted upon it in any way.[18]

Here, then, we have twenty-three out of our thirty-nine fathers "who framed the Government under which we live," who have, upon their official responsibility and their corporal oaths, acted upon the very question which the text affirms they "understood just as well, and even better than we do now;" and twenty-one of them—a clear majority of the whole "thirty-nine"—so acting upon it as to make them guilty of gross political impropriety and willful perjury, if, in their understanding, any proper division between local and federal authority, or anything in the Constitution they had made themselves, and sworn to support, forbade the Federal Government to control as to slavery in the federal territories. [*Cheers.*] Thus the twenty-one acted; and, as actions speak louder than words, so actions, under such responsibility, speak still louder.

Two of the twenty-three voted against Congressional prohibition of slavery in the federal territories, in the instances in which they acted upon the question. But for what reasons they so voted is not

---

by the present law, restriction; which you will see by the votes, I voted against. But it is at present of no moment; it is a vast tract, uninhabited, only by savages and wild beasts, in which not a foot of the Indian claims to soil is extinguished, and in which, according to the ideas prevalent, no land office will be opened for a great length of time. With respect, your obedient servant,

CHARLES PINCKNEY.

But conclusive evidence of Mr. Pinckney's views is furnished in the fact, that *he was himself a member of the Committee which reported the Ordinance of '87, and that on every occasion, when it was under the consideration of Congress, he voted against all amendments.*—Jour. Am. Congress, Sept. 29th, 1786. Oct. 4th. When the ordinance came up for its final passage, Mr. Pinckney was sitting in the Convention, and did not take part in the proceedings of the Congress.

18. By reference to notes 4, 6, 10, 13, 15, and 16, it will be seen that, of the twenty-three who acted upon the question of prohibition, twelve were from the present slaveholding States.

known. They may have done so because they thought a proper division of local from federal authority, or some provision or principle of the Constitution, stood in the way; or they may, without any such question, have voted against the prohibition, on what appeared to them to be sufficient grounds of expediency. No one who has sworn to support the Constitution can conscientiously vote for what he understands to be an unconstitutional measure, however expedient he may think it; but one may and ought to vote against a measure which he deems constitutional, if, at the same time, he deems it inexpedient. It, therefore, would be unsafe to set down even the two who voted against the prohibition, as having done so because, in their understanding, any proper division of local from federal authority, or anything in the Constitution, forbade the Federal Government to control as to slavery in federal territory.[19] [*Laughter and prolonged applause.*]

The remaining sixteen of the "thirty-nine," so far as I have discovered, have left no record of their understanding upon the direct question of federal control of slavery in the federal territories. But there is much reason to believe that their understanding upon that question would not have appeared different from that of their twenty-three compeers, had it been manifested at all.[20]

For the purpose of adhering rigidly to the text, I have purposely omitted whatever understanding may have been manifested by any person, however distinguished, other than the thirty-nine fathers who framed the original Constitution; and, for the same reason, I have also omitted whatever understanding may have been manifested by any of the "thirty-nine" even, on any other phase of the general question of slavery. If we should look into their acts and declarations on those other phases, as the foreign slave trade, and the morality and policy of slavery generally, it would appear to us that on the direct question of federal control of slavery in federal territories, the sixteen, if they had acted at all, would probably have acted just

---

19. *Vide* notes 5 and 17, *ante.*

20. "The remaining sixteen" were Nathaniel Gorham, Mass.; Alex. Hamilton, New-York; William Livingston and David Brearly, New Jersey; Benjamin Franklin, Jared Ingersoll, James Wilson and Gouverneur Morris, Penn.; Gunning Bradford, John Dickinson and Jacob Broom, Delaware; Daniel, of St. Thomas, Jenifer, Maryland; John Blair, Virginia; Richard Dobbs Spaight, North Carolina; and John Rutledge and Charles Cotesworth Pinckney, South Carolina.

as the twenty-three did. Among that sixteen were several of the most noted anti-slavery men of those times—as Dr. Franklin, Alexander Hamilton and Gouverneur Morris—while there was not one now known to have been otherwise, unless it may be John Rutledge, of South Carolina.[21] [*Applause.*]

The sum of the whole is, that of our thirty-nine fathers who framed the original Constitution, twenty-one—a clear majority of the whole—certainly understood that no proper division of local from federal authority, nor any part of the Constitution, forbade the Federal Government to control slavery in the federal territories; while all the rest probably had the same understanding. Such, unquestionably, was the understanding of our fathers who framed the original Constitution; and the text affirms that they understood the question "better than we." [*Laughter and cheers.*]

But, so far, I have been considering the understanding of the ques-

---

21. "The only distinction between freedom and slavery consists in this: in the former state, a man is governed by the laws to which he has given his consent, either in person or by his representative; in the latter, he is governed by the will of another. In the one case, his life and property are his own; in the other, they depend upon the pleasure of a master. It is easy to discern which of the two states is preferable. No man in his senses can hesitate in choosing to be free rather than slave. * * * * * * * * * * * * * * * * Were not the disadvantages of slavery too obvious to stand in need of it, I might enumerate and describe the tedious train of calamities inseparable from it. I might show that it is fatal to religion and morality; that it tends to debase the mind, and corrupt its noblest springs of action. I might show that it relaxes the sinews of industry and clips the wings of commerce, and works misery and indigence in every shape."— *Hamilton, Works,* vol. 2, pp. 3, 9.

"That you will be pleased to countenance the restoration of *liberty* to those unhappy *men,* who alone in this land of freedom, are degraded into perpetual bondage, and who, amidst the general joy of surrounding freemen, are groaning in servile subjection; that you will devise names for removing this inconsistency from the character of the American people; that you will promote mercy and *justice* toward this distressed race; and that you will step to the *very verge* of the power vested in you, for discouraging every species of traffic in the persons of our fellow-men."— *Philadelphia, Feb. 3d, 1790, Franklin's Petition to Congress for the Abolition of Slavery.*

Mr. Gouverneur Morris said:—"He never would concur in upholding domestic slavery. It was a nefarious institution. It was the curse of heaven on the States where it prevailed. * * * The admission of slavery into the representation, when fairly explained, comes to this—that the inhabitant of South Carolina or Georgia, who goes to the coast of Africa, and, in defiance of the most sacred laws of humanity, tears away his fellow-creatures from their dearest connections, and damns them to the most cruel bondage, shall have more votes, in a government instituted for the protection of the rights of mankind, than the citizen of Pennsylvania or New Jersey, who views, with a laudable horror, so nefarious a practice. * * * * * * * He would sooner submit himself to a tax for paying for all the negroes in the United States than saddle posterity with such a constitution"—*Debate on Slave Representation in the Convention.—Madison Papers.*

tion manifested by the framers of the original Constitution. In and by the original instrument, a mode was provided for amending it; and, as I have already stated, the present frame of "the Government under which we live" consists of that original, and twelve amendatory articles framed and adopted since. Those who now insist that federal control of slavery in federal territories violates the Constitution, point us to the provisions which they suppose it thus violates; and, as I understand, that all fix upon provisions in these amendatory articles, and not in the original instrument. The Supreme Court, in the Dred Scott case, plant themselves upon the fifth amendment, which provides that no person shall be deprived of "life, liberty or property without due process of law;" while Senator Douglas and his peculiar adherents plant themselves upon the tenth amendment, providing that "the powers not delegated to the United States by the Constitution," "are reserved to the States respectively, or to the people."[22]

Now, it so happens that these amendments were framed by the first Congress which sat under the Constitution—the identical Congress which passed the act already mentioned, enforcing the prohibition of slavery in the Northwestern Territory. [*Applause.*] Not only was it the same Congress, but they were the identical, same individual men who, at the same session, and at the same time within the session, had under consideration, and in progress toward maturity, these Constitutional amendments, and this act prohibiting slavery in all the territory the nation then owned. The Constitutional amendments were introduced before, and passed after the act enforc-

---

22. An eminent jurist (Chancellor Walworth) has said that "The preamble which was prefixed to these amendments, as adopted by Congress, is important to show in what light that body considered them." (8 *Wend. R.*, p. 100.) It declares that a number of the State Conventions "having at the time of their adopting the Constitution *expressed a desire*, in order to prevent *misconstruction or abuse of its powers*, that further *declaratory* and restrictive clauses should be added," resolved &c.

This preamble is in substance the preamble affixed to the "Conciliatory Resolutions" of Massachussetts, which were drawn by Chief Justice Parsons, and offered in the convention as a compromise by John Hancock. (*Life ch. J. Parsons*, p. 67.) They were afterward copied and adopted with some additions by New Hampshire.

The fifth amendment, on which the Supreme Court relies, is taken almost literally from the declaration of rights put forth by the convention of New-York, and the clause referred to forms the ninth paragraph of the declaration. The tenth amendment, on which Senator Douglas relies, is taken from the Conciliatory Resolutions, and is the first of those resolutions somewhat modified. Thus, these two amendments sought to be used for slavery, originated in the two great antislavery states, New-York and Massachussetts.

ing the Ordinance of '87; so that, during the whole pendency of the act to enforce the Ordinance, the Constitutional amendments were also pending.[23]

The seventy-six members of that Congress, including sixteen of the framers of the original Constitution, as before stated, were pre-eminently our fathers who framed that part of "the Government under which we live," which is now claimed as forbidding the Federal Government to control slavery in the federal territories.

Is it not a little presumptuous in any one at this day to affirm that the two things which that Congress deliberately framed, and carried to maturity at the same time, are absolutely inconsistent with each other? And does not such affirmation become impudently absurd when coupled with the other affirmation from the same mouth, that those who did the two things, alleged to be inconsistent, understood whether they really were inconsistent better than we—better than he who affirms that they are inconsistent? [*Applause and great merriment.*]

It is surely safe to assume that the thirty-nine framers of the original Constitution, and the seventy-six members of the Congress which framed the amendments thereto, taken together, do certainly include those who may be fairly called "our fathers who framed the Government under which we live."[24] And so assuming, I defy any man to show that any one of them ever, in his whole life, declared that, in his understanding, any proper division of local from federal authority, or any part of the Constitution, forbade the Federal Government to control as to slavery in the federal territories. [*Loud applause.*] I go a step further. I defy any one to show that any living man in the whole world ever did, prior to the beginning of the present century, (and I might almost say prior to the beginning of the last half of the present century,) declare that, in his understanding,

---

23. The amendments were proposed by Mr. Madison in the House of Representatives, June 8, 1789. They were adopted by the House, August 24, and some further amendments seem to have been transmitted by the Senate, September 9. The printed journals of the Senate do not state the time of the final passage, and the message transmitting them to the State Legislatures speaks of them as adopted at the first session, begun on the fourth day of March, 1789. The date of the introduction and passage of the act enforcing the ordinance of '87, will be found at note 9, *ante.*

24. It is singular that while two of the "thirty-nine" were in that Congress of 1819, there was but one (besides Mr. King) of the "seventy-six." The one was William Smith, of South Carolina. He was then a Senator and, like Mr. Pinckney, occupied extreme Southern ground.

any proper division of local from federal authority, or any part of the Constitution, forbade the Federal Government to control as to slavery in the federal territories. To those who now so declare, I give, not only "our fathers who framed the Government under which we live," but with them all other living men within the century in which it was framed, among whom to search, and they shall not be able to find the evidence of a single man agreeing with them.

Now, and here, let me guard a little against being misunderstood. I do not mean to say we are bound to follow implicitly in whatever our fathers did. To do so, would be to discard all the lights of current experience—to reject all progress—all improvement. What I do say is, that if we would supplant the opinions and policy of our fathers in any case, we should do so upon evidence so conclusive, and argument so clear, that even their great authority, fairly considered and weighed, cannot stand; and most surely not in a case whereof we ourselves declare they understood the question better than we. [*Laughter.*]

· If any man at this day sincerely believes that a proper division of local from federal authority, or any part of the Constitution, forbids the Federal Government to control as to slavery in the federal territories, he is right to say so, and to enforce his position by all truthful evidence and fair argument which he can. But he has no right to mislead others, who have less access to history, and less leisure to study it, into the false belief that "our fathers who framed the Government under which we live" were of the same opinion—thus substituting falsehood and deception for truthful evidence and fair argument. [*Applause.*] If any man at this day sincerely believes "our fathers who framed the Government under which we live," used and applied principles, in other cases, which ought to have led them to understand that a proper division of local from federal authority or some part of the Constitution, forbids the Federal Government to control as to slavery in the federal territories, he is right to say so. But he should, at the same time, brave the responsibility of declaring that, in his opinion, he understands their principles better than they did themselves; [*great laughter,*] and especially should he not shirk that responsibility by asserting that they "understood the question just as well, and even better, than we do now." [*Applause.*]

But enough! *Let all who believe that "our fathers, who framed the*

Government under which we live, understood this question just as well, and even better, than we do now," speak as they spoke, and act as they acted upon it. This is all Republicans ask—all Republicans desire—in relation to slavery. As those fathers marked it, so let it be again marked, as an evil not to be extended, but to be tolerated and protected only because of and so far as its actual presence among us makes that toleration and protection a necessity. [Loud applause.] Let all the guarantees those fathers gave it, be, not grudgingly, but fully and fairly, maintained. For this Republicans contend, and with this, so far as I know or believe, they will be content. [Applause.]

And now, if they would listen—as I suppose they will not—I would address a few words to the Southern people. [Laughter.]

I would say to them:—You consider yourselves a reasonable and a just people; and I consider that in the general qualities of reason and justice you are not inferior to any other people. Still, when you speak of us Republicans, you do so only to denounce us as reptiles, or, at the best, as no better than outlaws. You will grant a hearing to pirates or murderers, but nothing like it to "Black Republicans." [Laughter.] In all your contentions with one another, each of you deems an unconditional condemnation of "Black Republicanism" as the first thing to be attended to. [Laughter.] Indeed, such condemnation of us seems to be an indispensable prerequisite—license, so to speak—among you to be admitted or permitted to speak at all. Now, can you, or not, be prevailed upon to pause and to consider whether this is quite just to us, or even to yourselves? Bring forward your charges and specifications, and then be patient long enough to hear us deny or justify.

You say we are sectional. We deny it. [Loud applause.] That makes an issue; and the burden of proof is upon you. [Laughter and applause.] You produce your proof; and what is it? Why, that our party has no existence in your section—gets no votes in your section. The fact is substantially true; but does it prove the issue? If it does, then in case we should, without change of principle, begin to get votes in your section, we should thereby cease to be sectional. [Great merriment.] You cannot escape this conclusion; and yet, are you willing to abide by it? If you are, you will probably soon find that we have ceased to be sectional, for we shall get votes in your section this very year. [Loud cheers.] You will then begin to discover, as the truth plainly is, that your proof does not touch the issue. The fact that we get no votes in your section, is a fact of your making, and not of ours. And if there be fault in that fact, that fault is primarily yours, and remains until you show that we repel you by some wrong principle or practice. If we do repel you by any wrong principle or practice, the fault is ours; but this brings you to where you ought to have started—to a discussion of the right or wrong of our principle. [*Loud applause*.] If our principle, put in practice, would wrong your section for the benefit of ours, or for any other object, then our principle, and we with it, are sectional, and are justly opposed and denounced as such. Meet us, then, on the question of whether our principle, put in practice, would wrong your section; and so meet it as if it were possible that something may be said on our side. [*Laughter*.] Do you accept the challenge? No! Then you really believe that the principle which "our fathers who framed the Government under which we live" thought so clearly right as to adopt it, and indorse it again and again, upon their official oaths, is in fact so clearly wrong as to demand your condemnation without a moment's consideration. [*Applause*.]

Some of you delight to flaunt in our faces the warning against sectional parties given by Washington in his Farewell Address. Less than eight years before Washington gave that warning, he had, as President of the United States, approved and signed an act of Congress, enforcing the prohibition of slavery in the Northwestern Territory, which act embodied the policy of the Government upon that subject up to and at the very moment he penned that warning; and about one year after he penned it, he wrote La Fayette that he considered that prohibition a wise measure, expressing in the same connection his hope that we should at some time have a confederacy of free States.[25] [*Applause*.]

25. The following is an extract from the letter referred to:—
   "I agree with you cordially in your views in regard to negro slavery. I have long considered it a most serious evil, both socially and politically, and I should rejoice in any feasible scheme to rid our States of such a burden. The Congress of 1787 adopted an ordinance which prohibits the existence of involuntary servitude in our Northwestern Territory forever. I consider it a wise measure. It meets with the approval and assent of nearly every member from the States more immediately interested in Slave labor. The prevailing opinion in Virginia is against the spread of slavery in our new territories, and I trust we shall have a confederation of free States."

Bearing this in mind, and seeing that sectionalism has since arisen upon this same subject, is that warning a weapon in your hands against us, or in our hands against you? Could Washington himself speak, would he cast the blame of that sectionalism upon us, who sustain his policy, or upon you who repudiate it? [*Applause.*] We respect that warning of Washington, and we commend it to you, together with his example pointing to the right application of it. [*Applause.*]

But you say you are conservative—eminently conservative—while we are revolutionary, destructive, or something of the sort. What is conservatism? Is it not adherence to the old and tried, against the new and untried? We stick to, contend for, the identical old policy on the point in controversy which was adopted by "our fathers who framed the Government under which we live;" while you with one accord reject, and scout, and spit upon that old policy, and insist upon substituting something new. True, you disagree among yourselves as to what that substitute shall be. You are divided on new propositions and plans, but you are unanimous in rejecting and denouncing the old policy of the fathers. Some of you are for reviving the foreign slave trade; some for a Congressional Slave-Code for the Territories; some for Congress forbidding the Territories to prohibit Slavery within their limits; some for maintaining Slavery in the Territories through the judiciary; some for the "gur-reat pur-rinciple" [*laughter*] that "if one man would enslave another, no third man should object," fantastically called "Popular Sovereignty;" [*renewed laughter and applause*] but never a man among you is in favor of federal prohibition of slavery in federal territories, according to the practice of "our fathers who framed the Government under which we live." Not one of all your various plans can show a precedent or an advocate in the century within which our Government originated. Consider, then, whether your claim of conservatism for yourselves, and your charge of destructiveness against us, are based on the most clear and stable foundations.

The following extract from a letter of Washington to Robert Morris, April 12th, 1786, shows how strong were his views, and how clearly he deemed emancipation a subject for legislative enactment:—"I can only say that there is no man living who wishes more sincerely than I do to see a plan adopted for the abolition of it; but there is but one proper and effective mode by which it can be accomplished, and that is, BY LEGISLATIVE AUTHORITY, and that, as far as *my suffrage will go, shall never be wanting.*"

Again, you say we have made the slavery question more prominent than it formerly was. We deny it. We admit that it is more
prominent, but we deny that we made it so. It was not we, but you,
who discarded the old policy of the fathers. We resisted, and still
resist, your innovation; and thence comes the greater prominence
of the question. Would you have that question reduced to its former
proportions? Go back to that old policy. What has been will be
again, under the same conditions. If you would have the peace of
the old times, readopt the precepts and policy of the old times.
[*Applause.*]

You charge that we stir up insurrections among your slaves. We
deny it; and what is your proof? Harper's Ferry! [*Great laughter.*] John
Brown!! [*Renewed laughter.*] John Brown was no Republican; and you
have failed to implicate a single Republican in his Harper's Ferry
enterprise. [*Loud applause.*] If any member of our party is guilty in
that matter, you know it or you do not know it. If you do know it,
you are inexcusable for not designating the man and proving the
fact. If you do not know it, you are inexcusable for asserting it, and
especially for persisting in the assertion after you have tried and
failed to make the proof. [*Great applause.*] You need to be told that
persisting in a charge which one does not know to be true, is simply
malicious slander.[26] [*Applause*]

---

26. A Committee of five, consisting of Messrs. Mason, Davis and Fitch, (Democrats,) and
    Collamer and Doolittle, (Republicans,) was appointed Dec. 14, 1859, by the U.S.
    Senate, to investigate the Harper's Ferry affair. That Committee was directed, among
    other things, to inquire: (1.) "Whether such invasion and seizure was made under
    color of any organization intended to subvert the government of any of the States of
    the Union." (2.) "What was the character and extent of such organization." (3.)
    "And whether any citizen of the United States, not present, were implicated therein,
    or accessory thereto, by contributions of money, arms, munitions, or otherwise."
      The majority of the Committee, Messrs. Mason, Davis, and Fitch, reply to the
    inquiries as follows:
    1.   "There will be found in the Appendix, a copy of the proceedings of a Conven-
         tion held at Chatham, Canada, of the Provisional Form of Government there pre-
         tended to have been instituted, the object of which clearly was to subvert the
         government of one or more States, and of course, to that extent, the government of
         the United States." By reference to the copy of Proceedings it appears that *nineteen*
         persons were present at that Convention, *eight* of whom were killed or executed at
         Charlestown [site of John Brown's execution—ed.], and one examined before the
         Committee. [*Ed. note:* This and subsequent texts do *not* follow the nineteenth
         century practice, employed in original notes, of using open quotes to open each
         new line text for long quotations.]

Some of you admit that no Republican designedly aided or encouraged the Harper's Ferry affair, but still insist that our doctrines and declarations necessarily lead to such results. We do not believe it. We know we hold to no doctrine, and make no declaration, which were not held to and made by "our fathers who framed the Government under which we live." [*Applause.*] You never dealt fairly by us in relation to this affair. When it occurred, some important State elections were near at hand, and you were in evident glee with the belief that, by charging the blame upon us, you could get an advantage of us in those elections. The elections came, and your expectations were not quite fulfilled. [*Laughter.*] [Thayer & Eldridge version added: "You did not sweep New York, and New Jersey, and Wisconsin, and Minnesota, precisely like fire sweeps over the prairie in the high wind. (*Laughter.*) You are still drumming at this idea. Go on with it. If you think you can, by slandering a woman, make her love you, or by vilifying a man make him vote with you, go on and try it. (*Boisterous laughter, and prolonged applause.*)—*ed.*] Every Republican man knew that, as to himself at least, your charge was a slander, and he was not much inclined by it to cast his vote in your favor. Republican doctrines and declarations are accompanied with a continual protest against any interference whatever with your slaves, or with you about your slaves. Surely, this does not encourage them to revolt. True,

2.   "The character of the military organization appears, by the commissions issued to certain of the armed party as captains, lieutenants, &c., a specimen of which will be found in the Appendix."

   (These Commissions are signed by John Brown as Commander-in-Chief, under the Provisional Government, and by J. H. Kagi as Secretary.)

   "It clearly appeared that the scheme of Brown was to take with him comparatively but few men; but those had been carefully trained by military instruction previously, and were to act as officers. For his military force he relied, very clearly, on inciting insurrection amongst the Slaves."

3.   "It does not appear that the contributions were made with actual knowledge of the use for which they were designed by Brown, although it does appear that money was freely contributed by those styling themselves the friends of this man Brown, and friends alike of what they styled the cause of freedom, (of which they claimed him to be an especial apostle,) without inquiring as to the way in which the money would be used by him to advance such pretended cause."

   In concluding the report the majority of the Committee thus characterize the "invasion:" "It was simply the act of lawless ruffians, under the sanction of no public or political authority—distinguishable only from ordinary felons by the ulterior ends in contemplation by them," &c.

we do, in common with "Our fathers, who framed the Government under which we live," declare our belief that slavery is wrong; [*applause;*] but the slaves do not hear us declare even this. For anything we say or do, the slaves would scarcely know there is a Republican party. I believe they would not, in fact, generally know it but for your misrepresentations of us, in their hearing. In your political contests among yourselves, each faction charges the other with sympathy with Black Republicanism; and then, to give point to the charge, defines Black Republicanism to simply be insurrection, blood and thunder among the slaves. [*Boisterous laughter and applause.*]

Slave insurrections are no more common now than they were before the Republican party was organized. What induced the Southampton insurrection, twenty-eight years ago, in which, at least, three times as many lives were lost as at Harper's Ferry?[27] You can scarcely stretch your very elastic fancy to the conclusion that Southampton was "got up by Black Republicanism." [*Laughter.*] In the present state of things in the United States, I do not think a general, or even a very extensive slave insurrection, is possible. The indispensable concert of action cannot be attained. The slaves have no means of rapid communication; nor can incendiary freemen, black or white, supply it. The explosive materials are everywhere in parcels; but there neither are, nor can be supplied, the indispensable connecting trains.

Much is said by Southern people about the affection of slaves for their masters and mistresses; and a part of it, at least, is true. A plot for an uprising could scarcely be devised and communicated to twenty individuals before some one of them, to save the life of a favorite master or mistress, would divulge it. This is the rule; and the slave revolution in Hayti was not an exception to it, but a case occurring under

---

27. The Southampton insurrection, August, 1831, was induced by the remarkable ability of a slave calling himself General Nat Turner. He led his fellow bondmen to believe that he was acting under the order of Heaven. In proof of this he alleged that the singular appearance of the sun at that time was a divine signal for the commencement of the struggle which would result in the recovery of their freedom. This insurrection resulted in the death of sixty-four white persons, and more than one hundred slaves. The Southampton was the eleventh large insurrection in the Southern States, besides numerous attempts and revolts.

peculiar circumstances.[28] The gunpowder plot of British history, though not connected with slaves, was more in point. In that case, only about twenty were admitted to the secret; and yet one of them, in his anxiety to save a friend, betrayed the plot to that friend, and, by consequence, averted the calamity. Occasional poisonings from the kitchen, and open or stealthy assassinations in the field, and local revolts extending to a score or so, will continue to occur as the natural results of slavery; but no general insurrection of slaves, as I think, can happen in this country for a long time. Whoever much fears, or much hopes for such an event, will be alike disappointed.

In the language of Mr. Jefferson, uttered many years ago, "It is still in our power to direct the process of emancipation, and deportation, peaceably, and in such slow degrees, as that the evil will wear off insensibly; and their places be, *pari passu*, filled up by free white laborers. [*Loud applause.*] If, on the contrary, it is left to force itself on, human nature must shudder at the prospect held up."[29]

Mr. Jefferson did not mean to say, nor do I, that the power of emancipation is in the Federal Government. He spoke of Virginia; and, as to the power of emancipation, I speak of the slaveholding States only. The Federal Government, however, as we insist, has the power of restraining the extension of the institution—the power to

---

28. In March, 1790, the General Assembly of France, on the petition of the *free* people of color in St. Domingo, many of whom were intelligent and wealthy, passed a decree intended to be in their favor, but so ambiguous as to be construed in favor of both the whites and the blacks. The differences growing out of the decree created two parties—the *whites* and the people of color; and some blood was shed. In 1791, the blacks again petitioned, and a decree was passed declaring the colored people citizens, who were born of free parents on both sides. This produced great excitement among the whites, and the two parties armed against each other, and horrible massacres and conflagrations followed. Then the Assembly rescinded this last decree, and like results followed, the blacks being the exasperated parties and the aggressors. Then the decree giving citizenship to the blacks was restored, and commissioners were sent out to keep the peace. The commissioners, unable to sustain themselves, between the two parties, with the troops they had, issued a proclamation that all blacks who were willing to range themselves under the banner of the Republic should be free. As a result a very large proportion of the blacks became in fact free. In 1794, the Conventional Assembly *abolished slavery* throughout the French Colonies. Some years afterward the French government sought, with an army of 60,000 men to reinstate slavery, but were unsuccessful, and then the white planters were driven from the Island.

29. *Vide* Jefferson's Autobiography, commenced January 6th, 1821. Jefferson's Works, vol. 1, page 49.

insure that a slave insurrection shall never occur on any American soil which is now free from slavery. [*Applause.*]

John Brown's effort was peculiar. It was not a slave insurrection. It was an attempt by white men to get up a revolt among slaves, in which the slaves refused to participate. In fact, it was so absurd that the slaves, with all their ignorance, saw plainly enough it could not succeed. That affair, in its philosophy, corresponds with the many attempts, related in history, at the assassination of kings and emperors. An enthusiast broods over the oppression of a people till he fancies himself commissioned by Heaven to liberate them. He ventures the attempt, which ends in little else than his own execution. [Felice] Orsini's [unsuccessful assassination] attempt on Louis Napoleon [in 1858—ed.], and John Brown's attempt at Harper's Ferry were, in their philosophy, precisely the same. The eagerness to cast blame on old England in the one case, and on New England in the other, does not disprove the sameness of the two things.

And how much would it avail you, if you could, by the use of John Brown, [Hinton Rowan] Helper's Book [*The Impending Crisis of the South: How to Meet It,* published in 1857—ed.], and the like, break up the Republican organization? Human action can be modified to some extent, but human nature cannot be changed. There is a judgment and a feeling against slavery in this nation, which cast at least a million and a half of votes. You cannot destroy that judgment and feeling—that sentiment—by breaking up the political organization which rallies around it. You can scarcely scatter and disperse an army which has been formed into order in the face of your heaviest fire; but if you could, how much would you gain by forcing the sentiment which created it out of the peaceful channel of the ballot-box, into some other channel? What would that other channel probably be? Would the number of John Browns be lessened or enlarged by the operation?

But you will break up the Union rather than submit to a denial of your Constitutional rights.[30]

---

30. "I am not ashamed or afraid publicly to avow, that the election of William H. Seward or Salmon P. Chase, or any such representative of the Republican party, upon a sectional platform, ought to be resisted to the disruption of every tie that binds the Confederacy together. (Applause on the Democratic side of the House.)"—Mr. [Jabez L. M.] *Curry, of Alabama* [later in the Confederate army—ed.], *in the House of Representatives.*

  "Just so sure as the Republican party succeed in electing a sectional man, upon

That has a somewhat reckless sound; but it would be palliated, if not fully justified, were we proposing, by the mere force of numbers, to deprive you of some right, plainly written down in the Constitution. But we are proposing no such thing.

When you make these declarations, you have a specific and well-understood allusion to an assumed Constitutional right of yours, to take slaves into the federal territories, and to hold them there as property. But no such right is specifically written in the Constitution. That instrument is literally silent about any such right. We, on the contrary, deny that such a right has any existence in the Constitution, even by implication. [*Applause*.]

Your purpose, then, plainly stated, is that you will destroy the Government, unless you be allowed to construe and enforce the

---

their sectional, anti-slavery platform, breathing destruction and death to the rights of my people, just so sure, in my judgment, the time will have come when the South must and will take an unmistakable and decided action, and then he who dallies is a dastard, and he who doubts is damned! I need not tell what I, as a Southern man, will do. I think I may safely speak for the masses of the people of Georgia—that when that event happens, they, in my judgment, will consider it an overt act, a declaration of war, and meet immediately in convention, to take into consideration the mode and measure of redress. That is my position; and if that be treason to the Government, make the most of it."—*Mr. Gartell, of Georgia, in the House of Representatives.*

"I said to my constituents, and to the people of the capital of my State, on my way here, if such an event did occur,"—[*i.e.*, the election of a Republican President, upon a Republican platform,] "while it would be their duty to determine the course which the State would pursue, it would be my privilege to counsel with them as to what I believed to be the proper course; and I said to them, what I say now, and what I will always say in such an event, that my counsel would be to take independence out of the Union in preference to the loss of constitutional rights, and consequent degradation and dishonor, in it. That is my position, and it is the position which I know the Democratic party of the State of Mississippi will maintain."—*Gov. McRae, of Mississippi.*

"It is useless to attempt to conceal the fact that, in the present temper of the southern people, it" [*i.e.*, the election of a Republican President] "cannot be, and will not be submitted to. The 'irrepressible conflict' doctrine, announced and advocated by the ablest and most distinguished leader of the Republican party, is an open declaration of war against the institution of slavery, wherever it exists; and I would be disloyal to Virginia and the South, if I did not declare that the election of such a man, entertaining such sentiment, and advocating such doctrines, *ought to be resisted by the slaveholding States*. The idea of permitting such a man to have the control and direction of the army and navy of the United States, and the appointment of high judicial and executive officers, POSTMASTERS INCLUDED, *cannot* be entertained by the South for a moment."—*Gov.* [John] *Letcher, of Virginia* [who later led his state out of the Union and helped convince Robert E. Lee to fight for Virginia, not the Union—*ed.*].

"Slavery *must* be maintained—in the Union, if possible; out of it, if necessary; peaceably if we may; forcibly if we must.—*Senator* [Alfred] *Iverson, of Georgia* [radical Democratic "fire-eater" who resigned the Senate when Georgia seceded; his son became a Confederate general—*ed.*]. (*continued on following page*)

Constitution as you please, on all points in dispute between you and us. You will rule or ruin in all events.

This, plainly stated, is your language. Perhaps you will say the Supreme Court has decided the disputed Constitutional question in your favor. Not quite so. But waiving the lawyer's distinction between dictum and decision, the Court have decided the question for you in a sort of way. The Court have substantially said, it is your Constitutional right to take slaves into the federal territories, and to hold them there as property. When I say the decision was made in a sort of way, I mean it was made in a divided Court, by a bare majority of the Judges, and they not quite agreeing with one another in the reasons for making it;[31] that it is so made as that its avowed supporters disagree with one another about its meaning, and that it was mainly based upon a mistaken statement of fact—the statement in

(*continued from previous page*)"Lincoln and Hamlin, the Black Republican nominees, will be elected in November next, and the South will then decide the great question whether they will submit to the domination of Black Republican rule—the fundamental principle of their organization being an open, undisguised, and declared war upon our social institutions. I believe that the honor and safety of the South, in that contingency, will require the prompt secession of the slaveholding States from the Union; and failing then to obtain from the free States additional and higher guaranties for the protection of our rights and property, that the seceding States should proceed to establish a new government. But while I think such would be the imperative duty of the South, I should emphatically reprobate and repudiate any scheme having for its object the separate secession of South Carolina. If Georgia, Alabama and Mississippi alone—giving us a portion of the Atlantic and Gulf coasts—would unite with this State in common secession upon the election of a Black Republican, I would give my assent to the policy."—*Letter of Hon. James L. Orr, of S.C., to John Martin and others, July 23, 1860.*

31. The Hon. John A. Andrew, of the Boston Bar, made the following analysis of the Dred Scott case in the Massachusetts legislature. Hon. Caleb Cushing was then a member of that body, but did not question its correctness.

"On the question of possibility of citizenship to one of the Dred Scott color, extraction, and origin, three justices, viz., Taney, Wayne and Daniels, held the negative. Nelson and Campbell passed over the plea by which the question was raised. Grier agreed with Nelson. Catron said the question was not open. McLean agreed with Catron, but thought the plea bad. Curtis agreed that the question was open, but attacked the plea, met its averments, and decided that a free born colored person, native to any State, is a citizen thereof, by birth, and is therefore a citizen of the Union, and entitled to sue in the Federal Courts.

"Had a majority of the court directly sustained the plea in abatement, and denied the jurisdiction of the Circuit Court appealed from, then all else they could have said and done would have been done and said in a cause not theirs to try and not theirs to discuss. In the absence of such majority, one step more was to be taken. And the next step reveals an agreement of six of the Justices, on a point decisive of the cause, and putting an end to all the functions of the court.

the opinion that "the right of property in a slave is distinctly and expressly affirmed in the Constitution."[32]

An inspection of the Constitution will show that the right of property in a slave is not "*distinctly* and *expressly* affirmed" in it. [*Applause.*] Bear in mind, the Judges do not pledge their judicial opinion that such right is *impliedly* affirmed in the Constitution; but they pledge their veracity that it is "*distinctly and expressly*" affirmed there—"distinctly," that is, not mingled with anything else— "expressly," that is, in words meaning just that, without the aid of any inference, and susceptible of no other meaning.

If they had only pledged their judicial opinion that such right is

---

"It is this. Scott was first carried to Rock Island, in the state of Illinois, where he remained about two years, before going with his master to Fort Snelling, in the Territory of Wisconsin. His claim to freedom was rested on the alleged effect of his transition from a slave State, and again into a free territory. If, by his removal to Illinois, he became emancipated from his master, the subsequent continuance of his pilgrimage into the Louisiana purchase could not add to his freedom, nor alter the fact. If, by reason of any want or infirmity in the laws of Illinois, or of conformity on his part to their behests, Dred Scott remained a slave while he remained in that State, then—for the sake of learning the effect on him of his territorial residence beyond the Mississippi, and of his marriage and other proceedings there, and the effect of the sojourn and marriage of Harriet, in the same territory, upon herself and her children—it might become needful to advance one other step into the investigation of the law; to inspect the Missouri Compromise, banishing slavery to the south of the line of 36°30' in the Louisiana purchase.

"But no exigency of the cause ever demanded or justified that advance; for six of the Justices, including the Chief Justice himself, decided that the *status* of the plaintiff, as free or slave, was dependent, not upon the laws of the State into which he had been, but of the State of Missouri, in which he was at the commencement of the suit. The Chief Justice asserted that 'it is now firmly settled by the decision of the highest court in the State, that Scott and his family, on their return were not free, but were, by the laws of Missouri, the property of the defendant.' This was the burden of the opinion of Nelson, who declares 'the question is one solely depending upon the law of Missouri, and that the federal Court, sitting in the State, and trying the case before us, was bound to follow it.' It received the emphatic endorsement of Wayne, whose general concurrence was with the Chief Justice. Grier concurred in set terms with Nelson on all 'the questions discussed by him.' Campbell says, 'The claim of the plaintiff to freedom depends upon the effect to be given to his absence from Missouri, in company with his master in Illinois and Minnesota, *and this effect is to be ascertained by reference to the laws of Missouri.*' Five of the Justices, then, (if no more of them,) regard the law of Missouri as decisive of the plaintiff's rights."

32. "Now, as we have already said in an earlier part of this opinion upon a different point, the right of property in a slave is distinctly and expressly affirmed in the Constitution. The right to traffic in it, *like an ordinary article of merchandise and property*, was guaranteed to the citizens of the United States in every State that might desire it for twenty years."—Ch. J. Taney, 19 *How. U.S.R.*, p. 451. *Vide* language of Mr. Madison, note 34, as to "*merchandise.*"

affirmed in the instrument by implication, it would be open to others to show that neither the word "slave" nor "slavery" is to be found in the Constitution, nor the word "property" even, in any connection with language alluding to the things slave, or slavery, [*applause*,] and that wherever in that instrument the slave is alluded to, he is called a "person;"—and wherever his master's legal right in relation to him is alluded to, it is spoken of as "service or labor which may be due,"—as a debt payable in service or labor.[33] Also, it would be open to show, by contemporaneous history, that this mode of alluding to slaves and slavery, instead of speaking of them, was employed on purpose to exclude from the Constitution the idea that there could be property in man.

To show all this, is easy and certain.[34]

When this obvious mistake of the Judges shall be brought to their notice, is it not reasonable to expect that they will withdraw the mistaken statement, and reconsider the conclusion based upon it?

---

33. Not only was the right of property *not* intended to be "distinctly and expressly affirmed in the Constitution;" but the following extract from Mr. Madison demonstrates that the utmost care was taken to avoid so doing:—

"The clause as originally offered [respecting fugitive slaves] read 'If any person LEGALLY bound to service or labor in any of the United States shall escape into another State," etc., etc. (Vol. 3, p. 1456.) In regard to this, Mr. Madison says, "The term *'legally'* was struck out, and the words 'under the laws thereof,' inserted after the word State, in compliance with the wish of some who thought the term 'legally' equivocal and favoring the idea that slavery was legal in a moral point of view."—*Ib.*, p. 1589.

34. We subjoin a portion of the history alluded to by Mr. Lincoln. The following extract relates to the provision of the Constitution relative to the slave trade. (Article I, Sec. 9.)

25th August, 1787.—The report of the Committee of eleven being taken up, Gen [Charles Cotesworth] Pinckney moved to strike out the words "the year 1800," and insert the words "the year 1808."

Mr. Gorham seconded the motion.

Mr. Madison—Twenty years will produce all the mischief that can be apprehended from the liberty to import slaves. So long a term will be more dishonorable to the American character than to say nothing about it in the Constitution.

*   *   *   *   *   *   *   *   *   *

Mr. Gouverneur Morris was for making the clause read at once—

"The importation of slaves into North Carolina, South Carolina, and Georgia, shall not be prohibited," &c.

This, he said, would be most fair, and would avoid the ambiguity by which, under the power with regard to naturalization the liberty reserved to the States might be defeated. He wished it to be known, also, that this part of the Constitution was a compliance with those States. If the change of language, however, should be objected to by the members from those States, he should not urge it.

And then it is to be remembered that "our fathers, who framed the Government under which we live"—the men who made the Constitution—decided this same Constitutional question in our favor, long ago—decided it without division among themselves, when making the decision; without division among themselves about the meaning of it after it was made, and, so far as any evidence is left, without basing it upon any mistaken statement of facts.

Under all these circumstances, do you really feel yourselves justified to break up this Government unless such a court decision as yours is, shall be at once submitted to as a conclusive and final rule of political action? But you will not abide the election of a Republican president! In that supposed event, you say, you will destroy the Union; and then,

---

Col. Mason, (of Va.,) was not against using the term "slaves," but against naming North Carolina, South Carolina, and Georgia, lest it should give offence to the people of those States.

Mr. Sherman liked a description better than the terms proposed, which had been declined by the old Congress, and were not pleasing to some people.

Mr. Clymer concurred with Mr. Sherman.

Mr. Williamson, of North Carolina, said that *both in opinion and practice he was against slavery; but thought it more in favor of humanity, from a view of all circumstances, to let in South Carolina and Georgia, on those terms, than to exclude them from the Union.*

Mr. Morris withdrew his motion.

Mr. Dickinson wished the clause to be confined to the States which had not themselves prohibited the importation of slaves, and for that purpose moved to amend the clause so as to read—

"The importation of slaves into such of the States as shall permit the same, shall not be prohibited by the Legislature of the United States, until the year 1808," which was disagreed to, *nem. con.*

The first part of the report was then agreed to as follows:

"The migration or importation of such persons as the several states now existing shall think proper to admit, shall not be prohibited by the Legislature prior to the year 1808."

*   *   *   *   *   *   *   *   *   *

Mr. Sherman was against the second part, ["but a tax or duty may be imposed on such migration or importation at a rate not exceeding *the average of the duties laid on imports,*"] as acknowledging men to be property by taxing them as such under the character of slaves.

*   *   *   *   *   *   *   *   *   *

Mr. Madison *thought it wrong to admit in the Constitution the idea that there could be property in men.* The reason of duties did not hold, as slaves *are not, like merchandise,* consumed.

*   *   *   *   *   *   *   *   *   *

It was finally agreed, *nem., con.* to make the clause read—

"But a tax or duty may be imposed on such importation, not exceeding *ten dollars* for each PERSON."—*Madison Papers*, Aug. 25, 1787.

you say, the great crime of having destroyed it will be upon us! [*Laughter.*] That is cool. [*Great laughter.*] A highwayman holds a pistol to my ear, and mutters through his teeth, "Stand and deliver, or I shall kill you, and then you will be a murderer!".[*Continued laughter.*]

To be sure, what the robber demanded of me—my money—was my own; and I had a clear right to keep it; but it was no more my own than my vote is my own; [*"That's so," and applause,*] and the threat of death to me, to extort my money, and the threat of destruction to the Union, to extort my vote, can scarcely be distinguished in principle.

A few words now to Republicans. *It is exceedingly desirable that all parts of this great Confederacy shall be at peace; and in harmony, one with another. Let us Republicans do our part to have it so.* ["We will," and applause.] *Even though much provoked, let us do nothing through passion and ill temper. Even though the southern people will not so much as listen to us, let us calmly consider their demands, and yield to them if, in our deliberate view of our duty, we possibly can.*[35] Judging by all they say and do, and by the subject and nature of their controversy with us, let us determine, if we can, what will satisfy them.

Will they be satisfied if the Territories be unconditionally surrendered to them? We know they will not. In all their present complaints against us, the Territories are scarcely mentioned. Invasions and insurrections are the rage now. Will it satisfy them, if, in the future, we have nothing to do with invasions and insurrections? We know it will not. We so know, because we know we never had anything to do with invasions and insurrections; and yet this total abstaining does not exempt us from the charge and the denunciation.

The question recurs, what will satisfy them? Simply this: We must not only let them alone, but we must somehow, convince them that we do let them alone. This, we know by experience, is no easy task. We have been so trying to convince them from the very beginning of our organization, but with no success. In all our platforms and speeches we have constantly protested our purpose to let them alone; but this has had no tendency to convince them. Alike unavailing to convince them, is the fact that they have never detected a man of us in any attempt to disturb them.

---

35. Compare this noble passage and that at page 18 [in this book, pages 266–67], with the twaddle of Mr. Orr, (note 30) and the slang of Mr. Douglas (note 37).

These natural, and apparently adequate means all failing, what will convince them? This, and this only: cease to call slavery *wrong*, and join them in calling it *right*. And this must be done thoroughly—done in *acts* as well as in *words*. Silence will not be tolerated—we must place ourselves avowedly with them. Senator Douglas's new sedition law must be enacted and enforced, suppressing all declarations that slavery is wrong, whether made in politics, in presses, in pulpits, or in private. We must arrest and return their fugitive slaves with greedy pleasure. We must pull down our Free State constitutions. The whole atmosphere must be disinfected from all taint of opposition to slavery, before they will cease to believe that all their troubles proceed from us.

I am quite aware they do not state their case precisely in this way. Most of them would probably say to us, "Let us alone, do nothing to us, and say what you please about slavery." But we do let them alone—have never disturbed them—so that, after all, it is what we say, which dissatisfies them. They will continue to accuse us of doing, until we cease saying.

I am also aware they have not, as yet, in terms, demanded the overthrow of our Free-State Constitutions.[36] Yet those Constitutions

---

36. That demand has since been made. Says MR. O'CONOR, counsel for the State of Virginia in the *Lemon Case*, page 44: "We claim that under these various provisions of the Federal Constitution, a citizen of Virginia has an immunity against the operation of any law which the State of New-York can enact, whilst he is a stranger and wayfarer, or whilst passing through our territory; and that he has absolute protection for all his domestic rights, and for all his rights of property, which under the laws of the United States, and the laws of his own State, he was entitled to, whilst in his own State. We claim this, and neither more NOR LESS."

Throughout the whole of that case, in which the right to pass through New-York with slaves at the pleasure of the slave owners is maintained, it is nowhere contended that the statute is contrary to the Constitution of New-York; but that the statute and Constitution of the State are both contrary to the Constitution of the United States.

The State of Virginia, not content with the decision of our own courts upon the right claimed by them, is now engaged in carrying this, the Lemon case, to the Supreme Court of the United States, hoping by a decision there, in accordance with the intimations of the Dred Scott case, to overthrow the Constitution of New-York.

Senator [Robert] Toombs, of Georgia [future Confederate secretary of state—*ed.*] has claimed in the Senate, that laws of Connecticut, Maine, Massachusetts, Michigan, New Hampshire, Ohio, Rhode Island, Vermont, and Wisconsin, for the exclusion of slavery, conceded to be warranted by the State Constitutions, are contrary to the Constitution of the United States, and has asked for the enactment of laws by the General Government which shall override the laws of those States and the Constitutions which authorize them.

declare the wrong of slavery, with more solemn emphasis, than do all other sayings against it; and when all these other sayings shall have been silenced, the overthrow of these Constitutions will be demanded, and nothing be left to resist the demand. It is nothing to the contrary, that they do not demand the whole of this just now. Demanding what they do, and for the reason they do, they can voluntarily stop nowhere short of this consummation. Holding, as they do, that slavery is morally right, and socially elevating, they cannot cease to demand a full national recognition of it, as a legal right, and a social blessing.[37] [*Applause.*]

Nor can we justifiably withhold this, on any ground save our conviction that slavery is wrong. If slavery is right, all words, acts, laws, and constitutions against it, are themselves wrong, and should be silenced, and swept away. If it is right, we cannot justly object to its nationality—its universality; if it is wrong, they cannot justly insist upon its extension—its enlargement. All they ask, we could readily grant, if we thought slavery right; all we ask, they could as readily

---

37. "Policy, humanity, and Christianity, alike forbid the extension of the evils of free society to new people and coming generations."—*Richmond Enquirer, Jan. 22,* 1856.

"I am satisfied that the mind of the South has undergone a change to this great extent, that it is now *the almost universal belief* in the South, not only that the condition of African slavery in their midst, is the best condition to which the African race has ever been subjected, but that *it has the effect of ennobling both races, the white and the black.*"—*Senator* [James] *Mason, of Virginia* [later Confederate envoy to Great Britain—*ed.*].

"I declare again, as I did in reply to the Senator from Wisconsin (Mr. Doolittle,) that, in my opinion, slavery is a great moral, social and political blessing—a blessing to the slave, and a blessing to the master."—*Mr.* [Albert Gallatin] *Brown* [of Mississippi, later a Confederate officer and senator—*ed.*], *in the Senate, March 6,* 1860.

"I am a Southern States' Rights man; I am an African slave-trader. I am one of those Southern men who believe that slavery is right—morally, religiously, socially, and politically." (Applause) * * * * * * I represent the African Slave-trade interests of that section. (Applause.) I am proud of the position I occupy in that respect. I believe the African Slave-trader is a true missionary and a true Christian." (Applause)—*Mr. Gaulden, a delegate from First-Congressional District of Georgia, in the Charleston Convention, now a supporter of Mr. Douglas.*

"Ladies and gentlemen, I would gladly speak again, but you see from the tones of my voice, that I am unable to. This has been a happy, a glorious day. I shall never forget it. There is a charm about this beautiful day, about this sea air, and especially about that peculiar institution of yours—a clam bake. I think you have the advantage, in that respect, of Southerners. For my own part, I have much more fondness for your clams than I have for their niggers. But every man to his taste."—*Hon. Stephen A. Douglas's Address at Rocky Point, R. I., Aug. 2,* 1860.

grant, if they thought it wrong.[38] Their thinking it right, and our thinking it wrong, is the precise fact upon which depends the whole controversy. Thinking it right, as they do, they are not to blame for desiring its full recognition, as being right; but, thinking it wrong, as we do, can we yield to them? Can we cast our votes with their view, and against our own? In view of our moral, social, and political responsibilities, can we do this? [*"No, no," and applause.*]

Wrong as we think slavery is, we can yet afford to let it alone where it is, because that much is due to the necessity arising from its actual presence in the nation; but can we, while our votes will prevent it, allow it to spread into the National Territories, and to overrun us here in these Free States? [*"No, never," and applause. A voice—"Guess not." Laughter.*] If our sense of duty forbids this, then let us stand by our duty, fearlessly and effectively. Let us be diverted by none of those sophistical contrivances wherewith we are so industriously plied and belabored—contrivances such as groping for some middle ground between the right and the wrong, vain as the search for a man who should be neither a living man nor a dead man—such as a policy of "don't care" on a question about which all true men do care—such as Union appeals beseeching true Union men to yield to Disunionists, reversing the divine rule, and calling, not the sinners, but the righteous to repentance—[*prolonged cheers and laughter,*] such as invocations to Washington, imploring men to unsay what Washington said, and undo what Washington did.

---

38. It is interesting to observe how two profoundly logical minds, though holding extreme, opposite views, have deduced this common conclusion. Says Mr. O'Conor, the eminent leader of the New-York Bar, and the counsel for the State of Virginia in the Lemon case, in his speech at Cooper Institute, December 19th, 1859:—

"That is the point to which this great argument must come—Is negro slavery unjust? If it is unjust, it violates the first rule of human conduct—'Render to every man his due.' If it is unjust, it violates the law of God which says, 'Love thy neighbor as thyself,' for that requires that we should perpetuate no injustice. Gentlemen, if it could be maintained that negro slavery was unjust, perhaps I might be prepared—perhaps we all ought to be prepared—to go with that distinguished man to whom allusion is frequently made, and say, 'There is a higher law which compels us to trample beneath our feet the Constitution established by our fathers, with all the blessings it secures to our children' [the words of New York Senator William H. Seward, by then defeated by Lincoln for the presidential nomination—*ed.*]. But I insist—and that is the argument which we must meet, and on which we must come to a conclusion that shall govern our actions in the future selection of representatives in the Congress of the United States—I insist that negro slavery is not unjust."

Neither let us be slandered from our duty by false accusations against us, nor frightened from it by menaces of destruction to the Government nor of dungeons to ourselves. [*Applause*.] LET US HAVE FAITH THAT RIGHT MAKES MIGHT, AND IN THAT FAITH, LET US, TO THE END, DARE TO DO OUR DUTY AS WE UNDERSTAND IT.

["Three rousing cheers were given to the orator"—*The New York Times*; the *Evening Post* reported a standing ovation, with "the waving of handkerchiefs and hats, and repeated cheers."]

Glossary of Terms Used in Nott-Brainerd Footnotes and Lincoln Text

Ib.	*ibidem* (literally "there the same," referring to the previous book, chapter, or page)
Vide	*vide ante* ("see before") or *vide infra* ("see below")
Viz.	*videlicit* ("that is to say," or "for example")
Id.	*idem* ("same as previously mentioned")
Nem. Com.	*nemine contradicente* ("with no one contesting, or unanimously")
Ante	"Prior"
Pari passu	"At an equal pace or rate"

⊰ NOTES ⊱

INTRODUCTION

1. See Andrew Freeman, *Abraham Lincoln in New York* (New York: Coward-McCann, 1960). As of this writting, the only other significant study of the speech was a monograph, Benjamin Barondess, *Lincoln's Cooper Institute Speech* (New York: The Civil War Round Table of New York, 1954), which was later included in Barondess's book, *Three Lincoln Masterpieces* (Charleston: Education Foundation of West Virginia, 1954).

2. Don E. Fehrenbacher, *Prelude to Greatness: Lincoln in the 1850's* (Stanford: Stanford University Press, 1962), 102. Lincoln himself joined the throng that went off to hear another politician, Owen Lovejoy, give a speech after the first debate with Douglas at Ottawa on August 21, 1858. See Earl Schenck Miers, ed., *Lincoln Day by Day: A Chronology, 1809–1865*, 3 vols. (Washington: Lincoln Sesquicentennial Commission, 1960), 2:225.

3. Robert W. Johannsen, *Stephen A. Douglas* (New York: Oxford University Press, 1973), 641.

4. James D. Horan, *Mathew Brady: Historian with a Camera* (New York: Crown Publishers, 1952), 32. Horan quoted Lincoln's friend, later White House aide, and biographer, Ward Hill Lamon. For a subsequent paraphrasing, see Rufus Rockwell Wilson, *Intimate Memories of Lincoln* (New York: Primavera Press, 1945), 248.

CHAPTER ONE: "ABE LINCOLN MUST COME"

1. *Daily* (Springfield) *Illinois State Journal*, October 17, 1859; October 20, 1859; October 14, 1859.

2. "Great Popular Demonstration," ibid., October 17, 1859.

3. *Williams' Springfield Directory and City Guide for 1860–61* (Springfield: Johnson & Bradford, 1860), 143. The telegraph operator who received and printed the telegram was C. F. McIntyre.

4. Vote tallies, *Daily Illinois State Journal*, November 18, 1859. Republicans also won by twenty-four thousand in Pennsylvania, taking the legislature.

5. Original telegram in the Abraham Lincoln Papers, Library of Congress.

6. *Daily Illinois State Journal*, October 17, 1859; October 18, 1859.

7. Ibid., October 18, 1859, quoting the *Lancaster* (Pennsylvania) *Examiner & Journal*.

8. James A. Briggs to Lincoln, August 30, 1858, Abraham Lincoln Papers, Library of Congress.

9. See, for example, Ida M. Tarbell, *The Life of Abraham Lincoln*, orig. pub. 1895, 2 vols. (New York: Lincoln Memorial Assoc. and McClure, Phillips & Co., 1900), 1:326. Tarbell contended that Lincoln "feared he was not equal to an Eastern audience."

10. Ward H. Lamon, *The Life of Abraham Lincoln* . . . (Boston: James R. Osgood, 1872), 424.

11. Paul M. Angle, *Here I Have Lived: A History of Lincoln's Springfield, 1821–1865*, rev. ed. (Chicago: Abraham Lincoln Book Shop, 1971), 231.

12. This and the succeeding quotations are from William H. Herndon to Ward Hill Lamon, March 6, 1870. Original in the Henry E. Huntington Library, No. 346. Herndon's recollections were written ten years after the event, by which time he evidently had forgotten that Lincoln was invited to Brooklyn, not New York, which remained a separate city until 1898.

13. David Donald, *Lincoln's Herndon* (New York: Alfred A. Knopf, 1948), 115.

14. William H. Herndon, *Herndon's Lincoln: The True Story of a Great Life*. . . , 3 vols. (orig. pub. 1889; Springfield, Ill.: The Herndon's Lincoln Publishing Co., n.d.), 2:375.

15. See, for example, Willard L. King, *Lincoln's Manager, David Davis* (Chicago: University of Chicago Press, 1960), 131.

16. Herndon, *Herndon's Lincoln*, 3:454.

17. The occupations of the committee members are from Henry C. Bowen, "Recollections of Abraham Lincoln," in William Hayes Ward, ed., *Abraham Lincoln: Tributes from His Associates* (New York: Thomas Y. Crowell, 1895), 27.

18. Allen Thorndike Rice, ed., *Reminiscences of Abraham Lincoln by Distinguished Men of His Time* (New York: North American Publishing Co., 1886), 247.

19. James A. Briggs, "His Lecture at the Cooper Institute in 1860," *New York Evening Post*, August 16, 1867, reprinted in appendix of Charles Godfrey Leland, *Abraham Lincoln and the Abolition of Slavery in the United States* (New York: G. P. Putnam's Sons, 1881), 245. See also James A. Briggs, *An Authentic Account of Hon. Abraham Lincoln Being Invited to Give an Address in Cooper Institute, New York . . .* (Putnam, Conn.: privately printed, 1915).

20. The original is lost. Pettengill's letter was reproduced in part in the *Catalogue of the Oliver R. Barrett Lincoln Collection, February 19–20, 1952* (New York: Parke-Bernet Galleries, 1952), 87.

21. Briggs to Lincoln, November 1, 1859, Abraham Lincoln Papers, Library of Congress.

22. Lincoln was hired by relatives of murder victim James W. Bandy to ensure the vigorous prosecution of accused murderer Alexander W. Kilpatrick, who had fled the jurisdiction. See Donald G. Richter, *Lincoln: Twenty Years on the Eastern Prairie* (Montoon, Ill.: United Graphics, 1999), 239.

23. Roy P. Basler, ed., *The Collected Works of Abraham Lincoln*, 9 vols. (New Brunswick, N.J.: Rutgers University Press, 1953–55; hereinafter cited as *Collected Works*), 3:494. By the time Lincoln could respond to Briggs, the New York elections were over and Republicans had done well.

24. The most exhaustive study of Lincoln's career as a lecturer is Wayne C. Temple, "Lincoln the Lecturer," esp. Part 1, *Lincoln Herald* 3 (Fall 1999): 94–110.

25. Lyceums also gave entertainment-starved local residents something useful to do on lonely evenings that otherwise tempted citizens to mischief and worse. See Mary W. Graham, "The Lyceum Movement and Sectional Controversy, 1860," in J. Jeffrey Auer, ed., *Antislavery and Disunion, 1858–1861: Studies in the Rhetoric of Compromise and Conflict* (New York: Harper & Row, 1963), 108, 113.

26. *Collected Works*, 1:108–15. The best historiographical essay on the lecture, particularly in its analysis of Edmund Wilson's writings, is Mark E. Neely, Jr., "Lincoln's Lyceum Speech and the Origins of a Modern Myth," *Lincoln Lore*, Nos. 1776 and 1777 (February and March 1987).

27. His address to the Washington Temperance Society of Springfield was delivered on February 22, 1842; his address to the Wisconsin State Agricultural Society of Milwaukee, on September 30, 1859. Lincoln took his

"discoveries and inventions" talk to "small and waning audiences," in Henry Clay Whitney's words, at Bloomington, Jacksonville, Clinton, Decatur, and finally at Springfield, once to a house so small that Lincoln declined the honorarium and canceled the appearance. See description by J. H. Burnham in Harry E. Pratt, ed., *Concerning Mr. Lincoln* (Springfield: The Abraham Lincoln Association, 1944), 22. Henry Clay Whitney described Lincoln as "crestfallen" in *Life on the Circuit with Lincoln,* (Boston: Estes and Lauriat, 1892), 215.

28. Whitney, *Life on the Circuit with Lincoln,* 214.

29. The "Gus" letter was dated January 28, 1860. Pratt, *Concerning Mr. Lincoln,* 21.

30. "I must stick to the courts awhile," he explained to one writer. See Lincoln to William M. Morris, March 28, 1859, *Collected Works,* 3:374. For other invitations, see letters from Nathan B. Dodson, July 28, 1859; D. W. Young, February 10, 1859; F. Quinn, November 3, 1859; Dwight Deming, December 17, 1859; S. A. Holt, January 30, 1860—all in the Abraham Lincoln Papers, Library of Congress.

31. Lincoln to F. C. Herbruger, *Collected Works,* 4:40. By the time he wrote those words, the Cooper Union lecture was already behind him.

32. Whitney, *Life on the Circuit with Lincoln,* 214; Lamon, *The Life of Abraham Lincoln,* 1872, 421.

33. Herndon to Lamon, March 6, 1870.

34. Herndon, *Herndon's Lincoln,* 2:375; Herndon's own lecture on "The Sweep of Commerce," the pro-Lincoln *State Journal* reported awkwardly, was "altogether too good for the size of the audience."; see *Illinois State Journal,* March 16, 1860. Lincoln never lost enthusiasm for his "discoveries and inventions" talk. When, as president, he met Louis Agassiz, the celebrated Swiss-born naturalist who gave an Amazon River talk at Cooper Union, the famous scientist asked Lincoln if he had tried lecturing himself. Lincoln could not quite help recalling his own efforts with nostalgic pride. He proceeded to give "the outline of a lecture which he had partly written, to show the origin of inventions, and prove that there is nothing new under the sun." Even then, Lincoln regarded his lecture on discoveries and inventions as unfinished—a success waiting to happen. Politely, Agassiz "begged that Lincoln would finish the lecture some time," to which the president replied that "when I get out of this place, I'll finish it up," and perhaps "print it somewhere." Of course, he never got the chance. See Herbert Mitgang, ed., *Washington in Lincoln's Time by Noah Brooks* (New York: Rinehardt & Co., 1958), 268–69.

35. John S. Goff, *Robert Todd Lincoln: A Man in His Own Right* (Norman, Okla.: University of Oklahoma Press, 1969), 24.

36. Autobiography for John L. Scripps, *Collected Works*, 4: 62.

37. George Haven Putnam, *Abraham Lincoln: The People's Leader in the Struggle for National Existence* (New York: G. P. Putnam's, 1909), quoted in Louis A. Warren, "Copper Union Legends Scrutinized," *Lincoln Lore*, No. 1465 (March 1960).

38. Legends die hard. Elwin L. Page argued in 1929 that "the desire to visit Robert at his school, not the ambition to forward his own fortunes, was clearly the chief motive for accepting the invitation to make an address in the East. The chance to finance the trip to Exeter appealed to the father, not the politician." Echoed Robert's own biographer, John S. Goff: "The speech was merely a by-product of Lincoln's desire to see his son."

39. Justin G. Turner and Linda Levitt Turner, eds., *Mary Todd Lincoln: Her Life and Letters* (New York: Alfred A. Knopf, 1972), 58, 60.

40. Francis Fisher Browne, *The Every Day Life of Lincoln* . . . (New York and St. Louis: N. D. Thompson, 1886), 312–13.

41. D. D. T. Marshall and others to Lincoln, October 26, 1859, Abraham Lincoln Papers, Library of Congress. The other signatories were Owen W. Brennan, Thomas Little, S. B. Dutcher, E. F. Shepard. C. F. E. Luder, H. T. Cleveland, and George Sparrow.

42. Briggs in Leland, *Abraham Lincoln and the Abolition of Slavery in the United States*, 246; the ice-in-the-river explanation appears in the church's visitor pamphlet, *Historic Notes*, n.d. Historian Philip Van Doren Stern, for one, argued on the centennial of the speech that his hosts transferred the event to Cooper Union when they became convinced that he could "fill up the Great Hall." See Stern, "Cooper Union Talk a Success," *Illinois State Journal*, February 13, 1960.

43. Brigg's handwritten, signed comment about the Young Men's Republican group is on his personal copy of R. C. McCormick's published reminiscences, now in the Western Reserve Historical Society, Cleveland, Ohio.

44. Origins noted in prefatory notes to *An Oration Delivered by Hon. Charles Sumner under the Auspices of the Young Men's Republican Union of New York, November 27, 1861* (New York: Young Men's Republican Union, 1861). The roster of 1860 officers and elders is listed in *The Address of the Hon. Abraham Lincoln in Vindication of the Policy of the Framers of the Constitution* . . . (New York: George F. Nesbitt & Co., 1860). Reports of the other "young men's" activities are in the *New York Herald*, February 25 (Republican Committee) and February 28 (National Union), 1860.

45. Eveline D. Brainerd, "The Cooper Union Meeting," typescript in the Lincoln Museum, Fort Wayne, Indiana (Ms. Brainerd was the niece of Cephas Brainerd); George Haven Putnam, *Abraham Lincoln the Great Captain* (Oxford: Clarendon Press, 1928), 8.

46. Putnam, *Abraham Lincoln the Great Captain*, 8.

47. Brainerd, "The Cooper Union Meeting," *The Address of the Hon. Abraham Lincoln*. . . .

48. Charles C. Nott to Abraham Lincoln, February 9, 1860, Abraham Lincoln Papers, Library of Congress. His judicial candidacy at the time was reported in *Harper's Weekly*, December 5, 1896.

49. James A. Briggs to Abraham Lincoln, February 15, 1860, Abraham Lincoln Papers, Library of Congress. Briggs's reference to "this great Commercial Metropolis" should have offered Lincoln a clue that the venue for his lecture had shifted to New York.

CHAPTER TWO: "SO MUCH LABOR AS THIS"

1. William H. Herndon, *Herndon's Lincoln: The True Story of a Great Life*, 3 vols., orig. pub. 1889 (Springfield, Ill.: Herndon's Lincoln Publishing Co., n.d.), 3:514–15.

2. The quotations are from Lincoln's address at Bloomington, September 26, 1854, as reported in the *Peoria Weekly Republican*, *Collected Works*, 2:238–39.

3. Ibid., 461–62. Lincoln's response to both Kansas-Nebraska and Dred Scott are well detailed in Mark E. Neely, Jr., *The Abraham Lincoln Encyclopedia* (New York: McGraw-Hill, 1982), 90–91, 170–71.

4. *Collected Works*, 2:276.

5. *Collected Works*, 3:16.

6. See Lincoln's speech at Peoria, October 16, 1854, ibid., 2:255, 265.

7. *Collected Works*, 2:403.

8. Henry B. Rankin, *Personal Recollections of Abraham Lincoln* (New York: G. P. Putnam's Sons, 1916), 246. Rankin's prolific reminiscences on all manner of Lincoln subjects are discounted by most modern historians, yet he clearly observed or heard enough believable detail about Cooper Union at the time of its preparation to merit tolerant inclusion in any full treatment of the speech. Lincoln certainly knew Rankin; on February 23, 1858, he felt "honored" to sign his new autograph album. See *Collected Works*, 2:435.

9. *Collected Works*, 2:378.

10. Ibid., 246.

11. Gas lighting was installed in the State Capitol as early as 1855. See Sunderine Wilson Temple and Wayne C. Temple, *Illinois' Fifth Capitol: The House that Lincoln Built and Caused to be Rebuilt (1837–1865)* Springfield: Phillips Brothers, 1988), 127–29.

12. Henry B. Rankin, "Comments and Corrections on 'The Lincoln Life-Mask and How It Was Made,'" *Journal of the Illinois State Historical Society*, 8 (July 1915):250–51.

13. *New York Times*, March 12, 1859.

14. Lincoln to Thomas J. Pickett, editor of the *Rock Island* (Illinois) *Register*, April 16, 1859, in *Collected Works*, 3:377.

15. Earl Schenck Miers, ed., *Lincoln Day by Day: A Chronology, 1809–1865*, 3 vols. (Washington: Lincoln Sesquicentennial Commission, 1959), 2:266–73.

16. *Collected Works*, 3:376. The form letter requesting his presence in Boston was, technically, Lincoln's first invitation to speak in the East, but it was impersonal enough for him to decline.

17. Neither Lincoln's nor Douglas's name was actually on the 1858 ballot. But statewide Republican candidates won more than 125,000 votes, or 49.9%; Democrats over 121,000 votes, or 47%. See Harold Holzer, *The Lincoln-Douglas Debates: The First Complete Unexpurgated Text* (New York: HarperCollins, 1993), 373.

18. Robert W. Johannsen, *The Frontier, the Union, and Stephen A. Douglas* (Urbana: University of Illinois Press, 1989), 124, esp. the chapter, "Stephen A. Douglas, *Harper's Magazine*, and Popular Sovereignty."

19. Ibid., 125.

20. Robert W. Johannsen, *Stephen A. Douglas* (New York: Oxford University Press, 1973), 710. Ironically, four years later, as president, Lincoln would defend his administration's restrictions on civil liberties as likewise necessary to preserve the body politic, explaining with a similar use of metaphor: "By general law life *and* limb must be protected; yet often a limb must be amputated to save a life; but a life is never wisely given to save a limb." See Lincoln to Albert G. Hodges, April 4, 1864, *Collected Works*, 7:281.

21. Stephen A. Douglas, "The Dividing Line Between Federal and Local Authority: Popular Sovereignty in the Territories," *Harper's New Monthly Magazine*, 19 (September 1859):519. An excellent commentary on the article can be found in Harry V. Jaffa, *A New Birth of Freedom: Abraham Lincoln and The Coming of the Civil War* (Lanham, Md.: Rowman, Littlefield, Inc., 2000), 473–89. Jaffa points to Douglas's insistence that the rights of community trumped those of equality.

22. Stephen A. Douglas, "The Dividing Line Between Federal and Local Authority," 519, 521, 526, 528.

23. Historian Robert Johannsen discovered this subterfuge: See Johannsen, *The Frontier, the Union, and Stephen A. Douglas*, 130.

24. Ibid., 126–27.

25. William T. Bascomb to Abraham Lincoln, September 1, 1859, Abraham Lincoln Papers, Library of Congress; *Collected Works*, 3:399.

26. Ward H. Lamon, *The Life of Abraham Lincoln* (Boston: James R. Osgood, 1872), 424; *Chicago Press and Tribune*, September 14, 1859.

27. *Collected Works*, 3:403, 406, 412–13.

28. Ibid., 413, 411.

29. Justin G. Turner and Linda Levitt Turner, eds., *Mary Todd Lincoln: Her Life and Letters* (New York: Alfred A. Knopf, 1972), 59; "Speech of Senator Douglas at Cincinnati," *New York Times*, September 12, 1859.

30. *Collected Works*, 3:435, 457.

31. Ibid., 453.

32. Ibid., 465–66.

33. Lincoln to William E. Frazer, Ibid., 491.

34. Ibid., 398.

35. Ibid., 399.

36. Roy P. Basler, ed., *The Collected Works of Abraham Lincoln: Supplement 1832–1865* (Westport, Conn.: The Greenwood Press, 1974), 42.

37. Robert W. Johannsen, ed., *The Letters of Stephen A. Douglas* (Urbana: University of Illinois Press, 1961), 477–78.

38. *Collected Works*, 3:496.

39. Ibid., 502.

40. Ibid., 496, 501, 504.

41. Ibid., 504.

42. Ibid., 343; Holzer, ed., *The Lincoln-Douglas Debates*, 29.

43. *Collected Works*, 3:347, 373, 515.

44. Lincoln to Samuel Galloway, December 19, 1859, Basler, ed., *Collected Works of Abraham Lincoln: Supplement*, 47.

45. *Collected Works*, 3:511–12.

46. Willard King, *Lincoln's Manager, David Davis* (Chicago: The University of Chicago Press, 1960), 129–30; clippings on the controversy, including the libel suit, were sent to Lincoln by Wentworth—see esp. Wentworth to Lincoln, January 13, 1860, Abraham Lincoln Papers, Library of Congress.

47. Lincoln to Judd, December 9, 1859; Lincoln to George W. Dole, Gurdon S. Hubbard, and William H. Brown, December 14, 1859, in *Collected Works*, 3:505, 508.

48. Wentworth to Lincoln, February 9, 1860, Abraham Lincoln Papers, Library of Congress.

49. Lincoln to Judd, February 9, 1860, *Collected Works*, 3:517; Lincoln to Wentworth, Don E. Fehrenbacher, *Abraham Lincoln: Collected Speeches and Writings*, 2 vols. (New York: Library of America, 1989), 2:728-9n. See also Don E. Fehrenbacher, "Lincoln and the Mayor of Chicago," in *Lincoln in Text and Context: Collected Essays* (Stanford: Stanford University Press, 1987), 33–43.

50. *Chicago Press and Tribune*, February 16, 1860; Judd to Lincoln, February 21, 1860, Abraham Lincoln Papers, Library of Congress.

51. Basler, ed., *Collected Works of Abraham Lincoln: Supplement*, 48.

52. Wentworth to Lincoln, February 22, 1860, Abraham Lincoln Papers, Library of Congress.

53. Davis to Lincoln, February 21, 1860, Abraham Lincoln Papers, Library of Congress. Wentworth went on to secure the nomination, and win re-election as mayor of Chicago.

54. Henry B. Rankin, *Personal Recollections of Abraham Lincoln* (New York: G. P. Putnam's Sons, 1916), 246; Herndon, *Herndon's Lincoln*, 1:191.

55. Lamon, *Life of Abraham Lincoln*, 471.

56. Robert Todd Lincoln to Isaac Markens, November 4, 1917, original in the Chicago Historical Society. See also Paul M. Angle, ed., *A Portrait of Abraham Lincoln by His Oldest Son* (Chicago: Chicago Historical Society, 1968), 47.

57. Robert Taylor Conrad, *Sanderson's Biography of the Signers to the Declaration of Independence* (Philadelphia: Thomas, Cowperthwait & Co., 1847). The original owned by Lincoln resides today in the collection at Robert Todd Lincoln's "Hildene," his summer home in Manchester, Vermont. See Wayne C. Temple, "Lincoln the Lecturer," *Lincoln Herald*, 102 (Fall 1999):96.

58. *Collected Works*, 1:115; Herndon, *Herndon's Lincoln*, 3:455n. The private library of William H. Herndon, including the book cited, was sold at auction by W. O. Davie & Co. of Cincinnati on January 10 and 11, 1873; a broadside advertising the sale is in the Rare Books Division, Library of Congress.

59. *Collected Works*, 1:113.

60. *Elliott's Debates*, 5 vols. (Philadelphia: J. B. Lippincott, 1891), 3:534, 590.

61. Lincoln to Charles Lanman, June 9, 1860, *Collected Works*, 4:74. Hinton Rowan Helper, *The Impending Crisis of the South: How to Meet It* (New York: A. B. Burdick, 1860), 151.

62. *Collected Works*, 3:537n.26.

63. *Collected Works*, 5:537.

64. Leonard W. Volk, "The Lincoln Life-Mask and How it was Made," *Century Magazine*, 23 (December 1881): 223–28.

65. Charles C. Nott in George Haven Putnam, *Abraham Lincoln: The People's Leader in the Struggle for National Existence* (New York: G. P. Putnam's Sons, 1909), 219; Herndon, *Herndon's Lincoln*, 3:454.

66. Herndon, *Herndon's Lincoln*, 3:454.

CHAPTER THREE: "SOME CONFUSION IN THE ARRANGEMENTS"

1. J. A. Gano to Lincoln, January 18, 1860; Josiah M. Lucas, February 5, 1860, Abraham Lincoln Papers, Library of Congress.

2. Horace White to Lincoln, February 13, 1860, Abraham Lincoln Papers, Library of Congress.

3. *Illinois Daily State Journal*, February 20, 1865; *Chicago Press and Tribune*, February 16, 1860.

4. Henry B. Rankin, *Personal Recollections of Abraham Lincoln* (New York: G. P. Putnam's Sons, 1916), 246; R. C. McCormick, "Abraham Lincoln. Interesting Reminiscences. Lincoln's Visit to New York in 1860. . . ," *New York Times*, May 3, 1860, copy in the Illinois State Historical Library, Springfield, Illinois. Also published in *Littell's Living Age*, May 1860, copy in the Lincoln Museum, Fort Wayne, Indiana. "Foolscap" described in Christopher A. Schnell, *Stovepipe Hat and Quill Pen: The Artifacts of Abraham Lincoln's Law Practice* (Springfield: Illinois Historic Preservation Agency, 2002), 17.

5. Harry E. Pratt, *The Personal Finances of Abraham Lincoln* (Springfield: The Abraham Lincoln Association, 1943), 163, 170–71; Earl Schenck Miers, ed., *Lincoln Day by Day: A Chronology, 1809–1865*, 3 vols. (Washington: Lincoln Sesquicentennial Commission, 1959), 2:271; *Williams' Springfield Directory . . . for 1860–61* (Springfield: Johnson & Bradford, 1860), 144.

6. *Lincoln Day by Day*, 2:198; Justin G. Turner and Linda Levitt Turner, *Mary Todd Lincoln: Her Life and Letters* (New York: Alfred A. Knopf, 1972), 50.

7. Abraham Jonas to Lincoln, February 3, 1860, Abraham Lincoln Papers, Library of Congress.

8. Horace White to Abraham Lincoln, February 13, 1860, Abraham Lincoln Papers, Library of Congress; Lincoln to Horace White, February 13, 1860, *Collected Works*, 3:519.

9. *Illinois Daily State Journal*, February 22, 1860, February 23, 1860. The New York City weather was reported in the *New York Tribune*, February 23, 1860. Another stubborn Cooper Union myth, disproved by these reports, is that, as Henry B. Rankin asserted: "No notice of his departure, or purpose of the journey, was made by the local papers." See Henry B. Rankin, *Lincoln's Cooper Union Speech Fifty-Six Years Ago* (Springfield, Ill.: State Register Printers, 1917), 4.

10. Pratt, *Personal Finances*, 179; Rankin, *Personal Recollections of Abraham Lincoln*, 247.

11. The *Illinois State Register* announcement was picked up in the anti-Lincoln Chicago *Daily Times* on February 26, while Lincoln was in New York City.

12. "Lincoln and the Reporters," *Washington Post*, n.d., original clipping in the Lincoln Museum, Fort Wayne, Indiana; Andrew Freeman, *Abraham Lincoln Goes to New York* (New York: Coward-McCann, 1960), 54.

13. The legend has been printed in, among other places, Robert S. Harper, *Lincoln and the Press* (New York: McGraw-Hill, 1951), 44, and Andrew A. Freeman, *Abraham Lincoln Goes to New York* (New York: Coward-McCann, 1960), 54–55.

14. Louis A. Warren, "Cooper Union Legends Scrutinized: A Centennial Monograph," *Lincoln Lore*, No. 1465 (March 1960).

15. [Fort Wayne] *Dawson's Daily News*, February 23, 1860, ibid.

16. Wayne C. Temple, "When Lincoln Left Town with Another Woman," *Lincoln Herald*, 68 (Winter 1966); 175–77, 182. Mrs. Smith later claimed: "He learned much of his Cooper Institute speech" by repeating passages from his oration while marching Dudley up and down the streets "perched high on his shoulders." See "Friends of Lincoln. A Bloomington Lady Tells Some Interesting Incidents About That Great Man," *Bloomington Pantagraph*, February 19, 1895, copy in the Lincoln Museum, Fort Wayne, Indiana.

17. Ibid.; L. E. Chittenden, *Recollections of President Lincoln and his Administration* (New York: Harper & Brothers, 1891), 65.

18. Some trains of the day did feature a "sleeping coach." See Wayne C. Temple, "Lincoln the Lecturer, Part II," *Lincoln Herald*, 101 (Winter 1999), 53. Temple further believes that Mrs. Smith emphasized the absence of sleepers to make certain that no one suspected her of impropriety with the future president. Temple to Holzer, January 15, 2003.

19. "Friends of Lincoln"; John W. Starr, Jr., *Lincoln & the Railroads* (New York: Dodd, Mead & Co., 1927), 100.

20. Starr, *Lincoln & the Railroads*, 100.

21. Lincoln made the remarks as president-elect in an address to the Philadelphia Select council on February 22, 1861. See *Collected Works*, 4:240.

22. Mark E. Neely, Jr., "Lincoln's Theory of Representation: A Significant New Lincoln Document," *Lincoln Lore*, No. 1683 (May 1978).

23. Wilmot ultimately turned on Cameron and supported Lincoln at the Republican convention. Perhaps in exchange for its votes, Pennsylvania earned a cabinet post in the Lincoln administration, and Cameron was appointed, serving for a time as secretary of war. See Mark E. Neely, Jr., *The Abraham Lincoln Encyclopedia* (New York: McGraw-Hill, 1973), 45–47, 338.

24. *Collected Works*, 3:521. The "enclosed" Wilmot letter has never surfaced.

25. Louis A. Warren, "Cooper Union Legends Scrutinized"; John Steele Gordon, "Standard Time: We All Live by What Happened on November 18, 1863," *American Heritage* (July–August 2001), 22; ferry routes detailed in Kenneth T. Jackson, ed., *The Encyclopedia of New York City* (New Haven: Yale University Press, 1995), 198.

26. *New York Daily News*, February 27, 1860.

27. *New York Daily News*, March 3, 1860.

28. Ernest Duvergier de Hauranne, *A Frenchman in Lincoln's America: Huit Mois en Amérique—Lettres et Notes de Voyage, 1864–1865* (Chicago: R. R. Donnelley & Sons, 1974), 19–20.

29. Mary C. Henderson, *The City and the Theatre: New York Playhouses From Bowling Green to Times Square* (Clifton, N.J.: James T. White & Co., 1973), 102. For Lincoln's comments on Webster and Clay on yet another visit to the Astor House in 1861, see *Collected Works*, 4:230. The social season was covered in *New York Illustrated News*, January 14, 1860.

30. Edward K. Spann, *Gotham at War: New York City, 1860–1865* (Wilmington, Del.: SR Books, 2002), 84; Edwin G. Burrows and Mike Wallace, *Gotham: A History of New York City to 1898* (New York: Oxford University Press, 1999), 862.

31. Circulations compared in *New York Evening Sun*, March 2, 1860, *Washington National Era*, March 8, 1860; advertisements for the *Weekly Tribune* in *Tribune Tracts.—Number 4*, original in the Gilder Lehrman Collection, examined in Morgan Library, New York. See also *New York Sun* advertisement in *New York Tribune*, March 3, 1860.

32. *New York Sun* advertisement in the *New York Tribune*, March 3, 1860; *New York Times*, February 25, 1860.

33. *New York Times*, February 22, 1860; James G. Randall, *Lincoln the Presi-*

dent, 4 vols. (New York: Dodd Mead, 1945), 1:136; William Harlan Hale, *Horace Greeley: Voice of the People* (New York: Harper & Bros., 1950), 210; *New York Herald*, February 28, 1860; Howard K. Beale, ed., *The Diary of Edward Bates, 1859–1866* (Washington: U.S. Government Printing Office, 1933), 105.

34. Frederic A. Conningham, *Currier & Ives Prints: An Illustrated Check List*, rev. ed. (New York: Crown), 1970, 3, 299; Burrows and Wallace, *Gotham*, 369–70. I am indebted to Philip E. Schoenberg for sharing the text for his scholarly guided tour, *Lincoln's New York*.

35. Hauranne, *A Frenchman in Lincoln's America*, 20; Herbert Mitgang, ed., *Edward Dicey's Spectator of America* (Chicago: Quadrangle Books, 1971), 13.

36. *Frank Leslie's Illustrated Newspaper*, December 2, 1865; Clarence P. Hornung, *The Way it Was: New York, 1850–1890* (New York: Schocken, 1977), 30–33.

37. Hauranne, *A Frenchman in Lincoln's America*, 20–21.

38. *New York Daily News*, March 3, 1860; Allan Nevins and Milton Halsey-Thomas, eds., *The Diary of George Templeton Strong*, 4 vols. (New York: Macmillan, 1952), 2:12; *New York Times*, February 27, 1860.

39. Timothy J. Gilfoyle, *City of Eros: New York City, Prostitution, and the Commercialization of Sex, 1790–1829* (New York: W. W. Norton, 1992), 58, 230–31.

40. *Philadelphia Sun Dispatch*, March 4, 1860; reprint from the Morristown, New Jersey, *Burlington County Advertiser*.

41. Eric Homberger, *Scenes from the Life of a City: Corruption and Conscience in Old New York* (New Haven: Yale University Press, 1994), 38–39.

42. Ibid., 47–48.

43. Dicey, *Spectator of America*, 11.

44. David M. Potter, *Lincoln and His Party in the Secession Crisis*, orig. pub. 1942 (Baton Rouge: Louisiana State University Press, 1995), 117; Philip S. Foner, *Business and Slavery: The New York Merchants and the Irrepressible Conflict* (Chapel Hill: University of North Carolina Press, 1941), 4, 8; McKay, *The Civil War in New York*, 18.

45. *New York City Register* (New York: H. Wilson, 1859), 12–17, 21, 28–29, 33–35, 41.

46. George B. Lincoln to Cephas Brainerd, February 13, 1890, copy in the Lincoln Museum, Fort Wayne, Indiana; Nathan Silver, *Lost New York* (New York: American Legacy Press, 1967), 68; [New York] *Journal of Commerce*, February 28, 1860. For prices of hotels, see Henderson, *The City and the Theatre*, 102.

47. Lincoln to Cornelius F. McNeill, April 6, 1860, *Collected Works*, 4:38; *New York Tribune*, February 25, 1860.

48. Lincoln to Hannibal Hamlin, September 28, 1862, *Collected Works*, 5:444.

49. McCormick, "Lincoln's Visit to New York in 1860," *New York Times*, May 3, 1860.

50. George B. Lincoln to Brainerd, February 13, 1890.

51. *New York Independent*, March 15, 1860, February 23, 1860, March 16, 1860.

52. Henry B. Rankin, *Intimate Character Sketches of Abraham Lincoln* (Philadelphia: J. B. Lippincott, 1924), 178–81.

53. Ibid. I have broken Bowen's long reminiscence into paragraphs to make it easier to read—and appreciate.

54. Henry C. Bowen, "Recollections of Abraham Lincoln," in William Hayes Ward, ed., *Abraham Lincoln: Tributes from His Associates* (New York: Thomas Y. Crowell, 1895), 27.

55. Charles C. Nott to Cephas Brainerd, March 16, 1896, Gilder Lehrman Collection, GLC 4471.01, examined at the Morgan Library, New York.

56. Bowen, "Recollections of Abraham Lincoln," 27–28; Henry R. Stiles, *History of the City of Brooklyn* . . . 3 vols. (Brooklyn: Published by Subscription, 1867), 3:787.

57. *New York Evening Post*, February 25, 1860. This was surely the first time Lincoln had ever been called, however jokingly, a "pro-slavery man."

58. James H. Callender, *Yesterday on Brooklyn Heights* (New York: The Dorland Press, 1927), 152; Stephen M. Griswold, *Sixty Years with Plymouth Church* (New York: Fleming H. Revell, 1907), 28, 35.

59. Griswold, *Sixty Years with Plymouth Church*, 34–35, 52. For Parker, whose works Herndon owned, and Lincoln read, see Garry Wills, *Lincoln at Gettysburg: The Words that Remade America* (New York: Simon & Schuster, 1992), 111.

60. *Trow's Guide to New York, 1860*, 20; Stiles, *History of the City of Brooklyn*, 3:551; McKay, *The Civil War and New York City*, 17.

61. Wayne C. Temple, *Abraham Lincoln: From Skeptic to Prophet* (Mahomet, Ill.: Mayhaven 1995), 49.

62. George B. Lincoln to Brainerd, February 13, 1890.

63. Bowen, "Recollections of Abraham Lincoln," 28.

64. Ibid., *New York Independent*, March 1, 1860. Mrs. Beecher's "neuralgic" affliction described in the *Brooklyn Daily Eagle*, February 27, 1860, which carried no report of Lincoln's visit, or his speech at Cooper Union. Seward's Senate speech, on the other hand, was fully reported on March 1.

65. Bowen, "Recollections of Abraham Lincoln," 28–29.

66. Clarence Winthrop Bowen quoted in Callender, *Yesterdays on Brooklyn Heights*, 149–50.

67. Bowen, "Recollections of Abraham Lincoln," 29.

68. *New York Times*, January 25, 1860.

Chapter Four: "Much the Best Portrait"

1. *New York Times*, February 27, 1860.

2. *New York Tribune*, February 25, 1860; *The Mississippian*, quoted in *Illinois State Daily Journal*, February 18, 1860.

3. *New York Herald*, February 27, 1860.

4. Chase was invited to lecture on at least two occasions, September 26, 1859, and October 26, 1859. Original letters in the collection of the Lincoln Shrine, Redlands, California.

5. *New York Times*, January 26, 1860.

6. *New York Times*, March 8, 1860; *New York Evening Post*, February 16, 1860.

7. J. Jeffery Auer, "Cooper Institute: Tom Corwin and Abraham Lincoln," *New York History*, 32 (October 1951), 400, 402, 405, 406–7.

8. All these articles appeared on February 27, 1860.

9. *Speech of Hon. R. M. T. Hunter, of Virginia, on Invasion of States, Delivered in the Senate of the United States, January 30, 1860* (Printed by Lemuel Tucker, n.d.).

10. McCormick's reminiscence, first published in *The New York Times* on May 3, 1865, later appeared in several collections, including Rufus Rockwell Wilson, ed., *Intimate Memories of Lincoln* (Elmira, N.Y.: The Primavera Press, 1945), 250–55; Ward H. Lamon, *Life of Abraham Lincoln* (Boston: James R. Osgood, 1872), 425.

11. Louis A. Warren, *Preliminaries to the Cooper Union Masterpiece* (Madison: Lincoln Fellowship of Wisconsin, 1961), 14. Brayman claimed he was the first to reach Lincoln's hotel room on February 27; McCormick remembered running into Brayman later on the street.

12. Wilson, ed., *Intimate Memories of Lincoln*, 251.

13. Brayman to W. H. Bailhache, February 27, 1860, in Carl Sandburg, *Lincoln Collector: The Story of Oliver R. Barrett's Great Private Collection* (New York: Harcourt, Brace & Co., 1950), 160. The original is now in the Chicago Historical Society. See also Wayne C. Temple, *By Square and Compass: Saga of the Lincoln Home* (Mahomet, Ill.: Mayhaven Publishing, 2002), 76–78, 86–87.

14. Lamon, *The Life of Abraham Lincoln*, 425; Mary Panzer, *Mathew Brady*

and the Image of History (Washington: Smithsonian Institution Press, 1997), 37; Junius Henry Browne, *The Great Metropolis: A Mirror of New York,* orig. pub. 1869 (New York: Arno Press, 1975), 28.

15. Henry J. Raymond, *The Life and Public Services of Abraham Lincoln* (New York: Derby & Miller, 1865), 100.

16. Panzer, *Mathew Brady,* 220.

17. H. Wilson, *Trow's New York City Directory for the Year Ending May 1, 1860* (New York: John F. Trow, 1860), 99; the gallery's name is recorded on a surviving label reproduced in George E. Sullivan, "Brady's Gallery Discovered—the *True* Location of the Studio that Changed History," *The Rail Splitter,* 5 (December 1999), 13. *The New York Times* announced Brady's move on August 23, 1859. See also George Gilbert, "The Brady Photograph which Introduced Lincoln to the American Public," *Photographica,* 20 (October 1991), 4.

18. Panzer, *Mathew Brady,* 218.

19. James B. Horan, *Mathew Brady: Historian with a Camera* (New York: Crown, 1955), 28; Panzer, *Mathew Brady,* 44; *The New York Times* quoted in Bill Kaland, "The New York Galleries of Mathew Brady," *Photographica,* 11 (December 1979), 6.

20. The standard study is Charles Hamilton and Lloyd Ostendorf, *Lincoln in Photographs: An Album of Every Known Pose* (Norman: University of Oklahoma Press, 1963). For pre–Cooper Union beardless photos, see 369–73; for Shepherd advertisement, see 5. Lincoln's comment on the disheveled Hesler profile is in *Collected Works,* 4:114.

21. Hamilton and Ostendorf, *Lincoln in Photographs,* 14–15, 17, 21, 22–23, 373.

22. *Collected Works,* 4:30; Panzer, *Mathew Brady,* 200–201.

23. Quoted in Sarah McNair Vosmeier, "Photographing Lincoln, Part IV," *Lincoln Lore,* no. 1808 (October 1989).

24. Wilson, ed., *Intimate Memories,* 251. Six years later, the Civil War fought and won, Bancroft would be invited to deliver a Lincoln's Birthday address before Congress. Not everyone would be pleased with it. "It is hard for a man of purely intellectual temperament like the historian," suggested *Harper's Weekly,* "heartily to appreciate a simpler and more emotional nature like that of the late president." Perhaps Bancroft had first found it difficult to appreciate Lincoln's "simpler" nature at Brady's years before.

25. Wilson, ed., *Intimate Memories,* 251–52.

26. Roy Meredith, *Mathew Brady's Portrait of an Era* (New York: W. W. Norton, 1982), 69, 82.

27. Carl Schurz, *The Reminiscences of Carl Schurz*, 3 vols. (New York: McClure & Co., 1908), 2:90.

28. Roy Meredith, *Mr. Lincoln's Camera Man, Mathew B. Brady* (New York: Charles Scribner's Sons, 1946), 59.

29. George Ferguson, *Signs and Symbols in Christian Art* (New York: Oxford University Press, 1981), 171, 178.

30. Meredith, *Mr. Lincoln's Camera Man*, 59. Brady himself probably did not "man" the cameras at this time; his eyesight was failing, so he left the work to hired operators and instead specialized in "arranging" the sittings.

31. Lincoln to Harvey G. Eastman, April 7, 1860, *Collected Works*, 4:39–40.

32. *Boston Herald*, May 24, 1860.

33. *Harper's Weekly*, May 26, 1860; *Frank Leslie's Illustrated Newspaper*, October 20, 1860. *Harper's* republished the woodcut on its cover on November 10.

34. Originals in the author's collection, including Currier & Ives advertising sheet.

35. Charles Dickens, "Election Time in America," *All The Year Round: A Weekly Journal*, 103 (April 13, 1861), 68.

36. Originals in the author's collection.

37. Currier & Ives, *Abraham Lincoln,/Sixteenth President of the United States*, in the Lincoln Museum, Fort Wayne; *Hon. Abraham Lincoln, "Our Next President,"* in the collection of the Old Print Shop, New York City.

38. *Portraits and Sketches of the Lives of All the Candidates for the Presidency and Vice-Presidency, for 1860* . . . (New York: J. C. Buttre, 1860), back cover, 4.

39. James W. Milgram, *Abraham Lincoln Illustrated Envelopes and Letter Paper 1860–1865* (Northbrook, Ill.: Northbrook Publishing, 1984), 11, 21, 23–24; Roger A. Fischer and Edmund B. Sullivan, *American Political Ribbons and Ribbon Badges, 1825–1981* (Lincoln, Mass.: Quarterman Publications, 1985), 127; Edmund B. Sullivan, *Collecting Political Americana* (New York: Crown, 1980), 28; *Momus*, June 2, 1860.

40. In a similarly inventive juxtaposition, engraver H. S. Sadd reissued his 1850 print, *Union*, ironically placing the Cooper Union Lincoln portrait atop the body of a political opposite, the late proslavery secessionist John C. Calhoun. See Harold Holzer, Gabor S. Boritt, and Mark E. Neely, Jr., *The Lincoln Image: Abraham Lincoln and the Popular Print* (New York: Charles Scribner's Sons, 1984), 30; George Sullivan, *Picturing Lincoln: Famous Photographs that Popularized the President* (New York: Clarion Books, 2000), 24–41. Winfred Porter Truesdell listed seventeen adaptations in his incomplete *Engraved and Lithographed Portraits of Abraham*

Lincoln, vol. 2 (vol. 1 unpublished) (Champlain, N. Y.: Troutsdale Press, 1933), 67–71.

41. The current owner allowed the author to examine the picture, along with the auction catalogue.

42. Douglas L. Wilson and Rodney O. Davis, *Herndon's Informants: Letters, Interviews, and Statements about Abraham Lincoln* (Urbana: University of Illinois Press, 1998), 360–61. Mrs. Lincoln made this observation in an 1866 interview with her husband's former law partner and future biographer, William H. Herndon.

43. Currier & Ives, *Political "Blondins" Crossing Salt River*, 1860; Currier & Ives, *An Heir to the Throne, or the Next Republican Candidate*, 1860; *Vanity Fair*, June 2, 1860, all in the author's collection. *No Communion with Slaveholders* in *Harper's Weekly*, March 2, 1861; "The Humors of the Presidential Canvass," including "The Rail auld Western Gentleman," in *Comic Monthly*, August 1860; see Gary L. Bunker, *From Rail-Splitter to Icon: Lincoln's Image in Illustrated Periodicals, 1860–1865* (Kent, Ohio: Kent State University Press, 2001), 42.

44. Holzer, Boritt, and Neely, *The Lincoln Image*, 31.

45. Ibid., 70–72; Grace Bedell's letter, and Lincoln's reply, are in *Collected Works*, 4:129–30.

46. George H. Story quoted in Meredith, *Mr. Lincoln's Camera Man*, 67; Brady quoted in George Alfred Townsend, "Still Taking Pictures," *New York World*, April 12, 1891, in Mary Panzer, *Mathew Brady and the Image of History* (Washington: Smithsonian Institution Press, 1997), 224.

47. Francis B. Carpenter, *Six Months at the White House with Abraham Lincoln: The Story of a Picture* (New York: Hurd & Houghton, 1866), 46–47.

48. The McSorley's assertion was made on the public television documentary *McSorley's New York*, first airing on WNET on March 5, 1987; *Chicago Press and Tribune*, May 23, 1860; McCormick, "Lincoln's Visit to New York in 1860."

49. Ralph Gary, *Following in Lincoln's Footsteps* . . . (New York: Carroll & Graf, 2001), 269.

50. Five years later, ironically, Laura Keene would be on stage in a different play at Ford's Theatre in Washington at the very moment John Wilkes Booth took fatal aim at Lincoln.

51. Barnum's "What Is It?" was advertised in *The New York Times*, February 27, 1860, and reported in the *Philadelphia Sun Dispatch*, March 4, 1860. All other theatrical notices are from the February 27 *Times*.

52. All of these entertainment programs were advertised in a single issue of

The New York Times on the same day as Lincoln's Cooper Union address, February 27, 1860.

53. *New York Tribune*, February 23, 1860; *New York Times*, February 23, 1860.

54. *New York Tribune*, February 24, 1860.

55. *Register of Meteorological Observations, Under the Direction of the Smithsonian Institution, Adopted by the Commissioner of Agriculture for His Annual Report. Charts for February recorded at the Deaf & Dumb Institute, New York*, by O.W. Morris. Other surviving official records for the period confirm clear or partly cloudy skies for February 27, 1860. The idea that snow inhibited attendance on February 27—repeated in modern times by Carl Sandburg ("A snowstorm interfered with traffic," *Abraham Lincoln: The Prairie Years*, 2 vols. [New York: Harcourt Brace, 1926], 2:211) and Benjamin P. Thomas ("That night, despite a snowstorm . . ." *Abraham Lincoln: A Biography* [New York: Alfred A. Knopf, 1952], 202), among other biographers—was inexplicably introduced by organizers Cephas Brainerd and Charles Cooper Nott, both writing many years later. (See Brainerd to Nott, March 13, 1896, in Gilder Lehrman Collection: Nott testimony in George Haven Putnam, *Abraham Lincoln: The People's Leader in the Struggle for National Existence* (New York: G. P. Putnam's Sons, 1909), 219. "It was snowing heavily," Putnam stubbornly concurred, ibid., 17.

56. Edward C. Mack, *Peter Cooper, Citizen of New York* (New York: Duell, Sloan and Pearce, 1949), 260, 266; "The Free Reading-room at the Cooper Institute" (letter), *New York Times*, November 17, 1859; Andrew Freeman, *Abraham Lincoln Goes to New York* (New York: Coward McCann, 1960), 59–60.

57. *New York Times*, December 1, 1858.

58. William Aspenwall Bradley, *William Cullen Bryant* (New York: Macmillan, 1905), 139; *Collected Works*, 1:510.

59. Warren, "Preliminaries to the Cooper Union Masterpiece," 14; "Lincoln's Life Work. Lecture by Mr. Choate," *New York Times*, November 14, 1900.

CHAPTER FIVE: "NOTHING IMPRESSIVE ABOUT HIM"

1. Francis Fisher Browne, *The Every-day Life of Abraham Lincoln*, (New York and St. Louis: N. D. Thompson, 1886), 316; "Lincoln's Life Work, Lecture by Mr. Choate," *New York Times*, February 14, 1900; Henry C. Bowen, "Recollections of Abraham Lincoln," in William Ward Hayes,

ed., *Abraham Lincoln: Tributes from His Associates* (New York: Thomas Y. Crowell, 1895), 29; Carl Sandburg, *Lincoln Collector: The Story of Oliver R. Barrett's Great Private Collection* (New York: Harcourt, Brace & Co., 1950), 160; *New York Tribune*, February 28, 1860; Johnson E. Fairchild, "Lincoln at the Cooper Union," in Ralph G. Newman, ed., *Lincoln for the Ages* (Garden City, N.Y.: Doubleday, 1960), 139.

2. Louis A. Warren, *Preliminaries to the Cooper Union Masterpiece* (Madison: Lincoln Fellowship of Wisconsin, 1961), 14.

3. Andrew Freeman, *Abraham Lincoln Goes to New York* (New York: Coward-McCann, 1960), 79–80.

4. Ibid., 79.

5. An incomplete list was published in the *Illinois State Journal*, March 3, 1860. The list "Patrons on the Platform When Lincoln Spoke at Cooper Union" is in the Cooper Union research library. See also John G. Nicolay and John Hay, *Abraham Lincoln: A History*, 10 vols., orig. pub. 1890 (New York: The Century Co., 1914), 2:217; and Earl Schenck Miers, ed., *Lincoln Day by Day*, 3 vols. (Washington, D.C.: Lincoln Sesquicentennial Commission, 1960), 1:291.

6. Russell H. Conwell, *Personal Glimpses of Celebrated Men and Women*, in Wayne Whipple, ed., *The Story-Life of Lincoln* . . . (Philadelphia: John C. Winston, 1908), 308. The door is described in Henry M. Field, *The Life of David Dudley Field* (New York: Charles Scribner's Sons, 1898), 122. Field, the attorney's son, was there that night.

7. George Haven Putnam, *Abraham Lincoln the Great Captain: Personal Reminiscences by a Veteran of the Civil War* (Oxford: Clarendon Press, 1928), 10; *New York Herald*, February 28, 1860.

8. Edward Dicey, *Six Months in the Federal States*, 1863, quoted in Harold Holzer, ed., *Lincoln as I Knew Him* (New York: Algonquin, 1999), 120.

9. Louis A. Warren, "The First Lincoln Portrait," *Lincoln Lore*, No. 121 (August 3, 1931).

10. *New York Times*, February 28, 1860.

11. Dicey in Holzer, ed., *Lincoln as I Knew Him*, 120.

12. Joseph Hodges Choate, "Abraham Lincoln at Cooper Union," in Nathan William MacChesney, ed., *Abraham Lincoln: the Tribute of a Century, 1809–1909* (Chicago: A. C. McClurg, 1910), 277; some adjectives added from "Lincoln's Life Work. Lecture by Mr. Choate . . . ," *New York Times*, November 14, 1900.

13. Noah Brooks, "Some Reminiscences of Abraham Lincoln," Dixon (Illinois) *Appeal*, November 4, 1860, quoted in Michael Burlingame, ed.,

Lincoln Observed: Civil War Dispatches of Noah Brooks (Baltimore: The Johns Hopkins University Press, 1998), 6.

14. Noah Brooks, *Abraham Lincoln* (New York: G. P. Putnam's Sons, 1888), 186.

15. Eveline D. Brainerd, "The Cooper Union Meeting," manuscript in the Lincoln Museum, Fort Wayne, Indiana.

16. Rufus Rockwell Wilson, ed., *Intimate Memories of Lincoln* (Elmira, N.Y.: Primavera Press, 1945), 258.

17. Conwell, in Whipple, *The Story-Life of Lincoln*, 308; Putnam, *Personal Reminiscences*, 11.

18. Brooks, *Abraham Lincoln*, 186.

19. Margaret Clapp, *Forgotten First Citizen: John Bigelow* (Boston: Little Brown, 1947), 136.

20. William Herndon, *Herndon's Lincoln: The True Story of a Great Life...*, 3 vols. (orig. pub. 1889; Springfield, Ill.: The Herndon's Lincoln Publishing Co., n.d.). 3:346, 454–455n.

21. *New York Evening Post*, February 28, 1860; Freeman, *Abraham Lincoln Goes to New York*, 82. Henry M. Field testified to Lincoln's "high-pitched" voice in the Life of *David Dudley Field*, 123.

22. Herndon, *Herndon's Lincoln*, 2:407; David J. Burrell quoted in *New York Times*, February 8, 1860.

23. Truman H. Bartlett, "An Old Likeness of Lincoln," *Harper's Weekly*, February 10, 1912.

24. Herndon, *Herndon's Lincoln*, 2:384, 406–7; Melvin L. Hayes, *Mr. Lincoln Runs for President* (New York: Citadel Press, 1960), 24; *New York Herald*, February 28, 1860.

25. Herndon, *Herndon's Lincoln*, 2:408.

26. Ibid., 407; Douglas L. Wilson and Rodney O. Davis, eds., *Herndon's Informants: Letters, Interviews, and Statements about Abraham Lincoln* (Urbana: University of Illinois Press, 1998), 508; Carl Schurz, *The Reminiscences of Carl Schurz*, 3 vols. (New York: McClure Co., 1908), 2:95.

27. Moncure Daniel Conway, writing in the *Review of London*, June 1865, reprinted in Wilson, ed., *Intimate Memories of Lincoln*, 179–80.

28. Herndon, *Herndon's Lincoln*, 2:406; *New York Herald*, February 28, 1860; "Cooper Union, Reminiscence of Pres.," letter by "Tuttle" to *New York Independent*, January 7, 1869, copy in the Lincoln Museum, Fort Wayne; Field, *Life of David Dudley Field*, 123.

29. Putnam, *Personal Reminiscences*, 11.

30. McCormick, "Mr. Lincoln's Visit to New York in 1860."

31. Brooks, *Abraham Lincoln*, 186–87.
32. Joseph Hodges Choate, "Abraham Lincoln at Cooper Institute," in Nathan William MacChesney, ed., *Abraham Lincoln: The Tribute of a Century, 1809–1909* (Chicago: A. C. McClurg & Co., 1910), 278.
33. Russell H. Conwell, *Personal Glimpses of Celebrated Men and Women*, in Whipple, *The Story-Life of Lincoln*, 308.
34. Ibid.
35. Richard McCormick, "Abraham Lincoln. Interesting Reminiscences," *New York Times*, May 3, 1865.
36. A valuable exception is Michael C. Leff and Gerald P. Mohrmann, "Lincoln at Cooper Union: A Rhetorical Analysis of the Text," *Quarterly Journal of Speech*, 60 (1974), 346–58. See also Mohrmann and Leff, "Lincoln at Cooper Union: A Rationale for Neo-Classical Criticism," ibid., 459–67) and Michael C. Leff, "Neo-Classical Criticism Revisited," *Western Journal of Communications*, 65 (Summer 2001): 232–48.
37. Seward would take to the floor of the U.S. Senate within days to deliver what was widely regarded as a conciliatory speech aimed at regaining the Republican center—perhaps from the sudden challenge of Lincoln in New York.

CHAPTER SIX: "THE STRENGTH OF ABSOLUTE SIMPLICITY"

1. The Lyceum Address of January 27, 1838, is in *Collected Works*, 1:108–15.
2. Lois J. Einhorn, *Abraham Lincoln the Orator: Penetrating the Lincoln Legend* (Westport, Conn.: Greenwood Press, 1991), 27.
3. The scholarly debate over which document Lincoln held dearer—the Declaration or the Constitution—has been going on for generations. Historian Philip Shaw Paludan called Lincoln neither a constitutionalist nor an egalitarian, but rather "a 'process-based' egalitarian" who "believed that equality would be realized only through the proper operation of existing institutions." See Paludan, *The Presidency of Abraham Lincoln* (Lawrence: University Press of Kansas, 1994), 19.
4. Lincoln uses the most beneficial interpretation of "our fathers" to make his calculations. In all, sixty-five men were named to attend the Constitutional Convention. Ten did not participate, and of the fifty-five who did, sixteen did not sign the final document. Lincoln cleverly chose not to investigate the views of these more conservative men, implying that they do not deserve to be considered among "our fathers"; he restricts himself to the thirty-nine who labored to limit sectional differences and achieve compromise to craft the Constitution.

5. Lyman Abbott, "Lincoln as a Labor Leader," in Nathan William Mac-Chesney, *Abraham Lincoln: The Tribute of a Century, 1809–1909* (Chicago: A. C. McClurg, 1910), 281; Henry M. Field, *The Life of David Dudley Field* (New York: Charles Scribner's Sons, 1898), 123.

6. *Collected Works*, 3:465, 496; Jacques Barzun, *Lincoln the Literary Genius* (Evanston, Ill.: Evanston Publishing Co., 1960), 17, 23.

7. See the excellent essay, Michael C. Leff and Gerald P. Mohrmann, "Lincoln at Cooper Union: A Rhetorical Analysis of the Text," *Quarterly Journal of Speech*, 60 (1974), 346–58.

8. David Zarefsky, "The Cooper Union Speech, 1860," lecture number 18 of *Abraham Lincoln: In His Own Words*, twenty-four-lecture audio series (Springfield, Va.: The Teaching Co., 1999). I am indebted to Steven K. Rogstad, literary editor of the *Lincoln Herald*, for bringing this excellent lecture to my attention.

9. *Collected Works*, 4:271.

10. The uprising was masterminded by the slave Nat Turner, who convinced fellow slaves that he had been directed by God to revolt. Turner and his followers murdered his master's family and other whites in the area. He was tried, convicted, and executed that same year.

11. The best analysis of the Dred Scott decision is Don E. Fehrenbacher, *The Dred Scott Case: Its Significance in American Law and Politics* (New York: Oxford University Press, 1978). For commentary on the Fifth Amendment, see 363, 520–21.

12. *Collected Works*, 2:366, 3:501. The best study of the 1856 Kansas speeches is still Thomas I. Starr, ed., *Lincoln's Kalamazoo Address Against Extending Slavery* (Detroit: Fine Book Circle, 1941).

13. Many nineteenth-century Republicans argued that they opposed slavery out of benevolence for oppressed people, not a moral belief in racial equality, and even then were wary of admitting to philanthropic sentiments. As late as 1862, when he issued the preliminary Emancipation Proclamation, Lincoln took pains to tell a journalist he was acting out of military necessity, not from "the bosom of philanthropy." See LaWanda Cox, *Lincoln and Black Freedom: A Study in Presidential Leadership* (Columbia: University of South Carolina Press, 1981), 13.

14. David Zarefsky, *Lincoln, Douglas, and Slavery in the Crucible of Public Debate* (Chicago: University of Chicago Press, 1990), 213. Zarefsky believed that by couching his almost radical message in the tone of a "lawyer's brief," Lincoln widened his appeal.

15. *Collected Works*, 4:270; 8:333. Even the hundreds of thousands of Civil War dead could not alter Lincoln's belief that justice called for strength.

It was as if, with secession still only a remote possibility, "duty" could yet be defined by men—"as we understand it"—and manifested by ballots, not bullets. But the inconceivable, incomprehensible destruction that would soon follow could only be explained, absorbed, and justified if God had shown the way.

16. Francis Fisher Browne, *The Every-Day Life of Abraham Lincoln* . . . (New York: N. D. Thompson, 1886), 737.

17. Mason Brayman to William H. Bailhache, February 28, 1860, Illinois State Historical Library.

18. George Haven Putnam, *Abraham Lincoln, the Great Captain: Personal Reminiscences by a Veteran of the Civil War* (Oxford: Clarendon Press, 1928), 11.

19. Joseph H. Choate, "New York Commemoration," in MacChesney, *Abraham Lincoln: The Tribute of a Century*, 1910.

20. Henry C. Bowen, "Recollections of Abraham Lincoln . . . ," in William Hayes Ward, ed., *Abraham Lincoln: Tributes from His Associates* . . . (New York: Thomas Y. Crowell, 1895), 29–30. Lincoln had mocked Douglas's *"great principle"*—without the comic inflections—in Indianapolis on September 15, 1859; see *Collected Works*, 3:466.

21. McCormick, "Abraham Lincoln, Interesting Reminiscences," *New York Times*, May 3, 1865; *New York Tribune*, February 28, 1860.

22. *New York Tribune*, February 28, 1860. Brooks was not on the scene himself, as the article implied, but in distant California on February 27, 1860. See Wayne C. Temple, "Lincoln's Castine: Noah Brooks, Part IV: The Plains Across," *Lincoln Herald*, 73 (Spring 1971), 27–45.

23. *New York Times*, February 28, 1860.

24. Ibid., with last lines from *New York Herald*, February 28, 1860.

25. "James A. Briggs Tells of a Prediction He Made in February, 1860," *New York Evening Post*, April 29, 1887; James A. Briggs to Salmon P. Chase, March 17, 1860, original in the Chase Papers, Library of Congress.

26. Henry J. Raymond, *The Life and Public Services of Abraham Lincoln* (New York: Derby & Miller, 1865), 99–100.

CHAPTER SEVEN: "SUCH AN IMPRESSION"

1. Richard C. McCormick, "Abraham Lincoln. Interesting Reminiscences," *New York Times*, May 3, 1865.

2. A year later, he entrusted his only copy of the First Inaugural Address to his son, who lost track of its whereabouts in Indianapolis, earning a stern tongue-lashing from his father. See Helen Nicolay, *Lincoln's Secretary: A*

Biography of John G. Nicolay (New York: Longmans, Green & Co., 1949), 64–65; Michael Burlingame, ed., *An Oral History of Abraham Lincoln: John G. Nicolay's Interviews and Essays* (Carbondale: Southern Illinois University Press, 1996), 108–9.

3. Stefan Lorant, *Lincoln: A Picture Story of His Life* (New York: W. W. Norton, 1969), 247; Ronald C. White, *Lincoln's Greatest Speech: the Second Inaugural* (New York: Simon & Schuster, 2002), 207.

4. Richard C. McCormick, "Abraham Lincoln. Interesting Reminiscences"; Charles C. Nott in George Haven Putnam, *Abraham Lincoln: The People's Leader in the Struggle for National Existence* (New York: G. P. Putnam's Sons, 1909), 218.

5. McCormick, "Abraham Lincoln. Interesting Reminiscences"; Nott in Putnam, *Abraham Lincoln*, 218.

6. Nott in Putnam, *Abraham Lincoln*, 221.

7. Nott's story of their trip downtown is in Putnam, *Abraham Lincoln*, 219–21.

8. Edwin Earle Sparks, *The Lincoln-Douglas Debates of 1858* (Springfield, Ill.: Illinois State Historical Library, 1908), 83–84; *Chicago Press and Tribune*, October 11, 1858.

9. James Parton quoted in Andrew A. Freeman, *Abraham Lincoln Goes to New York* (New York: Coward-McCann, 1960), 92; Charles S. Zane quoted in Don E. Fehrenbacher and Virginia Fehrenbacher, *Recollected Words of Abraham Lincoln* (Stanford: Stanford University Press, 1996), 510.

10. Henry B. Rankin, *Intimate Character Sketches of Abraham Lincoln* (Philadelphia: J. B. Lippincott, 1924), 190–91; Rankin, *Lincoln's Cooper Institute Speech Fifty-Six Years Ago* (Springfield, Ill.: State Register Printing, 1917).

11. Rankin, *Intimate Character Sketches*, 190–91.

12. *New York Herald*, February 28, 1860.

13. *New York Tribune*, February 28, 1860.

14. *Brooklyn Daily Times*, February 28, 1860.

15. *New York Tribune*, February 28, 1860; *New York Evening Post*, February 28, 1860, March 7, 1860.

16. William H. Herndon, *Herndon's Lincoln: The True Story of a Great Life . . .* , 3 vols. (orig. pub. 1889, Springfield, Ill.: Herndon's Lincoln Publishing Co., n.d.) 3:455.

17. John W. Starr, Jr., *Lincoln and the Railroads: A Biographical Study* (New York: Dodd, Mead & Co., 1927), 126–30.

18. Ibid., 130–31.

19. Paul M. Angle, ed., *A Portrait of Abraham Lincoln in Letters by his Oldest Son* (Chicago: Chicago Historical Society, 968), 73.

20. *New York Tribune*, February 28, 1860.

21. *Chicago Daily Evening Journal*, March 1, 1860.

22. *Chicago Press and Tribune*, February 29, 1860; *Chicago Daily Journal*, March 1, 1860.

23. *Richmond Enquirer*, March 2, 1860. The correspondent's report was filed the day after Lincoln's speech.

24. *New York Daily News*, March 1, 1860.

25. *New York Herald*, February 29, 1860.

26. *Illinois State Register*, March 3, 1860.

27. Ibid., March 6, 1860.

28. *Illinois Daily State Journal*, March 6, 1860.

29. John M. Taylor, *William Henry Seward: Lincoln's Right Hand* (New York: HarperCollins, 1991), 115.

30. Donald B. Cooke and John J. McDonough, *Benjamin Brown French: Witness to the Young Republic—A Yankee's Journal, 1832–1870* (Hanover, N.H.: University Press of New England, 1989), 320.

31. Taylor, *William Henry Seward*, 116; *New York Tribune*, March 5, 1860.

32. *Albany Evening Journal*, March 5, 1860.

33. *New York Tribune*, March 1, 1860.

34. *New York Evening Post*, March 2, 1860; *New York Tribune*, March 2, 1860; the *Sun* quoted in the *Albany Evening Journal*, March 2, 1860. The pro-Democratic *New York Journal of Commerce* (March 2, 1860) now "conceded as a settled fact" that Seward would be the Republican "standard-bearer at the Presidential election."

35. Taylor, *William Henry Seward*, 10–11, 23–24.

36. *Albany Evening Journal*, February 28, 1860; March 6, 1860.

37. Ibid., May 19, 1860.

38. Alan Nevins, *The Emergence of Lincoln*, 2 vols. (New York: Charles Scribner's Sons, 1950), 2:87–88. Nevins believed Seward's speech had "nobler eloquence," but Lincoln's boasted more "bold candor, intellectual vigor, and positiveness of moral conviction."

39. Philip S. Foner and Yuval Taylor, eds., *Frederick Douglass: Selected Speeches and Writings* (Chicago: Lawrence Hill Books, 1999), 380–81, 388.

40. Ibid., xi, 390.

41. Don E. Fehrenbacher and Ward M. McAfee, *The Slaveholding Republic: An Account of the United States Government's Relations to Slavery* (New York: Oxford University Press, 2001), 298, 438n.16.

42. Foner and Taylor, *Frederick Douglass*, 390.

43. Allen Thorndike Rice, ed., *Reminiscences of Abraham Lincoln by Distinguished Men of His Time* (New York: North American Publishing Co., 1886), 193, 195; Frederick Douglass, *My Bondage and My Freedom*, orig. pub. 1855 (New York: Dover, 1969, ed. Philip S. Foner), 336.

44. Frederick Douglass, *The Constitution of the United States: Is it Pro-Slavery or Anti-Slavery? By Frederick Douglass. A Speech Delivered in Glasgow, March 26, 1860* . . . (Halifax: T. & W. Birtwhistle Printers, 1860).

45. Barney to Lincoln, February 28, 1860, Abraham Lincoln Papers, Library of Congress. Barney's son later served in the Union army. See James N. Adams, "Lincoln and Hiram Barney," *Journal of the Illinois State Historical Society* 50 (Winter 1957): 344n.

46. "An Appeal to the Republicans of Kings County," *New York Evening Post*, February 29, 1860.

47. Letters from "A.G.L." and "Templar," *New York Evening Post*, March 7, March 6, 1860.

CHAPTER EIGHT: "UNABLE TO ESCAPE THIS TOIL"

1. White to Lincoln, February 25, 1860, Abraham Lincoln Papers, Library of Congress.

2. Frank J. Williams, "A Candidate Speaks in Rhode Island: Abraham Lincoln Visits Providence and Woonsocket, 1860," *Rhode Island History*, 51 (November 1993), 109–10.

3. *Collected Works*, 4:270; 1:115.

4. Robert T. Lincoln to James Schouler, January 29, 1908, Robert Todd Lincoln Letter Press, 41 (January 25, 1908–January 6, 1909), 370, Illinois State Historical Library.

5. Thomas C. Hayden, "Abraham Lincoln and the formation of the Republican Party in New Hampshire," *The Phillips Exeter Bulletin* (Winter 1983), 72.

6. Lincoln to Joshua Speed, August 24, 1855, *Collected Works*, 2:323. See also Charles Granville Hamilton, *Lincoln and the Know Nothing Movement* (Washington: Public Affairs Press, 1954).

7. Elwin L. Page, *Abraham Lincoln in New Hampshire* (Boston: Houghton Mifflin, 1929), 9. Greeley believed "you couldn't elect Seward if you could nominate him." See Rufus Rockwell Wilson, ed., *Lincoln Among His Friends* (Caldwell, Idaho: Caxton Printers, 1942), 205. Frederick Douglass, on the other hand, charged that Greeley abandoned Seward because he had a "passion for making political nominations from the

ranks of his enemies." See Eric Foner and Yuval Taylor, eds., *Frederick Douglass: Selected Speeches and Writings* (Chicago: Lawrence Hill Books, 1999), 394.

8. Michael Burlingame, ed., *Lincoln Observed: Civil War Dispatches of Noah Brooks* (Baltimore: The Johns Hopkins University Press, 1998), 8.

9. Wilkinson to Lincoln, February 25, 1860, Abraham Lincoln Papers, Library of Congress.

10. Still, Robert Lincoln never wavered from his belief that his father came to Exeter primarily "to see how I was getting along." See Robert T. Lincoln to George H. Putnam, July 27, 1909, vol. 43, entry 159, Robert T. Lincoln letter press collection, Illinois State Historical Library.

11. *Providence Journal*, February 27, 1860.

12. Earl Schenck Miers, *Lincoln Day by Day: A Chronology, 1809–1865*, 3 vols. (Washington: Lincoln Sesquicentennial Commission, 1959), 1:319–21. The *Boston Atlas* described him on this tour as "a capital specimen of a 'Sucker' Whig" (Ibid., 320).

13. *Collected Works*, 4:5–6; Allen Thorndike Rice, ed., *Reminiscences of Abraham Lincoln by Distinguished Men of His Time* (New York: North American Publishing Co., 1886), 297. Clay actually insisted he had met Lincoln once before, in Springfield in 1856 (see Rice, *Reminiscences*, 293).

14. *Providence Journal*, February 28, 1860; Williams, "A Candidate Speaks in Rhode Island," 109.

15. *Providence Journal*, February 28, 1860.

16. Robert Perkins Bernard et al., *Memories of Brown* (Providence: Brown University, 1909), 188–89.

17. Ibid.; *Collected Works*, 3:550.

18. Williams, "A Candidate Speaks in Rhode Island," 114; *Providence Daily Post*, March 1, 1860.

19. *Providence Daily Journal*, March 1, 1860.

20. Williams, "A Candidate Speaks in Rhode Island," 115.

21. Ibid., 114; Miers, ed.; *Lincoln Day by Day*, 2:274; "Mr. Lincoln in New York. His Addresses in New England . . . ," in William Hayes Ward, ed., *Abraham Lincoln: Tributes from His Associates* . . . (New York: Thomas Y. Crowell, 1895), 266.

22. William B. Morrill to Lincoln, February 28, 1860, Abraham Lincoln Papers, Library of Congress.

23. The Robert Lincoln and George Latham school records are in Catalogue of the Affairs of Phillips Exeter Academy for the Year 1859–1860, original in the archives of the academy; cost of school detailed in William J.

Cox, "Abraham Lincoln in Exeter," *The Phillips Exeter Bulletin* (February 1960), 3.

24. Tuck to Lincoln, May 14, 1860, Abraham Lincoln Papers, Library of Congress. Tuck did point out that he had subsequently invited Lincoln's "promising son" to tea.

25. Page, *Abraham Lincoln in New Hampshire*, 15, 18. Tuck probably had a hand in encouraging Lincoln to send Robert to Exeter in 1859 (6). Listed in most histories as Lincoln's Exeter host, Tuck wrote Lincoln on May 14: "I very much regretted that I was absent when you were at Exeter, and was sorry you did not call upon my family, in my absence." Abraham Lincoln Papers, Library of Congress.

26. Page, *Abraham Lincoln in New Hampshire*, 40–41; "Mr. Lincoln in New Hampshire," *Illinois Daily State Journal*, March 14, 1860. For Rollins conversion see Hayden, "Abraham Lincoln and the Formation of the Republican Party in New Hampshire," 72.

27. Page, *Abraham Lincoln in New Hampshire*, 44–45, 65.

28. *Collected Works*, 3:551–52.

29. *New Hampshire Mirror* quoted in *Illinois Daily State Journal*, March 14, 1860.

30. Page, *Abraham Lincoln in New Hampshire*, 26–27.

31. Ibid., 76–78; *Collected Works*, 3:552–54.

32. John Goff, *Robert Todd Lincoln: A Man in His Own Right* (Norman, Okla.: University of Oklahoma Press, 1969), 20.

33. Page, *Abraham Lincoln in New Hampshire*, 101–2; Cox, "Abraham Lincoln in Exeter," 3–4.

34. "When Lincoln Spoke at Exeter," *Journal of the Illinois State Historical Society*, 1 (Winter 1957), 418–19.

35. Marshall S. Snow, reminiscences in *Washington University Record*, reprinted in *Bulletin of the Phillips Exeter Academy* (September 1909), 30–32.

36. Walter B. Stevens, *A Reporter's Lincoln*, ed. Michael Burlingame (Lincoln: University of Nebraska Press, 1998), 95–96.

37. Lewis B. Smith and Henry D. Lord to Lincoln, March 2, 1860 (handed by Samuel R. Leavitt); Edward H. Rollins to Lincoln, March 2, 1860 (handed by William B. Morrill), Abraham Lincoln Papers, Library of Congress.

38. Pomeroy to Lincoln at Exeter, February 28, 1860, Abraham Lincoln Papers, Library of Congress; Lincoln to Pomeroy, March 3, 1860, *Collected Works*, 3:554.

39. F. C. Herbruger to Lincoln, March 14, 1860; D. L. Pope to Lincoln, March 4, 1860; John D. Candee to Lincoln, February 28, 1860, Abraham Lincoln Papers, Library of Congress. Reading invitation noted in *Illinois Daily State Journal*, March 12, 1860.

40. Roy P. Basler, ed., *The Collected Works of Abraham Lincoln: Supplement, 1832–1865* (Westport, Conn.: Greenwood Press, 1974), 49–50.

41. Lincoln to James A. Briggs, March 4, 1860, Roy P. Basler and Christian O. Basler, eds., *The Collected Works of Abraham Lincoln, Second Supplement 1848–1865* (New Brunswick, N.J.: Rutgers University Press, 1990), 20.

42. Page, *Abraham Lincoln in New Hampshire*, 111–13.

43. Ibid.; Albert Blair reminiscences quoted in "When Lincoln Spoke at Exeter," *Journal of the Illinois State Historical Society*, 1 (Winter 1957), 420.

44. *Hartford Press*, March 6, 1860; *Collected Works*, 4:6–7, 12.

45. *Collected Works*, 4:8, 13.

46. Ibid., 1.

47. *Hartford Daily Times*, March 6, 1860, March 8, 1860.

48. *Hartford Daily Courant*, March 6, 1860.

49. Daniel D. Bidwell, "Lincoln in Hartford," in Ward, ed., *Abraham Lincoln: Tributes from His Associates*, 182–83.

50. Bidwell, "Lincoln in Hartford," 184; Albert Mordell, ed., *Lincoln's Administration: Selected Essays by Gideon Welles* (New York: Twayne Publishers, 1960), 17; Gideon Welles, *Lincoln and Seward* (New York: Sheldon & Co., 1874), 32; Welles quoted in Edward J. Kempf, *Abraham Lincoln's Philosophy of Common Sense* (New York: New York Academy of Sciences, 1965), 800.

51. Basler, ed., *Collected Works of Abraham Lincoln, Supplement*, 50.

52. *New Haven Daily Palladium*, March 7, 1860.

53. *Collected Works*, 4:18.

54. Matthew M. Miller, "A Memory of Abraham Lincoln," *Money Magic*, September 7, 1907, 1320.

55. The excerpts cited here and in the preceding paragraphs are in *Collected Works*, 4:23, 24, 26–27, 29–30. Lincoln's impassioned New Haven address has eluded deserved acknowledgment as a major speech, probably because of its similarity to Cooper Union. Significantly, Lincoln moved well beyond Cooper Union at New Haven, charging that the Democrats' attempt to raise fears about a "struggle between the white man and negro" was "an ingenious falsehood, to degrade and brutalize the negro" (20). He had expressed no such sympathy for the slaves in his New York speech.

56. *Collected Works*, 4:30.

57. Miers, ed., *Lincoln Day by Day*, 2:275; *New Haven Palladium* quoted in *Chicago Press and Tribune*, March 14, 1860.

58. Miller, "A Memory of Abraham Lincoln."

59. *New Haven Daily Register*, March 8, 1860; *New Haven Daily Palladium*, March 7, 1860. The article was reprinted in the *Illinois Daily State Journal*, March 16, 1860.

60. *Providence Journal*, reprinted in *Illinois Daily State Journal*, March 16, 1860; Williams, "A Candidate Speaks in Rhode Island," 115; *Providence Journal*, March 9, 1860.

61. *Providence Journal*, March 2, 1860, March 8, 1860.

62. Williams, "A Candidate Speaks in Rhode Island," 115, 117.

63. Hugh H. Osgood quoted in Ward, ed., *Abraham Lincoln: Tributes from His Associates*, 266; Percy C. Eggleston, *Lincoln in New England* (New York: Steward, Warren & Co., 1922), 23.

64. John Gulliver, "A Talk with Abraham Lincoln," The *Independent*, September 1, 1864.

65. William H. Herndon, "Lincoln and Strangers," undated ms. in Herndon-Weik Collection, Library of Congress, Nos. 3527–32. Transcription provided by the Lincoln Studies Center at Knox College, Galesburg, Illinois.

66. John P. Gulliver, "A Talk with Abraham Lincoln," [New York] *Independent*, September 1, 1864. The reminiscence was reprinted two years later in the best-selling Francis B. Carpenter, *Six Months at the White House with President Lincoln: The Story of a Picture* (New York: Hurd & Houghton, 1866), 308–17.

67. Ibid., and Gulliver to Lincoln, August 26, 1864, Abraham Lincoln Papers, Library of Congress.

68. *New York Times*, March 6, 1860; *New York Tribune*, March 12, 1860.

69. *New York Tribune*, March 5, 1860.

70. James A. Briggs, "A Reminiscence of Abraham Lincoln," *New York Evening Post*, August 16, 1867.

71. Carpenter, *Six Months at the White House*, 134–35; Rice, *Reminiscences of Abraham Lincoln*, 247.

72. *New York Times*, February 22, 1860; Charles Dickens, *American Notes: A Journey*, orig. pub. 1842 (New York: Forum International, 1985), 88.

73. J. H. Bartlett, *Life of Abraham Lincoln* . . . (Cincinnati: Moore, Wilstach, Keys & Co., 1860), 189.

74. Francis Fisher Browne, *The Every-day Life of Abraham Lincoln* (New York: N. D. Thompson, 1886), 323. Browne claimed that Illinois con-

gressman Elihu Washburne also accompanied Lincoln to the Five Points, a story accepted by Tyler Anbinder in *Five Points . . .* (New York: Free Press, 2001), 236. But other sources place Washburne elsewhere on March 8, 1860, and there is good reason to doubt that he was part of the tour on March 11. Mary's December 31, 1860, letter to Samuel Byram Halliday, a future pastor of the Plymouth Church, is in Justin G. Turner and Linda Levitt Turner, *Mary Todd Lincoln: Her Life and Letters* (New York: Alfred A. Knopf, 1972), 67–68.

75. *Collected Works*, 4:24.

76. Julia Tappan reminiscence in James N. Adams, "Lincoln and Hiram Barney," *Journal of the Illinois State Historical Society*, 50 (Winter 1957), 345.

77. James A. Briggs to Salmon P. Chase, March 17, 1860, Chase Papers, Library of Congress. Briggs told Chase that "He [Lincoln] was very much pleased with Mr. Barney."

78. James A. Briggs, "A Reminiscence of Abraham Lincoln."

CHAPTER NINE: "PRESERVE IT FOR YOUR CHILDREN"

1. Louis A. Warren, "Cooper Union Legends Scrutinized: A Centennial Monograph," *Lincoln Lore*, No. 1465 (March 1960), 4.

2. Earl Schenck Miers, ed., *Lincoln Day by Day: A Chronology, 1809–1865*, 3 vols. (Washington: Lincoln Sesquicentennial Commission, 1960), 2:14; Louis A. Warren, "Cooper Union Legends Scrutinized," *Lincoln Lore*, No.1465 (March 1960).

3. Lincoln to William Gooding, April 6, 1860, *Collected Works*, 4:36; William H. Herndon, *Herndon's Lincoln; The True Story of a Great Life . . .*, 3 vols. (orig. pub. 1889; Springfield, Ill.: The Herndon's Lincoln Publishing Co., n.d.), 3:457.

4. *Collected Works*, 4:30–31.

5. Ibid., 32.

6. Lincoln to Mark W. Delahay, March 16, 1860, ibid., 4:32; to E. Stafford, March 17, 1860, 4:33.

7. Lincoln To James W. Somers, March 17, 1860, ibid., 4:33.

8. *Johnston* v. *Jones and Marsh* was a complex civil dispute over valuable new shorefront land that had accumulated because of the steady accretions of Lake Michigan. In his final turn as a railroad lawyer, Lincoln represented his most important client, the Illinois Central Railroad. Lincoln won the case and a $350 fee. See Allen D. Spiegel, *A. Lincoln Esquire: A Shrewd, Sophisticated Lawyer in His Time* (Macon: Mercer University Press, 2002), 242.

9. Lincoln to Samuel Galloway, March 24, 1860, *Collected Works*, 4:34.

10. Benjamin P. Thomas, *Abraham Lincoln: A Biography* (New York: Alfred A. Knopf, 1952), 205.

11. From his fragment on slavery, *Collected Works*, 2:482; Lincoln to Richard M. Corwine, April 6, 1860, *Collected Works*, 4:36; to William C. Hobbs and William H. Hanna, April 6, 1860, 4:37; Lincoln to Edward Wallace, May 12, 1860, 4:49.

12. Ibid., 4:41–42; Miers, ed., *Lincoln Day by Day*, 2:279.

13. James F. Babcock to Lincoln, April 9, 1860, Abraham Lincoln Papers, Library of Congress.

14. Lincoln to James F. Babcock, April 14, 1860, *Collected Works*, 4:43; to Hawkins Taylor, April 21, 1860, 4:45; to Lyman Trumbull, April 29, 1860, 4:45.

15. Original of the *Journal* edition in the Lincoln Museum, Fort Wayne, Indiana; see also Louis A. Warren, "Printing the Cooper Institute Address," *Lincoln Lore*, No. 589 (July 22, 1940). But Warren erred when he said that Lincoln arranged this edition when he returned to Springfield. The *Journal* was advertising its publication by March 13, before Lincoln reached home. See advertisements in *Illinois Daily State Journal*, March 13, 14, 15, 16, 17, 19, 1860, and for "hasty supervising," *Collected Works*, 4:59.

16. A copy of the *Tribune* pamphlet is in the Gilder Lehrman Collection (GLC-4471), examined at the Morgan Library, New York.

17. *The Campaign of 1860. Comprising the Speeches of Abraham Lincoln, William H. Seward, Henry Wilson, Benjamin F. Wade, Carl Schurz, Charles Sumner, William M. Evarts, &c.* (Albany: Weed, Parsons & Co., 1860), not paginated.

18. *Tribune* edition of Cooper Union pamphlet; advertisement in *New York Tribune*, March 6, 1860.

19. Louis A. Warren, "Pre-Convention Cooper Union Pamphlets," *Lincoln Lore*, No. 988 (March 15, 1948); Jay Monaghan, ed., *Lincoln Bibliography, 1839–1939*. 2 vols. (Springfield: Illinois State Historical Library, 1943), 1:14–15.

20. *Collected Works*, 4:38–39.

21. *Chicago Press and Tribune*, March 2, 1860; William Baringer, *Lincoln's Rise to Power* (Boston: Little, Brown & Co., 1937), 152.

22. Louis A. Warren, "Lincoln's $200 Speech," *Lincoln Lore*, No. 1378 (September 5, 1955).

23. Ibid.

24. Melvin L. Hayes, *Mr. Lincoln Runs for President* (New York; Citadel Press, 1960), 25.

25. Lincoln to Cornelius F. McNeill, April 6, 1860, *Collected Works*, 4:38.

26. Lincoln's March 15 deposit of $604 is in Miers, *Lincoln Day by Day*, 2:276; Briggs's estimate in Warren, "Lincoln's $200 Speech" and Briggs to Lincoln, February 29, 1860, Abraham Lincoln Papers, Library of Congress.

27. *Collected Works*, 4:38.

28. "Mr. Lincoln's Lecture at the Cooper Institute," *New York Times*, March 13, 1860.

29. Associated Press proceedings of the convention reported in *The New York Times*, May 19, 1860. For the delegate votes, ballot by ballot, see Paul M. Angle and Earl Schenck Miers, eds., *Fire the Salute!: Abe Lincoln is Nominated: Murat Halstead Reports the Republican National Convention ...* (Kingsport, Tenn.: Kingsport Press, 1960), 39–43.

30. Ibid.; Francis B. Carpenter, *Six Months at the White House: The Story of A Picture* (New York: Hurd & Houghton, 1866), 46 (recollection by Montgomery Blair, Lincoln's future postmaster general).

31. James A. Briggs to Lincoln, May 28, 1860, Abraham Lincoln Papers, Library of Congress; *Collected Works*, 4:60.

32. Miers, *Lincoln Day by Day*, 2:284; for the photograph, see Lloyd Ostendorf, *Lincoln's Photographs: A Complete Album* (Dayton, Ohio: Rockwood Press, 1998), 60–61; see Joseph Peters to Lincoln, March 20, 1861, Matt Anderson collection.

33. Lincoln to L. Montgomery Bond, October 15, 1860, *Collected Works*, 4:128.

34. Harold Holzer, *The Lincoln-Douglas Debates: The First Complete, Unexpurgated Text* (New York: HarperCollins, 1993), 30; Jay Monaghan, "The Lincoln-Douglas Debates," *Lincoln Herald*, 45 (June 1943), 2. Douglas had in fact been given no opportunity to review and edit his own debate transcripts.

35. Jay Monaghan, ed., *Lincoln Bibliography 1839–1939*, 2 vols. (Springfield: Illinois State Historical Library, 1943), 2:405, 407. An original copy of the *New-Yorker Demokrat* version is in the John Hay Library, Brown University Library. I examined most of these original imprints in the Alexander Sheff Collection at The Cooper Union Library.

36. *The Rail Mauler*, July 20, 1860 (endorsement), and August 10, 1860 (reprint of speech), originals in the Gilder Lehrman Collection, then in the Morgan Library, New York.

37. B. F. Lemen to Lincoln, April 1, 1860; Edward L. Pierce to Lincoln, July 20, 1860, Abraham Lincoln Papers, Library of Congress.

38. Both letters in the Abraham Lincoln Papers, Library of Congress.

39. Nott to Lincoln, May 23, 1860, in George Haven Putnam, *Abraham Lincoln: The People's Leader in the Struggle for National Existence* (New York: G. P. Putnam's Sons, 1909), 224–25.

40. Lincoln to Charles C. Nott, May 31, 1860, *Collected Works*, 4:58.

41. Brainerd and Nott statements in Putnam, *Abraham Lincoln: The People's Leader*, 212.

42. The marked-up copy of the pamphlet that Lincoln reviewed has not survived, and therefore some of his comments are difficult to match to a particular section of the speech. What emerges from the totality of the letter is his attention to the nuances of his own writing.

43. Lincoln to Charles C. Nott, May 31, 1860, *Collected Works*, 4:58–59. It is difficult to imagine the point in the text in which his editors proposed inserting the word "residences," though it probably referred to settlers in the Territories.

44. Nott to Lincoln, February 1, 1860, Abraham Lincoln Papers, Library of Congress.

45. Nott to Lincoln August 28, 1860, Abraham Lincoln Papers, Library of Congress.

46. Lincoln to Charles C. Nott, September 6, 1860, *Collected Works*, 4:113, September 22, 1860, 4:119.

47. Lincoln to Charles C. Nott, September 22, 1860, Ibid., 4:118.

48. Charles C. Nott and Cephas Brainerd, eds., *The Address of the Hon. Abraham Lincoln, in vindication of the policy of the framers of the Constitution and the principles of the Republican party, Delivered at Cooper Institute, February 27, 1860, issued by the Young Men's Republican Union . . .* (New York: George F. Nesbitt & Co., 1860), 3.

49. Ibid. Original copy, autographed by the editors, examined in the Gilder Lehrman Collection (GLC 4471.05), then in the Morgan Library, New York.

50. Nott to Brainerd, February 8, 1907, original in the Gilder Lehrman Collection (GLC 4471.02).

51. *The Address of the Hon. Abraham Lincoln*, rev. ed. of 1860 Nott-Brainerd pamphlet (New York: n.p., 1907), "explanatory note." Original in the Gilder Lehrman Collection (GLC 4471.06).

52. Nott to "Mr. Leonard," April 2, 1913, State Historical Society of Wisconsin.

53. Nott to "Professor Osgood," March 9, 1911, Department of Rare Books and Special Collections, Princeton University Library.

54. Ibid.

55. Ernest James Wessen, "Campaign Lives of Abraham Lincoln 1860: An Annotated Bibliography . . . ," *Papers in Illinois History and Transactions for the Year 1937* (Springfield: Illinois State Historical Society, 1938), 188.

56. The first edition was published in New York by Rudd & Carlton. A variant was examined in the Frank J. and Virginia Williams Collection, Hope Valley, Rhode Island. The Lincoln quotation comes from Lincoln to George Ashmun, June 4, 1860, *Collected Works*, 4:68.

57. *The Life and Public Services of Hon. Abraham Lincoln, of Illinois, and Hon. Hannibal Hamlin, of Maine* (Boston: Thayer & Eldridge, 1860), 241–63; J. H. Barrett, *Life of Abraham Lincoln (of Illinois)*. . . (Cincinnati: Moore, Wilstach, Keys & Co., 1860), 187–89.

58. D. W. Bartlett, *Presidential Candidates: Containing Sketches, Biographical, Personal, and Political, of Prominent Candidates for the Presidency* (New York: A. B. Burdick, 1859); Bartlett, *The Life and Public Services of Hon. Abraham Lincoln* . . . (New York : Derby & Jackson, 1860), 306–25.

59. Bartlett, *Life and Public Services of Hon. Abraham Lincoln*, 107.

60. W. D. Howells, *Life of Abraham Lincoln* (Columbus, Ohio: Follett, Foster & Co., 1860), 86–87.

61. As it happened, the new House—before many of its Southern members resigned and swore allegiance to the new Confederacy—would boast 108 Republicans and 129 in opposition, nearly all Democrats. See E. B. Long, ed., *The Civil War Day By Day: An Almanac, 1861–1865* (Garden City, N.Y.: Doubleday, 1971), 3.

62. *The Tribune Almanac for the Years 1838 to 1856* . . . (New York: The New York Tribune, 1868), 46. Lincoln likely consulted his own copy of this volume back in Springfield.

63. James A. Briggs to Abraham Lincoln, November 7, 1860, Abraham Lincoln Papers, Library of Congress.

64. *The Tribune Almanac for the Years 1838 to 1864, Inclusive* . . . (New York: The New York Tribune, 1868), 41.

65. Isaac N. Arnold, *The Life of Abraham Lincoln* (Chicago: Jansen, McClurg & Co., 1884), 158.

66. *Harper's Weekly*, November 24, 1860; *The Liberator*, December 14, 1860, both consulted on HarpWeek's Lincolnandthecivilwar.com.

67. Lincoln to William C. Kellogg, December 11, 1860, *Collected Works*, 4:150.

68. The sole exception came on August 8, 1860, when a Republican rally gathered at his Springfield home and Lincoln was obliged to offer a greeting. Although "profoundly gratified for this manifestation of your feelings," he reminded his supporters that he appeared before them only because they wished "to see me" and because "it is certainly my wish to see you." Then he begged the crowd to "kindly let me be silent." See *Collected Works*, 4:91.

EPILOGUE

1. Barney to Lincoln, January 11, 1865, Bowen to Lincoln, August 21, 1862, both in Abraham Lincoln Papers, Library of Congress; Mark E. Neely, Jr., *The Union Divided: Party Conflict in the Civil War North* (Cambridge, Mass.: Harvard University Press, 2002), 23–26.

2. *Collected Works*, 5:339, 366–67, 403.

3. Frederick Seward to Cephas Brainerd, September 28, 1862, original in the Gilder Lehrman Institute, GLC 4471.03, examined at the Morgan Library, New York; Walter B. Stevens, *A Reporter's Lincoln*, ed. Michael Burlingame (Lincoln: University of Nebraska Press, 1998), 264.

4. "The Chief Justice of the Court of Claims," *Harper's Weekly*, December 5, 1896; Douglas L. Wilson and Rodney O. Davis, *Herndon's Informants: Letters, Interviews, and Statements About Abraham Lincoln* (Urbana: University of Illinois Press, 1998), 232, 742.

5. Andrew Freeman, *Abraham Lincoln Goes to New York* (New York: Coward-McCann, 1960), 107–8; Ida Tarbell, *The Life of Abraham Lincoln*, 2 vols. (New York: S. S. McClure, 1895), 1:396.

6. Harold Holzer and Hans L. Trefousse, "A State of War," in Holzer, ed., *The Union Preserved . . .* (New York: Fordham University Press, 1999), 2; *Collected Works*, 4:232–33.

7. *Collected Works*, 4:261–271.

8. Harold G. Villard and Oswald Garrison Villard, eds., *Lincoln on the Eve of '61: A Journalist's Story by Henry Villard* (New York: Alfred A. Knopf, 1941), 93.

9. *New York Times*, April 14, 1860, June 8, 9, 1860, October 9, 18, 25, 16, 1860.

10. Edward K. Spann, *Gotham at War: New York City, 1860–1865* (Wilmington: Scholarly Resources, 2002), 125; "Resolutions Unanimously Adopted by the Citizens of New York by a Mass Meeting Held at Cooper Institute on Thursday Evening, March 6, 1862," Abraham Lincoln Papers, Library of Congress.

11. George Opdyke and others to Lincoln, November 28, 1863, Abraham Lincoln Papers, Library of Congress. One of the signatories to the invitation, Benjamin F. Manierre, had been a member of the Young Men's Central Republican Union in 1860.

12. *Collected Works*, 7:32.

13. William E. Buckingham and John N. Fisher to Lincoln, March 14, 1865. Abraham Lincoln Papers, Library of Congress.

14. Merrill D. Peterson, *Lincoln in American Memory* (New York: Oxford University Press, 1994), 365–6.

15. deanforamerica.com (accessed 11/6/03).

16. Robert Lincoln to J. G. Holland, June 6, 1865, in Rufus Rockwell Wilson, ed., *Intimate Memories of Lincoln* (Elmira, N.Y.: Primavera Press, 1945), 499.

17. Lincoln to Latham, July 23, 1860, original in the Gilder Lehrman Collection (GLC 3876). See also Harold Holzer, *"In the end you are sure to succeed": Lincoln on Perseverance* (New York: The Gilder Lehrman Institute of American History, 2001), 5–9.

18. Patrick McCarty and others to Lincoln, October 16, 1863, Abraham Lincoln Papers, Library of Congress. I reprinted this letter in *The Lincoln Mailbag: America Writes to the President, 1861–1865* (Carbondale, Ill.: Southern Illinois University Press, 1998), 107.

19. John Rhodehamel and Louise Taper, eds., *"Right or Wrong, God Judge Me": The Writings of John Wilkes Booth* (Urbana: University of Illinois Press, 1997), 144.

20. David B. Cheesebrough, *"No Sorrow Like Our Sorrow": Northern Protestant Ministers and the Assassination of Lincoln* (Kent, Ohio: Kent State University Press, 1994), 80. Sixteen years later, Beecher was embroiled in a sex scandal that would seriously tarnish his reputation.

21. A. Dallas Williams, ed., *The Praise of Lincoln: An Anthology* (Indianapolis: Bobbs-Merrill, 1911), 2.

22. The ribbon is illustrated in James L. Swanson and Daniel R. Weinberg, *Lincoln's Assassins: Their Trial and Execution* (Santa Fe, N.M.: Arena Editions, 2001), 47; Cooper Union was described in David E. Valentine, ed., *Obsequies of President Lincoln in the City of New York, Under the Auspices of the Common Council* (New York: Edmund Jones & Co., 1865), 91.

23. David M. Scobey, *Empire City: The Making and Meaning of the New York City Landscape* (Philadelphia: Temple University Press, 2002), 55.

24. Edward Steers, Jr., *Blood on the Moon: The Assassination of Abraham Lincoln* (Lexington, Ky.: University Press of Kentucky, 2001), 233.

⊰ ACKNOWLEDGMENTS ⊱

Lincoln may have researched and written his Cooper Union speech alone, but in the long process of investigating and writing that story, I have received an avalanche of essential, deeply appreciated help, encouragement, and support.

First, I must express my gratitude to the Pulitzer Foundation for its early and generous research grant, which made so much preliminary travel and study possible. Special thanks for their faith and friendship go, with both affection and respect, to Michael and Ceil Pulitzer. Later, I was honored with a Gilder Lehrman Institute of American History fellowship, which facilitated further research at the New York Public Library and the Morgan Library. For this I particularly thank GLI executive director Lesley Herrmann, President James Basker, and of course, Richard Gilder and Lewis Lehrman, who provide much crucial support to the study of American history on many levels. Finally, my research was supported through the Columbia University history research assistant program, for whose interest and help I sincerely thank its highly competent administrator, Patricia O'Toole.

Among the excellent research assistants who helped unearth some of the raw material for this book, I want particularly to recognize and thank three: Margot Kahn, Elizabeth Gold, and Randy Hartwell. Their tenacity and energy helped me a great deal along the road to preparing this study.

Many treasured colleagues within the Lincoln community came forth with essential guidance and criticism, and I have benefited much from their patient readings and sound advice. Wayne C. Temple, Chief Deputy Director of the Illinois State Archives in Springfield, gave the earliest drafts the benefit of his usual expert review, applying his customary scrupulous attention to detail. No expert knows more about Lincoln's Springfield years, and Wayne saved me from more errors of fact and interpretation than I would care to admit.

Additional, beneficial readings were provided by Lincoln scholar Frank J. Williams, and by historians John Y. Simon, Ronald C. White, and Douglas L. Wilson, all of whom identified innumerable areas for improvement. Additionally, Professor Wilson was generous enough to invite me to deliver my first talk about Lincoln's Cooper Union address at the Lincoln Studies Center at Knox College in Galesburg, Illinois, where I enjoyed his generous hospitality, along with that of Professor and Mrs. Rodney O. Davis. I thank all of them.

I am grateful for their help as well to David Zarefsky, the Owen L. Coon Professor of Communications Studies at Northwestern University, and to Steven K. Rogstad of the *Lincoln Herald* for pointing me to Dr. Zarefsky's excellent lectures on Lincoln's oratory; to the generous Doris Kearns Goodwin for so thoughtfully sharing a piece of research she unearthed for her own Lincoln project; to Richard Moe, president of the National Trust for Historic Preservation, for his many good suggestions; to Kenneth M. Jackson, then president of the New-York Historical Society, for his guidance on how to find a particularly elusive piece of meteorological information; to author Geoffrey C. Ward for directing me to a wonderful old book about the Brooklyn that Abraham Lincoln saw; to Sam Waterston and Mario Cuomo for their patient readings and good advice; and to historian Michael Beschloss for his friendship and counsel.

I launched my research efforts in 2001 with a trip to no ordinary library—but to the private archive maintained by my best friend in the Lincoln world, Chief Justice Frank J. Williams of Rhode Island, chairman of the Lincoln Forum and a colleague on the U.S. Lincoln Bicentennial Commission. Frank and his wonderful wife, Virginia, offered my wife and me access, lodging, home-cooked Italian food, and at the end of each work day, great wine and great company. In the months that followed, whenever another book or pamphlet caught my interest, Frank uncomplainingly dug into his collection on evenings and weekends, found the material for me, and promptly copied and shipped it. How does one begin to thank this generous man? He has provided support and encouragement for every book I have ever written; he is not only a loyal friend, but an indispensable one.

At libraries, museums, and research institutions throughout the country, I was given access and information by curators and archivists whose help opened many crucial doors. It is a pleasure to thank: John R. Sellers, Chief of

Nineteenth Century Manuscripts at the Library of Congress, and his colleague in the Rare Books division, Clark Evans; Albert C. Jerman, former historian of Robert Todd Lincoln's Hildene; Don McCue, Curator at the Lincoln Memorial Shrine in Redlands, California; Ann K. Sindelar, reference supervisor, and Harold L. Miller, reference archivist, at the Wisconsin Historical Society; Lois Rosebrooks of the Plymouth Church in Brooklyn (and Tim Goeglein, special Assistant to President Bush, for sharing one of my visits there); Mary-Jo Kline at the Brown University libraries; Daniel W. Stowell at the Abraham Lincoln Papers Project in Springfield; Russell Lewis, Andrew W. Mellon Director for Collections and Research at the Chicago Historical Society; Bernard Reilly, the Society's Director of Research and Access; and Lesley Martin, a Society research specialist.

I am particularly grateful to Kim L. Bauer, curator of the Henry Horner Lincoln Collection at the Illinois State Historical Library in Springfield, who not only provided access to the published sources that Lincoln consulted to prepare his Cooper Union speech but let me hold in my hand the priceless letter that Lincoln wrote after Cooper Union, begging his host to arrange no new speaking engagements. Thanks, too, to: Cindy VanHorn, Registrar at the Lincoln Museum in Fort Wayne, and of course CEO Joan Flinspach; Judy Hohmann at the New York State Archives in Albany; John Rhodehamel, Norris Foundation Curator of American Manuscripts at the Huntington Library in San Marino, California; Valerie Komor, head of the department of prints and photographs at the New-York Historical Society; Shelley C. Bronk, Archives Assistant at the Phillips Exeter Academy, along with the academy's Edward Derocher; and AnnaLee Pauls at the Princeton University Library's Department of Rare Books and Special Collections.

Leslie Fields, Sandra Trenholm, and, earlier, Paul W. Romaine, provided expert guidance through the vast Gilder Lehrman Collection of American manuscripts. And the staffs at the New York Public Library, the Morgan Library, and the Illinois State Historical Society offered patient help during repeated research visits. I am especially grateful to all the guards at Cooper Union, who were kind enough to let me slip into the basement every time I was in the neighborhood, no matter what the hour, to inhale again the atmosphere of the auditorium where Lincoln spoke in 1860. And Cooper Union's Claire McCarthy, Peter Buckley, Ula Volk, Gina Pollara, and Carol Salomon were most helpful and enthusiastic.

The list goes on. John Adler of HarpWeek offered access to his superb website together with sharp reprints, with help from his colleagues Susan Severtson and Greg Weber. Jonathan Mann, publisher of the Lincoln collectors' newsletter, *The Rail Splitter*, offered advice on Cooper Union ephemera, as did Daniel R. Weinberg, proprietor of the Abraham Lincoln Book Shop in Chicago. Don Pollard expertly photographed some rare printings of the address at Cooper Union, and was brave enough to take pictures of me there as well. And my fellow Lincoln Group of New York members Larry J. West and Philip E. Schoenberg provided important articles and maps, while President Joseph E. Garrera supplied endless encouragement.

I will never forget the October 2001 morning when I had the opportunity to thank Senator Hillary Rodham Clinton, at a New York political breakfast, for reintroducing Lincoln's Cooper Union "right makes might" peroration to soothe a city wounded by the World Trade Center terrorist attacks of the previous month. In response, she quoted the speech one more time that very day—wisely noting that "Lincoln used those words to anticipate a crisis, but they are just as appropriate in the aftermath of a crisis." Nineteen months later, during a visit I made to her office in Washington, Senator Clinton not only remembered that I had been working on this book, she was thoughtful enough—in the midst of the hoopla surrounding her own new book—to ask, "How's Lincoln?" Lincoln is fine, and I am most grateful to Mrs. Clinton for caring, and for trying to ensure that the words of Cooper Union endure.

At Simon & Schuster, I have been particularly blessed to have the support, advice, and occasionally, the direct orders, of my editor Alice Mayhew. For years, those of my colleagues who have written books for her have spoken almost mystically about the "Alice factor." Now I know for myself what it means. Much as I initially resisted some of her suggestions for cuts, reorganization, and refinements, she has unquestionably made this a far better book. I am truly grateful to her, to her unflappable Simon & Schuster colleague Roger Labrie, and to copy editor Celia Knight, for all their efforts and attention.

My agent, Geri Thoma, shopped and cheered the book from the proposal stage, and as always looked out for my interests on many occasions. My treasured friends John O'Keefe and Tim Mulligan championed the project from the precise moment it was unexpectedly conceived at a Lincoln banquet, appropriately enough, in Gettysburg. Chuck Platt, treasurer of the Lincoln Forum, was kind enough to administer the Pulitzer Foundation grant. And my assistants, Mary Jane Crook and, more recently, John Paul Conti, handled phone calls and correspondence with much skill and good humor—and young Mr. Conti, it turns out, is quite a good researcher in his own right!

I must admit that my Lincoln life is "interrupted" five days a week, ten hours a day—at least—by my full-time work at The Metropolitan Museum of Art, where I am further privileged to have the full-time understanding of

Director Philippe de Montebello. His encouragement of my scholarship over the years has been an essential, and deeply appreciated, benefit of serving with this inspiring leader on the staff of the greatest cultural institution in the world.

My family, too, has been more than encouraging during the course of this project. My wife, Edith, accompanied me enthusiastically on nearly all my research trips, allowed me to bounce new ideas and discoveries past her any time, anywhere, and reviewed the entire manuscript more than once, offering many more useful suggestions than I can count. I am eternally grateful to her for all her love, support, wisdom, and understanding.

Our wonderful writer children, daughter Remy and son-in-law Adam Kirsch, were always available to commiserate about research and deadlines, and to provide inspiration and affection. And our new extended family, Jonathan, Ann, and Jenny Kirsch, offered advice and encouragement on writing, contracts, and promotion, as both Jonathan and I coincidentally raced to complete books at precisely the same time.

Last but never least, our adored and accomplished younger daughter, Meg, played several important roles as well during her last summer of freedom before starting classes at the NYU School of Law. She made an exceptionally useful research trip to Exeter, where she found largely untapped records of Robert Lincoln's studies there, and while she later charged a dollar a page to proofread the manuscript, her exceptional editing skills would have made her work cheap at twice the price.

⇥ ACKNOWLEDGMENTS ⇤
TO THE PAPERBACK EDITION

I am grateful to have the additional opportunity here to express appreciation to those who have been so helpful since the first edition of this book was published.

First and foremost, I thank my friend Sam Waterston—who made the Cooper Union address again come alive. Thanks, too, to C-SPAN, particularly Brian Lamb, Mark Farkas, and Amy Roach, for telecasting it.

I am grateful to: journalist Glenn Collins for capturing the Waterston re-creation in the *New York Times*; President George Campbell, Jr., and communications chief Claire McCarthy for welcoming us to Cooper Union; Martin Segal for hosting a book reception at New York's Century Association; and James Swanson of the Heritage Foundation who, together with Michael Bishop of the Lincoln Bicentennial Commission, did likewise at James's Lincolniana-filled Washington town house. There, my U.S. Senator Hillary Rodham Clinton did me the great honor of serving as co-host and speaking glowingly about the book.

Special acknowledgment, too, goes to Daniel Weinberg of the Abraham Lincoln Book Shop, who unearthed and shared the long-lost Lincoln letter to Thomas Corwin, and who was kind enough to hold a book reception at his Chicago headquarters. Chief Justice Frank Williams, along with the Lincoln Museum's Cindy VanHorn and Sara Gabbard, helped with last-minute research questions.

Along the way between hardcover and paperback editions, many Lincoln and Civil War groups invited me to address them, and I am grateful for those opportunities. I thank: Joan Flinspach of the Lincoln Museum in Fort Wayne; Julie Johnas of the Highland Park Library in

Illinois; Seth Bongartz of Robert Todd Lincoln's "Hildene" in Manchester, Vermont; and Daniel and Ann Pearson of the Lincoln Fellowship of Wisconsin, before whose dinner George Buss, a gifted Lincoln performer in his own right, spoke the words Lincoln delivered in Beloit a few days before receiving his invitation to New York. I will not soon forget standing in Hanchett Hall, wreck though it now is, where Lincoln stood in 1859 to declare that the founders believed the federal government could control the spread of slavery—a theme to which he would so unforgettably return at Cooper Union.

I thank, too: Burris Carnahan and Charles Doty of the Lincoln Group of the District of Columbia; Sam Anthony of the National Archives (along with that institution's best research team, Budge and Russ Weidman); Nancy Newcomb, Louise Mirrer, and Steve Turtell of the New-York Historical Society; William Hanna of the Lincoln Group of Boston; Gerridine La Ravere of the Civil War Round Table of Palm Beach; Steve Laird and Guy de Masi of the Civil War Round Table of Connecticut; Frank J. Williams, Charles D. Platt, and Annette Westerby of the Lincoln Forum; Bob Willard of the Abraham Lincoln Institute; Len Rehner of the Civil War Round Table of New York; and, again, James Swanson of the Heritage Foundation, along with my new friends at Florida's Prologue Society and the Society of the Four Arts, along with Arlynn Greenbaum of Authors Unlimited.

Two organizations in my hometown—the town Lincoln took by storm in 1860—bestowed their annual book awards on *Lincoln at Cooper Union*. I am deeply honored by both the Award of Achievement of the Lincoln Group of New York, and the Barondess/Lincoln Award of the Civil War Round Table.

As a marketing man in my day-to-day professional life, I count every promotional success as a special blessing. So I want to thank for their generosity: David Carey and his staff at the New Yorker; Larry Warsh of *Museums New York*; Harvey Schulman, Margaret Mercer, and Annie Bergen at WQXR Radio; and Dianne Doctor at CBS-2. Rachel Nagler, the book's publicist at Simon & Schuster, has been a most effective advocate. John Paul Conti, my executive assistant, has been an absolute rock. And my family and friends sat through so many Cooper Union lectures they probably wish they had never heard of the school, the speech, the book, or its author.

Finally, special gratitude goes to the sharp-eyed readers who spotted errors in the first edition: Dennis Swanson of CBS, who clearly knows the road from Clinton to Springfield, Illinois, better than I; Jonathan Mann of *The Rail Splitter*; Richard Sloan of the Lincoln Group of New York; E. A. "Bud" Livingston of New York's Civil War Round Table; Craig Symonds of the U. S. Naval Academy, and the readers who understandably (but maybe a bit too gleefully) pointed out my clumsy—and, I promise, inadvertent—implication that Lincoln had six fingers on his right hand! Thanks to them, these mistakes have been corrected for this edition—for whose beautiful appearance I thank, again and always, my editors Alice Mayhew and Roger Labrie.

INDEX

ABOUT THE AUTHOR

HAROLD HOLZER is Senior Vice President for External Affairs at The Metropolitan Museum of Art. He is the author, coauthor, or editor of twenty-one previous books about Lincoln and the Civil War, including *The Lincoln Image*, *Lincoln As I Knew Him*, *Lincoln Seen and Heard*, *Mine Eyes Have Seen the Glory*, and *The Lincoln Family Album*. The winner of many awards and cochairman of the U.S. Lincoln Bicentennial Commission, he lives in Rye, New York. Visit his website at www.haroldholzer.com.